GENSHIKEN

3

KIO SHIMOKU

TRANSLATED AND ADAPTED BY
David Ury

LETTERED BY
Michaelis/Carpelis Design

BALLANTINE BOOKS • NEW YORK

Genshiken, Volume 3 is a work of fiction. Names, characters, places, and incidents are the products of the author's imagination or are used fictitiously. Any resemblance to actual events, locales, or persons, living or dead, is entirely coincidental.

A Del Rey Books Trade Paperback Original

Published in the United States by
Del Rey Books, an imprint of
The Random House Publishing Group, a
division of Random House, Inc., New York.

DEL REY is a registered trademark and the Del Rey colophon is a trademark of Random House, Inc.

First published in Japan in 2003 by
Kodansha Ltd., Tokyo
This publication rights arranged through
Kodansha Ltd.

Library of Congress Control Number:
2005922043

ISBN 0-345-48171-2

Printed in the United States of America

www.delreymanga.com

10 9 8 7 6 5 4 3 2

Lettering—Michaelis/Carpelis Design

げんしけん

THE SOCIETY FOR THE STUDY OF MODERN VISUAL CULTURE

もちろん！
OF COURSE!
じ、実は冗談
A-ACTUALLY, I'M KIDDING.
大野さん
OHNO-SAN
ほんとに…ほんとに私でいいんですか？
DO...DO YOU REALLY WANT ME?
Save
Load
Menu

KIO SHIMOKU

Contents

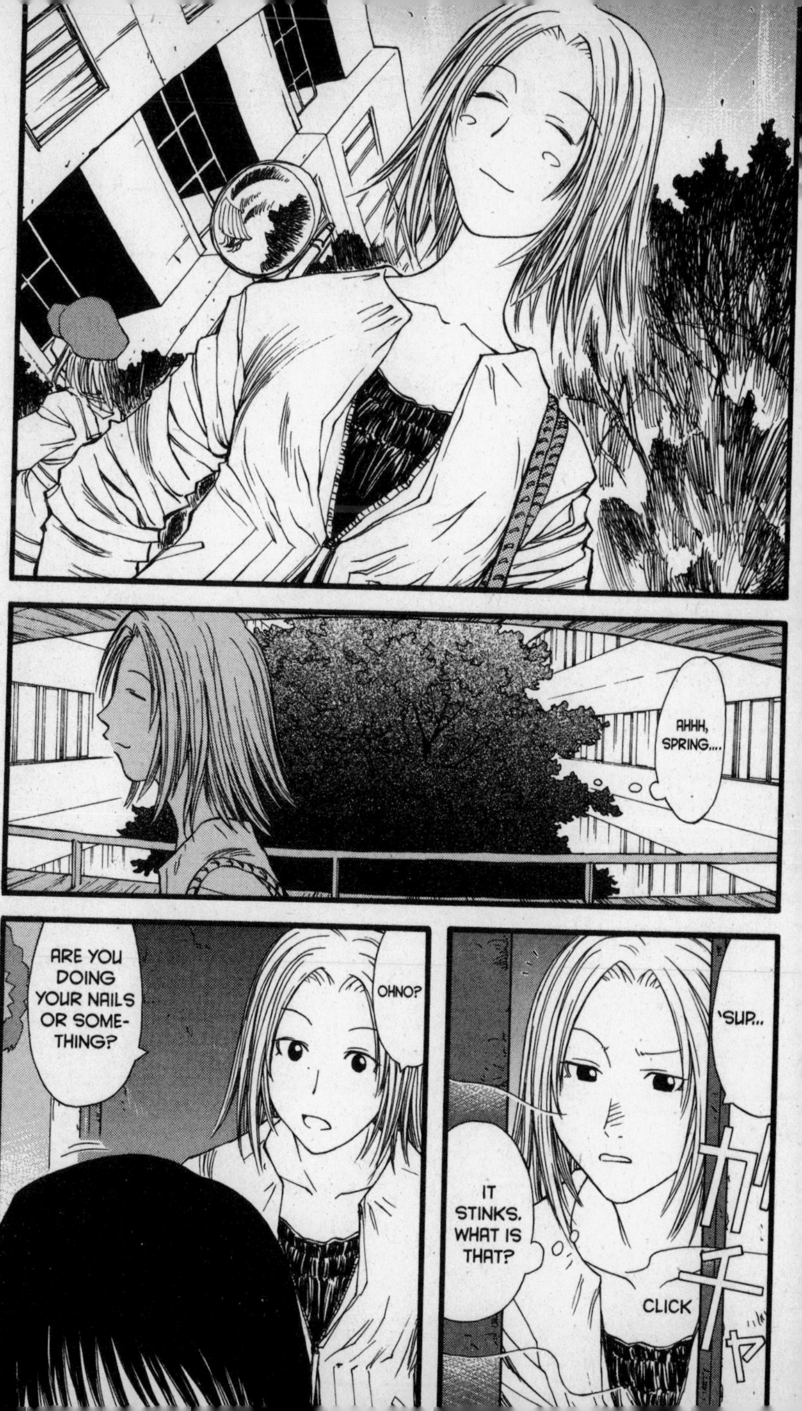
AHHH, SPRING....
'SUP...
IT STINKS. WHAT IS THAT?
CLICK
OHNO?
ARE YOU DOING YOUR NAILS OR SOME-THING?

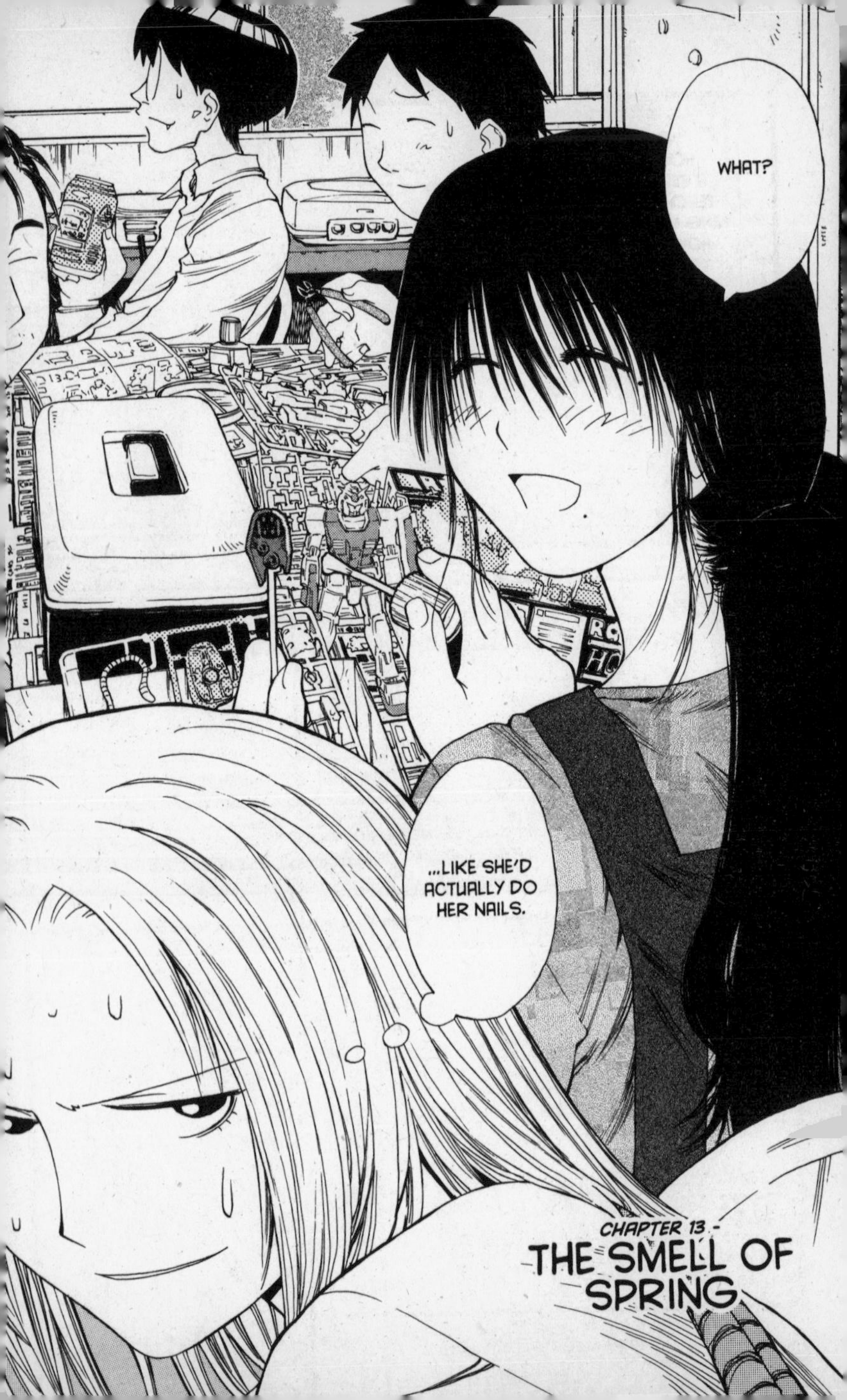
WHAT?
...LIKE SHE'D ACTUALLY DO HER NAILS.
CHAPTER 13 -
THE SMELL OF SPRING

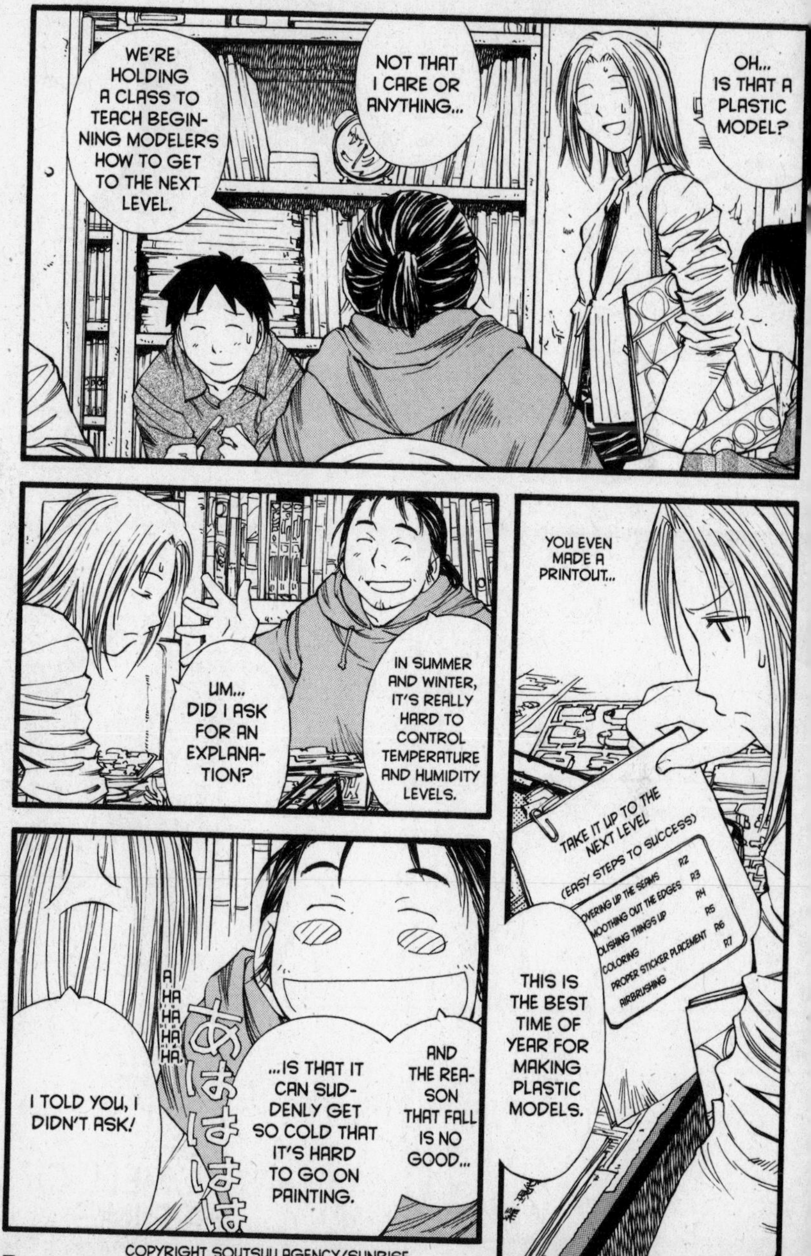

OH... IS THAT A PLASTIC MODEL?
NOT THAT I CARE OR ANYTHING...
WE'RE HOLDING A CLASS TO TEACH BEGINNING MODELERS HOW TO GET TO THE NEXT LEVEL.
YOU EVEN MADE A PRINTOUT...
TAKE IT UP TO THE NEXT LEVEL
(EASY STEPS TO SUCCESS)
OVERING UP THE SEAMS P2
MOOTHING OUT THE EDGES P3
OLISHING THINGS UP P4
COLORING P5
PROPER STICKER PLACEMENT P6
AIRBRUSHING P7
THIS IS THE BEST TIME OF YEAR FOR MAKING PLASTIC MODELS.
IN SUMMER AND WINTER, IT'S REALLY HARD TO CONTROL TEMPERATURE AND HUMIDITY LEVELS.
UM... DID I ASK FOR AN EXPLANATION?
AND THE REASON THAT FALL IS NO GOOD...
...IS THAT IT CAN SUDDENLY GET SO COLD THAT IT'S HARD TO GO ON PAINTING.
あははは
A HA HA HA HA.
I TOLD YOU, I DIDN'T ASK!

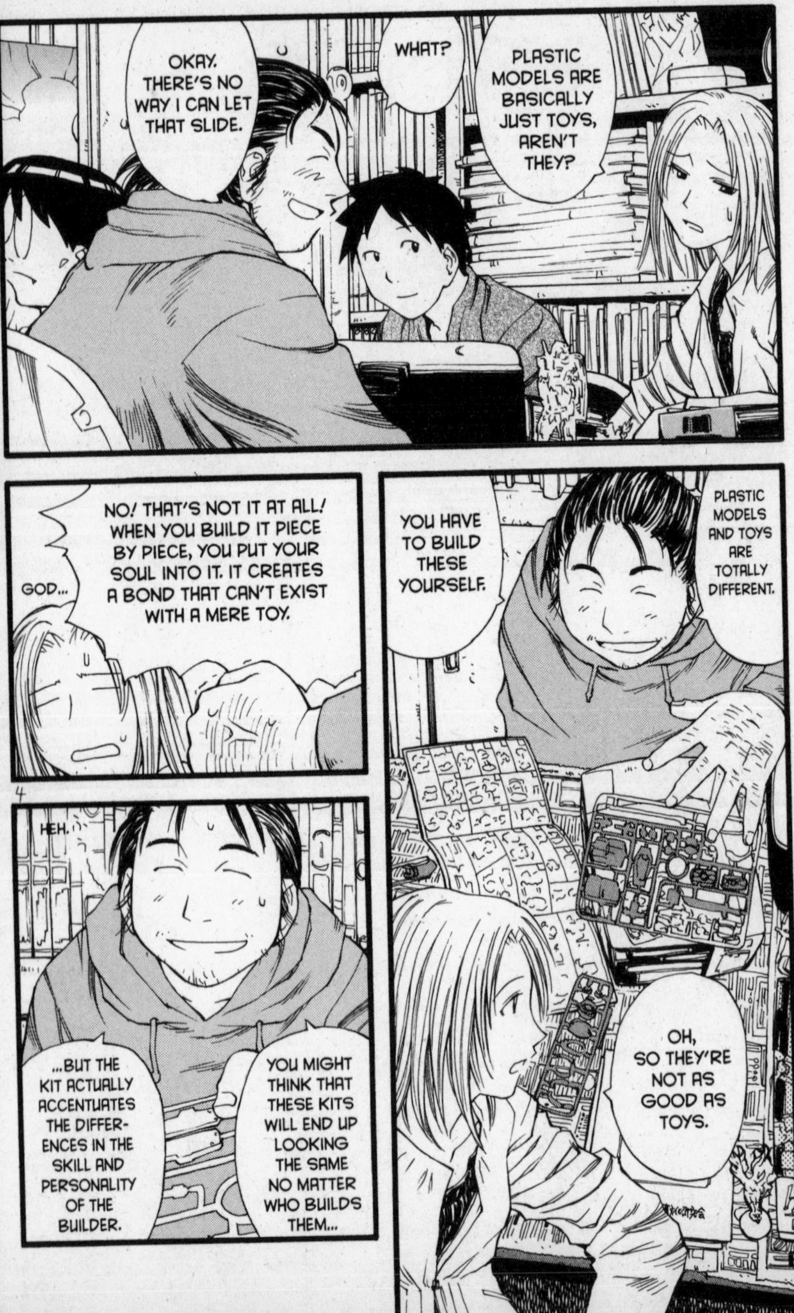
PLASTIC MODELS ARE BASICALLY JUST TOYS, AREN'T THEY?
WHAT?
OKAY. THERE'S NO WAY I CAN LET THAT SLIDE.
PLASTIC MODELS AND TOYS ARE TOTALLY DIFFERENT.
YOU HAVE TO BUILD THESE YOURSELF.
OH, SO THEY'RE NOT AS GOOD AS TOYS.
NO! THAT'S NOT IT AT ALL! WHEN YOU BUILD IT PIECE BY PIECE, YOU PUT YOUR SOUL INTO IT. IT CREATES A BOND THAT CAN'T EXIST WITH A MERE TOY.
GOD...
HEH.
YOU MIGHT THINK THAT THESE KITS WILL END UP LOOKING THE SAME NO MATTER WHO BUILDS THEM...
...BUT THE KIT ACTUALLY ACCENTUATES THE DIFFER-ENCES IN THE SKILL AND PERSONALITY OF THE BUILDER.

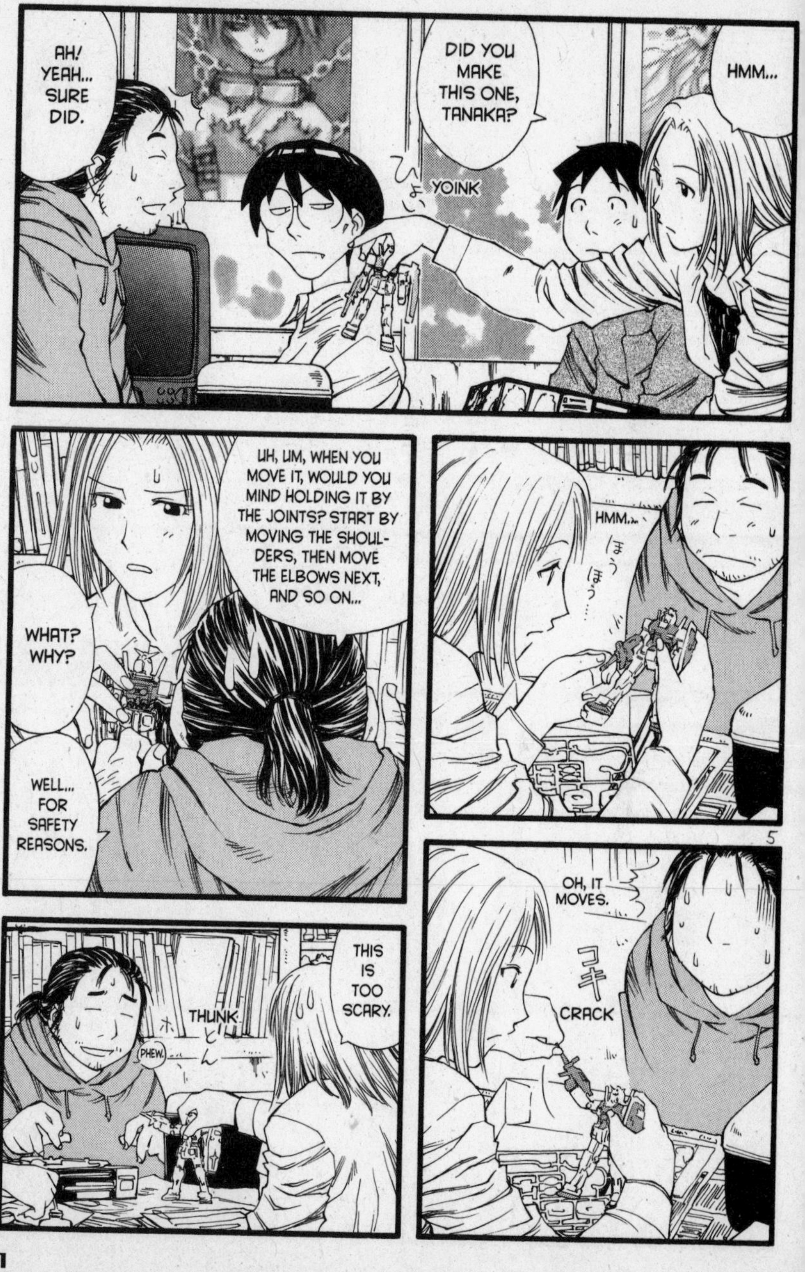
HMM...
DID YOU MAKE THIS ONE, TANAKA?
ひょい
YOINK
AH! YEAH... SURE DID.
HMM...
ほう ほう...
UH, UM, WHEN YOU MOVE IT, WOULD YOU MIND HOLDING IT BY THE JOINTS? START BY MOVING THE SHOUL-DERS, THEN MOVE THE ELBOWS NEXT, AND SO ON...
WHAT? WHY?
WELL... FOR SAFETY REASONS.
OH, IT MOVES.
コキ
CRACK
THIS IS TOO SCARY.
THUNK
どん
ホッ
PHEW.

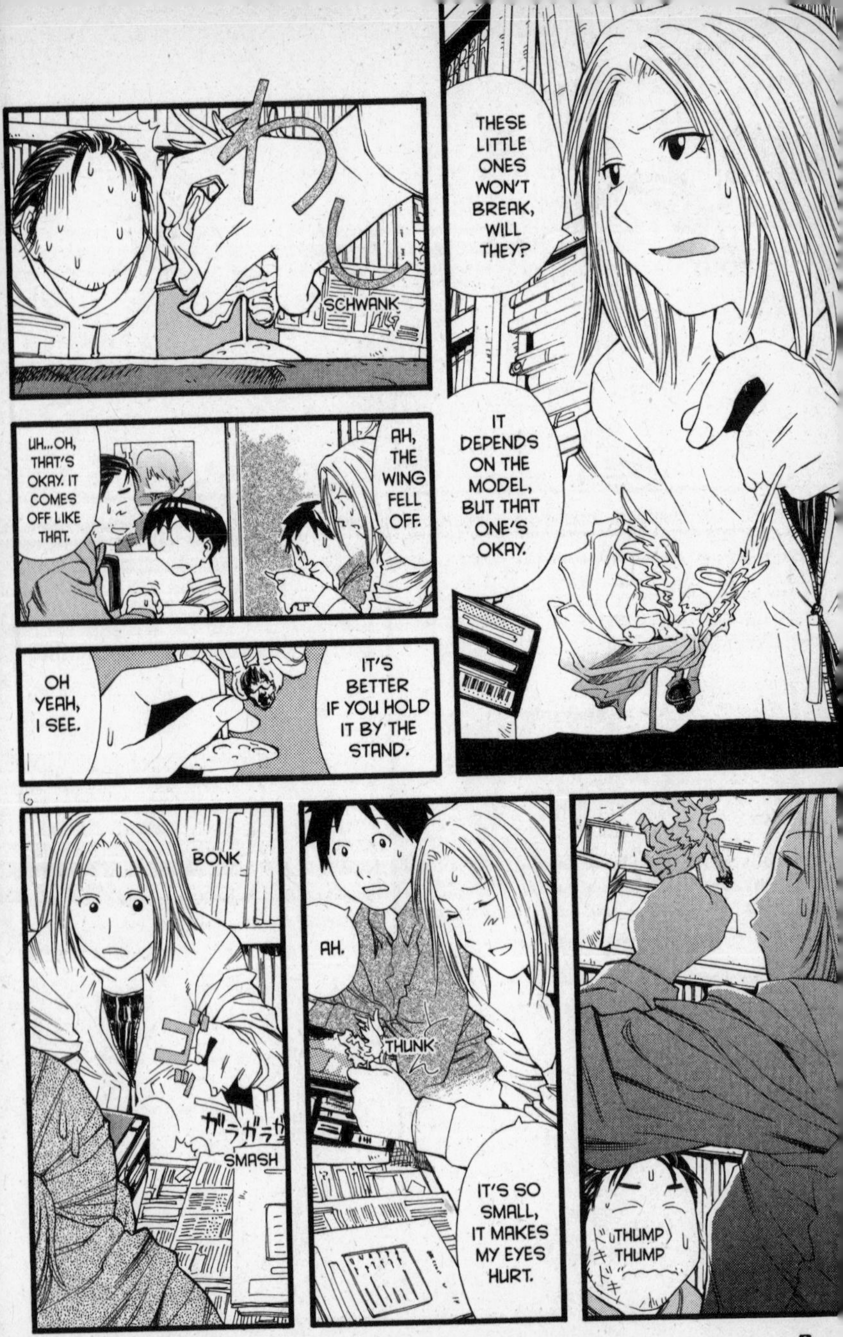
THESE LITTLE ONES WON'T BREAK, WILL THEY?
IT DEPENDS ON THE MODEL, BUT THAT ONE'S OKAY.
わし
SCHWANK
AH, THE WING FELL OFF.
UH...OH, THAT'S OKAY. IT COMES OFF LIKE THAT.
IT'S BETTER IF YOU HOLD IT BY THE STAND.
OH YEAH, I SEE.
THUMP THUMP
IT'S SO SMALL, IT MAKES MY EYES HURT.
AH.
THUNK
BONK
SMASH

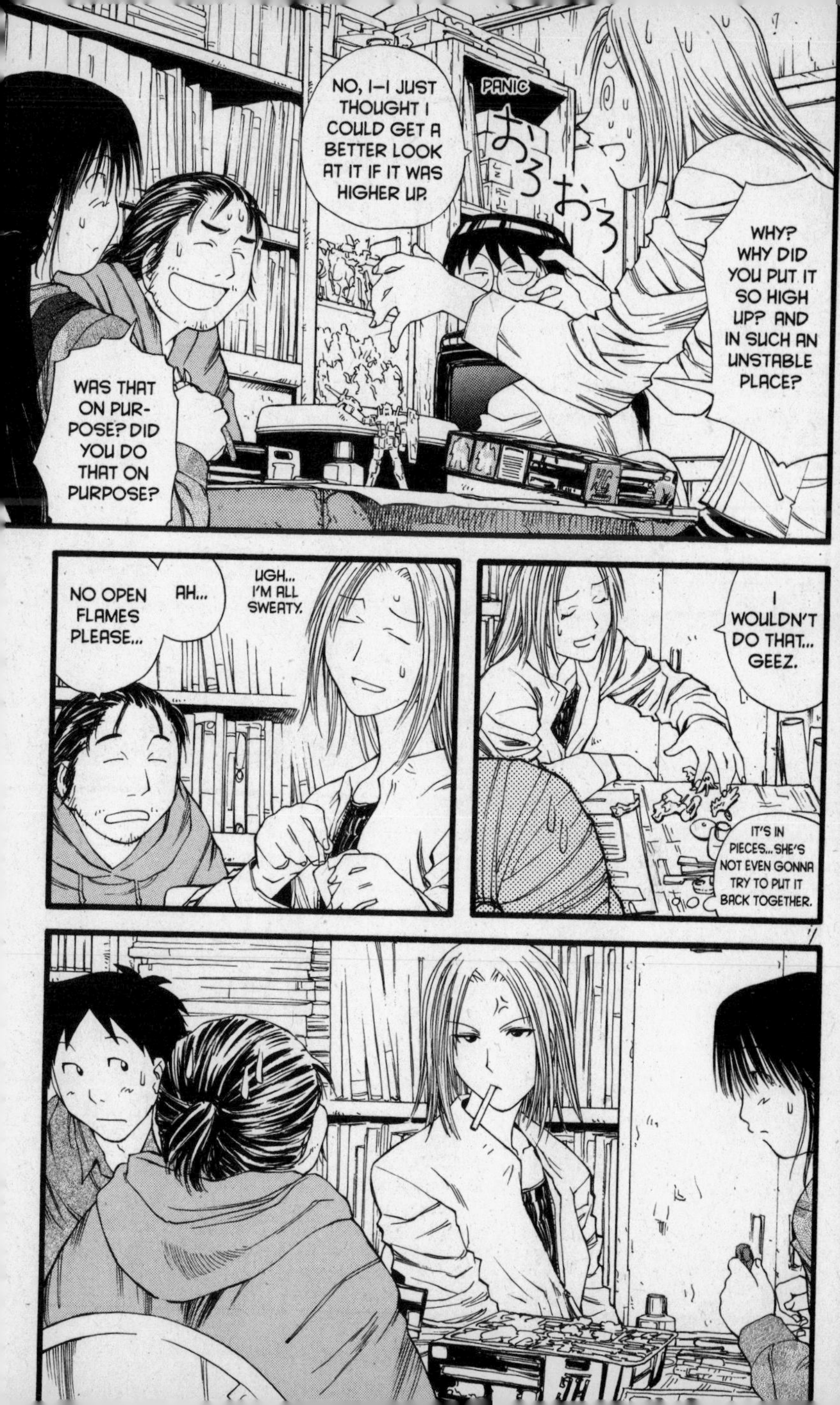
WHY? WHY DID YOU PUT IT SO HIGH UP? AND IN SUCH AN UNSTABLE PLACE?
PANIC
おろおろ
NO, I—I JUST THOUGHT I COULD GET A BETTER LOOK AT IT IF IT WAS HIGHER UP.
WAS THAT ON PURPOSE? DID YOU DO THAT ON PURPOSE?
I WOULDN'T DO THAT... GEEZ.
IT'S IN PIECES... SHE'S NOT EVEN GONNA TRY TO PUT IT BACK TOGETHER.
UGH... I'M ALL SWEATY.
AH...
NO OPEN FLAMES PLEASE...

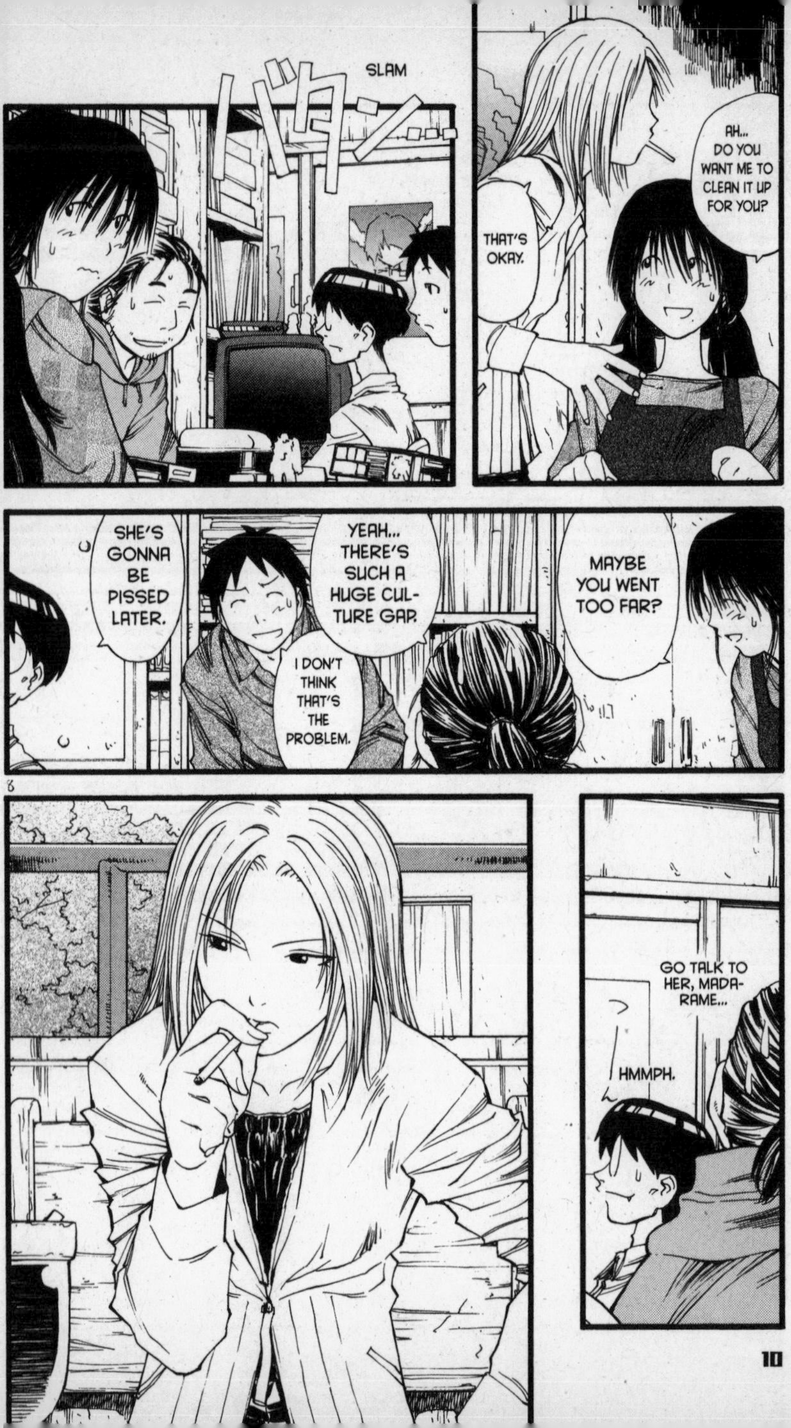
AH... DO YOU WANT ME TO CLEAN IT UP FOR YOU?
THAT'S OKAY.
SLAM
MAYBE YOU WENT TOO FAR?
YEAH... THERE'S SUCH A HUGE CUL-TURE GAP.
I DON'T THINK THAT'S THE PROBLEM.
SHE'S GONNA BE PISSED LATER.
GO TALK TO HER, MADA-RAME...
HMMPH.

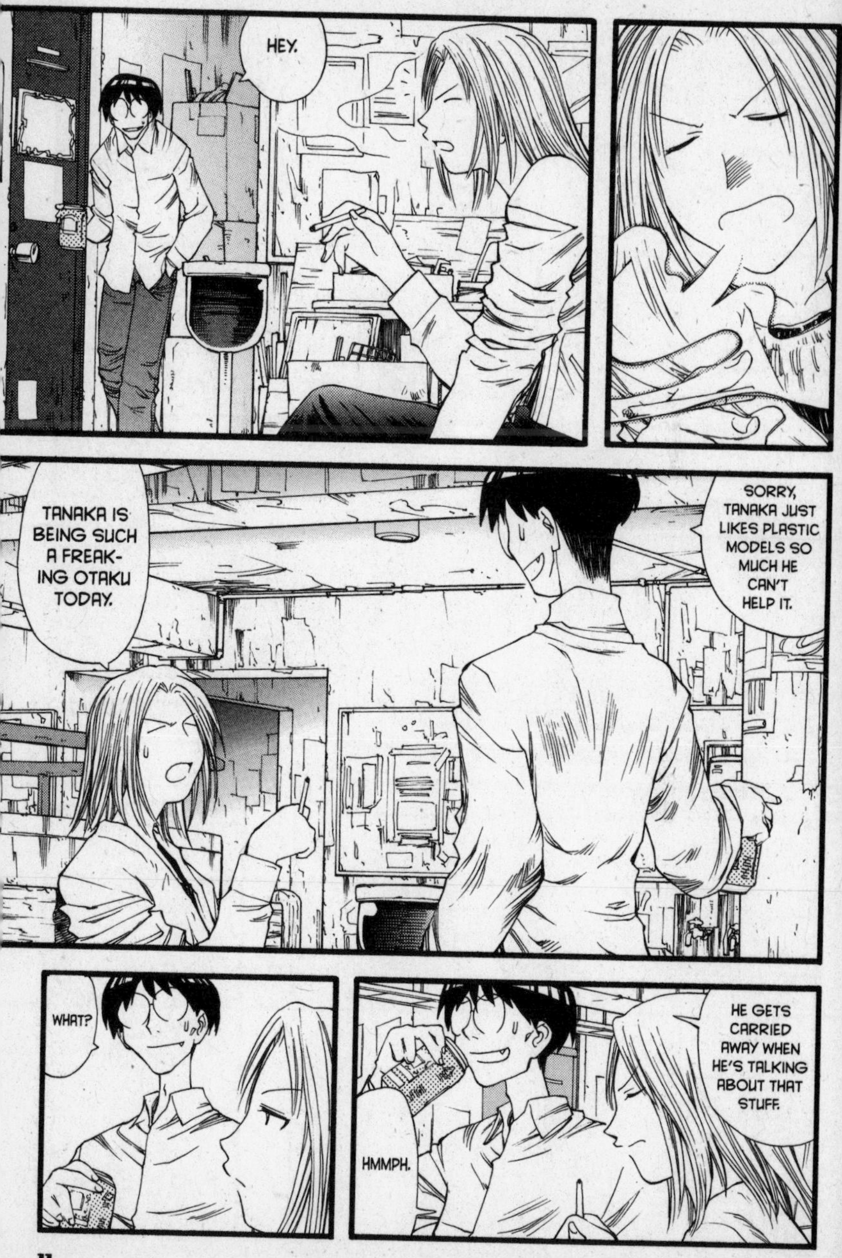
HEY.
TANAKA IS BEING SUCH A FREAK-ING OTAKU TODAY.
SORRY, TANAKA JUST LIKES PLASTIC MODELS SO MUCH HE CAN'T HELP IT.
HE GETS CARRIED AWAY WHEN HE'S TALKING ABOUT THAT STUFF.
HMMPH.
WHAT?

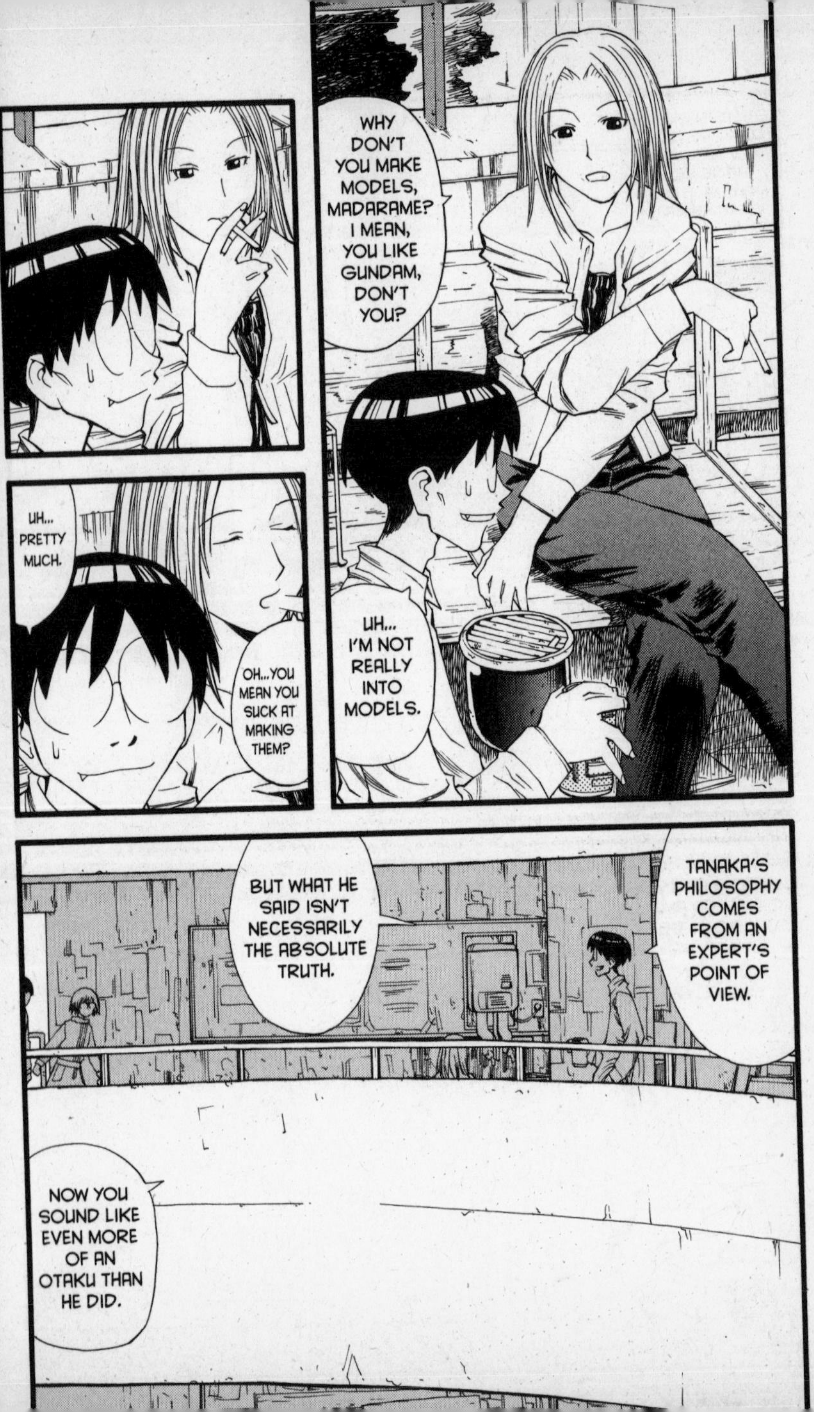
WHY DON'T YOU MAKE MODELS, MADARAME? I MEAN, YOU LIKE GUNDAM, DON'T YOU?
UH... I'M NOT REALLY INTO MODELS.
OH...YOU MEAN YOU SUCK AT MAKING THEM?
UH... PRETTY MUCH.
TANAKA'S PHILOSOPHY COMES FROM AN EXPERT'S POINT OF VIEW.
BUT WHAT HE SAID ISN'T NECESSARILY THE ABSOLUTE TRUTH.
NOW YOU SOUND LIKE EVEN MORE OF AN OTAKU THAN HE DID.

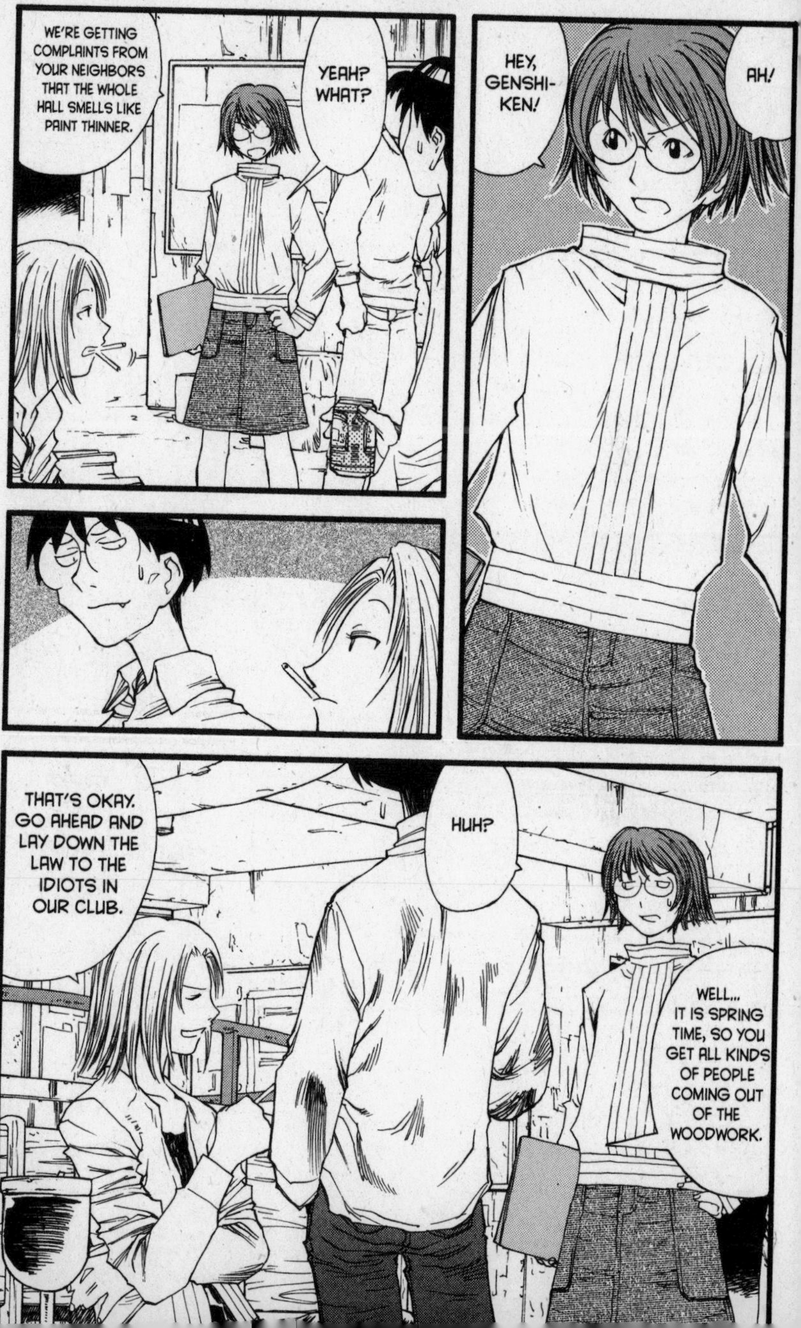
AH!
HEY, GENSHIKEN!
YEAH? WHAT?
WE'RE GETTING COMPLAINTS FROM YOUR NEIGHBORS THAT THE WHOLE HALL SMELLS LIKE PAINT THINNER.
HUH?
THAT'S OKAY. GO AHEAD AND LAY DOWN THE LAW TO THE IDIOTS IN OUR CLUB.
WELL... IT IS SPRING TIME, SO YOU GET ALL KINDS OF PEOPLE COMING OUT OF THE WOODWORK.

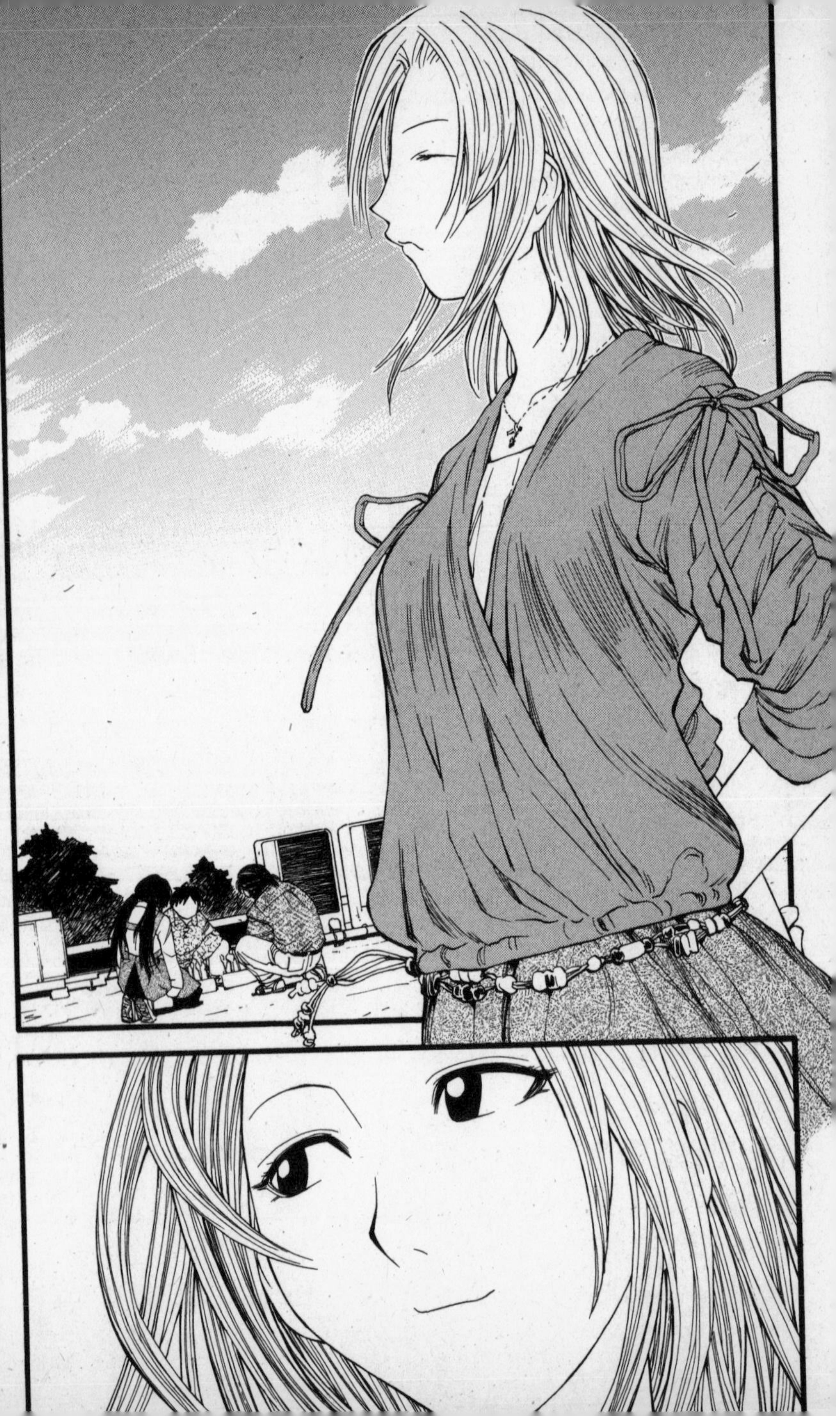

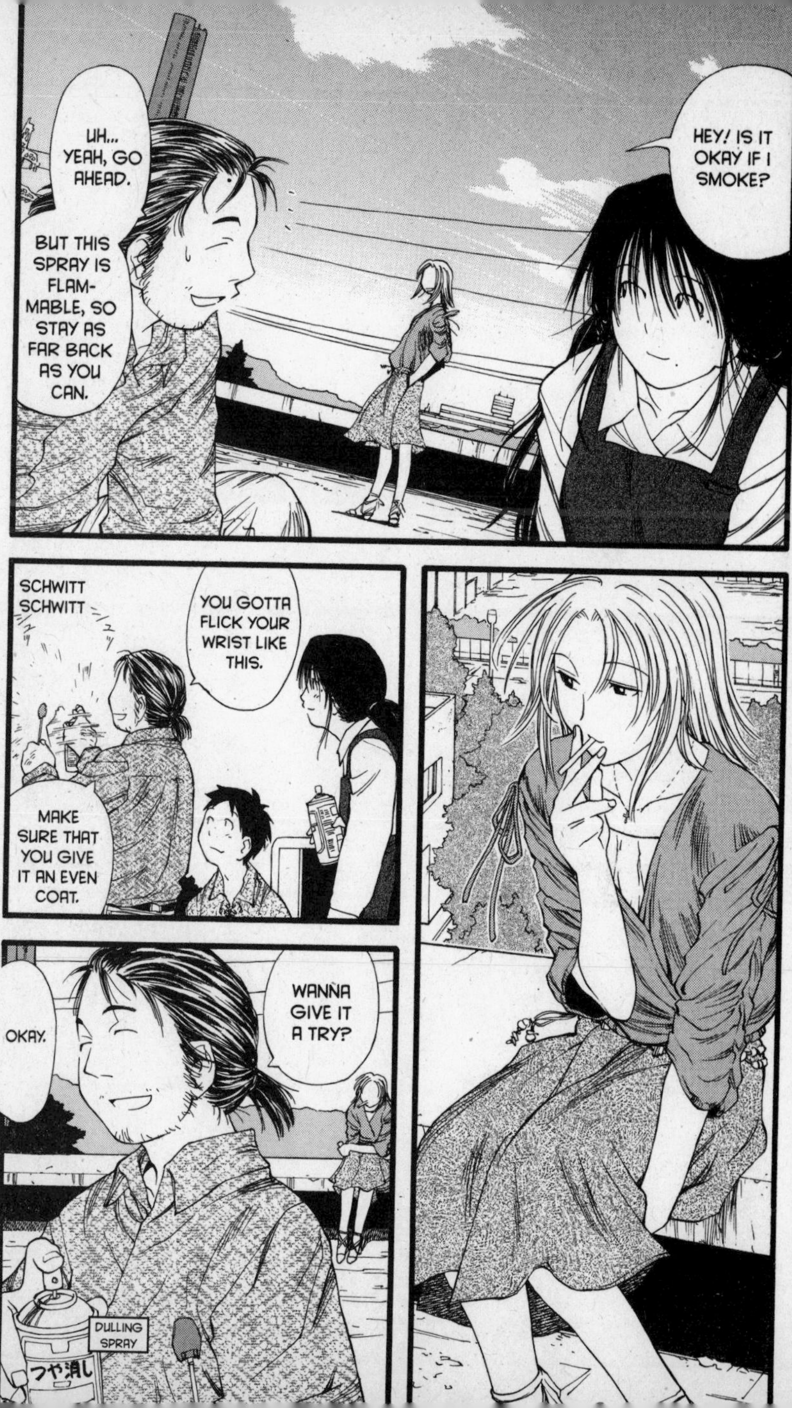
HEY! IS IT OKAY IF I SMOKE?
UH... YEAH, GO AHEAD.
BUT THIS SPRAY IS FLAM-MABLE, SO STAY AS FAR BACK AS YOU CAN.
YOU GOTTA FLICK YOUR WRIST LIKE THIS.
SCHWITT SCHWITT
MAKE SURE THAT YOU GIVE IT AN EVEN COAT.
WANNA GIVE IT A TRY?
OKAY.
DULLING SPRAY
つや消し

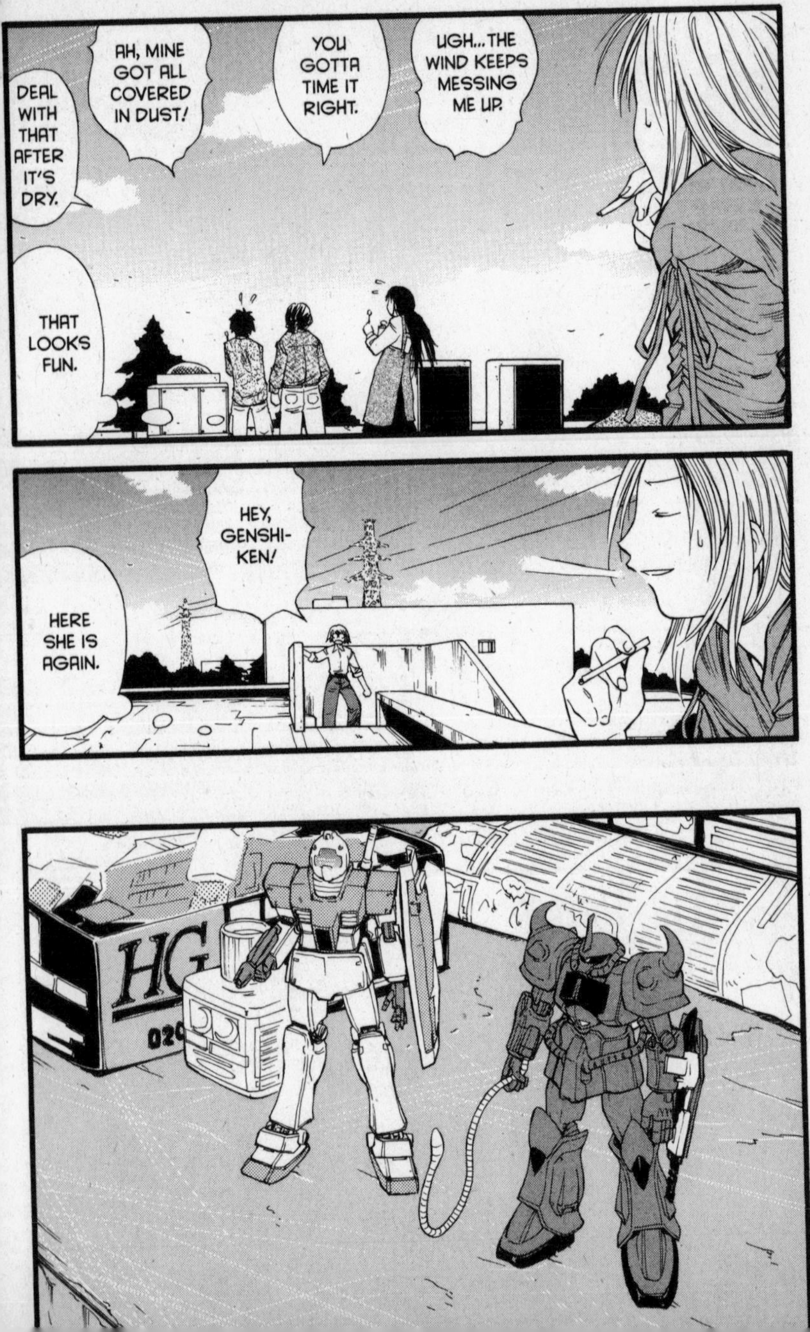
UGH... THE WIND KEEPS MESSING ME UP.
YOU GOTTA TIME IT RIGHT.
AH, MINE GOT ALL COVERED IN DUST!
DEAL WITH THAT AFTER IT'S DRY.
THAT LOOKS FUN.
HEY, GENSHIKEN!
HERE SHE IS AGAIN.
HG
020

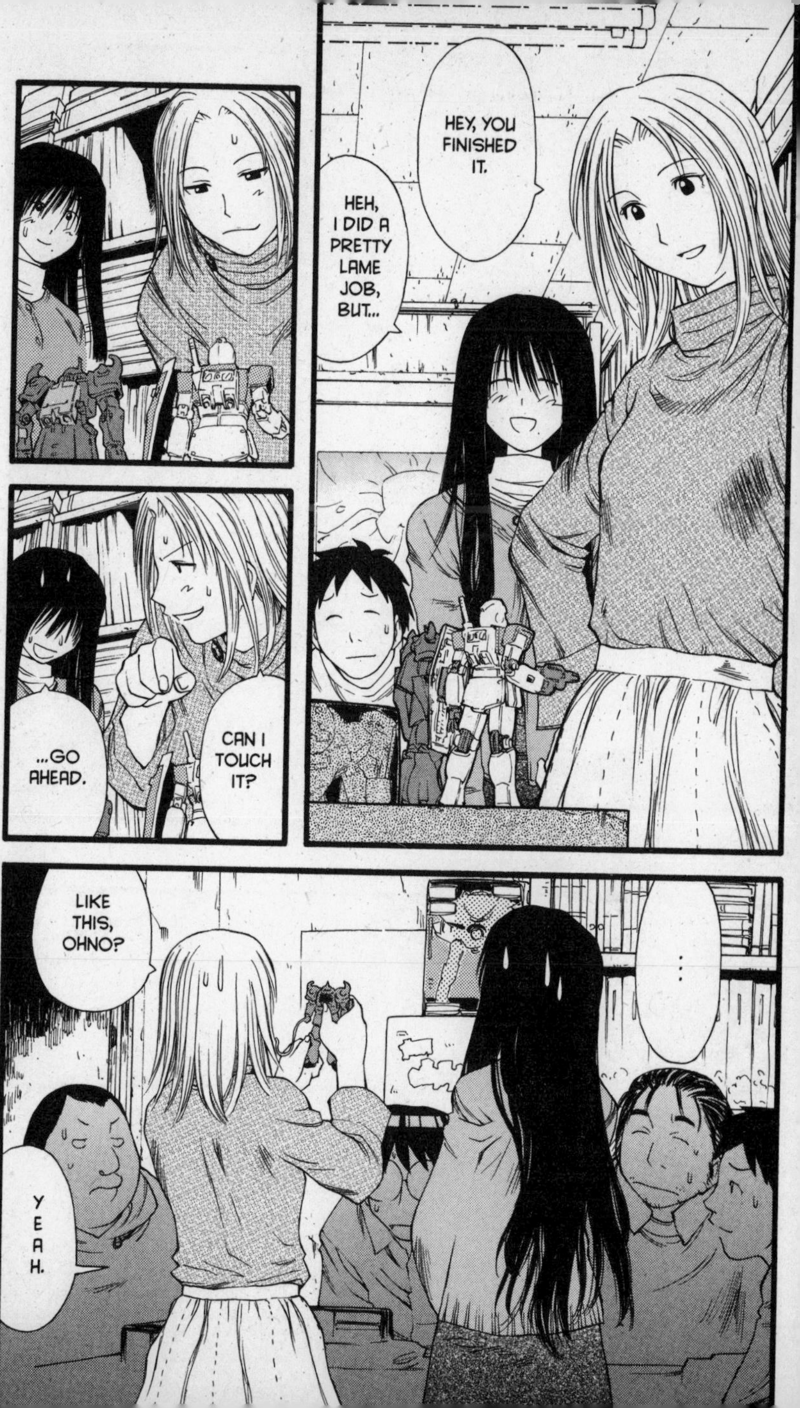
HEY, YOU FINISHED IT.
HEH, I DID A PRETTY LAME JOB, BUT...
CAN I TOUCH IT?
...GO AHEAD.
...
LIKE THIS, OHNO?
YEAH.

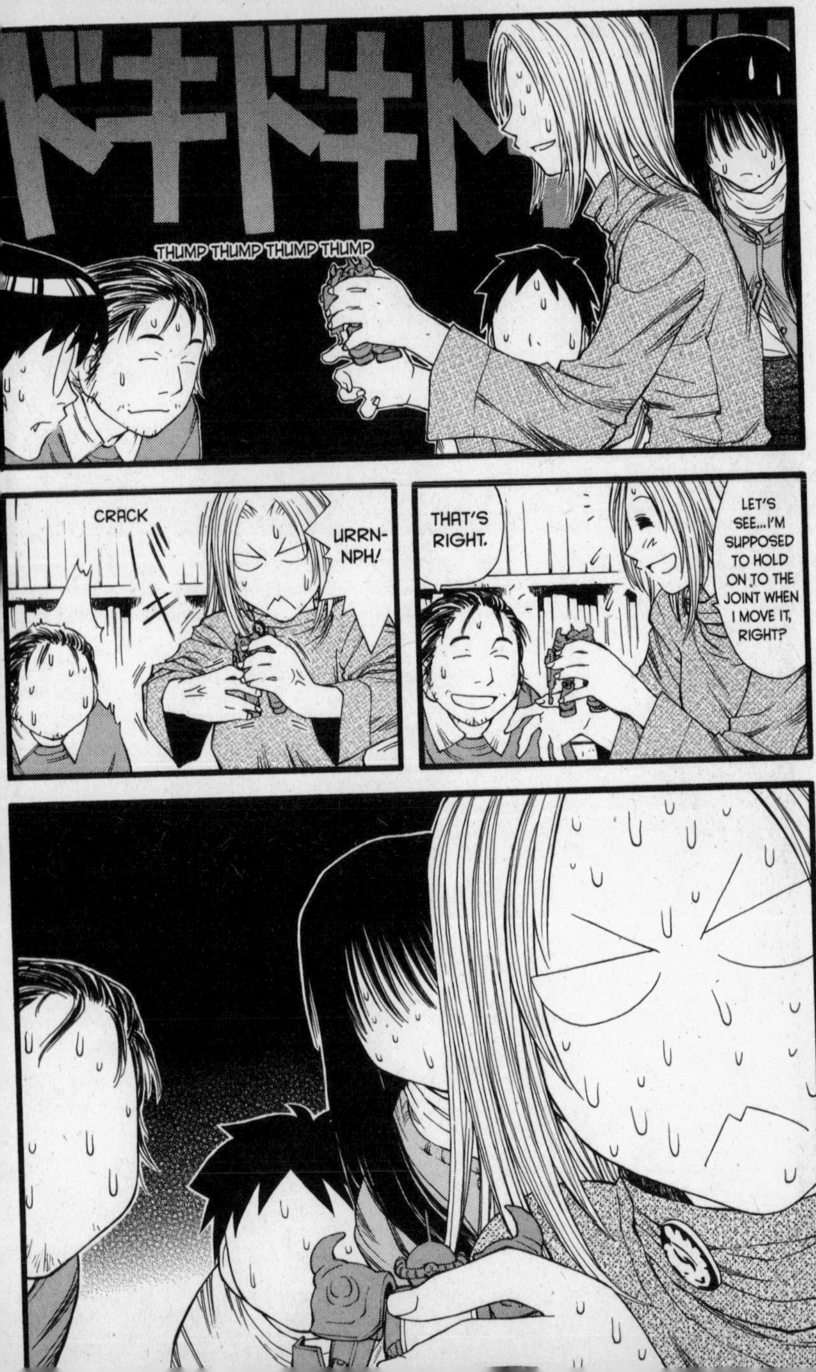
ドキドキド
THUMP THUMP THUMP THUMP
LET'S SEE...I'M SUPPOSED TO HOLD ON TO THE JOINT WHEN I MOVE IT, RIGHT?
THAT'S RIGHT.
URRN-NPH!
CRACK

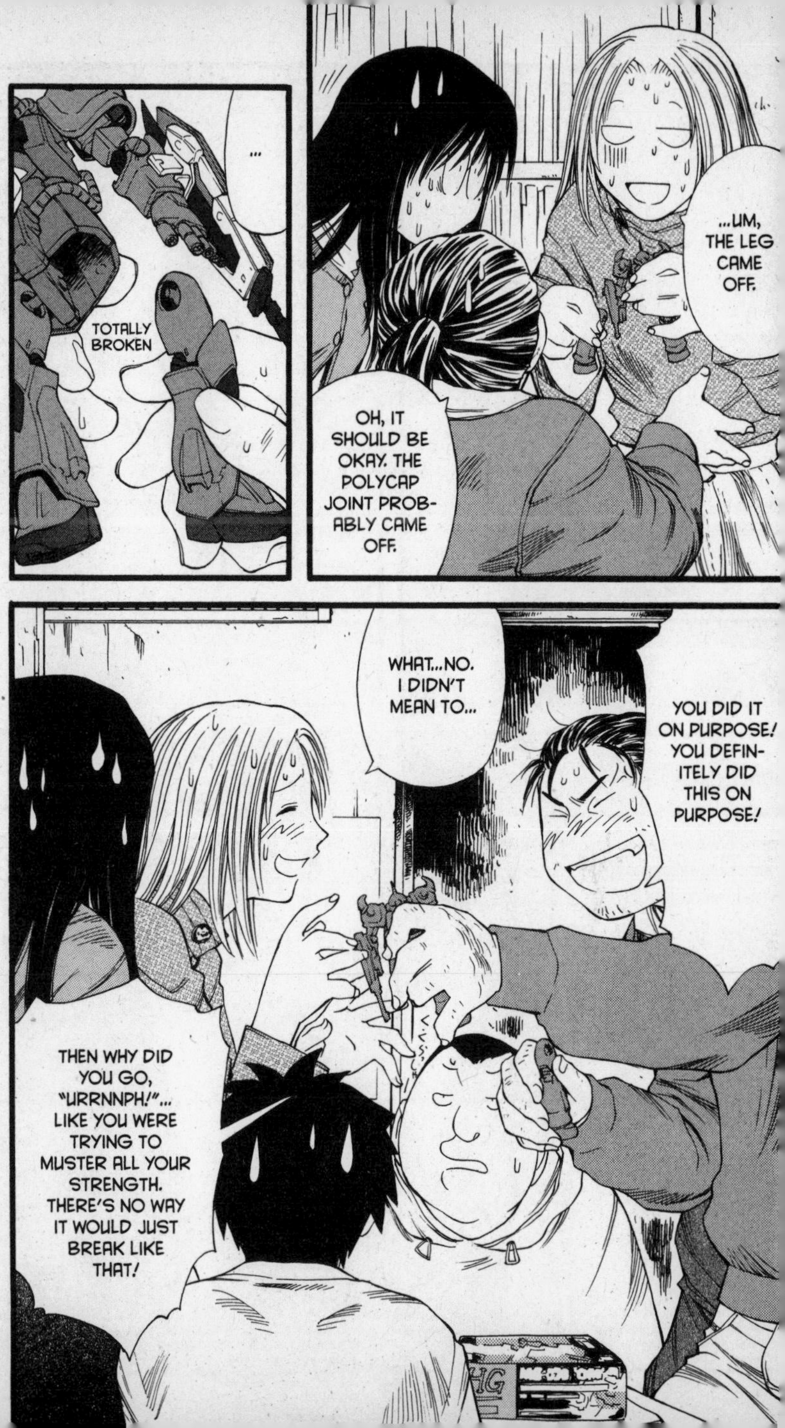
...UM, THE LEG CAME OFF.
OH, IT SHOULD BE OKAY. THE POLYCAP JOINT PROBABLY CAME OFF.
...
TOTALLY BROKEN
YOU DID IT ON PURPOSE! YOU DEFINITELY DID THIS ON PURPOSE!
WHAT...NO. I DIDN'T MEAN TO...
THEN WHY DID YOU GO, "URRNNPH!"... LIKE YOU WERE TRYING TO MUSTER ALL YOUR STRENGTH. THERE'S NO WAY IT WOULD JUST BREAK LIKE THAT!

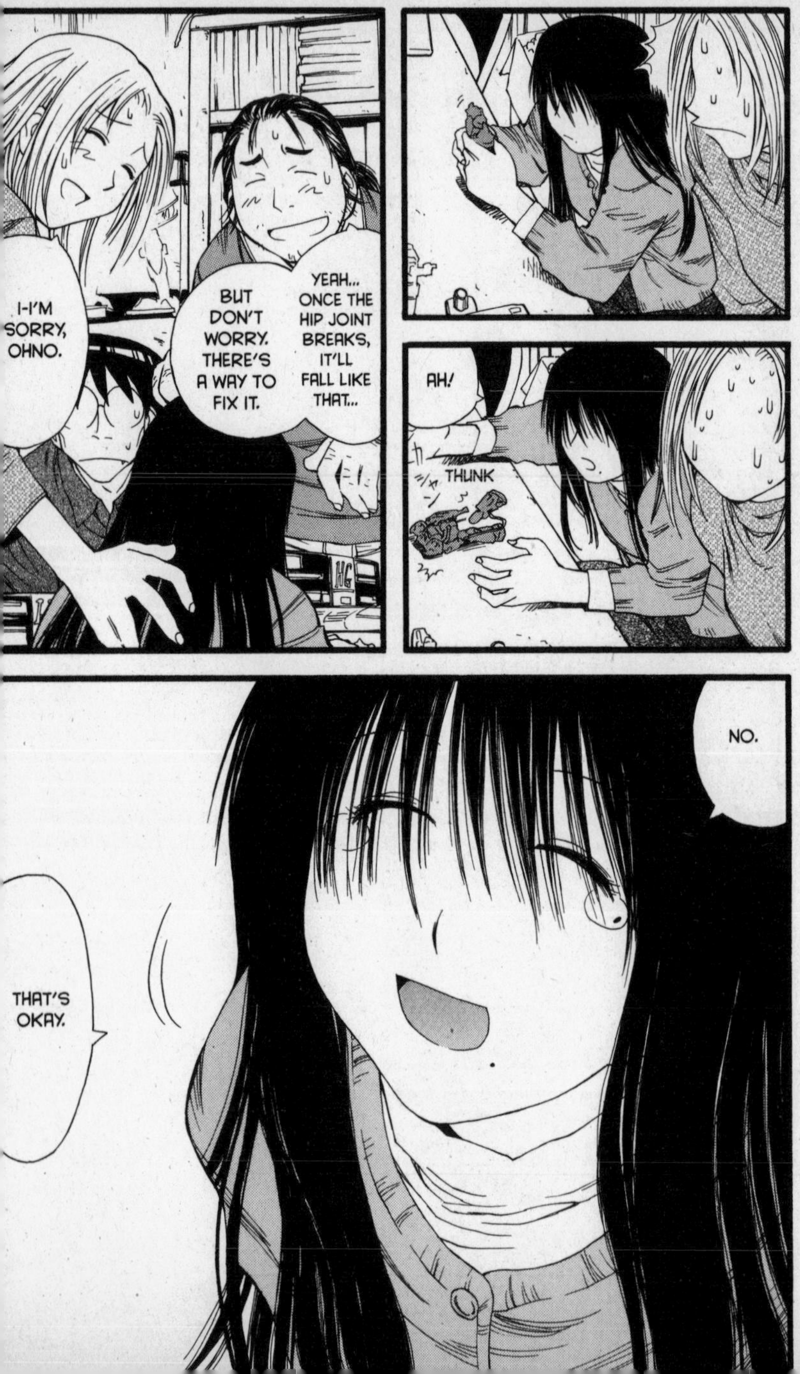
AH!
THUNK
YEAH... ONCE THE HIP JOINT BREAKS, IT'LL FALL LIKE THAT...
BUT DON'T WORRY. THERE'S A WAY TO FIX IT.
I-I'M SORRY, OHNO.
NO.
THAT'S OKAY.

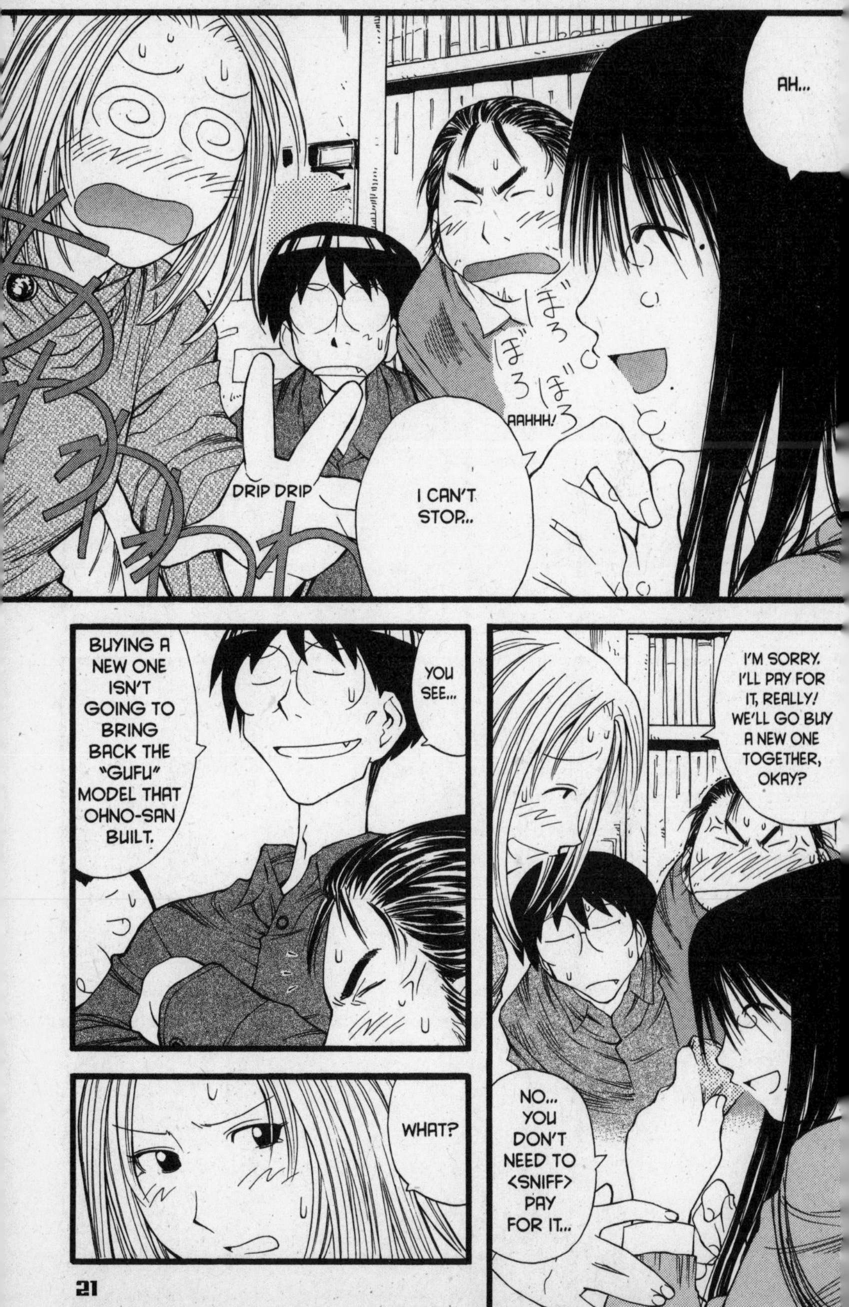
AH...
ぼろぼろ ぼろぼろ
AAHHH!
I CAN'T STOP...
DRIP DRIP
I'M SORRY. I'LL PAY FOR IT, REALLY! WE'LL GO BUY A NEW ONE TOGETHER, OKAY?
NO... YOU DON'T NEED TO <SNIFF> PAY FOR IT...
YOU SEE...
BUYING A NEW ONE ISN'T GOING TO BRING BACK THE "GUFU" MODEL THAT OHNO-SAN BUILT.
WHAT?

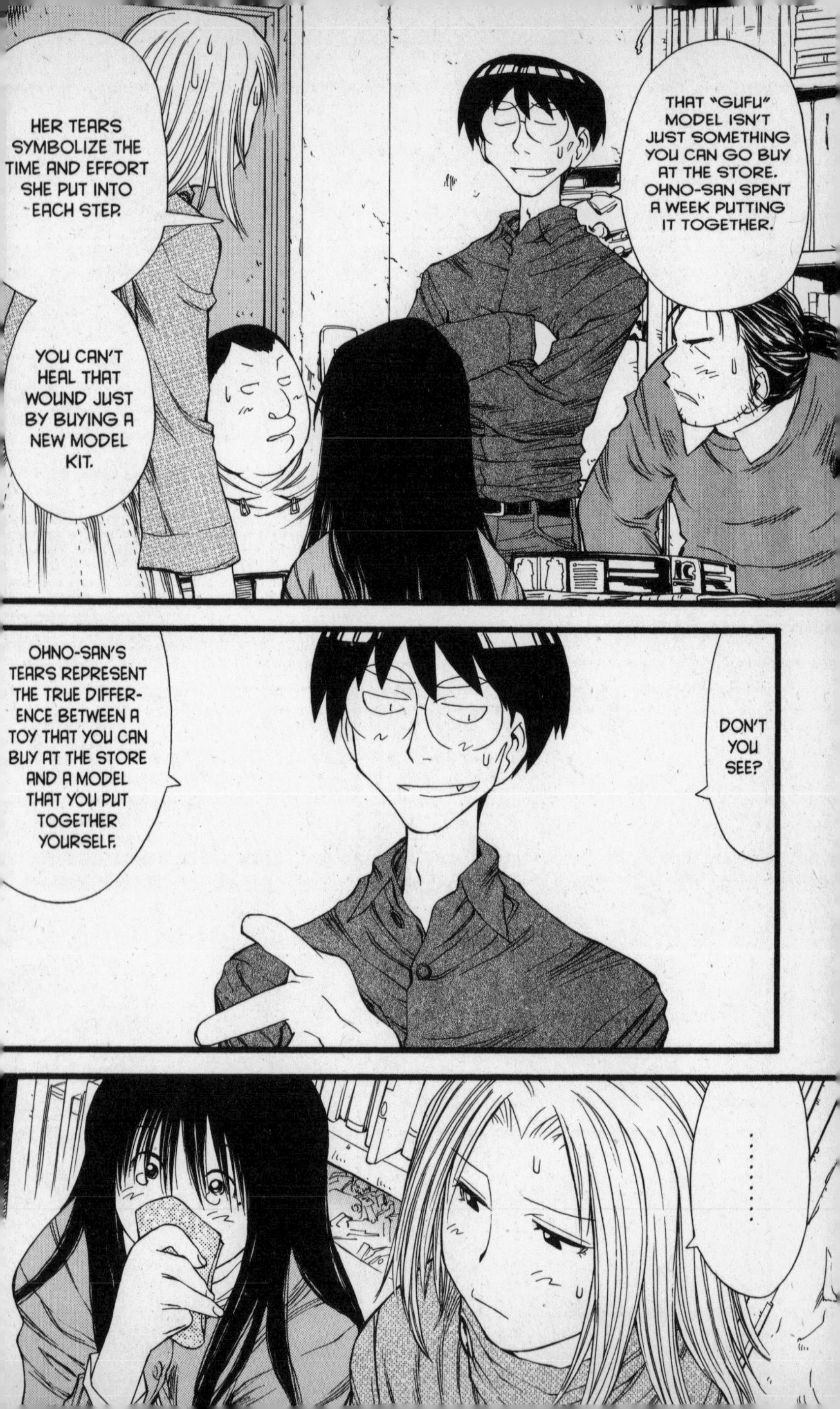
THAT "GUFU" MODEL ISN'T JUST SOMETHING YOU CAN GO BUY AT THE STORE. OHNO-SAN SPENT A WEEK PUTTING IT TOGETHER.
HER TEARS SYMBOLIZE THE TIME AND EFFORT SHE PUT INTO EACH STEP.
YOU CAN'T HEAL THAT WOUND JUST BY BUYING A NEW MODEL KIT.
DON'T YOU SEE?
OHNO-SAN'S TEARS REPRESENT THE TRUE DIFFER-ENCE BETWEEN A TOY THAT YOU CAN BUY AT THE STORE AND A MODEL THAT YOU PUT TOGETHER YOURSELF.
....

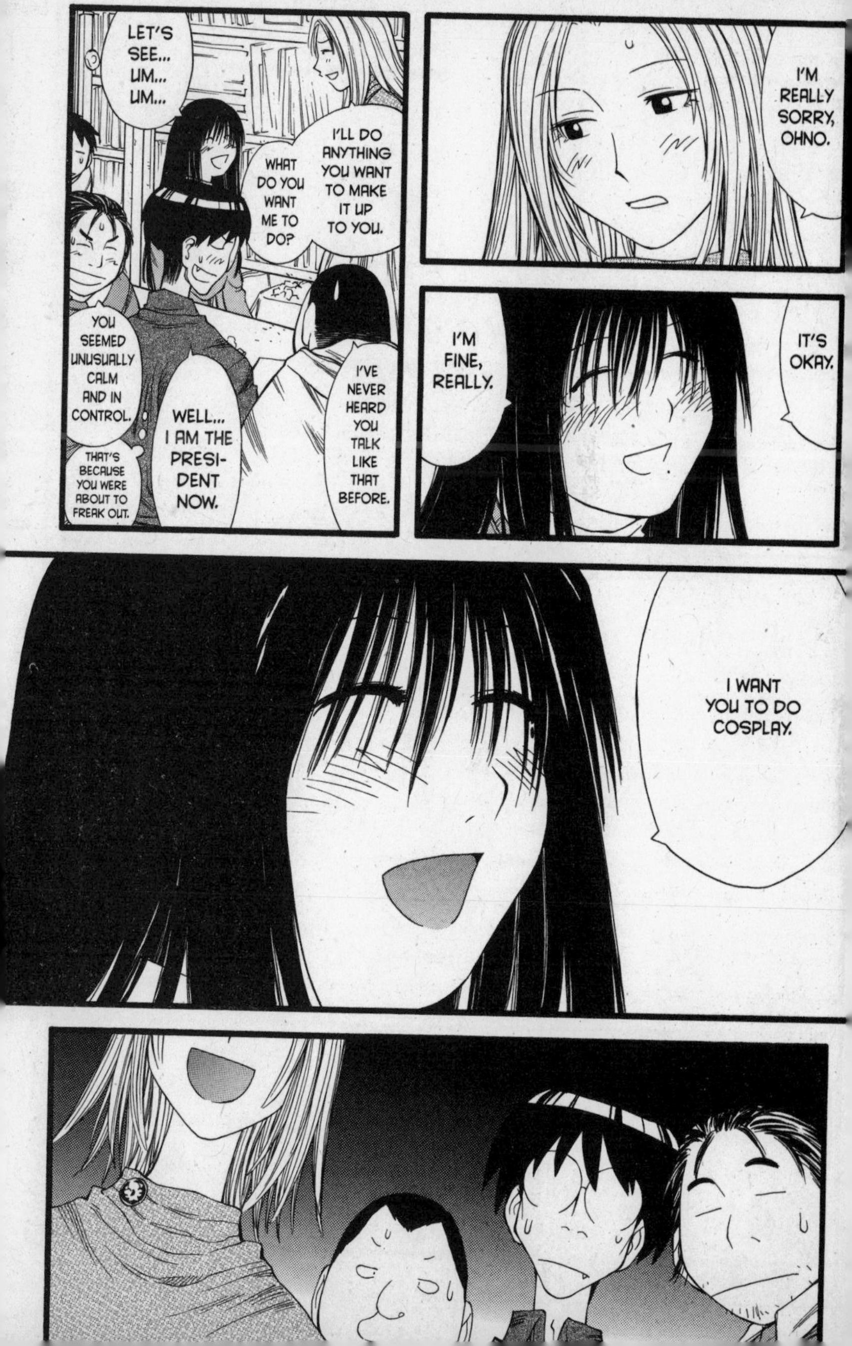
I'M REALLY SORRY, OHNO.
IT'S OKAY.
I'M FINE, REALLY.
I'LL DO ANYTHING YOU WANT TO MAKE IT UP TO YOU.
WHAT DO YOU WANT ME TO DO?
LET'S SEE... UM... UM...
I'VE NEVER HEARD YOU TALK LIKE THAT BEFORE.
WELL... I AM THE PRESIDENT NOW.
YOU SEEMED UNUSUALLY CALM AND IN CONTROL.
THAT'S BECAUSE YOU WERE ABOUT TO FREAK OUT.
I WANT YOU TO DO COSPLAY.

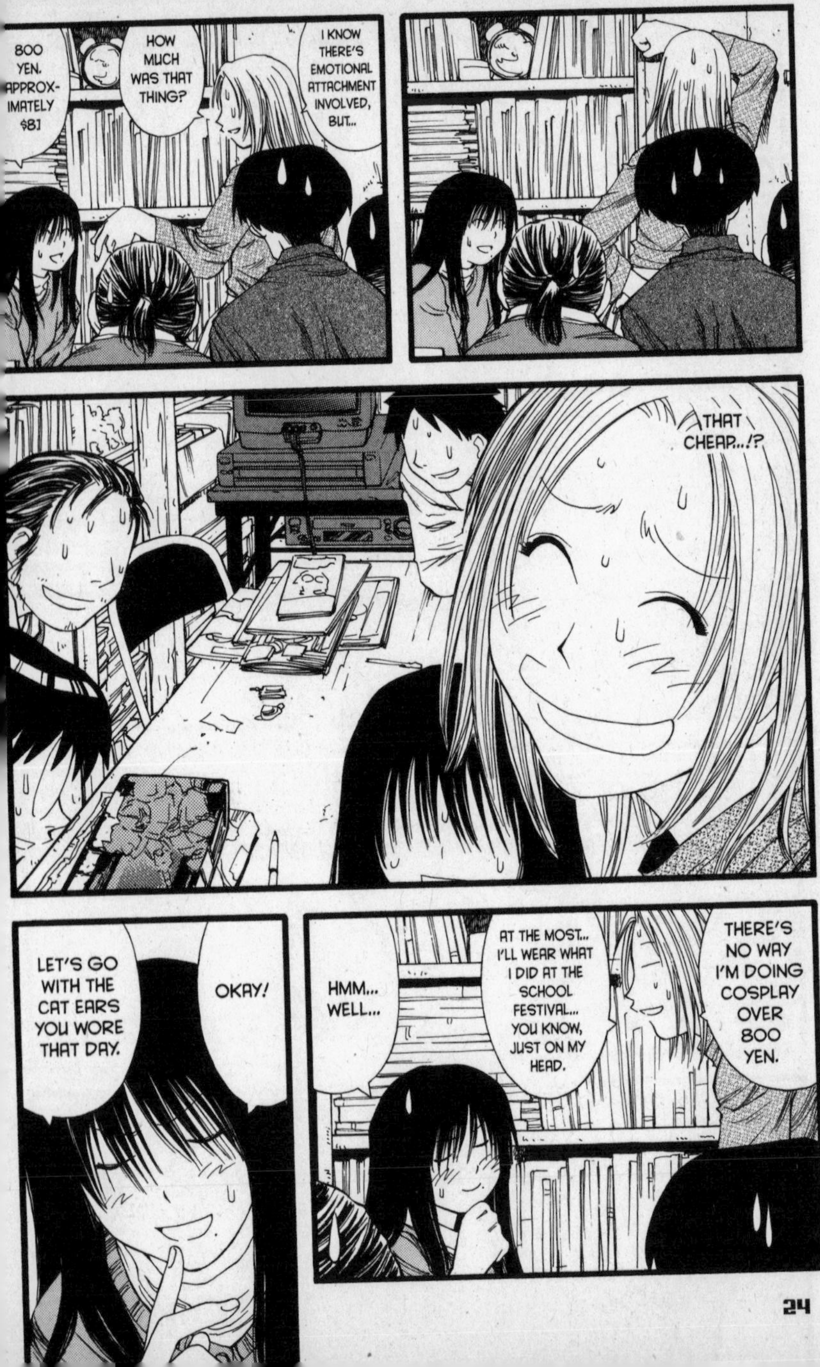
I KNOW THERE'S EMOTIONAL ATTACHMENT INVOLVED, BUT...
HOW MUCH WAS THAT THING?
800 YEN. [APPROXIMATELY $8]
THAT CHEAP...!?
THERE'S NO WAY I'M DOING COSPLAY OVER 800 YEN.
AT THE MOST... I'LL WEAR WHAT I DID AT THE SCHOOL FESTIVAL... YOU KNOW, JUST ON MY HEAD.
HMM... WELL...
OKAY!
LET'S GO WITH THE CAT EARS YOU WORE THAT DAY.

THE LACE
IS STUCK
ON WITH
SUPER
GLUE.

YANK
YANK

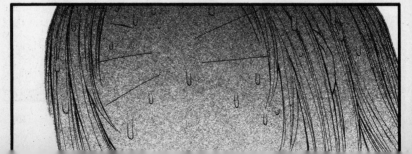

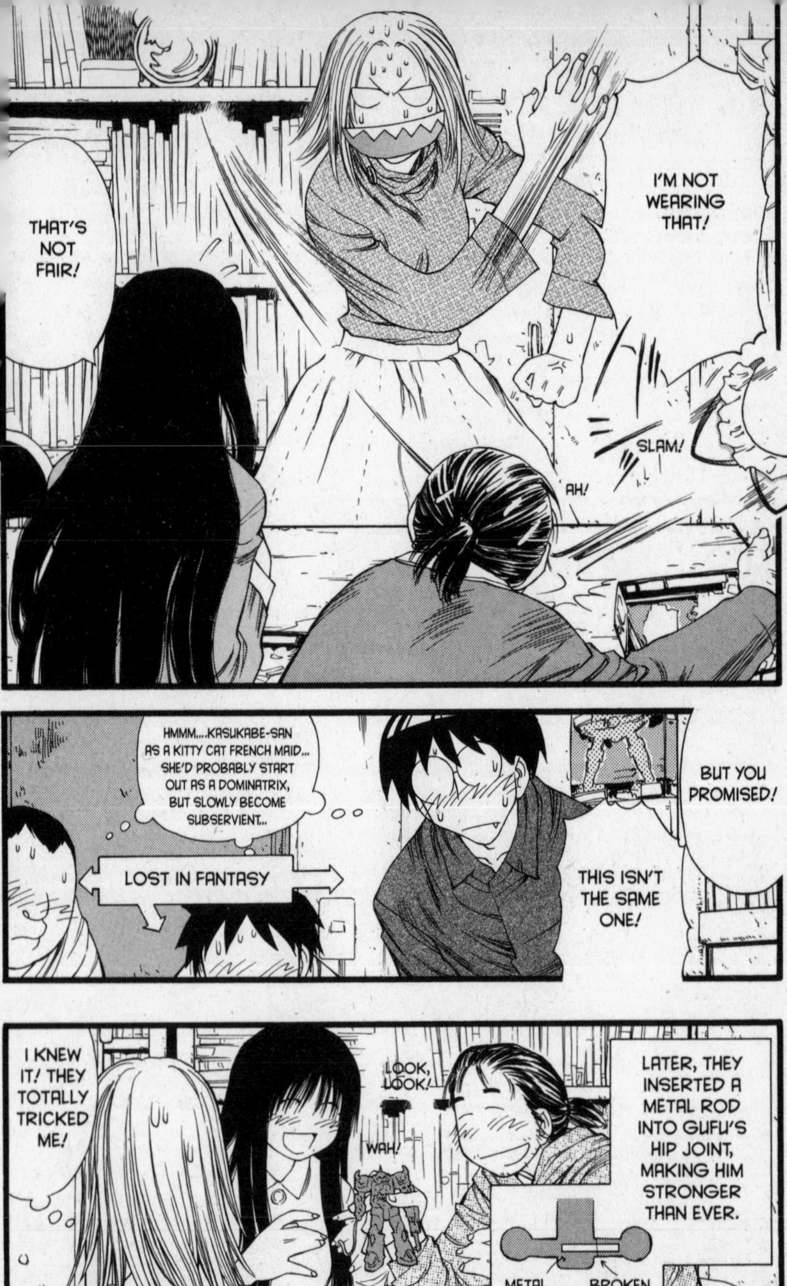
I'M NOT WEARING THAT!
SLAM!
AH!
THAT'S NOT FAIR!
BUT YOU PROMISED!
THIS ISN'T THE SAME ONE!
HMMM....KASUKABE-SAN AS A KITTY CAT FRENCH MAID... SHE'D PROBABLY START OUT AS A DOMINATRIX, BUT SLOWLY BECOME SUBSERVIENT...
LOST IN FANTASY
LATER, THEY INSERTED A METAL ROD INTO GUFU'S HIP JOINT, MAKING HIM STRONGER THAN EVER.
METAL ROD
BROKEN SECTION
LOOK, LOOK!
WAH!
I KNEW IT! THEY TOTALLY TRICKED ME!

END OF CHAPTER 13

1   RENKO KAMISHAKUJII AND HER FOLLOWERS

WRITTEN BY 72-YEAR-OLD PIT VIPER

HEY! PIT VIPER HERE. TODAY, I'M GOING TO TALK ABOUT THE DOUJIN FAN GAME "UNBALANCED FIGHTER." AS YOU CAN TELL BY THE TITLE, THE CHARACTER BALANCE IN THIS GAME IS TOTALLY WHACKED. (LAUGHS) THE CHARACTER SETTINGS ARE REALLY ECCENTRIC, JUST AS YOU WOULD EXPECT FROM A DOUJIN GAME. THE PHILOSOPHY IS SORT OF LIKE "WE IGNORE THE QUALITY OF THE GAME ITSELF, BUT OUR LOVE FOR THE CHARACTERS EXPLODES ONTO THE SCREEN." I REALLY LIKE IT.

WELL, I THINK I'LL JUST GET RIGHT TO IT, AND INTRO-DUCE THE CHARACTER I USE. KYA! ★

IT'S RENKO-CHAN, CLAP, CLAP, CLAP... "YOU MEAN, IT'S NOT SHINOBU-SENSEI?" SHINOBU'S TECHNIQUE OF TAKING OFF HER GLASSES IS TOO "ORIGINAL COMBO" STYLE FOR ME. I DON'T REALLY LIKE "ORIGINAL COMBO" (LAUGHS). IT'S TOUGH ON OLD FOLKS LIKE ME. HEH, HEH. THAT'S WHY I CHOSE RENKO AND YAMADA. I SAID HER "FOLLOWERS" ABOVE, BUT IT'S REALLY JUST YAMADA. THE OTHER TWO GUYS ONLY COME OUT WHEN SHE'S DOING HER TECHNIQUE.

I DON'T REALLY WANNA CRITICIZE SHINOBU-SENSEI HERE, BUT RENKO IS A VERY TECHNICAL CHARACTER. YAMADA'S STANCE IS KIND OF LIKE THAT OF THE CHARACTER "DADA." THE WAY YOU USE YAMADA TO ATTACK IS A LOT LIKE "DADA," TOO.

YAMADA CAN ALSO BE USED FOR DEFENSE. (I MEAN, TO BLOCK.) BUT WHEN YAMADA ISN'T THERE, IT'S IMPOSSIBLE TO GUARD RENKO. RENKO-CHAN DOESN'T HAVE MUCH REACH, SO SHE HAS TO FIGHT CLOSE UP. BUT, MY FELLOW SOLDIERS, IT FEELS GOOD T ATTACK USING RENKO-CHAN'S SHORT LITTLE ARMS AND LEGS!

SLIDING KICK

IF YOU PRESS D WHILE YAMADA KICKS, YOU END UP WITH A SLIDIN ATTACK. THE TRICK TO GETTING THROUGH YOUR OPPONENT'S GUAR IS TO KEEP DOING THAT SLIDE WHILE MAKING RENKO ATTACK WITH HI JUMP KICK. WHEN YAMADA GETS HIT, YOU LOSE POINTS, BUT THERE'S N DAMAGE, SO YAMADA'S GREAT FOR DEFENSE. YOU CAN ALSO USE RENK CHAN FOR AN AIRBORNE ATTACK. SHE'S GOOD AT SNEAK ATTACKS TOO SO USE THAT AS THE PRINCIPLE ATTACK METHOD.

YAMADA'S "GIANT SWING" IS EXACTLY WHAT IT SOUNDS LIK (LAUGHS). YOU COULD ALMOST SAY THAT'S THE REASON I CHOOS RENKO-CHAN. IT'S KIND OF SLOW, BUT THE YAMADA CHARACTER GO AROUND THE OPPONENT, AND CAN REALLY PENETRATE THE DEFENSE. IT EFFECTIVE MORE OFTEN THAN YOU WOULD EXPECT. THE MORE REPET TIVE ATTACKS YOU DO, THE FASTER YOU SPIN. MY PERSONAL BEST 6 IN A ROW.

SPIN, SPIN, SPIN

IN THE "FINAL CRUSHER" ATTACK, YOU ACTUALLY THROW THE SPIN NING YAMADA AT YOUR OPPONENT (LAUGHS). THERE'S NO WAY FOR TH OPPONENT TO GUARD AGAINST THAT. IT'S A VERY POWERFUL ATTACK SO YOU ONLY WANT TO USE IT TO DEAL THE FINAL BLOW. AFTER BOT THE "SWING" AND THE "CRUSHER" ATTACKS , YAMADA NEEDS TIME T RECOVER. THE MORE YOU SPIN HER, THE MORE TIRED SHE GETS. BU DON'T WORRY ABOUT THAT. SPIN, SPIN, SPIN! [PIT VIPER]

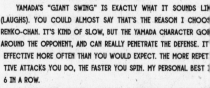

ABANDONING LOGIC

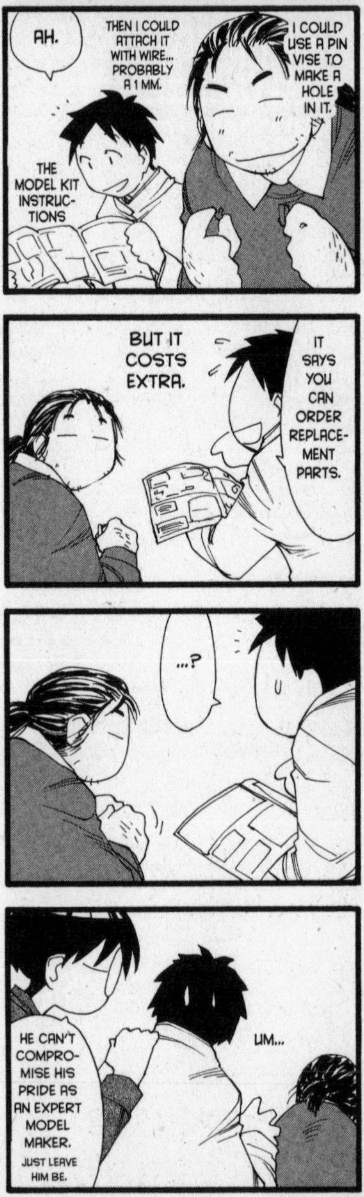
I COULD USE A PIN VISE TO MAKE A HOLE IN IT.
THEN I COULD ATTACH IT WITH WIRE... PROBABLY A 1 MM.
AH.
THE MODEL KIT INSTRUCTIONS
IT SAYS YOU CAN ORDER REPLACEMENT PARTS.
BUT IT COSTS EXTRA.
...?
UM...
HE CAN'T COMPROMISE HIS PRIDE AS AN EXPERT MODEL MAKER.
JUST LEAVE HIM BE.

LIFE IN 2003

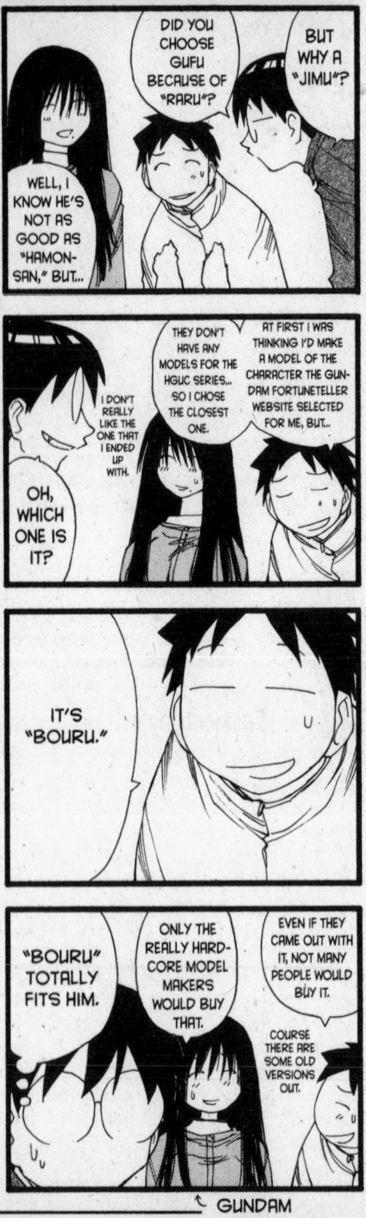
BUT WHY A "JIMU"?
DID YOU CHOOSE GUFU BECAUSE OF "RARU"?
WELL, I KNOW HE'S NOT AS GOOD AS "HAMON-SAN," BUT...
AT FIRST I WAS THINKING I'D MAKE A MODEL OF THE CHARACTER THE GUNDAM FORTUNETELLER WEBSITE SELECTED FOR ME, BUT...
THEY DON'T HAVE ANY MODELS FOR THE HGUC SERIES... SO I CHOSE THE CLOSEST ONE.
I DON'T REALLY LIKE THE ONE THAT I ENDED UP WITH.
OH, WHICH ONE IS IT?
IT'S "BOURU."
EVEN IF THEY CAME OUT WITH IT, NOT MANY PEOPLE WOULD BUY IT.
ONLY THE REALLY HARDCORE MODEL MAKERS WOULD BUY THAT.
COURSE THERE ARE SOME OLD VERSIONS OUT.
"BOURU" TOTALLY FITS HIM.
GUNDAM

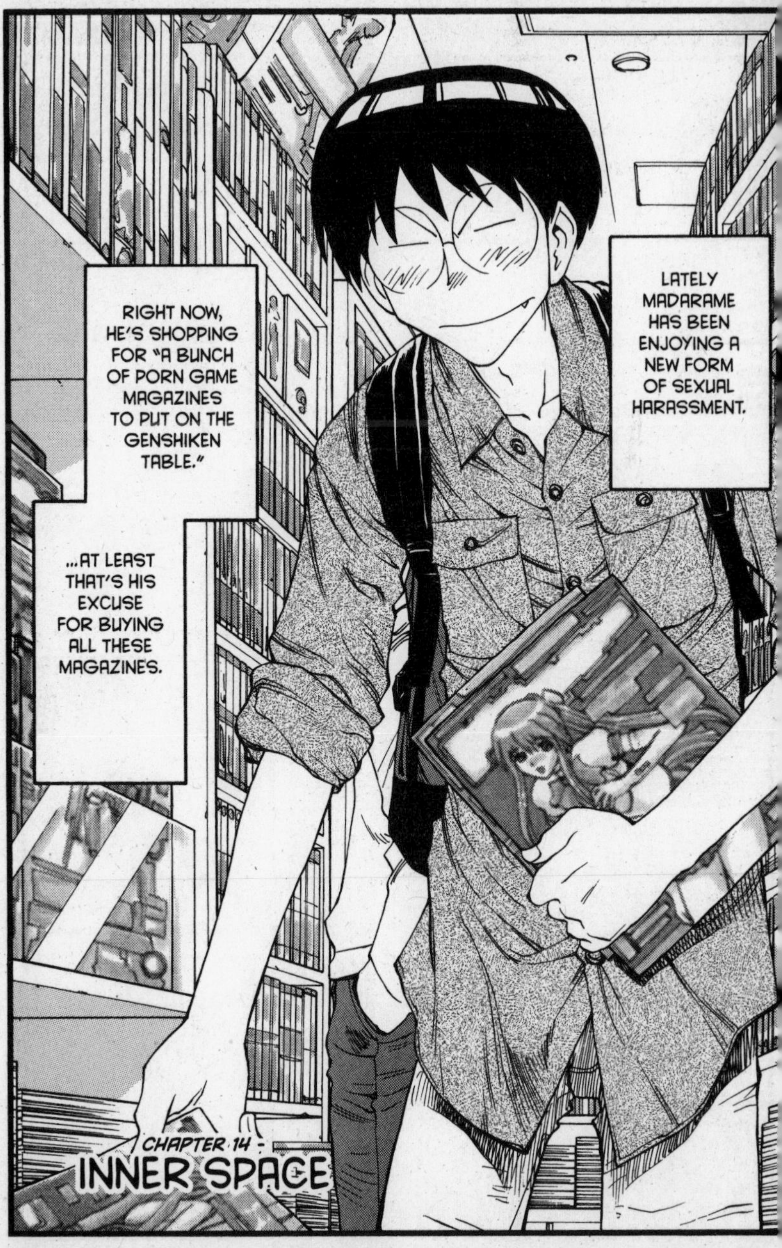
LATELY MADARAME HAS BEEN ENJOYING A NEW FORM OF SEXUAL HARASSMENT.
RIGHT NOW, HE'S SHOPPING FOR "A BUNCH OF PORN GAME MAGAZINES TO PUT ON THE GENSHIKEN TABLE."
...AT LEAST THAT'S HIS EXCUSE FOR BUYING ALL THESE MAGAZINES.
CHAPTER 14
INNER SPACE

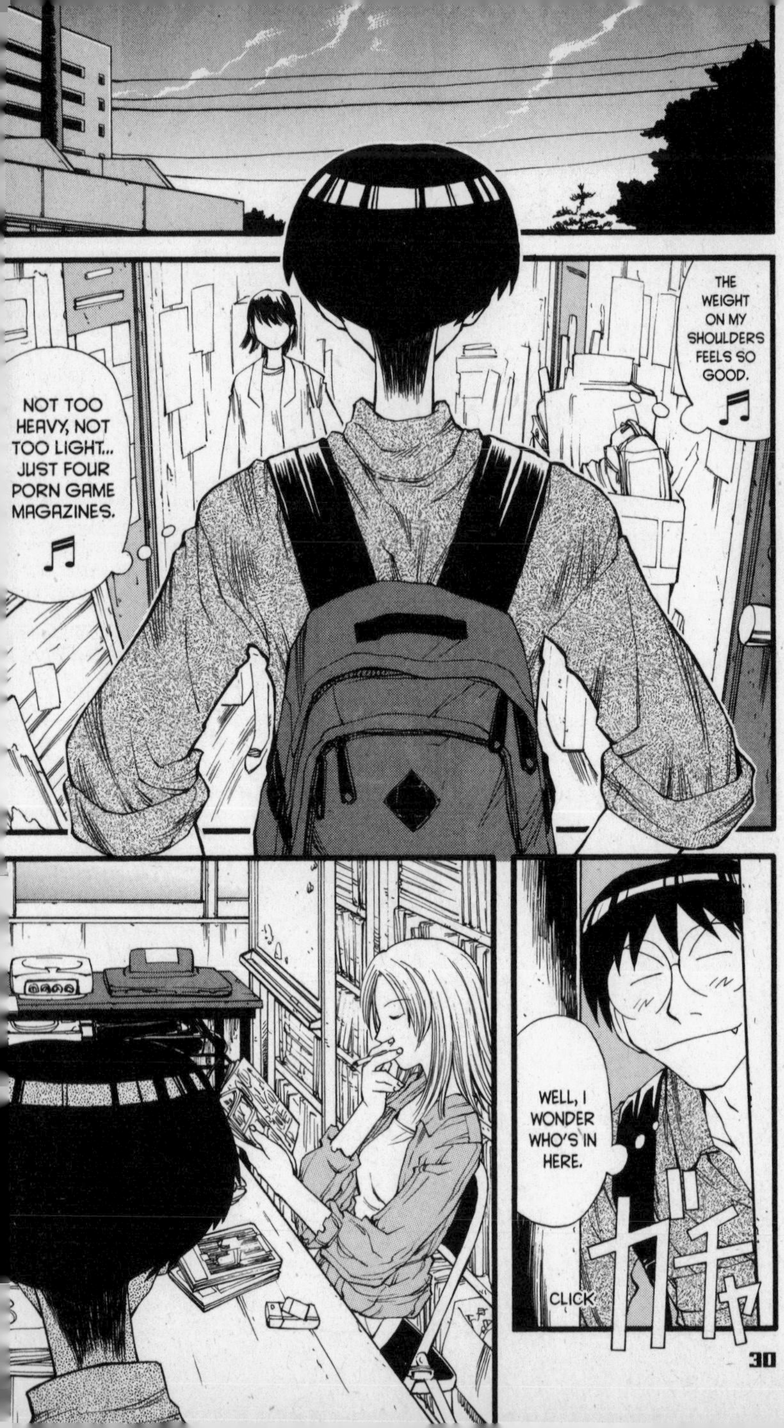
THE WEIGHT ON MY SHOULDERS FEELS SO GOOD. ♫
NOT TOO HEAVY, NOT TOO LIGHT... JUST FOUR PORN GAME MAGAZINES. ♫
WELL, I WONDER WHO'S IN HERE.
ガチャ
CLICK

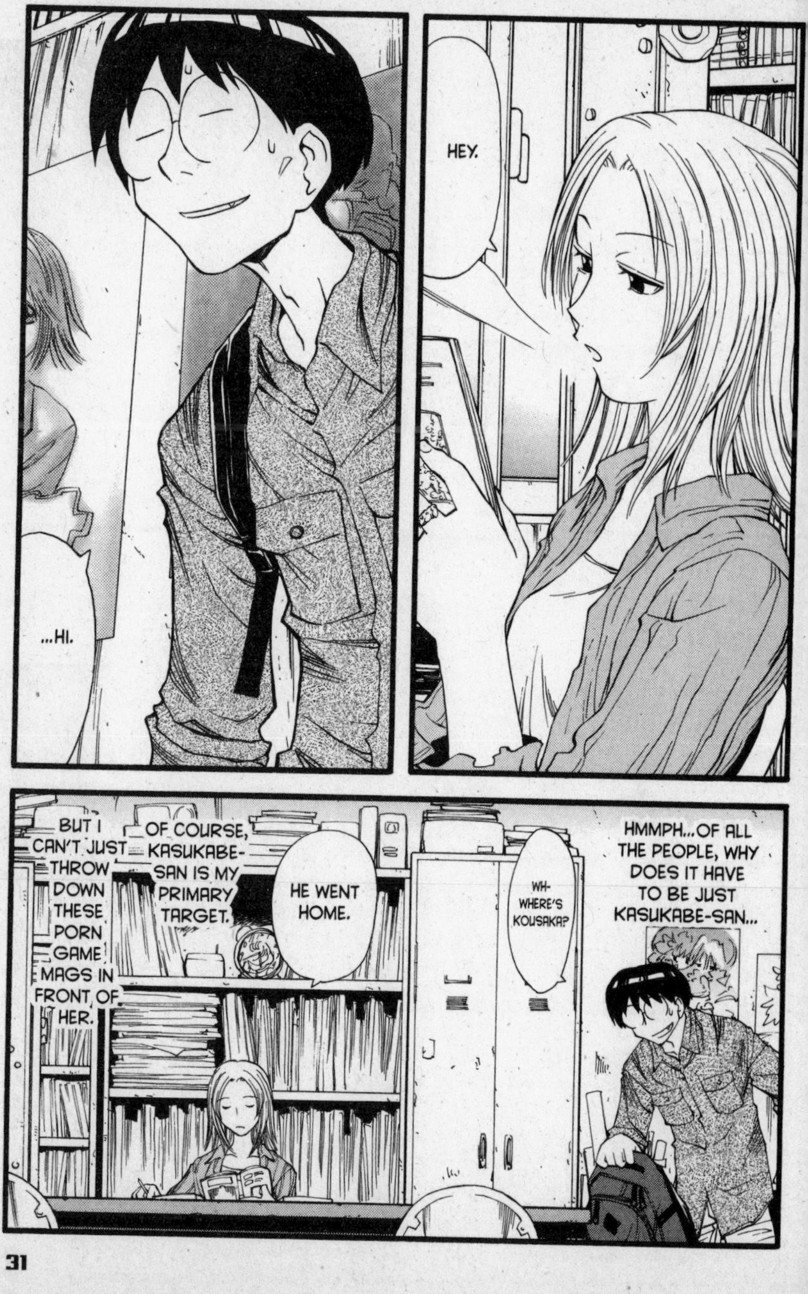
HEY.
...HI.
HMMPH...OF ALL THE PEOPLE, WHY DOES IT HAVE TO BE JUST KASUKABE-SAN...
WH-WHERE'S KOUSAKA?
HE WENT HOME.
OF COURSE, KASUKABE-SAN IS MY PRIMARY TARGET.
BUT I CAN'T JUST THROW DOWN THESE PORN GAME MAGS IN FRONT OF HER.

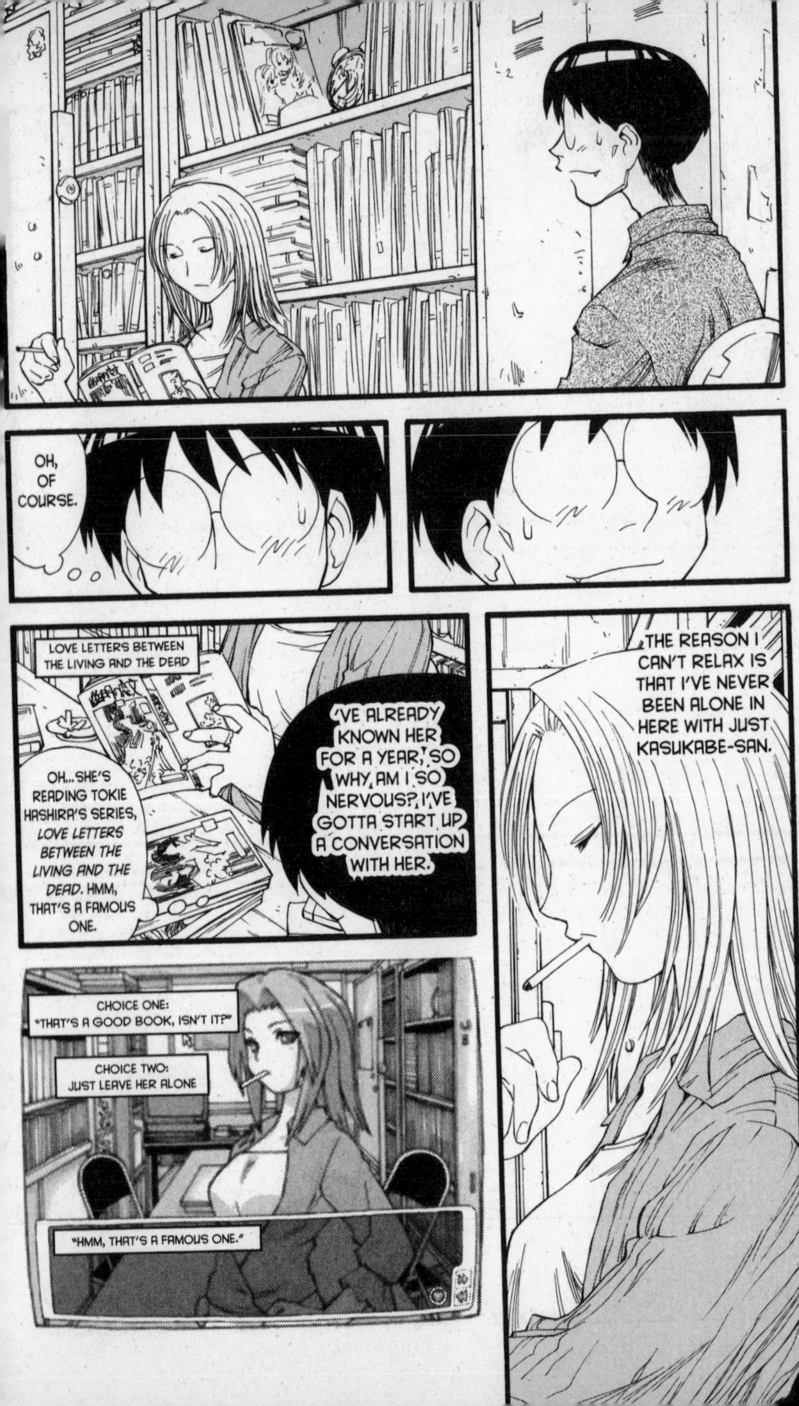
OH, OF COURSE.
THE REASON I CAN'T RELAX IS THAT I'VE NEVER BEEN ALONE IN HERE WITH JUST KASUKABE-SAN.
LOVE LETTERS BETWEEN THE LIVING AND THE DEAD
'VE ALREADY KNOWN HER FOR A YEAR, SO WHY AM I SO NERVOUS? I'VE GOTTA START UP A CONVERSATION WITH HER.
OH...SHE'S READING TOKIE HASHIRA'S SERIES, *LOVE LETTERS BETWEEN THE LIVING AND THE DEAD*. HMM, THAT'S A FAMOUS ONE.
CHOICE ONE: "THAT'S A GOOD BOOK, ISN'T IT?"
CHOICE TWO: JUST LEAVE HER ALONE
"HMM, THAT'S A FAMOUS ONE."

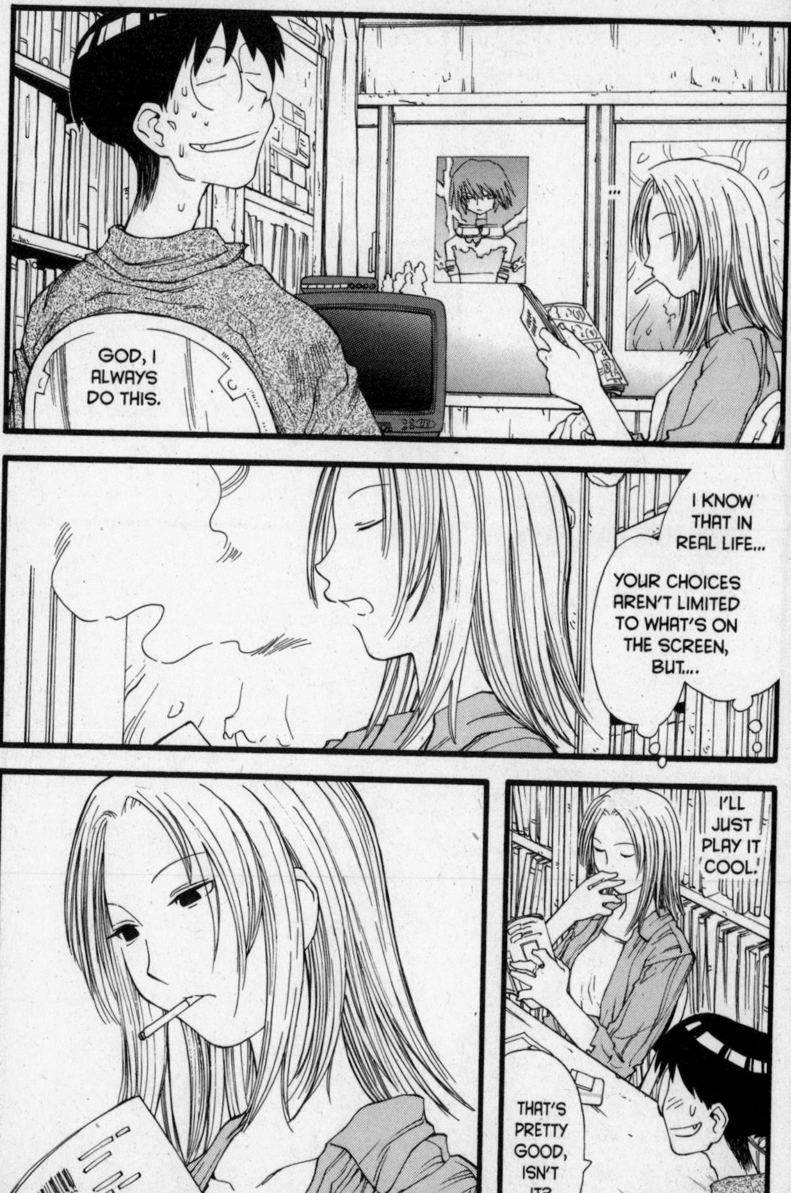
...
GOD, I ALWAYS DO THIS.
I KNOW THAT IN REAL LIFE...
YOUR CHOICES AREN'T LIMITED TO WHAT'S ON THE SCREEN, BUT....
I'LL JUST PLAY IT COOL.
THAT'S PRETTY GOOD, ISN'T IT?

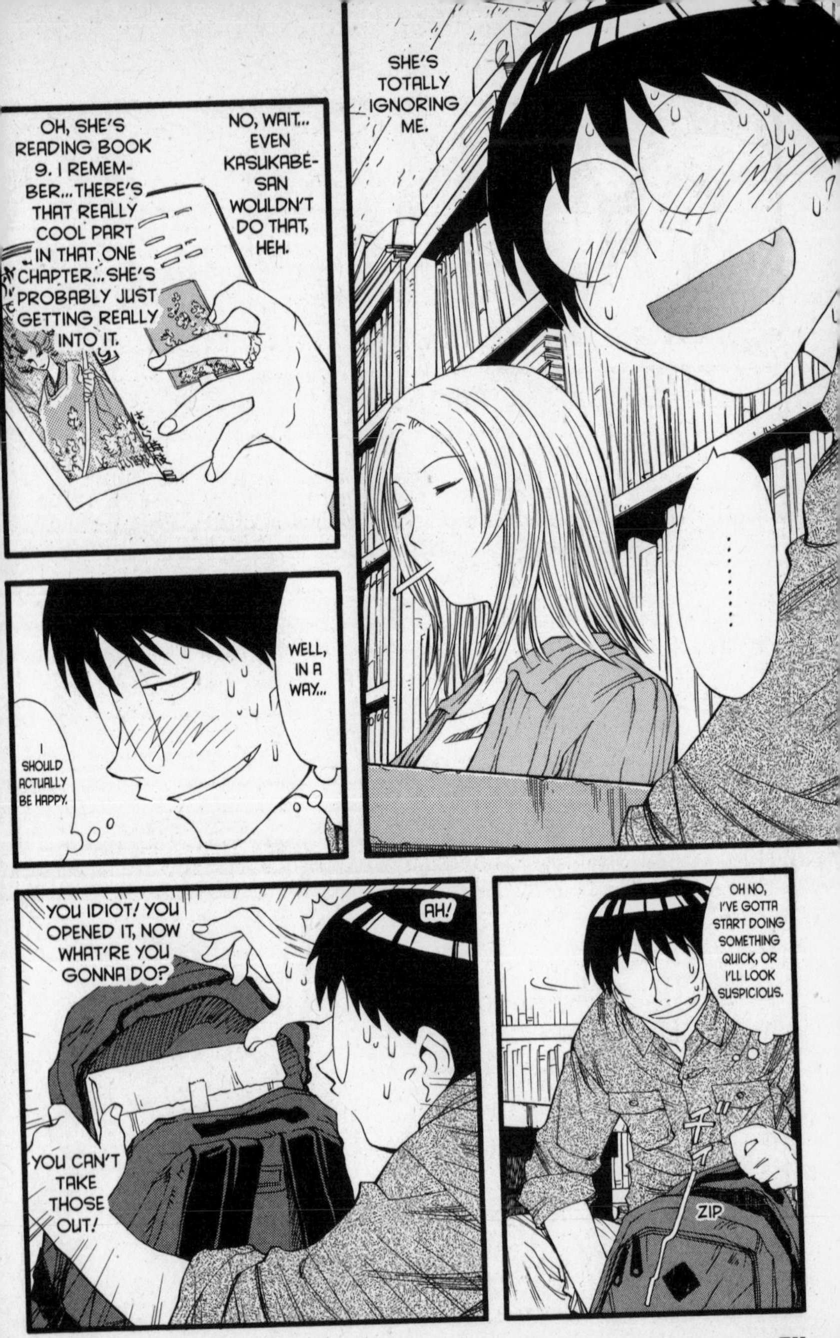
SHE'S TOTALLY IGNORING ME.
....
NO, WAIT... EVEN KASUKABE-SAN WOULDN'T DO THAT, HEH.
OH, SHE'S READING BOOK 9. I REMEMBER... THERE'S THAT REALLY COOL PART IN THAT ONE CHAPTER... SHE'S PROBABLY JUST GETTING REALLY INTO IT.
WELL, IN A WAY...
I SHOULD ACTUALLY BE HAPPY.
OH NO, I'VE GOTTA START DOING SOMETHING QUICK, OR I'LL LOOK SUSPICIOUS.
ZIP
AH!
YOU IDIOT! YOU OPENED IT, NOW WHAT'RE YOU GONNA DO?
YOU CAN'T TAKE THOSE OUT!

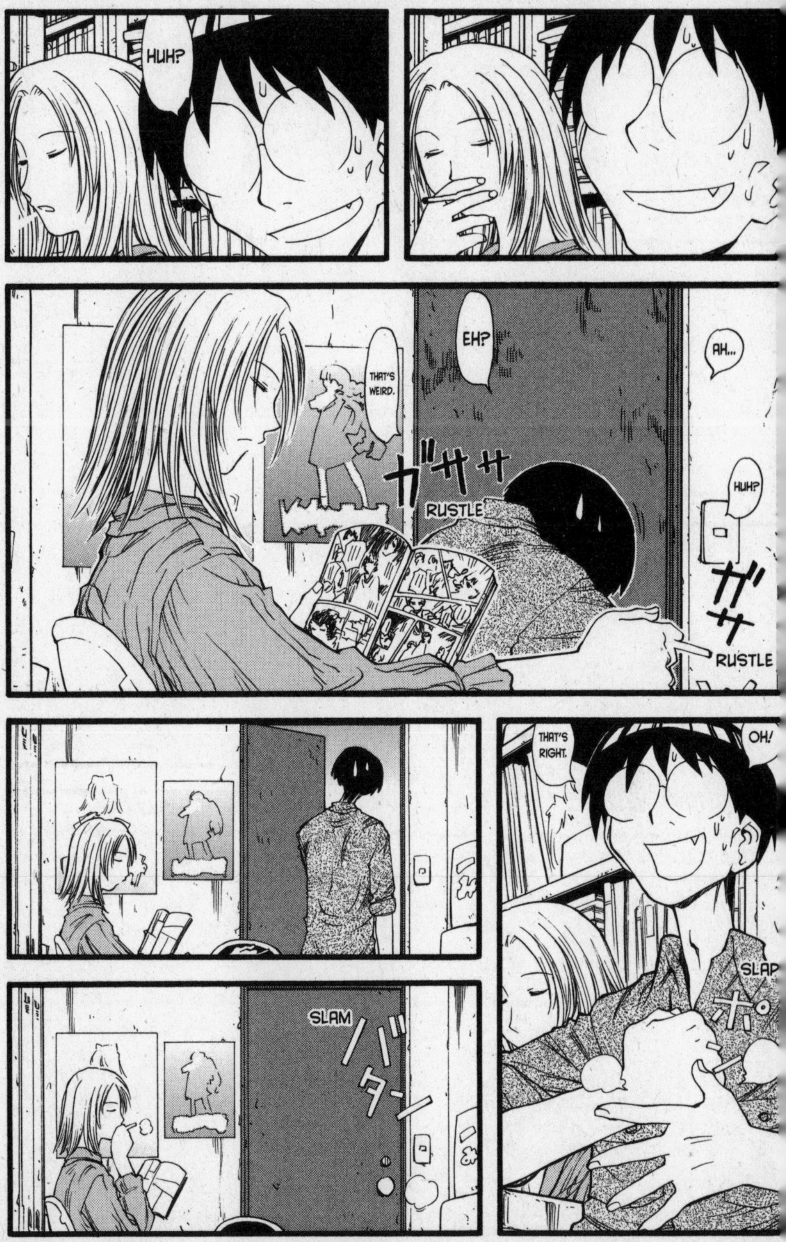
HUH?
AH...
HUH?
ガサ
RUSTLE
EH?
THAT'S WEIRD.
ガサササ
RUSTLE
OH!
THAT'S RIGHT.
SLAP
ポ
SLAM
バターン

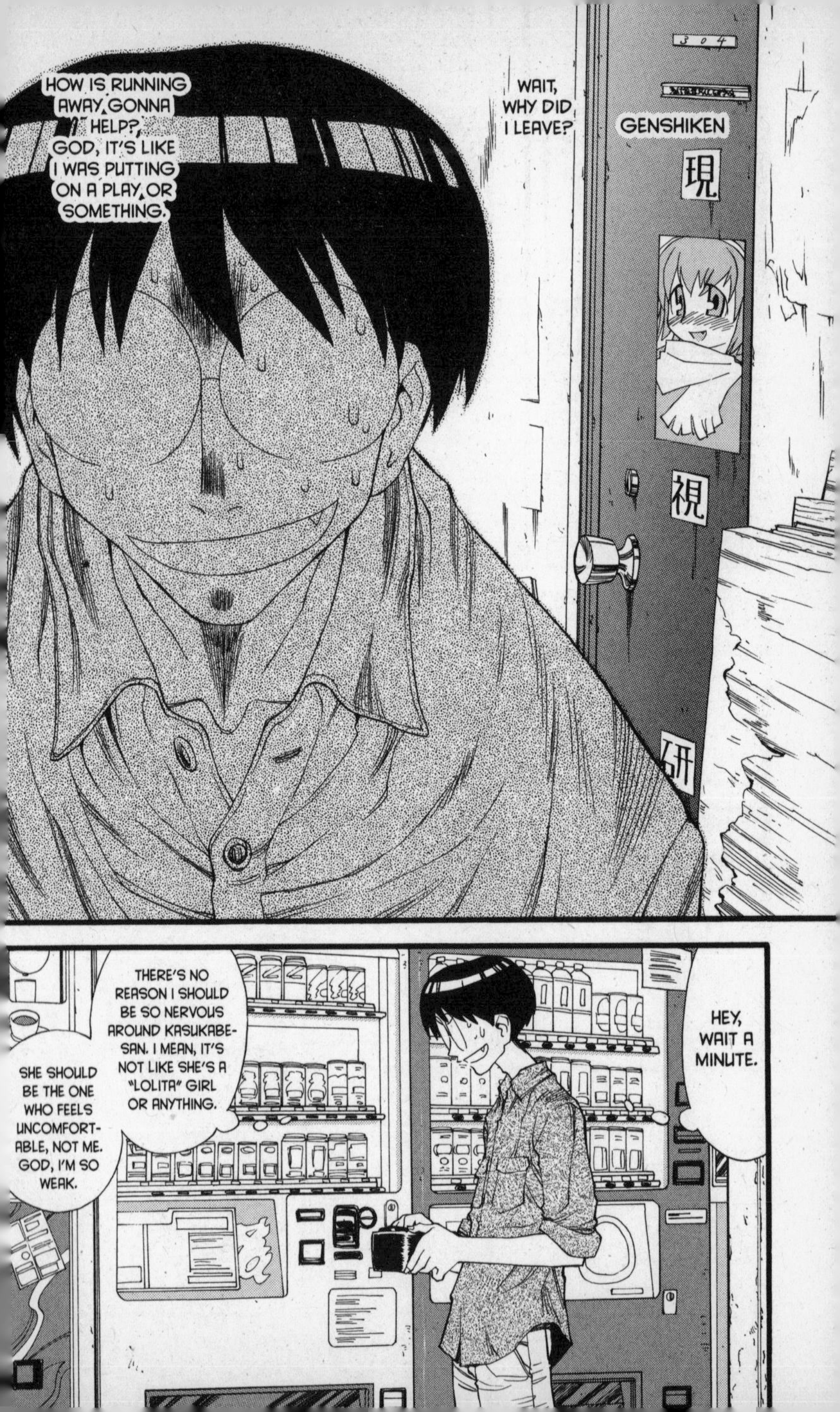
304
GENSHIKEN
現
視
研
WAIT, WHY DID I LEAVE?
HOW IS RUNNING AWAY GONNA HELP? GOD, IT'S LIKE I WAS PUTTING ON A PLAY OR SOMETHING.
HEY, WAIT A MINUTE.
THERE'S NO REASON I SHOULD BE SO NERVOUS AROUND KASUKABE-SAN. I MEAN, IT'S NOT LIKE SHE'S A "LOLITA" GIRL OR ANYTHING.
SHE SHOULD BE THE ONE WHO FEELS UNCOMFORTABLE, NOT ME. GOD, I'M SO WEAK.

...

I'VE GOTTA TRY...

...TO BE MORE NATURAL WHEN I TALK TO HER.

HUH?

WANT SOME TEA?

OH E YAMA HA
大江山花
ROYAL
MILK TEA
ロイヤル ミルクティー
牛乳使用100%絞
牛乳23%

UTY COFFEE

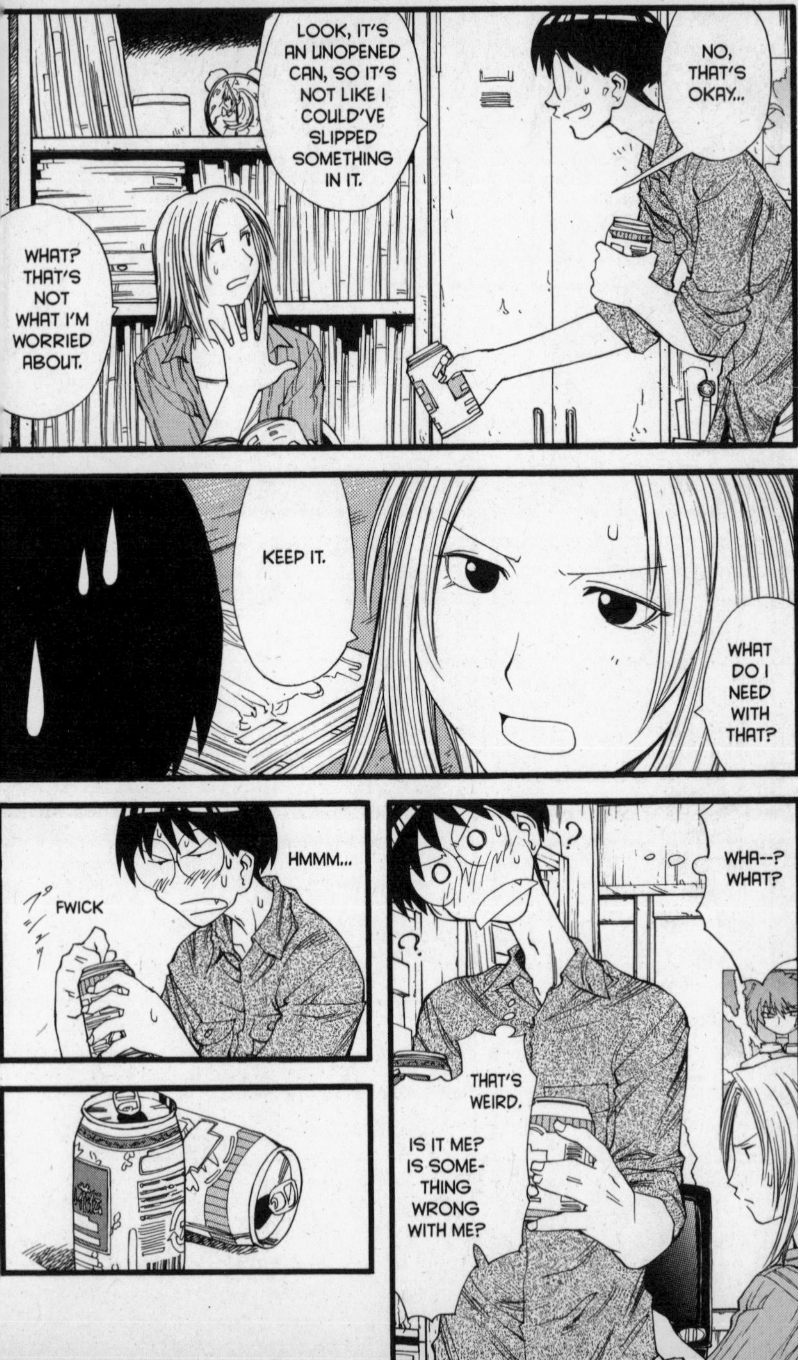
NO, THAT'S OKAY...
LOOK, IT'S AN UNOPENED CAN, SO IT'S NOT LIKE I COULD'VE SLIPPED SOMETHING IN IT.
WHAT? THAT'S NOT WHAT I'M WORRIED ABOUT.
WHAT DO I NEED WITH THAT?
KEEP IT.
WHA--? WHAT?
THAT'S WEIRD.
IS IT ME? IS SOME-THING WRONG WITH ME?
HMMM...
FWICK

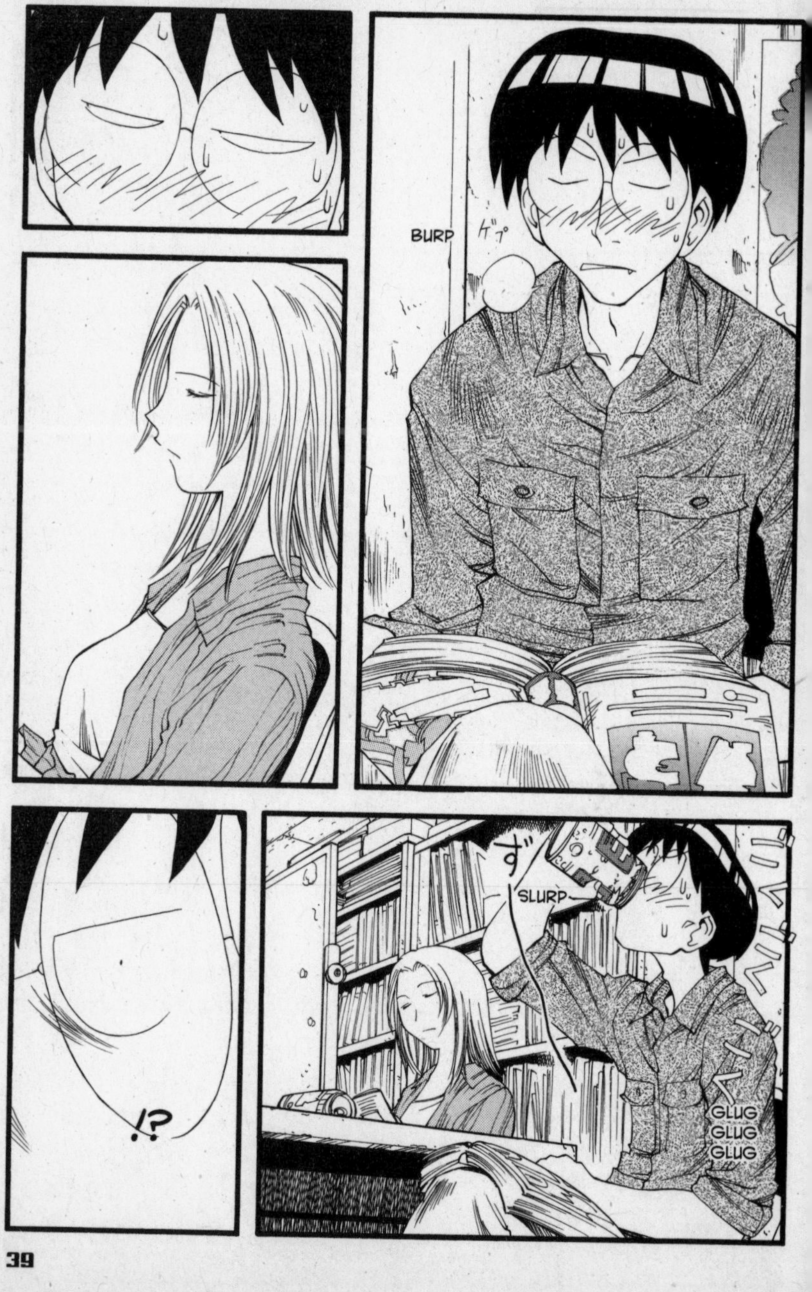
BURP
ゲプ
ず
SLURP
GLUG
GLUG
GLUG
!?

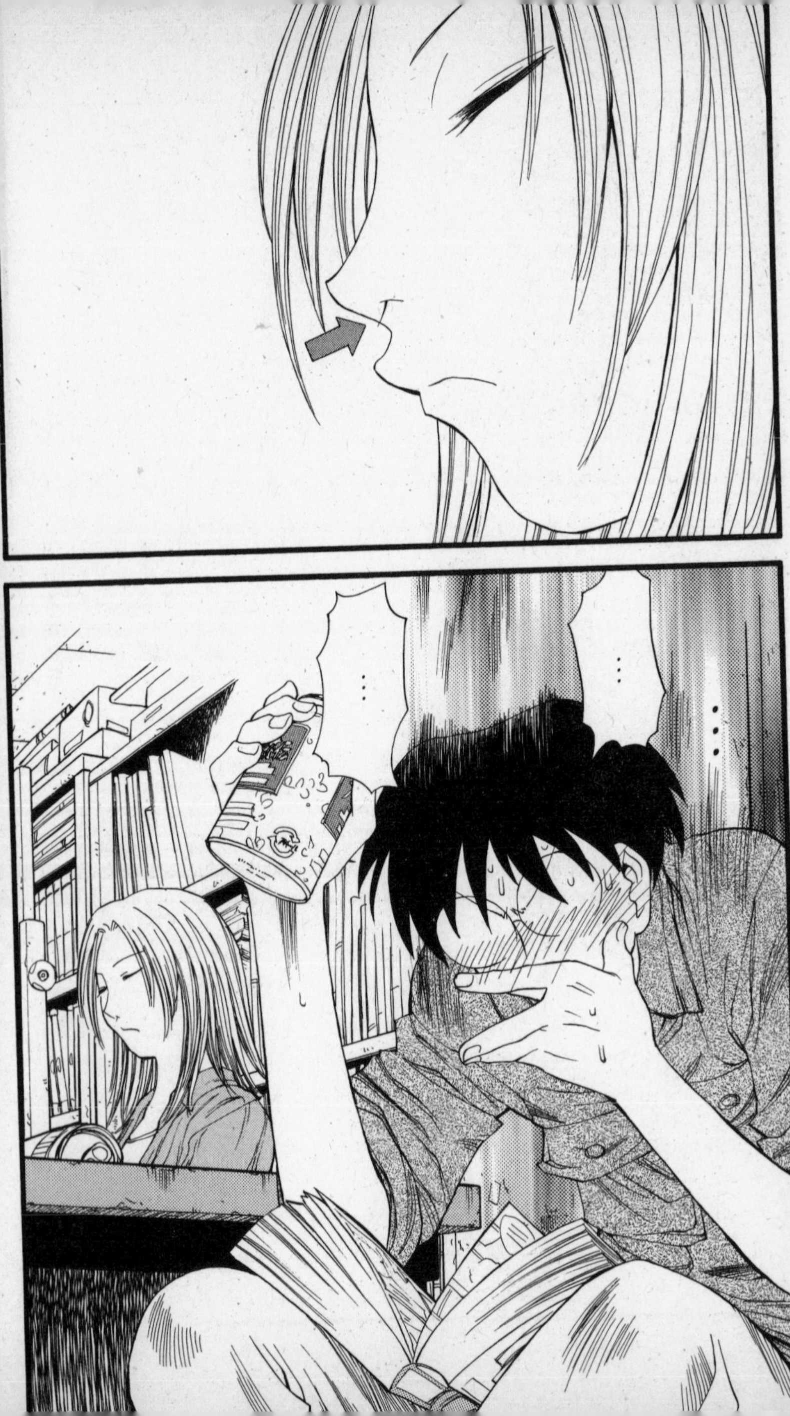

…
…
…

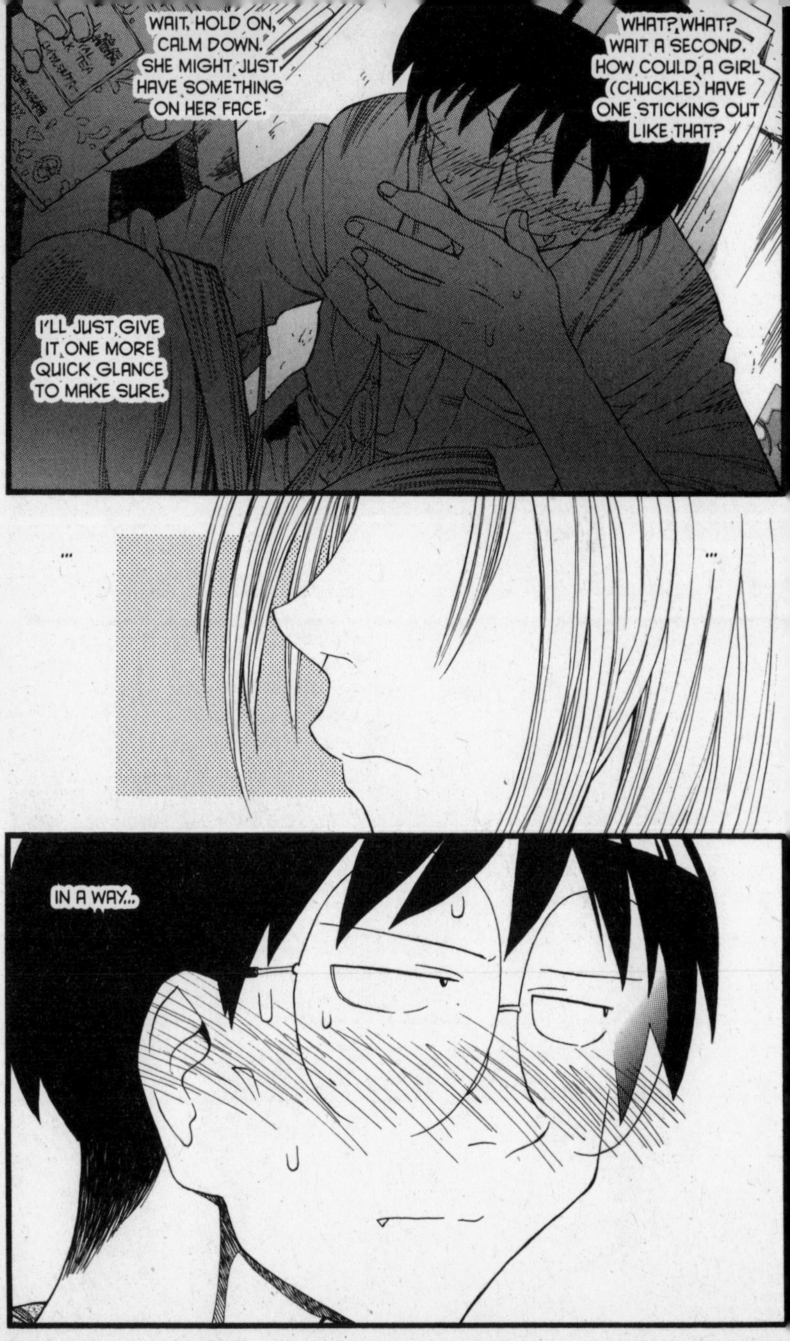
WHAT? WHAT? WAIT A SECOND. HOW COULD A GIRL (CHUCKLE) HAVE ONE STICKING OUT LIKE THAT?
WAIT, HOLD ON, CALM DOWN. SHE MIGHT JUST HAVE SOMETHING ON HER FACE.
I'LL JUST GIVE IT ONE MORE QUICK GLANCE TO MAKE SURE.
...
...
IN A WAY...

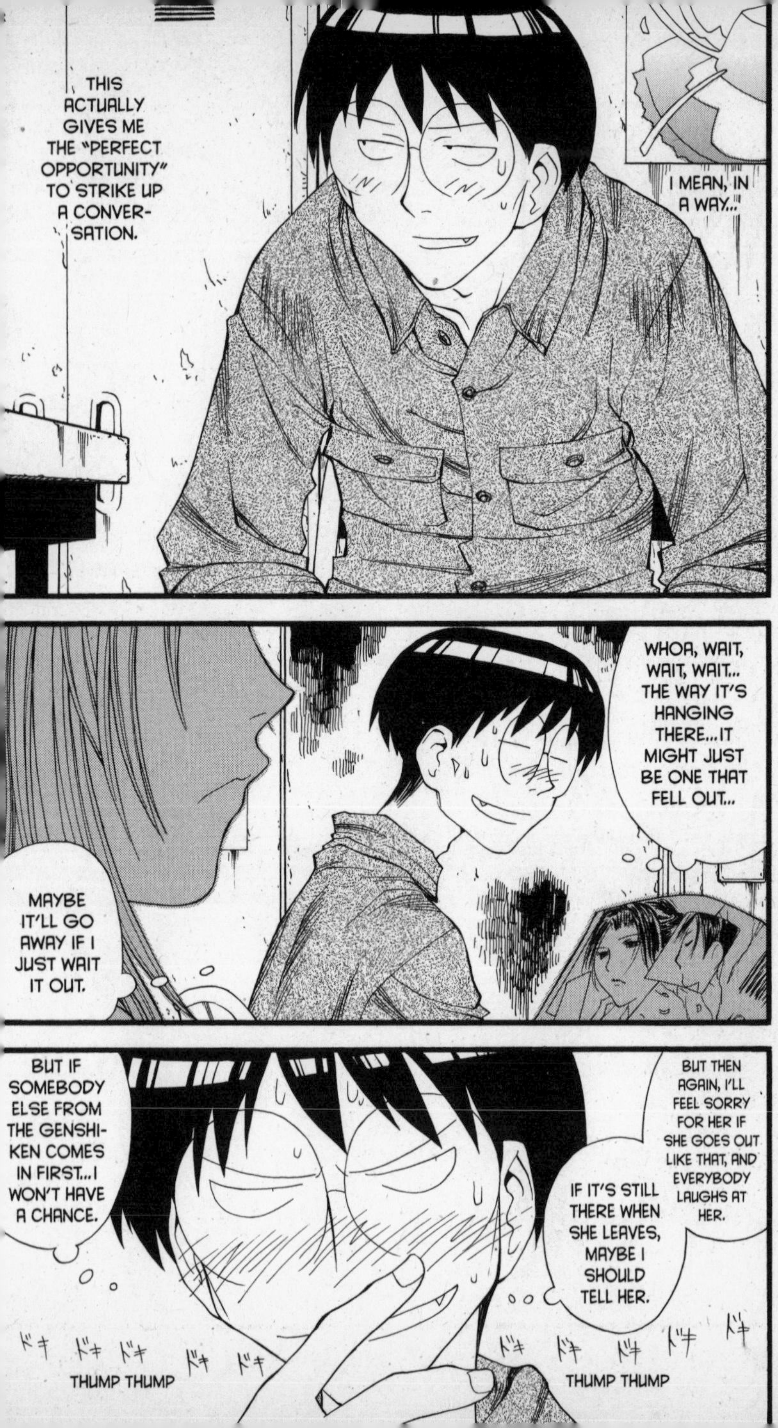
I MEAN, IN A WAY...
THIS ACTUALLY GIVES ME THE "PERFECT OPPORTUNITY" TO STRIKE UP A CONVER-SATION.
WHOA, WAIT, WAIT, WAIT... THE WAY IT'S HANGING THERE...IT MIGHT JUST BE ONE THAT FELL OUT...
MAYBE IT'LL GO AWAY IF I JUST WAIT IT OUT.
BUT THEN AGAIN, I'LL FEEL SORRY FOR HER IF SHE GOES OUT LIKE THAT, AND EVERYBODY LAUGHS AT HER.
IF IT'S STILL THERE WHEN SHE LEAVES, MAYBE I SHOULD TELL HER.
ドキ ドキ ドキ ドキ ドキ
THUMP THUMP
BUT IF SOMEBODY ELSE FROM THE GENSHI-KEN COMES IN FIRST...I WON'T HAVE A CHANCE.
ドキ ドキ ドキ ドキ ドキ
THUMP THUMP

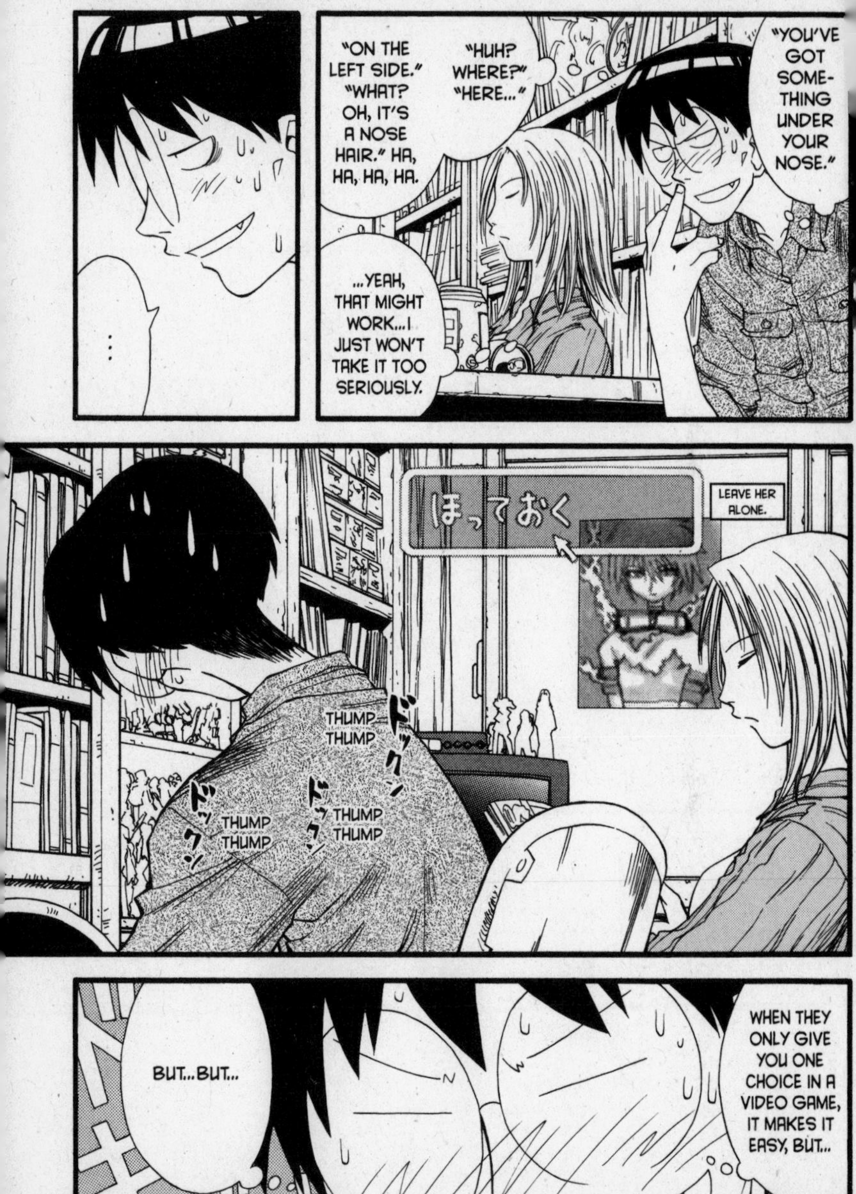
"YOU'VE GOT SOMETHING UNDER YOUR NOSE."
"HUH? WHERE?" "HERE..."
"ON THE LEFT SIDE." "WHAT? OH, IT'S A NOSE HAIR." HA, HA, HA, HA.
...YEAH, THAT MIGHT WORK...I JUST WON'T TAKE IT TOO SERIOUSLY.
...
ほっておく
LEAVE HER ALONE.
ドックン
THUMP THUMP
ドックン
THUMP THUMP
ドックン
THUMP THUMP
WHEN THEY ONLY GIVE YOU ONE CHOICE IN A VIDEO GAME, IT MAKES IT EASY, BUT...
BUT...BUT...
THUMP THUMP

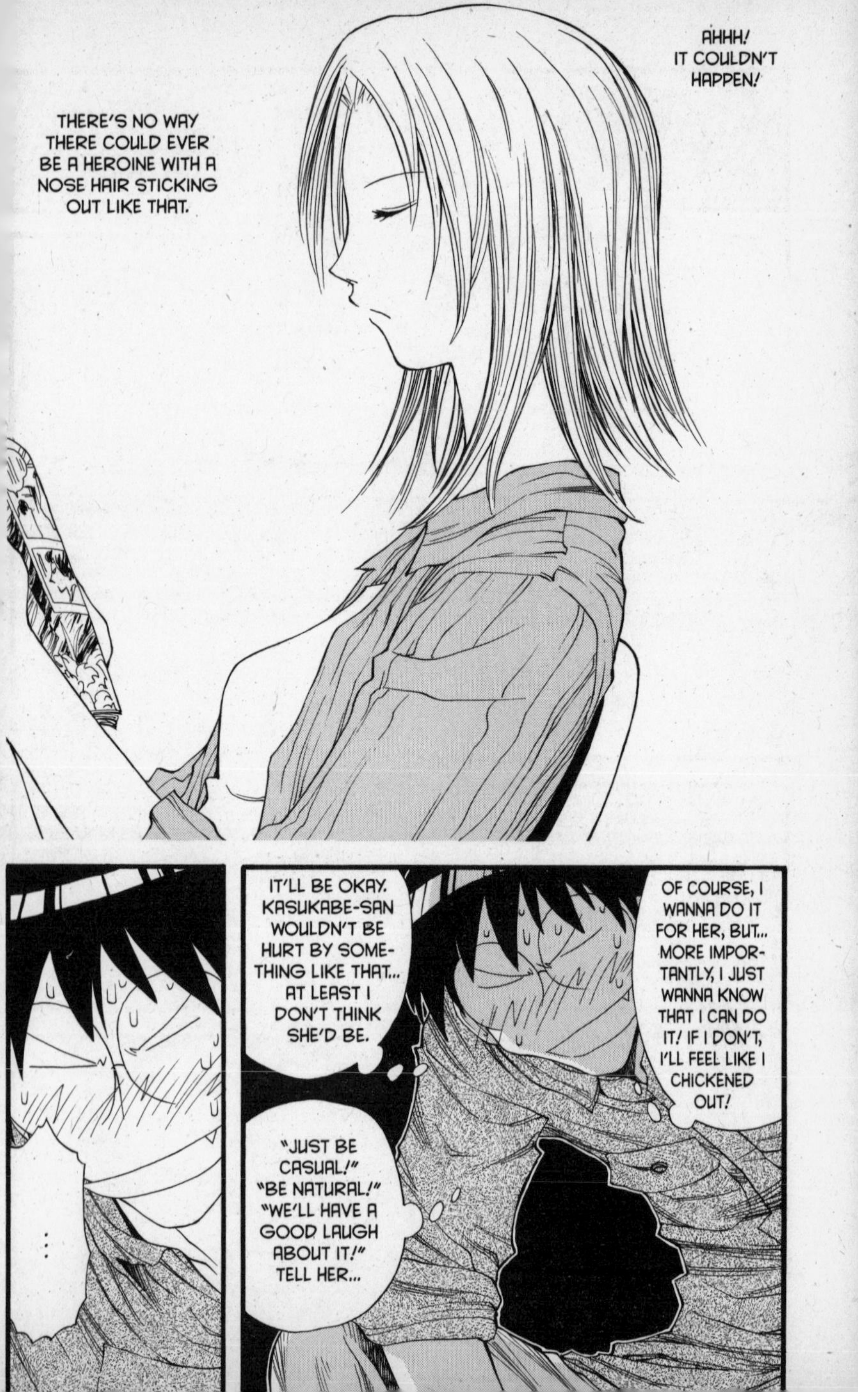
AHHH! IT COULDN'T HAPPEN!
THERE'S NO WAY THERE COULD EVER BE A HEROINE WITH A NOSE HAIR STICKING OUT LIKE THAT.
OF COURSE, I WANNA DO IT FOR HER, BUT... MORE IMPORTANTLY, I JUST WANNA KNOW THAT I CAN DO IT! IF I DON'T, I'LL FEEL LIKE I CHICKENED OUT!
IT'LL BE OKAY. KASUKABE-SAN WOULDN'T BE HURT BY SOMETHING LIKE THAT... AT LEAST I DON'T THINK SHE'D BE.
"JUST BE CASUAL!" "BE NATURAL!" "WE'LL HAVE A GOOD LAUGH ABOUT IT!" TELL HER...
...

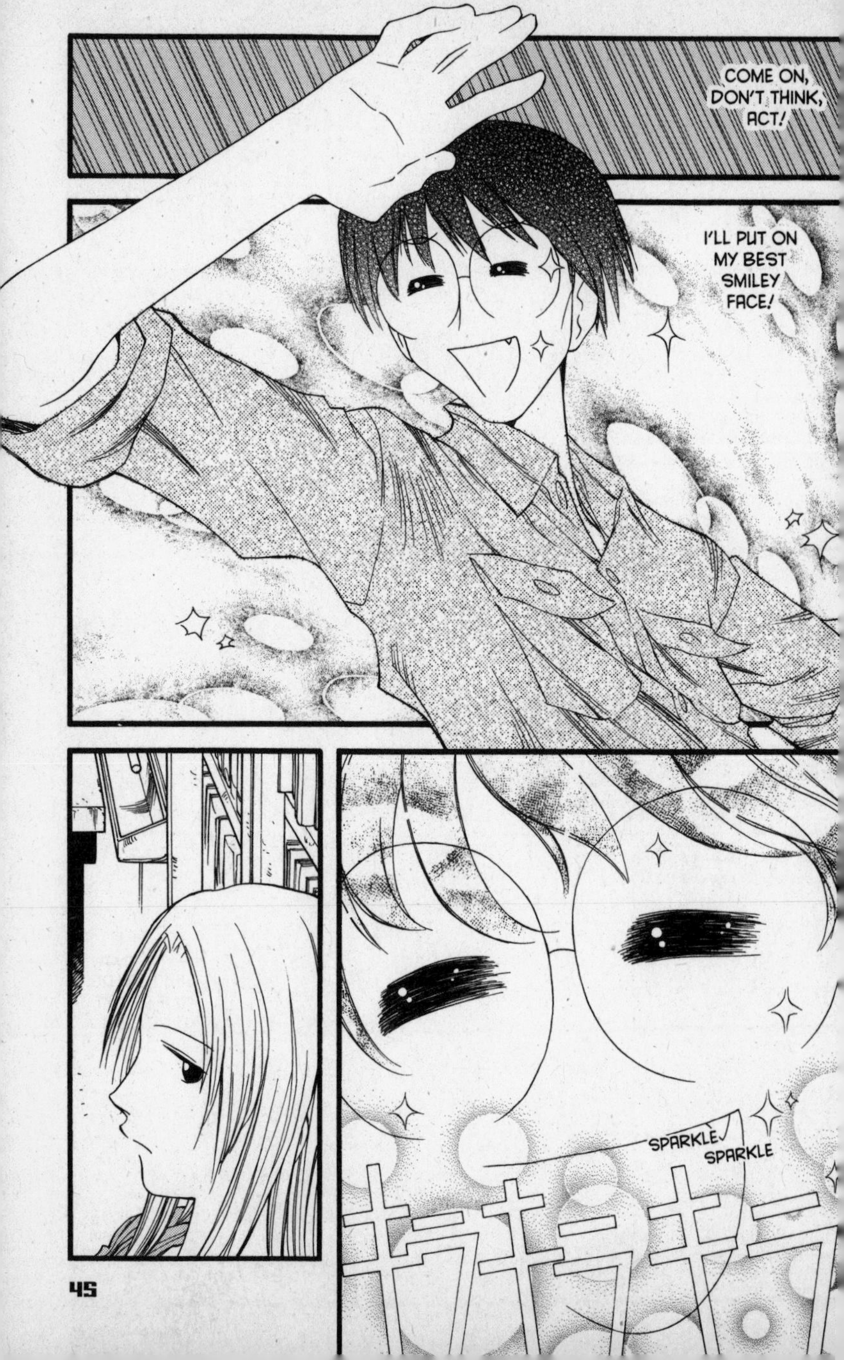
COME ON, DON'T THINK, ACT!
I'LL PUT ON MY BEST SMILEY FACE!
SPARKLE SPARKLE
キラキラキラ

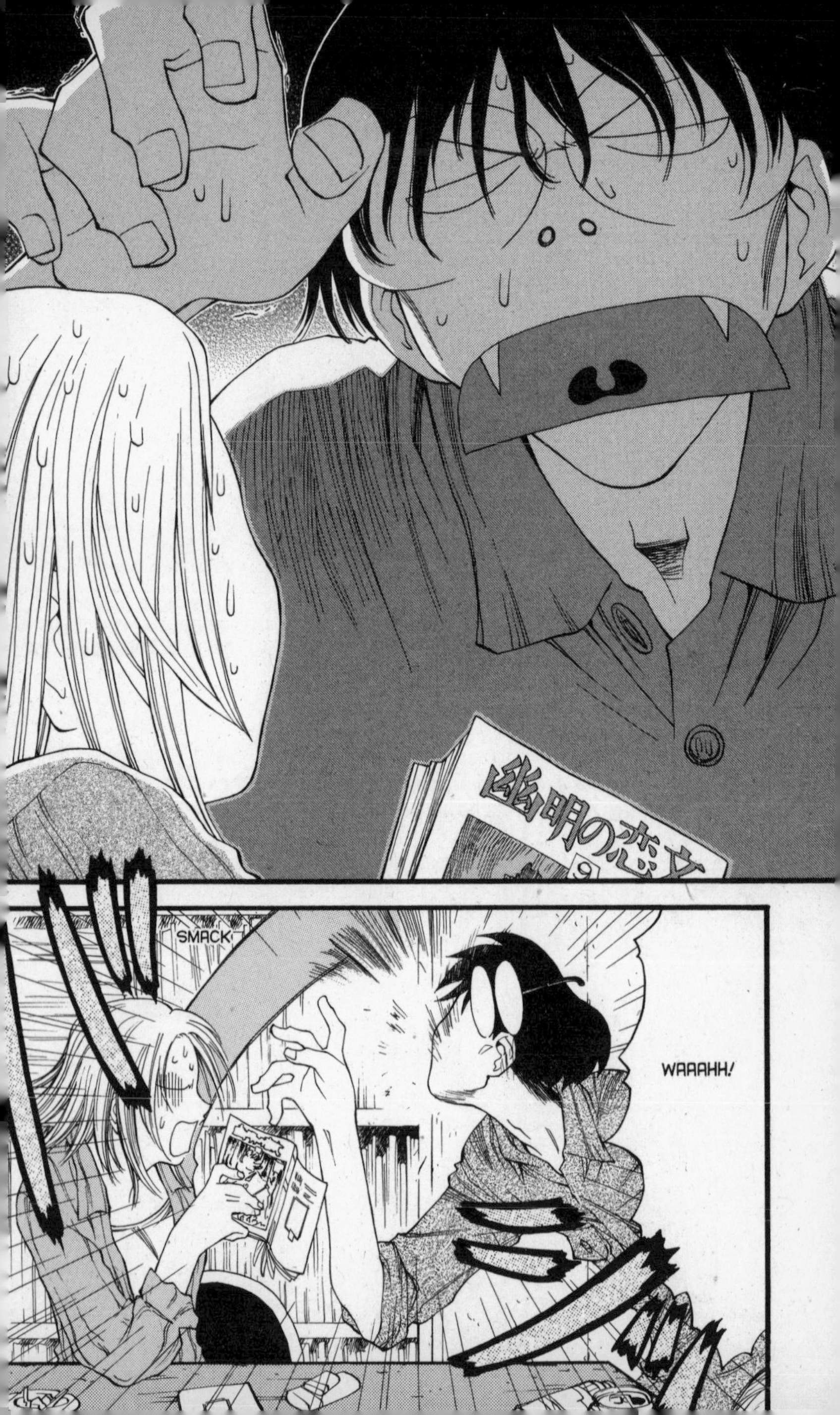
幽明の恋文
SMACK
WAAAHH!

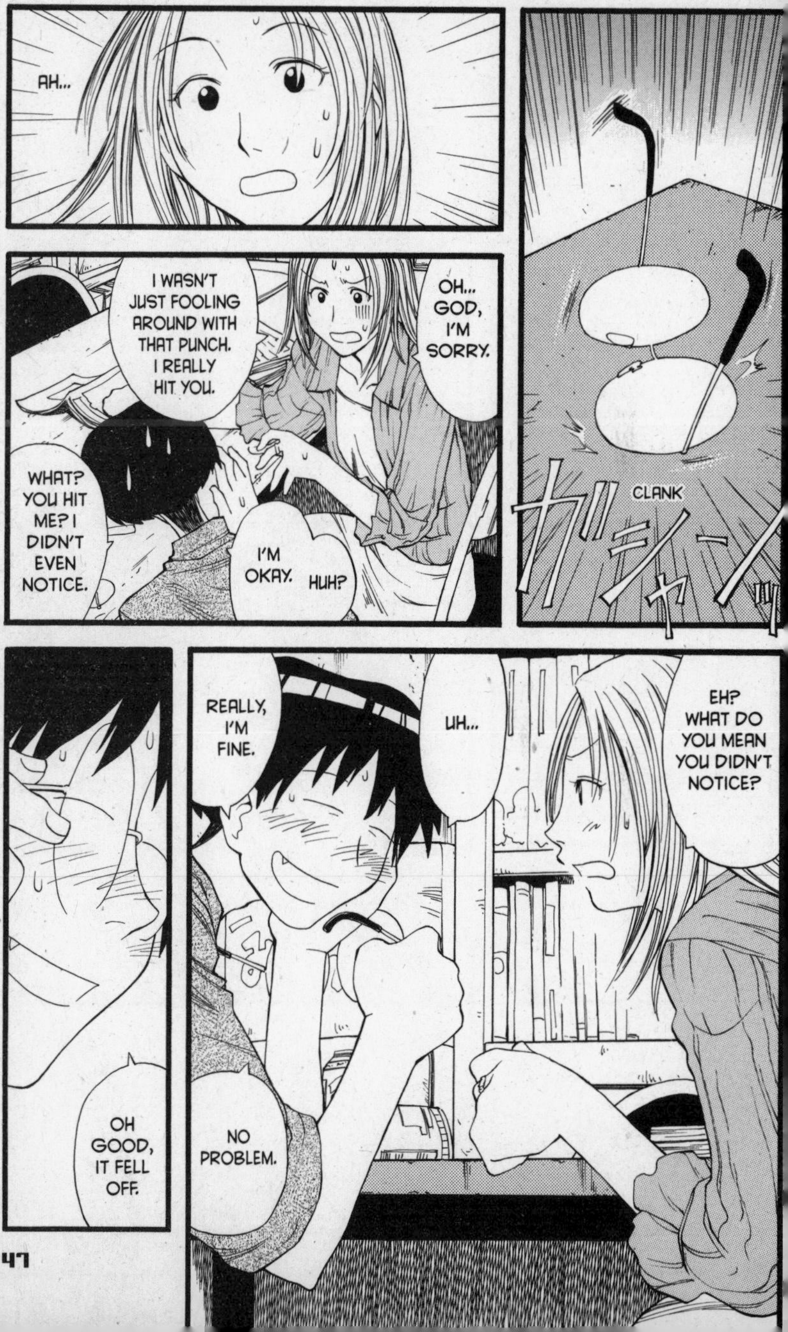
CLANK
ガシャーンッ
AH...
OH... GOD, I'M SORRY.
I WASN'T JUST FOOLING AROUND WITH THAT PUNCH. I REALLY HIT YOU.
HUH?
I'M OKAY.
WHAT? YOU HIT ME? I DIDN'T EVEN NOTICE.
EH? WHAT DO YOU MEAN YOU DIDN'T NOTICE?
UH...
REALLY, I'M FINE.
NO PROBLEM.
OH GOOD, IT FELL OFF.

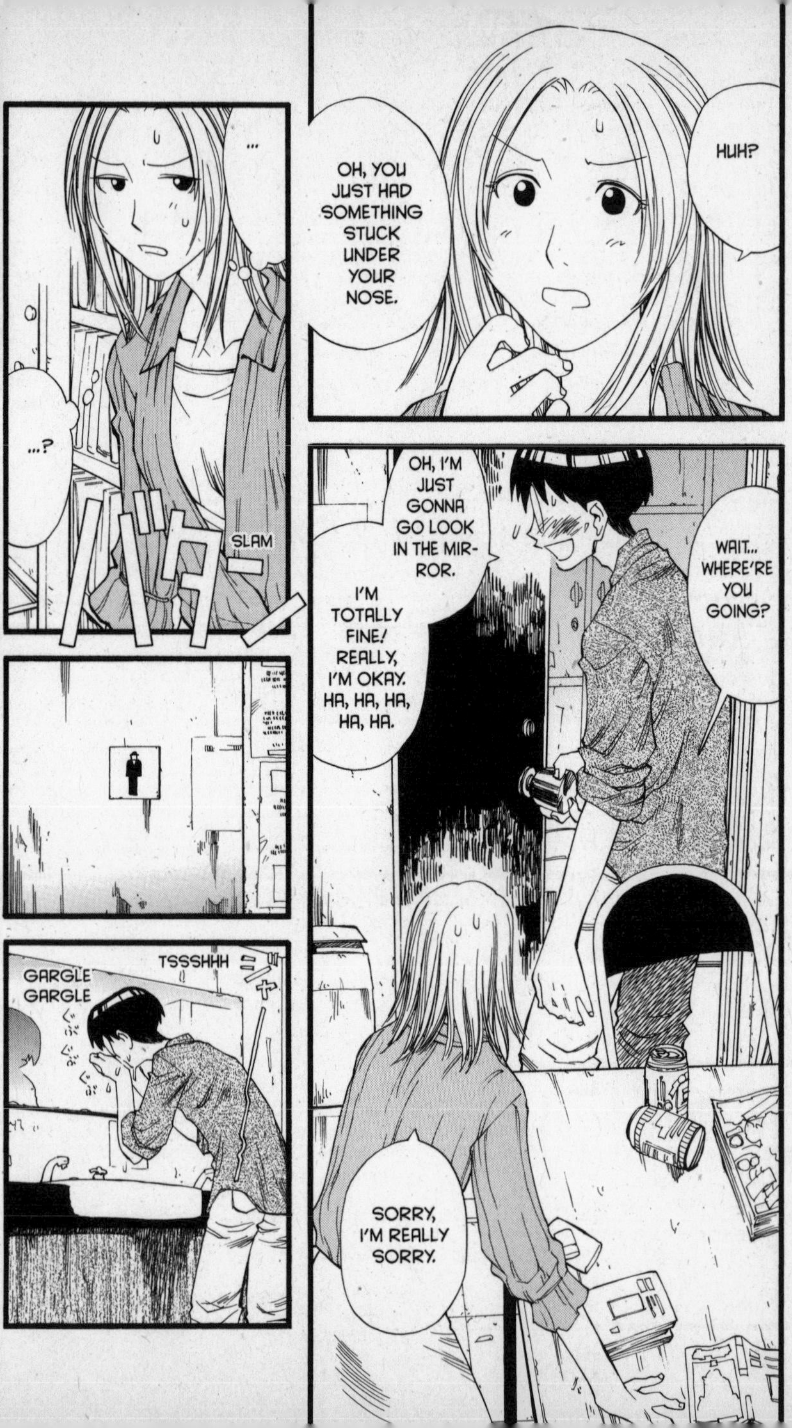
HUH?
OH, YOU JUST HAD SOMETHING STUCK UNDER YOUR NOSE.
...
...?
SLAM
WAIT... WHERE'RE YOU GOING?
OH, I'M JUST GONNA GO LOOK IN THE MIR-ROR.
I'M TOTALLY FINE! REALLY, I'M OKAY. HA, HA, HA, HA, HA.
SORRY, I'M REALLY SORRY.
TSSSHHH
GARGLE GARGLE

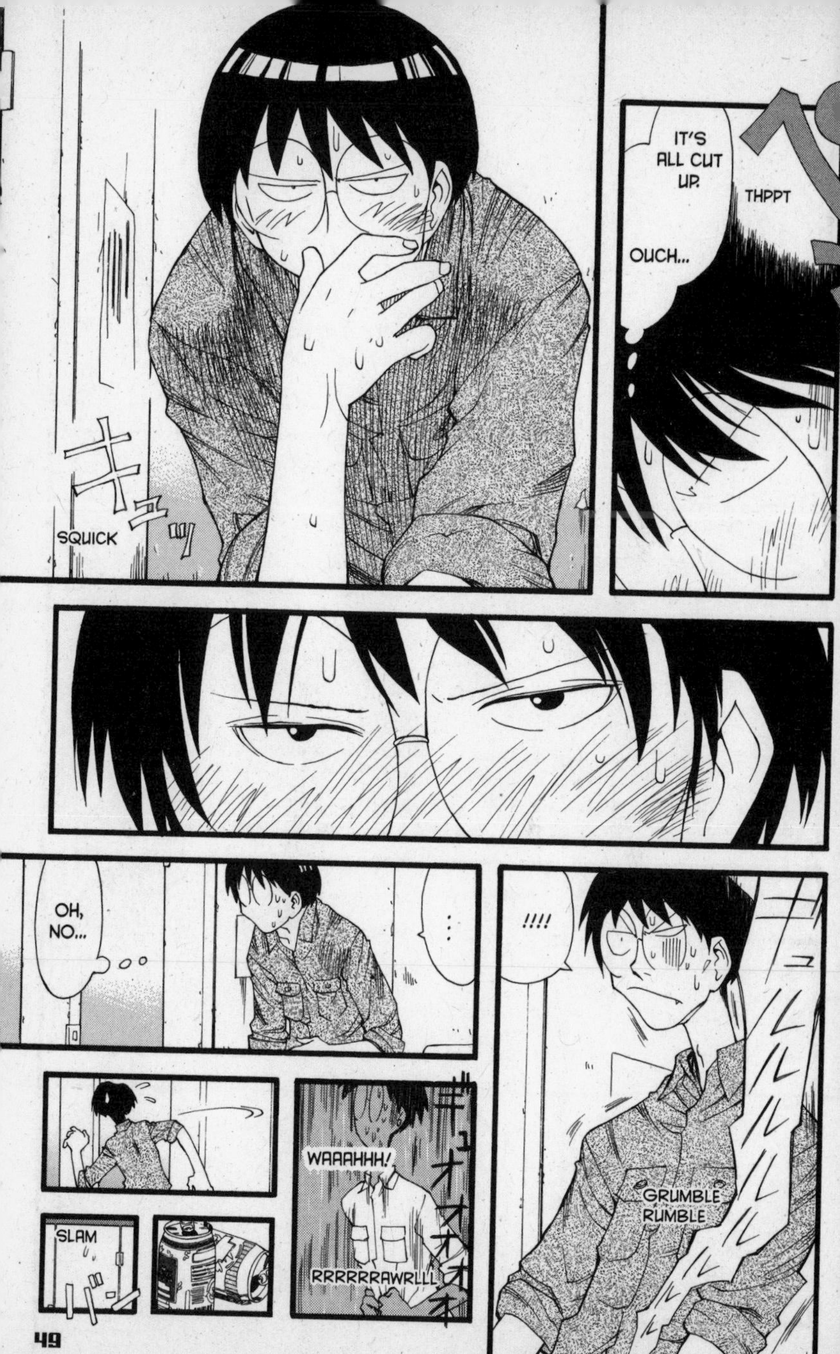
IT'S ALL CUT UP.
THPPT
OUCH...
SQUICK
!!!!
GRUMBLE RUMBLE
OH, NO...
...
WAAAHHH!
RRRRRRAWRLLL
SLAM

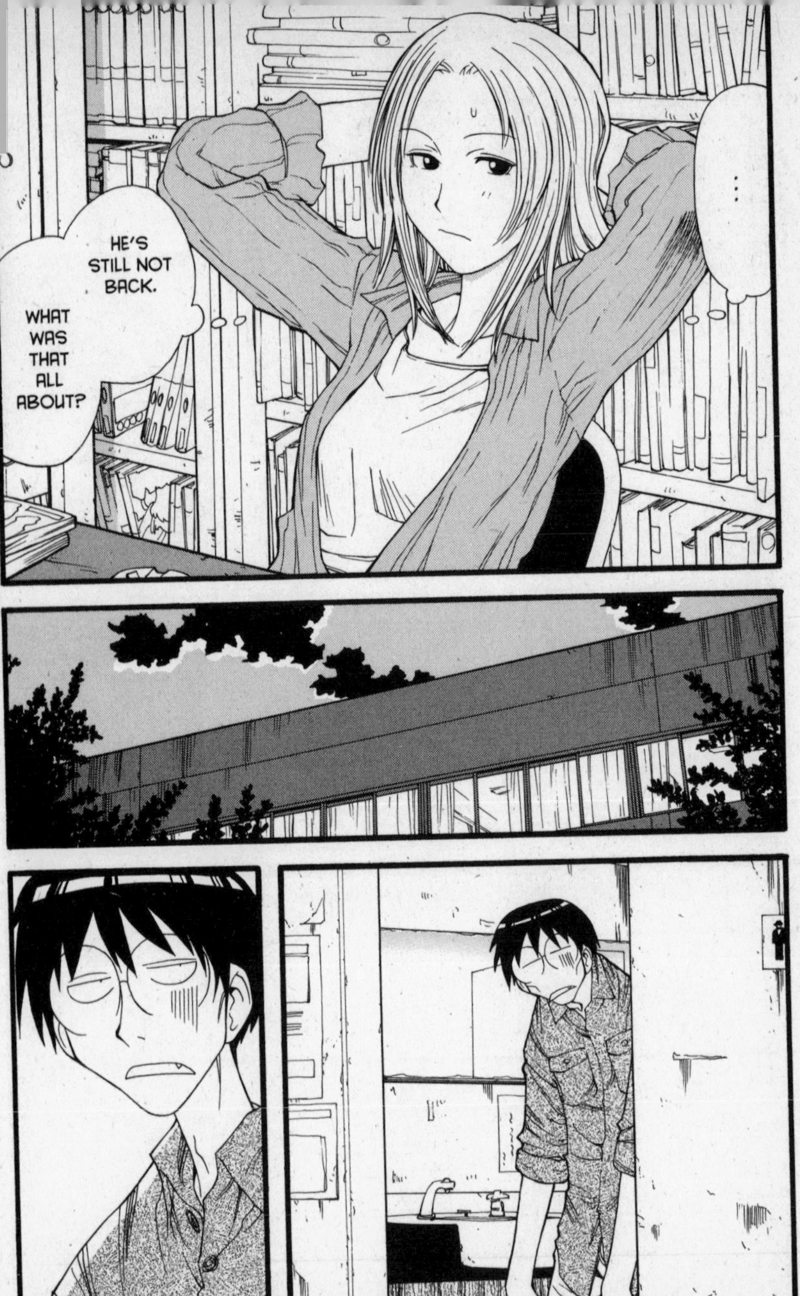
...
HE'S STILL NOT BACK.
WHAT WAS THAT ALL ABOUT?

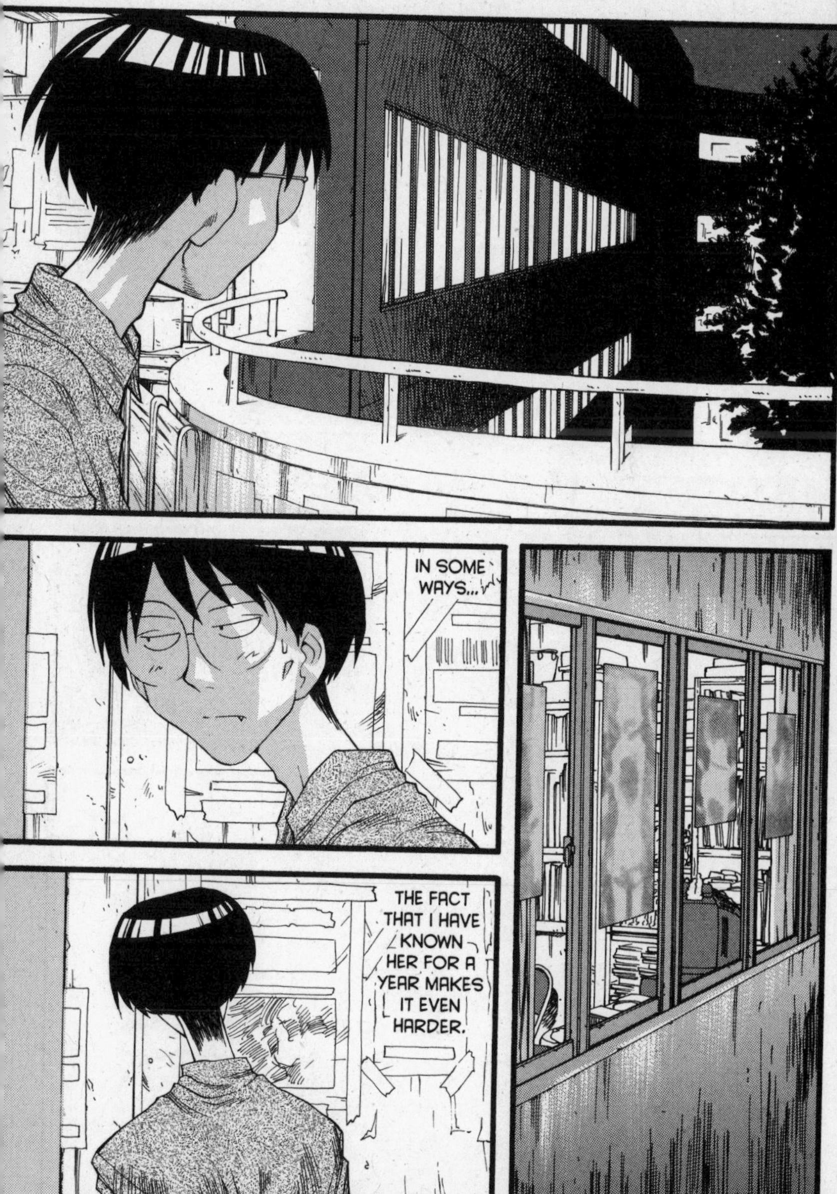
IN SOME WAYS...
THE FACT THAT I HAVE KNOWN HER FOR A YEAR MAKES IT EVEN HARDER.

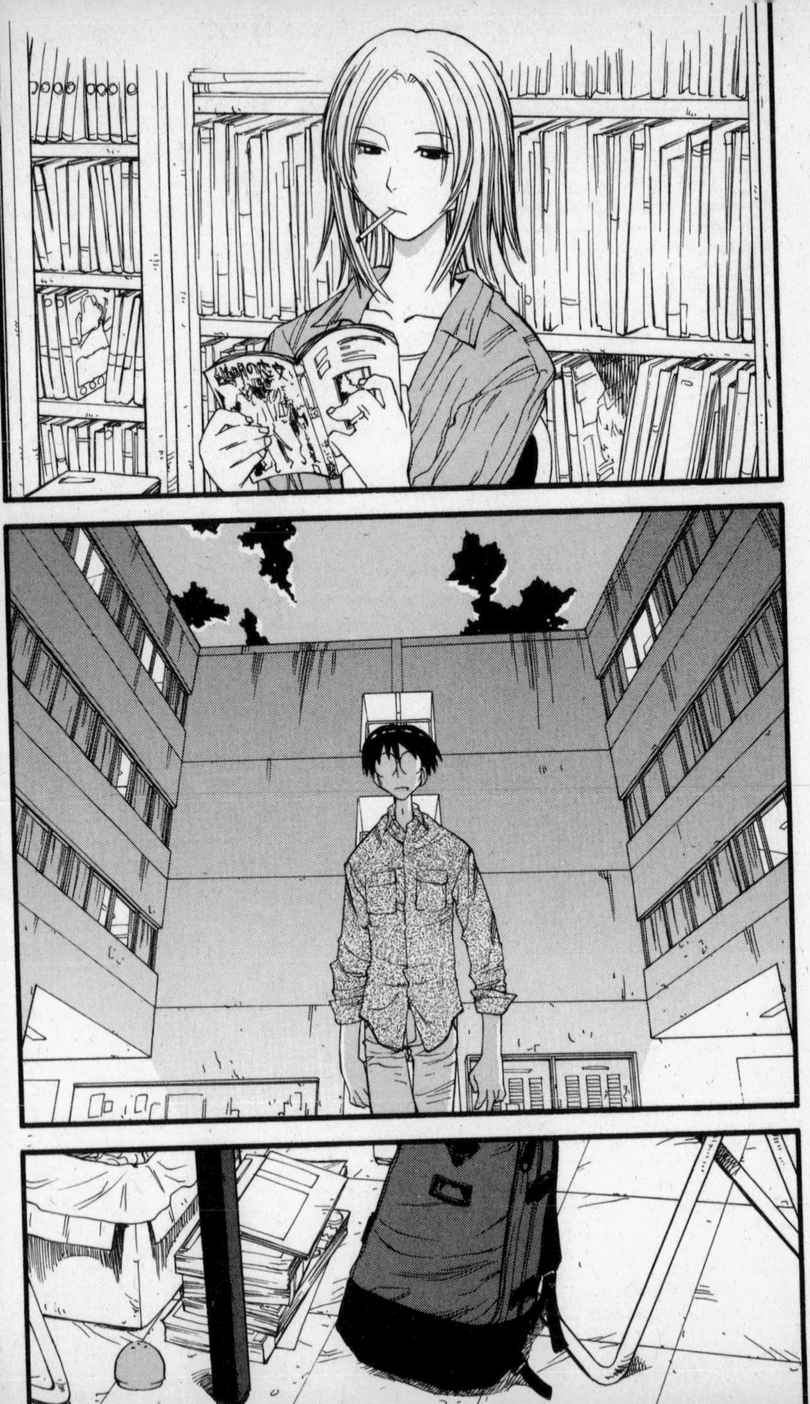

2 RITSUKO K. KETTENKRAD

WRITTEN BY BENJAMIN TAKEYO

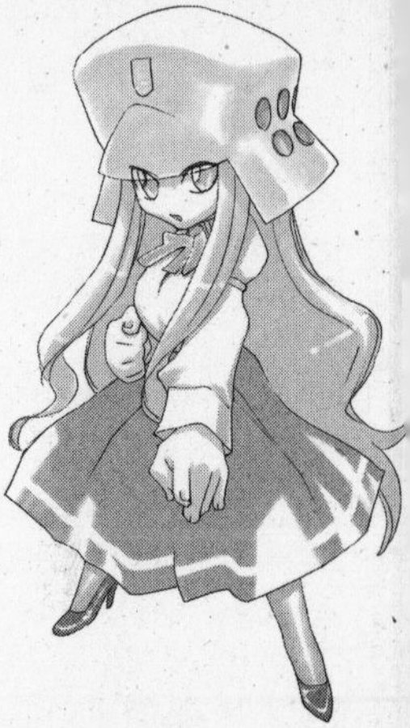

HI, IT'S BENJAMIN. IT'S TOO BAD. IT SEEMS THAT THE PIT VIPER IS STARTING TO SHOW HIS AGE. I THINK HE SHOULD'VE GONE WITH SHINOBU-SENSEI. HEH, HEH.

I'M GOING WITH THE PRESIDENT, OF COURSE, EVEN IF SHE IS WEAK. AMONG ALL THE KUJI-UN GAME CHARACTERS WE TALK ABOUT IN THE GENSHIKEN, SHE'S PROBABLY THE WEAKEST ONE (TEARS). OF COURSE IF YOU USE HER PROPERLY, SHE CAN BE PRETTY STRONG. SO, I'M GOING TO PROVIDE AN EXPLANATION OF HER MOVES.

FIRST OF ALL...FOR SOME REASON, SHE USES HAKKYOKUKEN STYLE MARTIAL ARTS. (LAUGHS) WELL, I GUESS IT DOES SUIT HER WELL. THE PRESIDENT IS HORRIBLE WHEN IT COMES TO ATHLETICS, SO SHE'S NOT MUCH FOR JUMP ATTACKS. SHE DOES BETTER WITH REPETITIVE KICKS. ALTHOUGH I'M A LITTLE CONCERNED ABOUT HOW SHE CAN KICK WITH THOSE HIGH HEELS ON.

ONE OF HER WEAKNESSES IS THAT SHE MOVES VERY SLOWLY. SHE TAKES HER FIGHTING STANCE AND JUST SORT OF INCHES ALONG. ON TOP OF THAT, WHENEVER SHE TRIES TO SPRINT, SHE ENDS UP FALLING. (LAUGHS) SHE'S TOO TOP HEAVY. IF SHE FALLS, IT GIVES HER OPPONENT A CHANCE TO ATTACK, SO SPRINTING IS PROHIBITED. IF SHE FALLS FORWARD, THERE'S A CHANCE THAT HER HELMET WILL STRIKE THE OPPONENT, BUT ONCE SHE'S DOWN, THE OPPONENT CAN ATTACK, SO THIS IS ONLY EFFECTIVE WHEN DEALING THE FINAL BLOW. HOWEVER, WHEN THIS FALL TECHNIQUE IS USED TO DELIVER THE FINAL BLOW, YOU GET TO SEE A UNIQUE VICTORY POSE, IN WHICH SHE STAYS ON THE GROUND AND HOLDS HER HEAD IN HER ARMS WITH AN EMBARRASSED LOOK ON HER FACE. I TRY TO DO THAT WHENEVER I CAN.

HER REACH IS ALSO VERY LIMITED. HAKKYOKUKEN IS A TECHNIQUE DESIGNED FOR CLOSE CONTACT FIGHTING, AND THE PRESIDENT IS VERY SMALL. THE WAY THE PRESIDENT MOVES TOWARDS HER OPPONENT WITHOUT BACKING AWAY IS SO BRAVE, IT ALMOST BRINGS A TEAR TO MY EYE. SHE USUALLY AIMS RIGHT FOR THE OPPONENT'S TORSO. OF COURSE, SHE CAN NEVER WIN WITH JUST ONE MOVE.

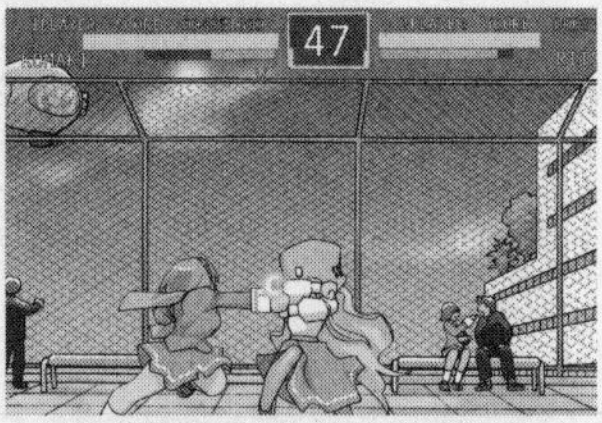
47

YOU GET EXTRA POINTS FOR USING THE "BACK DOOR" TECHNIQUE.

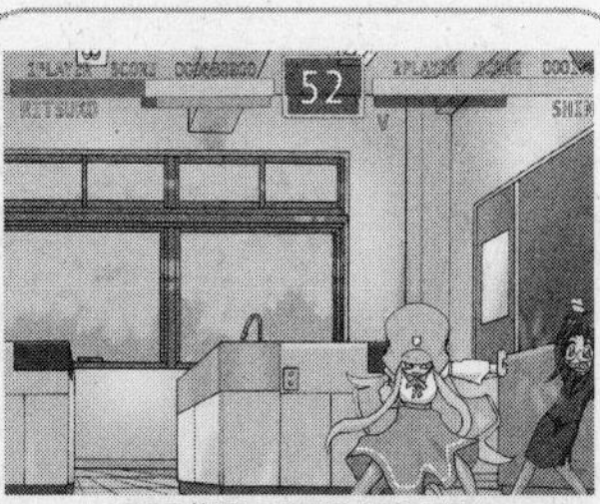
52

JUST KEEP GOING FORWARD, NO MATTER WHAT!

ONE OF HER GREAT STRENGTHS IS THAT HER HELMET REDUCES THE DAMAGE DONE BY HER OPPONENT'S JUMP KICKS BY HALF. HER HELMET ALSO ACTS AS "SUPER ARMOR," BUT I'M NOT EXACTLY SURE HOW TO USE IT TO MY ADVANTAGE.

HER SPECIAL ATTACK TECHNIQUES HAVE THEIR GOOD POINTS AND THEIR BAD POINTS. FIRST OF ALL, ALL OF HER TECHNIQUES USE THE REPETITIVE KICK EFFECT ALONG WITH DEFENSE PENETRATION POWER. WHEN YOU USE THE REPETITIVE KICK TECHNIQUE AT FULL POWER, IT CAN REACH THE OTHER SIDE OF THE SCREEN, SO IT HELPS TO USE IT ALONG WITH YOUR FLIGHT TOOLS. HER DEFENSE PENETRATION POWER IS GREAT, BUT ALL OF HER TECHNIQUES LEAVE HER VULNERABLE ONCE SHE FINISHES THE MOVE. THE ONLY WAY TO AVOID BEING ATTACKED IS TO STAY CLOSE TO EITHER EDGE OF THE SCREEN, UNLESS YOU'RE DOING THE SPRINTING ATTACK. (LAUGHS) AS LONG AS SHE'S BLOCKING PROPERLY, SHE WON'T BE AFFECTED BY THE ATTACKS. BUT WHEN SHE PUNCHES RIGHT AFTER COMING OUT OF A BLOCK, SHE MOVES REALLY SLOWLY. IT MAKES HER ATTACK SEEM EVEN MORE PRONOUNCED.

ANYWAY, JUST REMEMBER TO KEEP MOVING FORWARD. THAT'S WHAT THE PRESIDENT DOES BEST. BREAK DOWN THE DEFENSE, AND MOVE FORWARD, FORWARD, FORWARD! [BENJAMIN]

ACTUALLY I THINK THE PRESIDENT IS PRETTY STRONG. HER TECHNIQUES ARE DIVIDED INTO MID-TORSO ATTACKS AND LOWER BODY ATTACKS. SHE'S THE NATURAL ENEMY OF RENKO-CHAN OR ANY CHARACTER THAT PREFERS CLOSE CONTACT FIGHTING. IF YOU GET TOO CLOSE, THEN...WHACK....AND WHACK AGAIN...AAAHHH! I SURE DO LOVE TO SEE RENKO-CHAN AND THE PRESIDENT FIGHT. ♡ I THINK YOU ALWAYS LOSE BECAUSE YOU ALWAYS MISS WITH THAT SPRINT AND FALL TECHNIQUE. DON'T BE SUCH A CHICKEN. (LAUGHS) JUST RELAX. [PIT VIPER]

BREAKING THROUGH

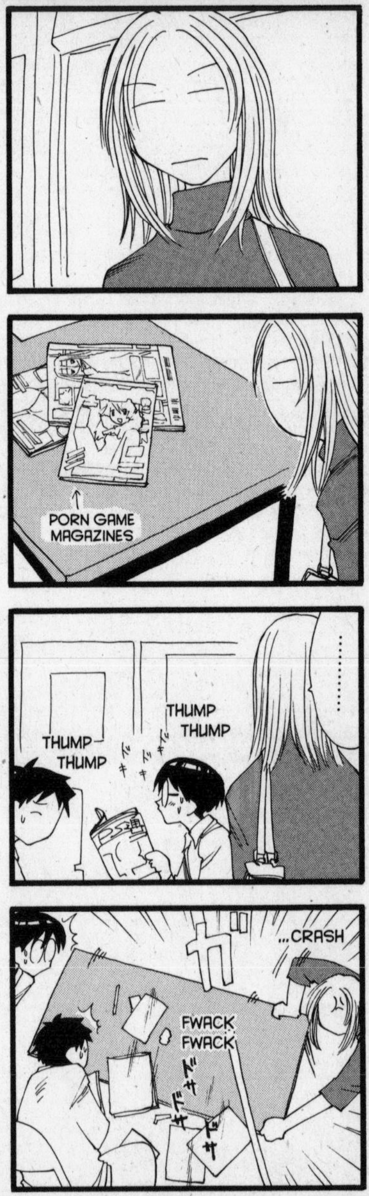
PORN GAME MAGAZINES
......
THUMP THUMP
THUMP-THUMP
...CRASH
FWACK FWACK

SIGNS OF THE TIMES

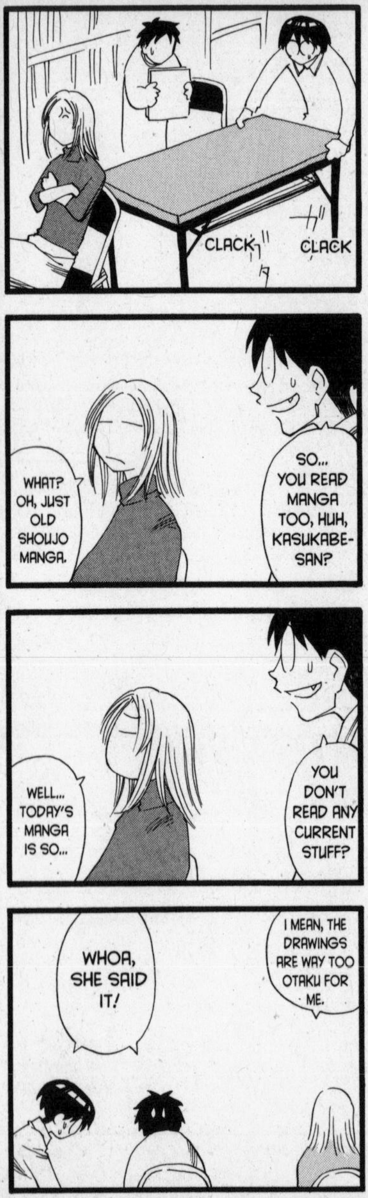
CLACK
CLACK
SO... YOU READ MANGA TOO, HUH, KASUKABE-SAN?
WHAT? OH, JUST OLD SHOUJO MANGA.
YOU DON'T READ ANY CURRENT STUFF?
WELL... TODAY'S MANGA IS SO...
I MEAN, THE DRAWINGS ARE WAY TOO OTAKU FOR ME.
WHOA, SHE SAID IT!

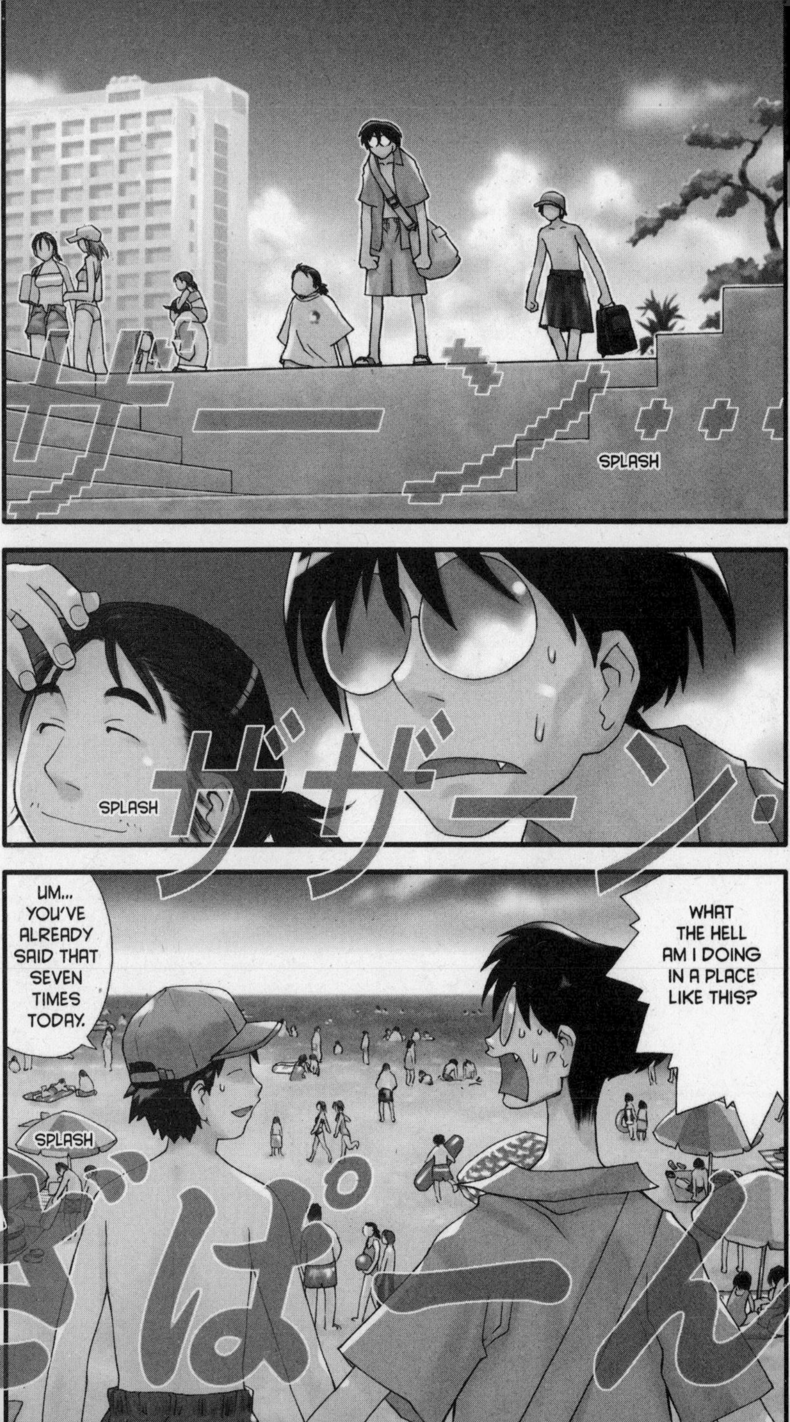
SPLASH
SPLASH
WHAT THE HELL AM I DOING IN A PLACE LIKE THIS?
UM... YOU'VE ALREADY SAID THAT SEVEN TIMES TODAY.
SPLASH

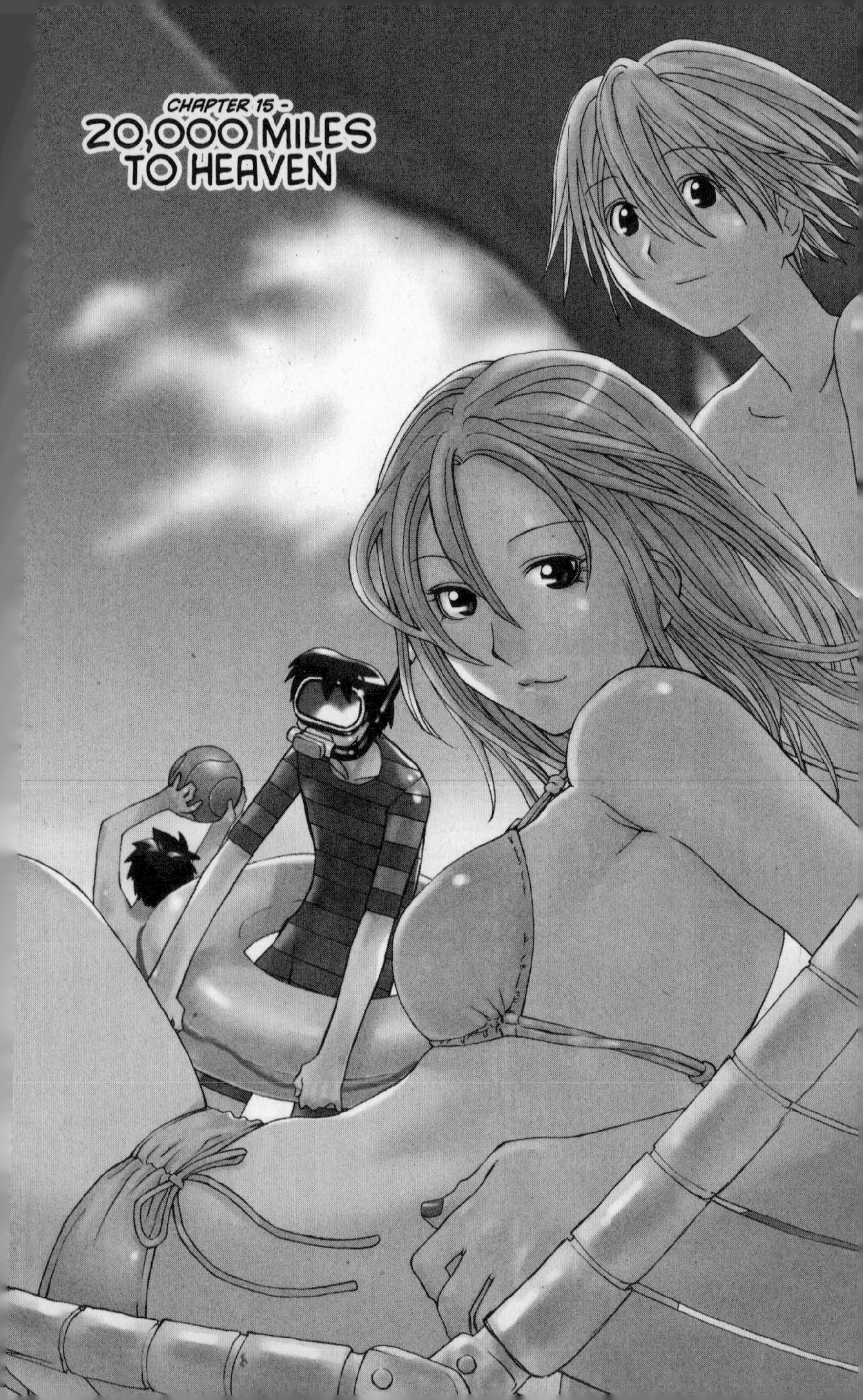
CHAPTER 15 -
20,000 MILES TO HEAVEN

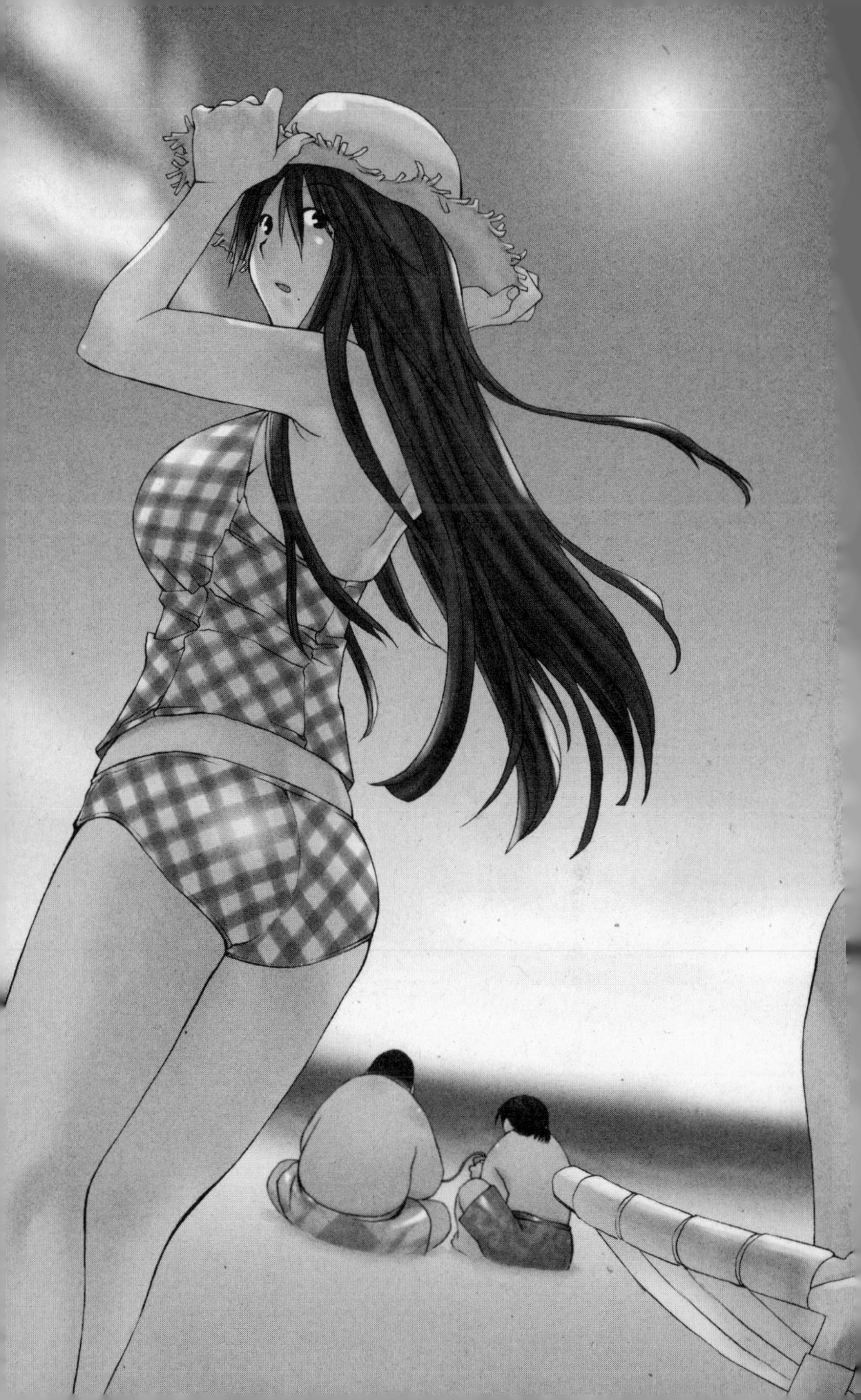

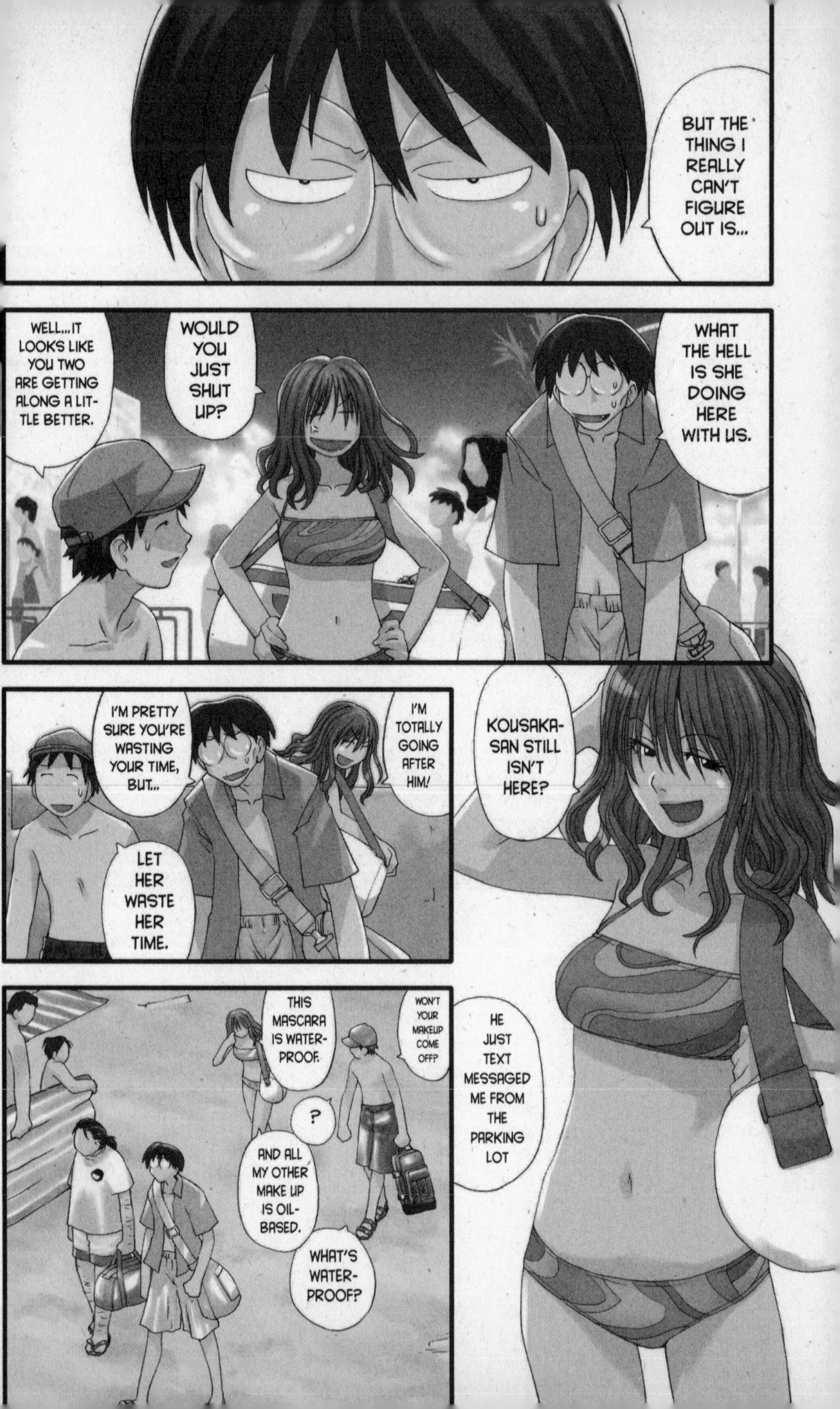
BUT THE THING I REALLY CAN'T FIGURE OUT IS...
WHAT THE HELL IS SHE DOING HERE WITH US.
WOULD YOU JUST SHUT UP?
WELL...IT LOOKS LIKE YOU TWO ARE GETTING ALONG A LITTLE BETTER.
KOUSAKA-SAN STILL ISN'T HERE?
HE JUST TEXT MESSAGED ME FROM THE PARKING LOT
I'M TOTALLY GOING AFTER HIM!
I'M PRETTY SURE YOU'RE WASTING YOUR TIME, BUT...
LET HER WASTE HER TIME.
WON'T YOUR MAKEUP COME OFF?
THIS MASCARA IS WATERPROOF.
?
AND ALL MY OTHER MAKE UP IS OIL-BASED.
WHAT'S WATERPROOF?

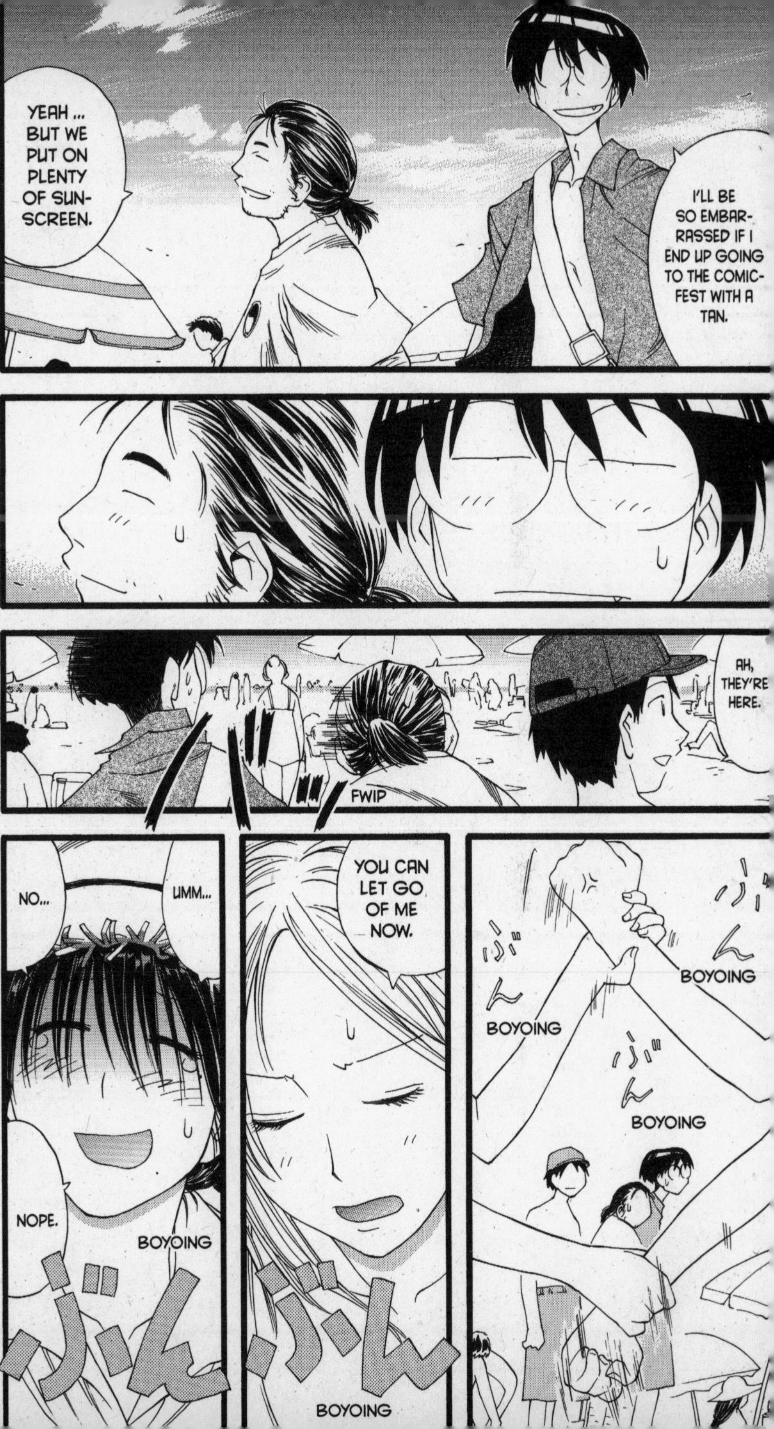
I'LL BE SO EMBAR-RASSED IF I END UP GOING TO THE COMIC-FEST WITH A TAN.
YEAH ... BUT WE PUT ON PLENTY OF SUN-SCREEN.
AH, THEY'RE HERE.
FWIP
ぶん
BOYOING
ぶん
BOYOING
ぶん
BOYOING
YOU CAN LET GO OF ME NOW.
ぶん
BOYOING
UMM...
NO...
NOPE.
BOYOING
ぶん

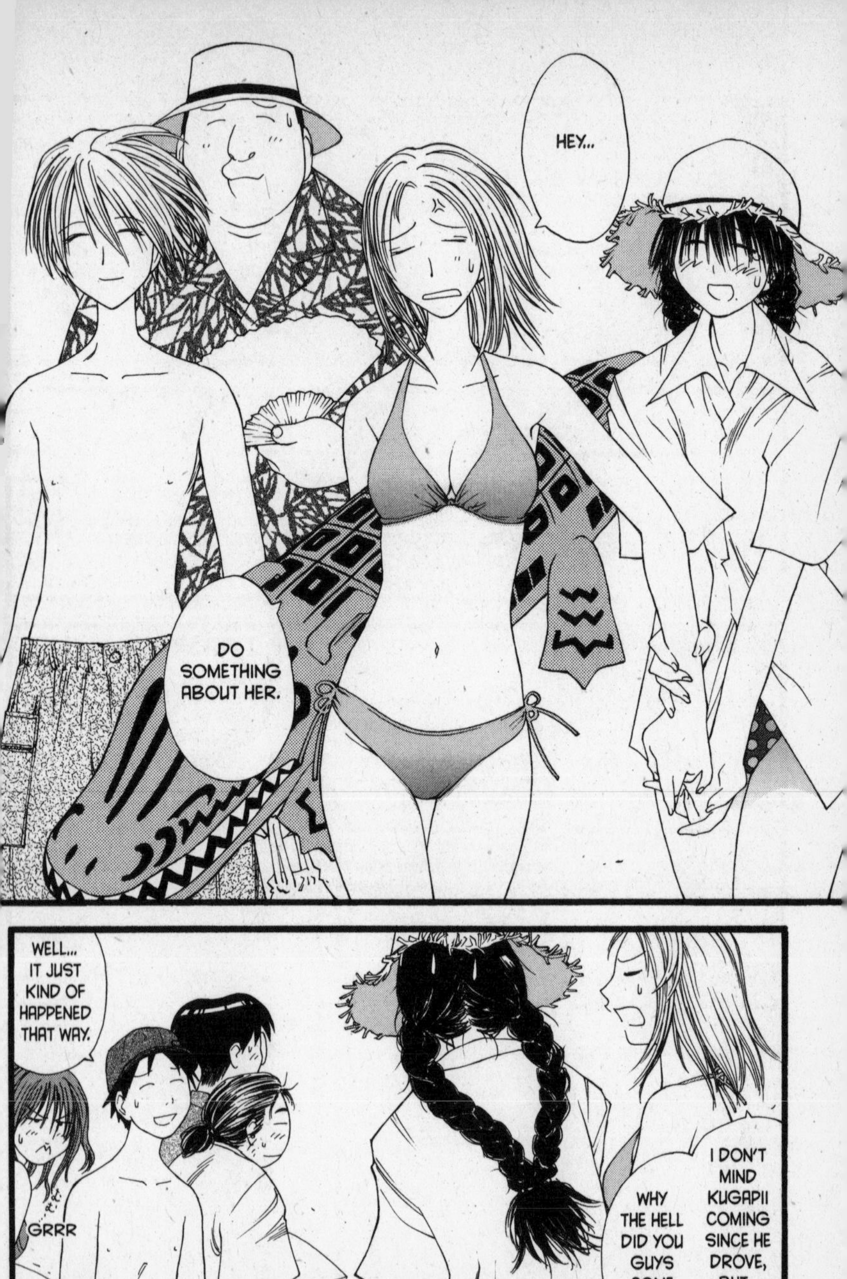
HEY...
DO SOMETHING ABOUT HER.
I DON'T MIND KUGAPII COMING SINCE HE DROVE, BUT...
WHY THE HELL DID YOU GUYS COME TOO?
WELL... IT JUST KIND OF HAPPENED THAT WAY.
GRRR

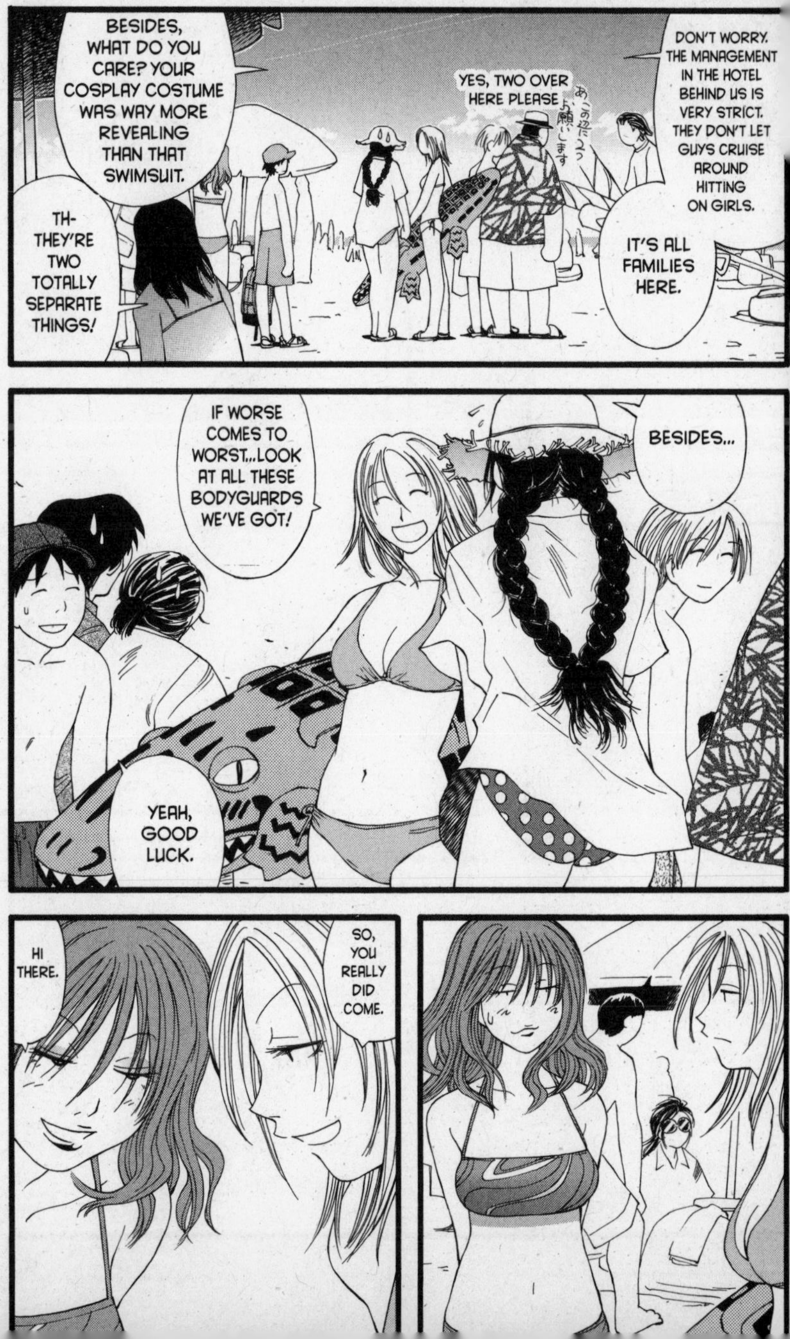
DON'T WORRY. THE MANAGEMENT IN THE HOTEL BEHIND US IS VERY STRICT. THEY DON'T LET GUYS CRUISE AROUND HITTING ON GIRLS.
IT'S ALL FAMILIES HERE.
YES, TWO OVER HERE PLEASE
あ、この辺に2つお願いします
BESIDES, WHAT DO YOU CARE? YOUR COSPLAY COSTUME WAS WAY MORE REVEALING THAN THAT SWIMSUIT.
TH- THEY'RE TWO TOTALLY SEPARATE THINGS!
BESIDES...
IF WORSE COMES TO WORST...LOOK AT ALL THESE BODYGUARDS WE'VE GOT!
YEAH, GOOD LUCK.
SO, YOU REALLY DID COME.
HI THERE.

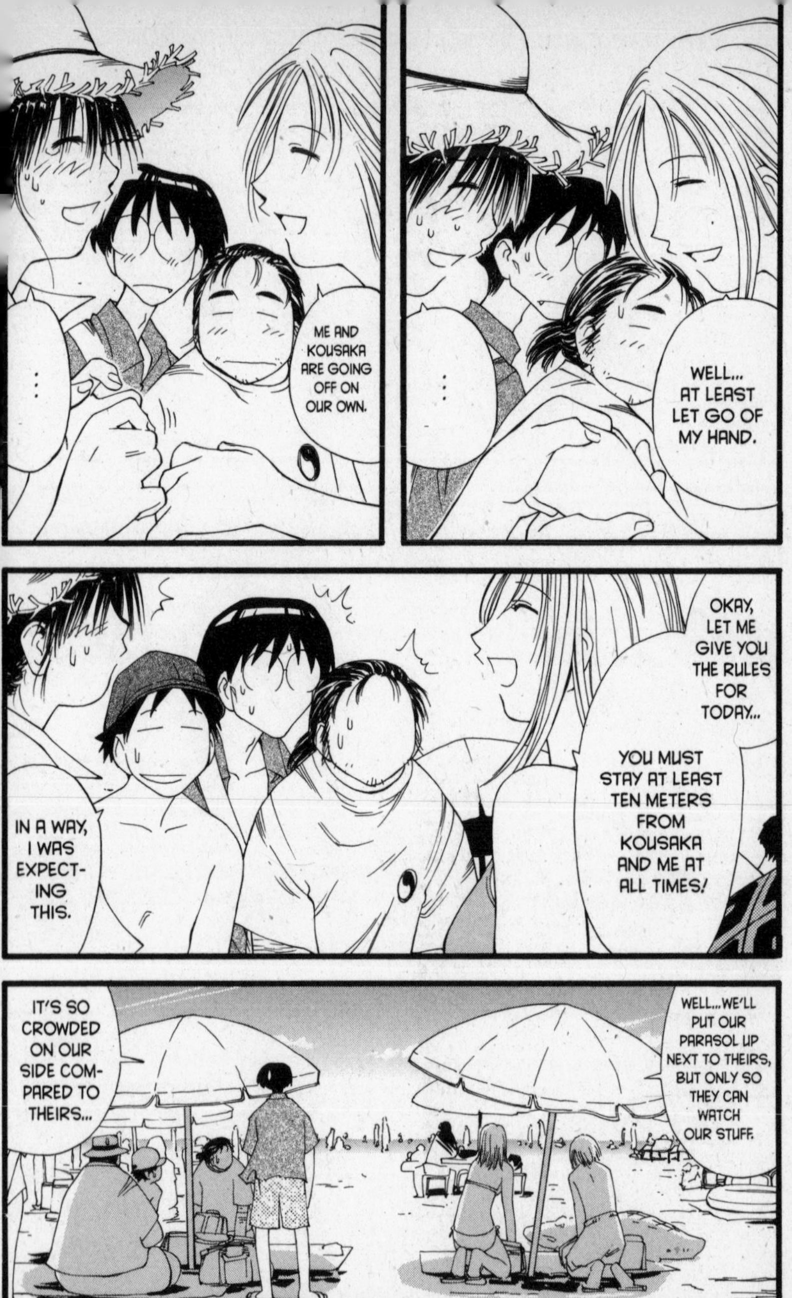
WELL... AT LEAST LET GO OF MY HAND.
...
ME AND KOUSAKA ARE GOING OFF ON OUR OWN.
...
OKAY, LET ME GIVE YOU THE RULES FOR TODAY...
YOU MUST STAY AT LEAST TEN METERS FROM KOUSAKA AND ME AT ALL TIMES!
IN A WAY, I WAS EXPECTING THIS.
WELL...WE'LL PUT OUR PARASOL UP NEXT TO THEIRS, BUT ONLY SO THEY CAN WATCH OUR STUFF.
IT'S SO CROWDED ON OUR SIDE COMPARED TO THEIRS...

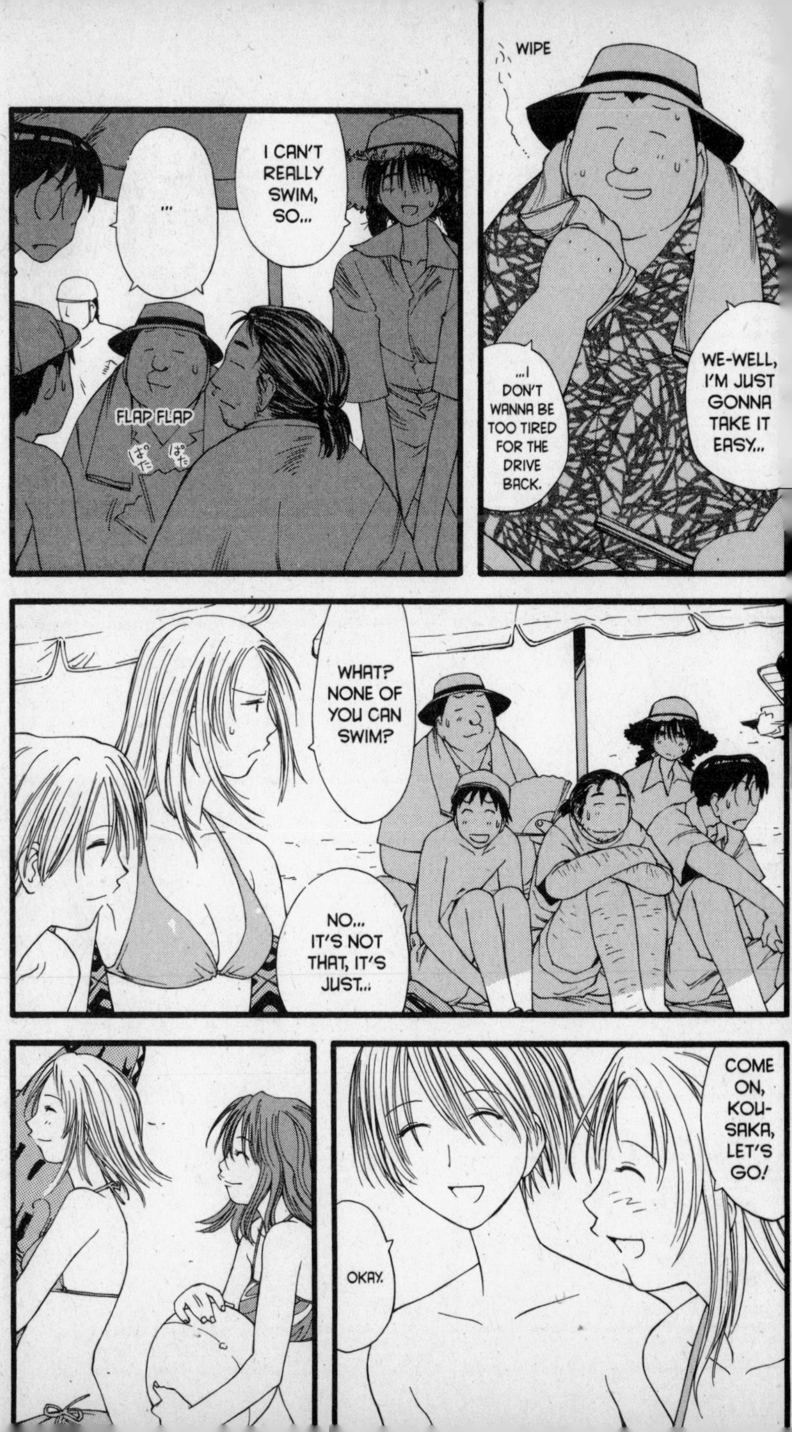
WIPE
ふい
WE-WELL, I'M JUST GONNA TAKE IT EASY...
...I DON'T WANNA BE TOO TIRED FOR THE DRIVE BACK.
I CAN'T REALLY SWIM, SO...
...
FLAP FLAP
ぱた ぱた
WHAT? NONE OF YOU CAN SWIM?
NO... IT'S NOT THAT, IT'S JUST...
COME ON, KOU-SAKA, LET'S GO!
OKAY.
...

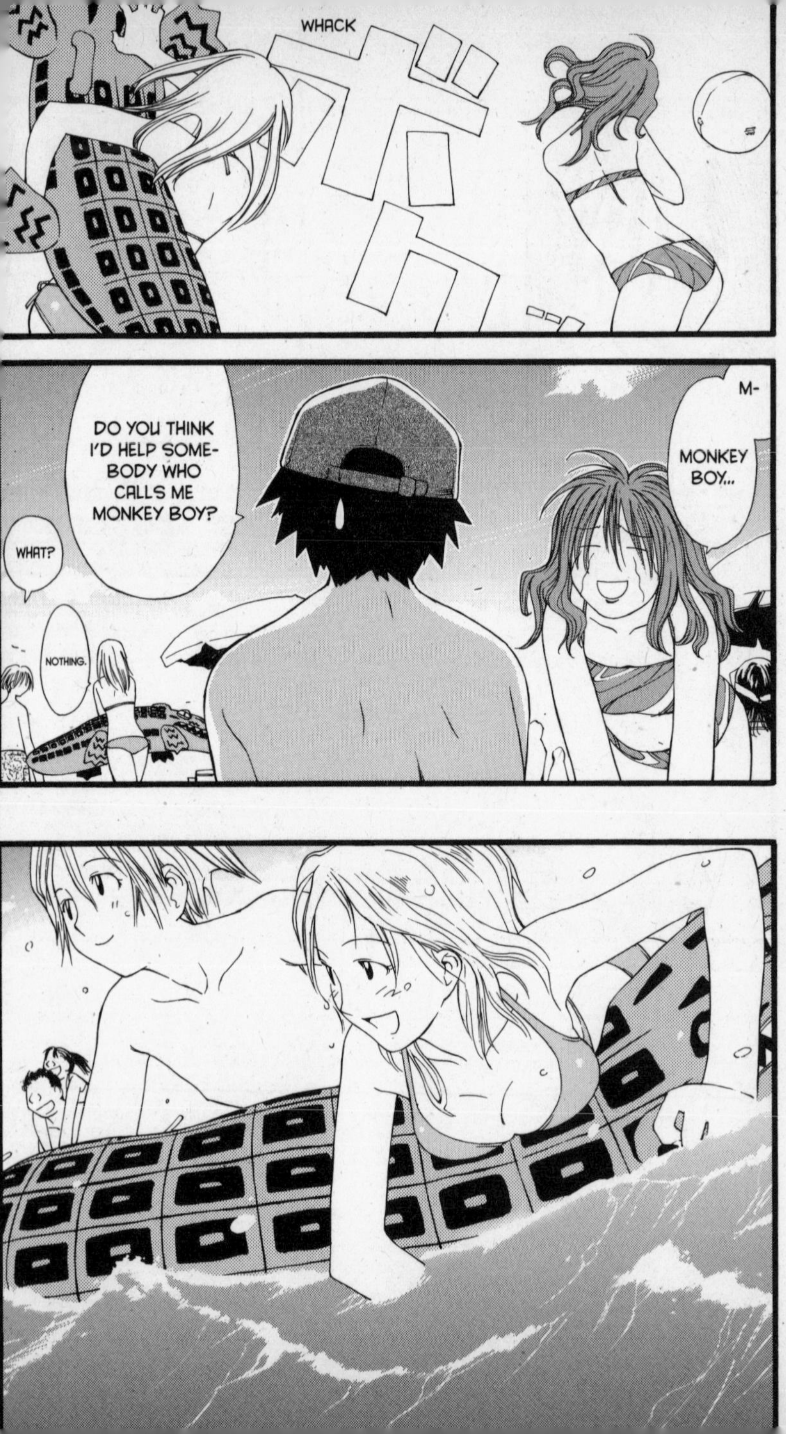
WHACK
M-
MONKEY BOY...
DO YOU THINK I'D HELP SOME-BODY WHO CALLS ME MONKEY BOY?
WHAT?
NOTHING.

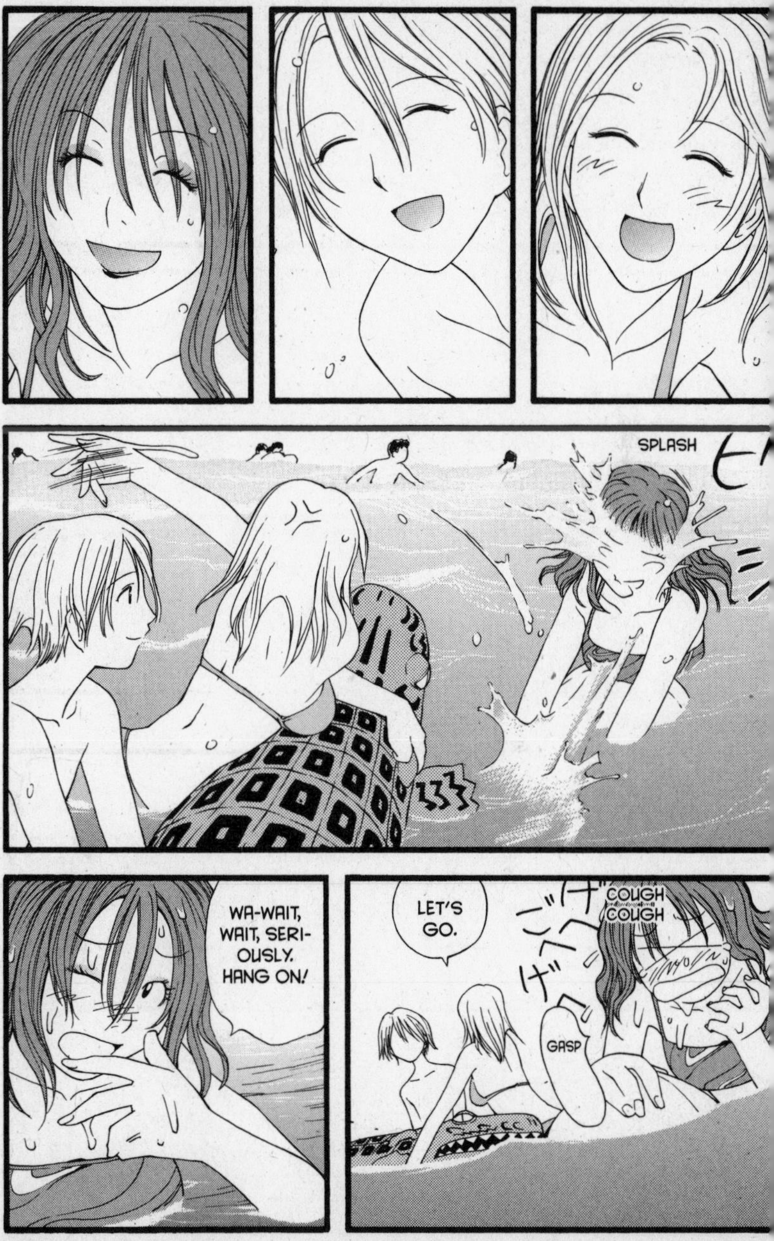
SPLASH
COUGH COUGH
LET'S GO.
GASP
WA-WAIT, WAIT, SERIOUSLY. HANG ON!

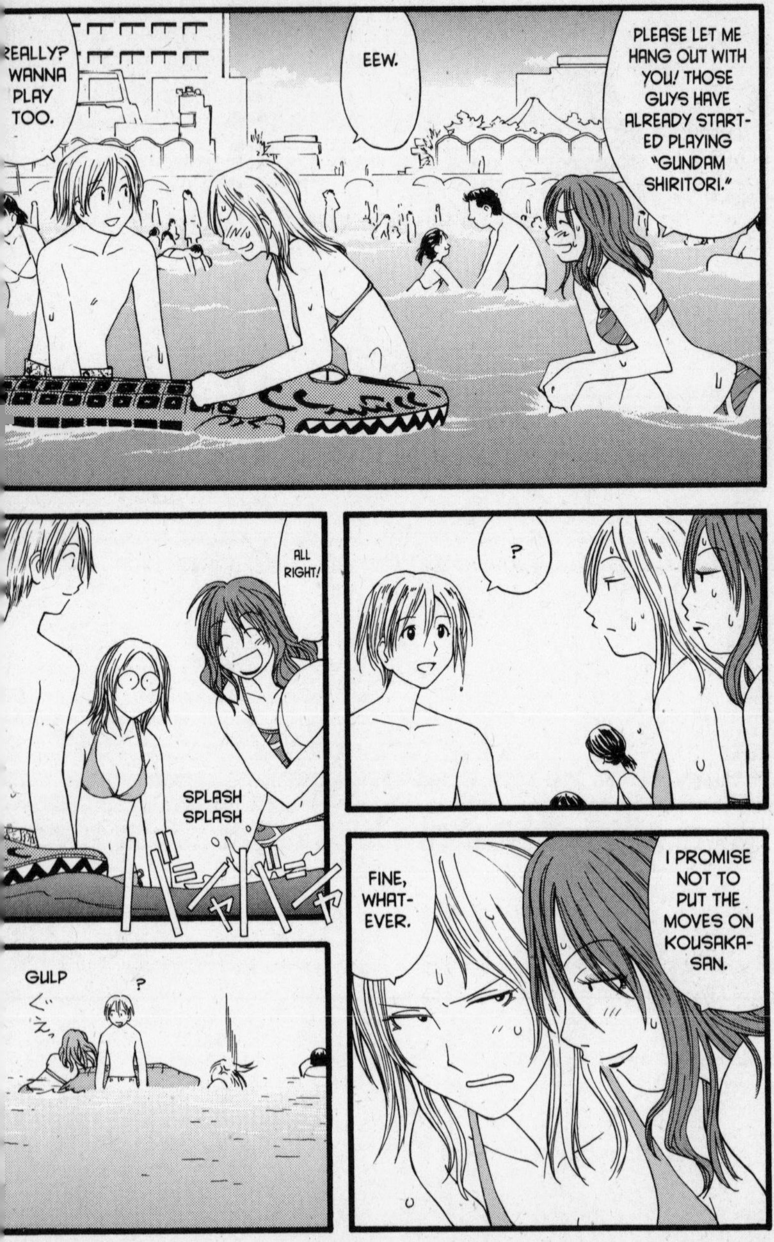
PLEASE LET ME HANG OUT WITH YOU! THOSE GUYS HAVE ALREADY START-ED PLAYING "GUNDAM SHIRITORI."
EEW.
REALLY? WANNA PLAY TOO.
?
ALL RIGHT!
SPLASH SPLASH
I PROMISE NOT TO PUT THE MOVES ON KOUSAKA-SAN.
FINE, WHAT-EVER.
GULP
?

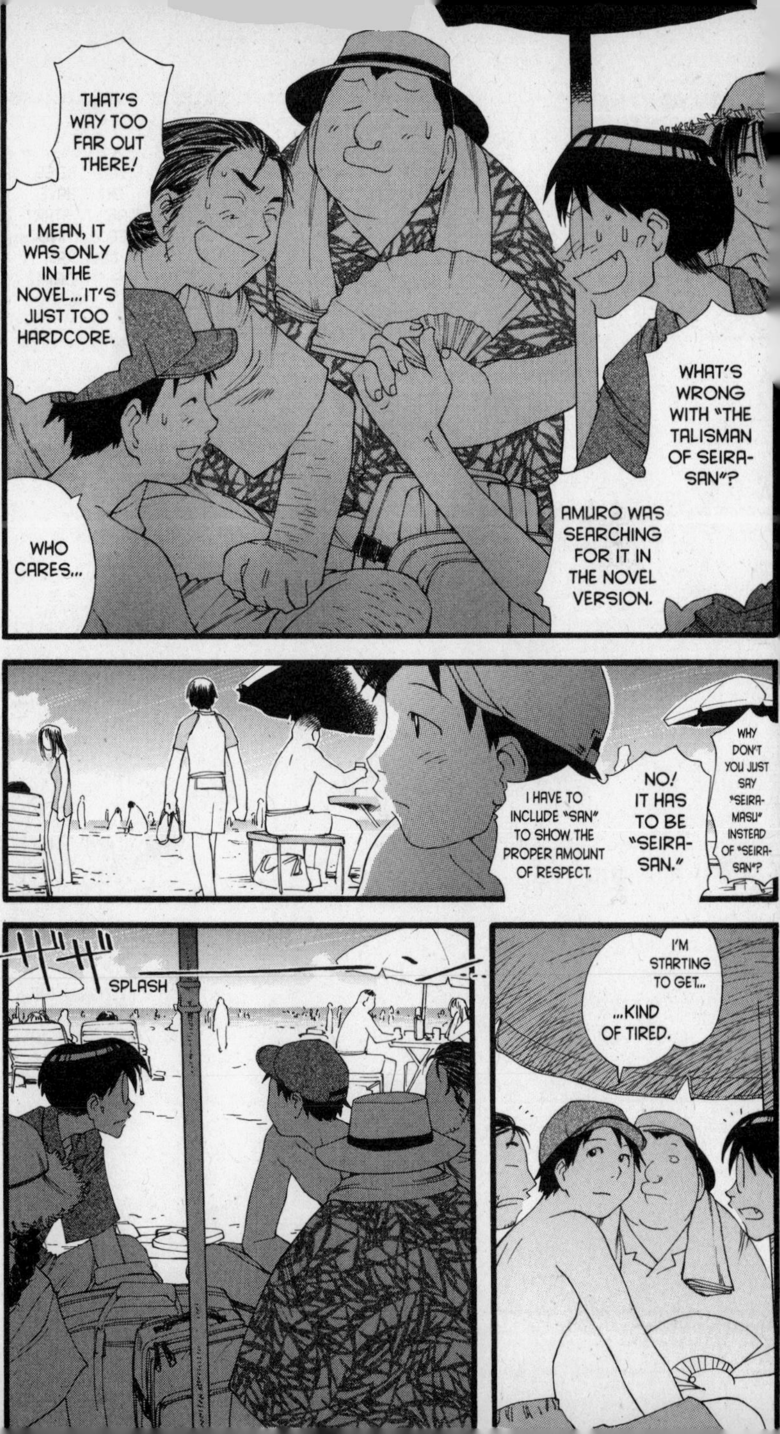
WHAT'S WRONG WITH "THE TALISMAN OF SEIRA-SAN"?
AMURO WAS SEARCHING FOR IT IN THE NOVEL VERSION.
THAT'S WAY TOO FAR OUT THERE!
I MEAN, IT WAS ONLY IN THE NOVEL...IT'S JUST TOO HARDCORE.
WHO CARES...
WHY DON'T YOU JUST SAY "SEIRA-MASU" INSTEAD OF "SEIRA-SAN"?
NO! IT HAS TO BE "SEIRA-SAN."
I HAVE TO INCLUDE "SAN" TO SHOW THE PROPER AMOUNT OF RESPECT.
I'M STARTING TO GET...
...KIND OF TIRED.
SPLASH

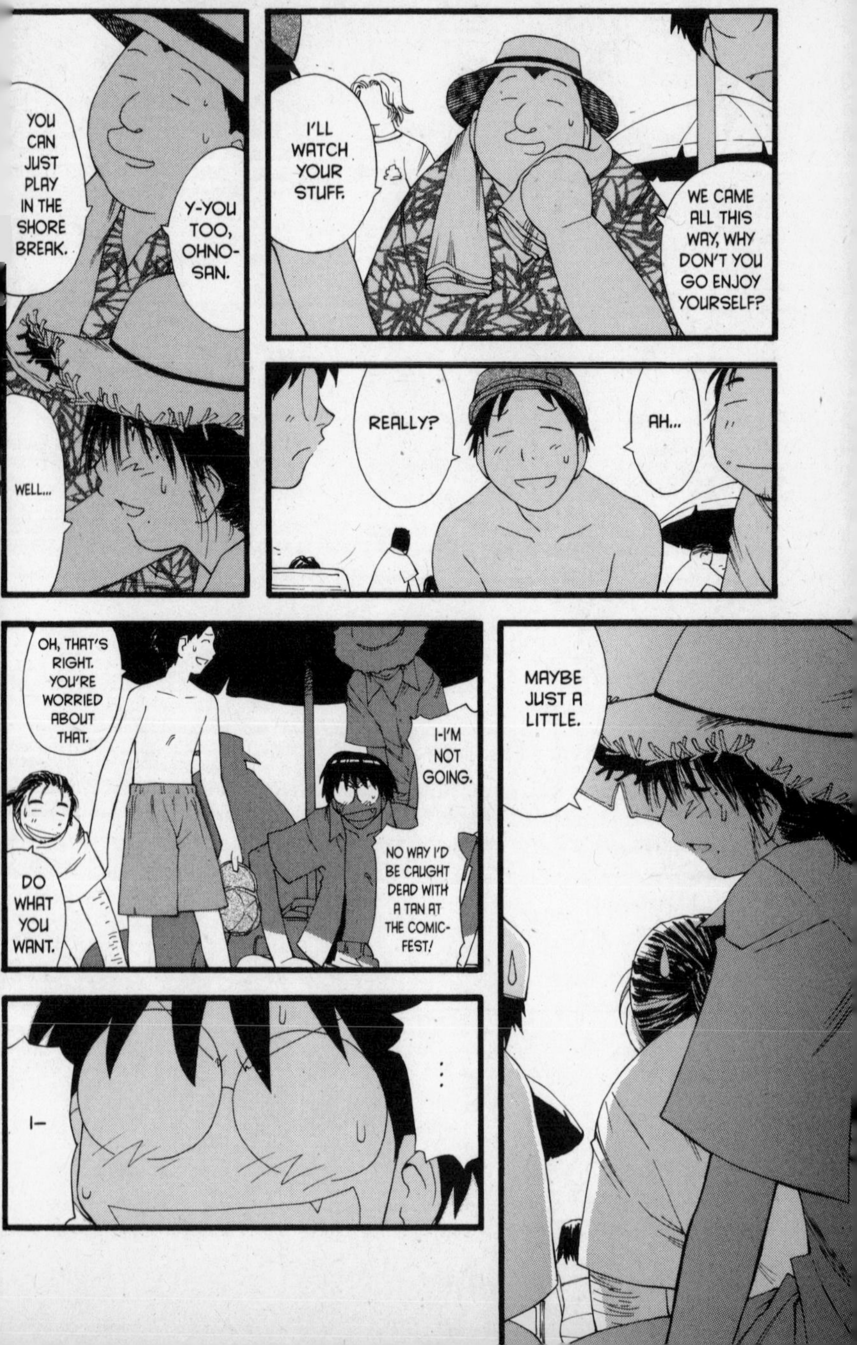
WE CAME ALL THIS WAY, WHY DON'T YOU GO ENJOY YOURSELF?
I'LL WATCH YOUR STUFF.
AH...
REALLY?
Y-YOU TOO, OHNO-SAN.
YOU CAN JUST PLAY IN THE SHORE BREAK.
WELL...
MAYBE JUST A LITTLE.
I-I'M NOT GOING.
NO WAY I'D BE CAUGHT DEAD WITH A TAN AT THE COMIC-FEST!
OH, THAT'S RIGHT. YOU'RE WORRIED ABOUT THAT.
DO WHAT YOU WANT.
...
I—

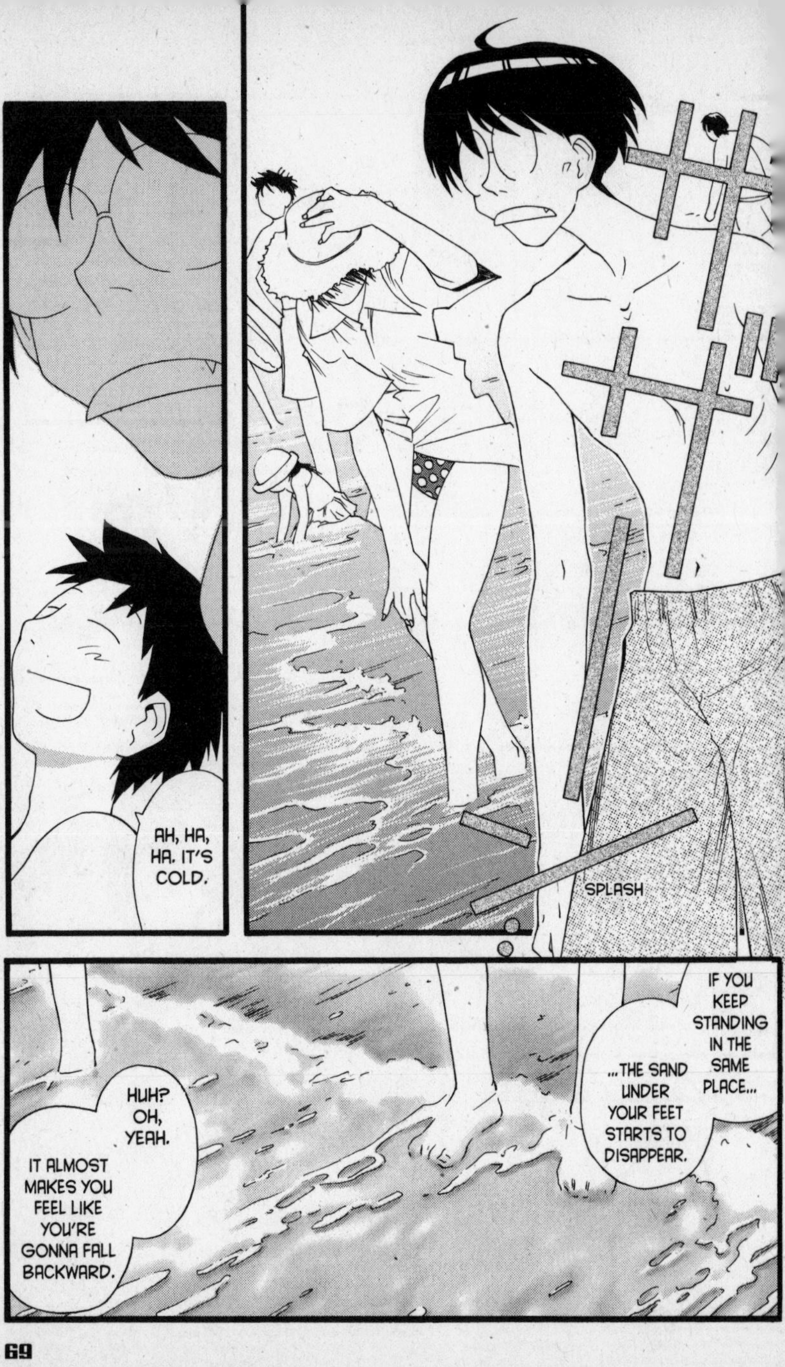
SPLASH
AH, HA, HA. IT'S COLD.
IF YOU KEEP STANDING IN THE SAME PLACE...
...THE SAND UNDER YOUR FEET STARTS TO DISAPPEAR.
HUH? OH, YEAH.
IT ALMOST MAKES YOU FEEL LIKE YOU'RE GONNA FALL BACKWARD.

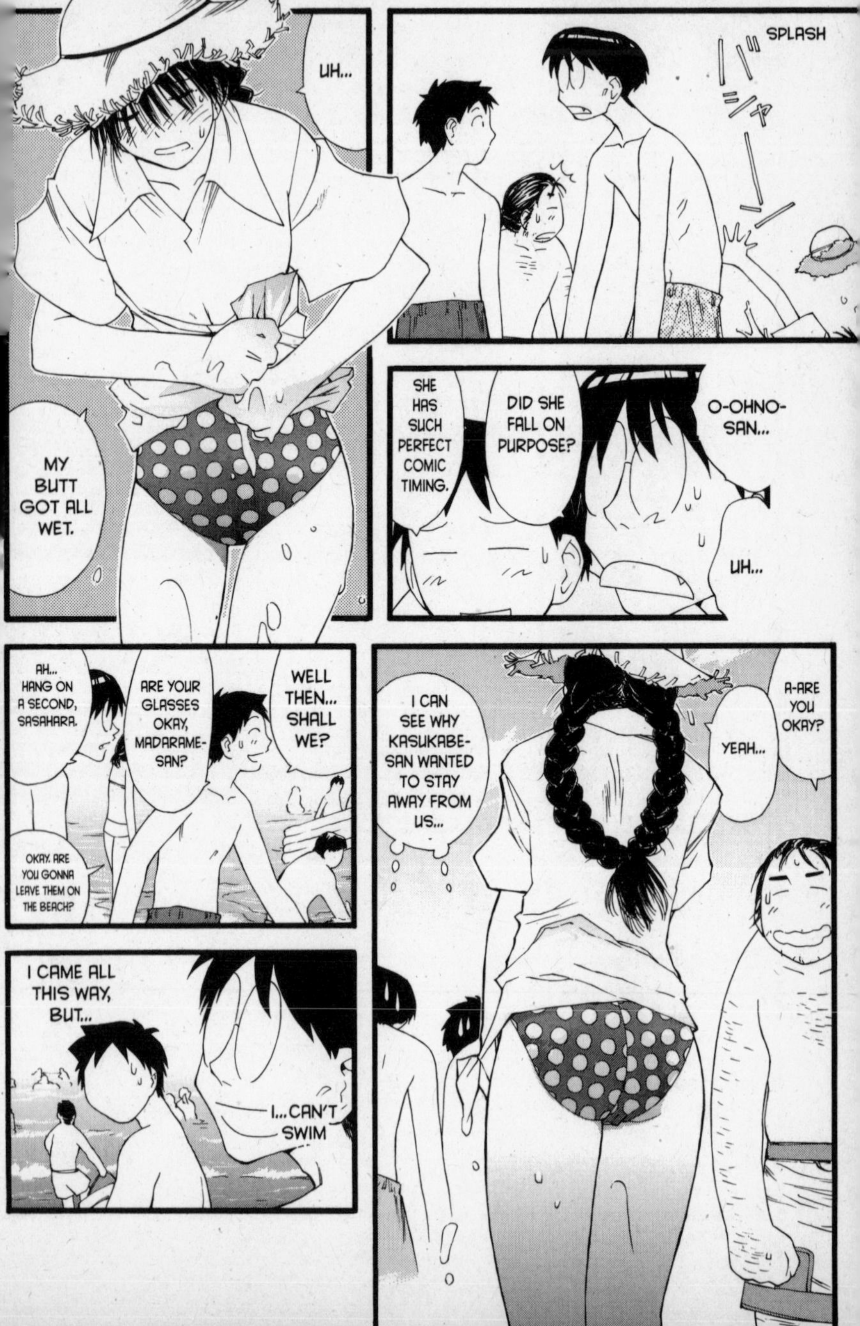
SPLASH
バシャー
O-OHNO-SAN...
DID SHE FALL ON PURPOSE?
SHE HAS SUCH PERFECT COMIC TIMING.
UH...
UH...
MY BUTT GOT ALL WET.
A-ARE YOU OKAY?
YEAH...
I CAN SEE WHY KASUKABE-SAN WANTED TO STAY AWAY FROM US...
WELL THEN... SHALL WE?
ARE YOUR GLASSES OKAY, MADARAME-SAN?
AH... HANG ON A SECOND, SASAHARA.
OKAY. ARE YOU GONNA LEAVE THEM ON THE BEACH?
I CAME ALL THIS WAY, BUT...
I...CAN'T SWIM

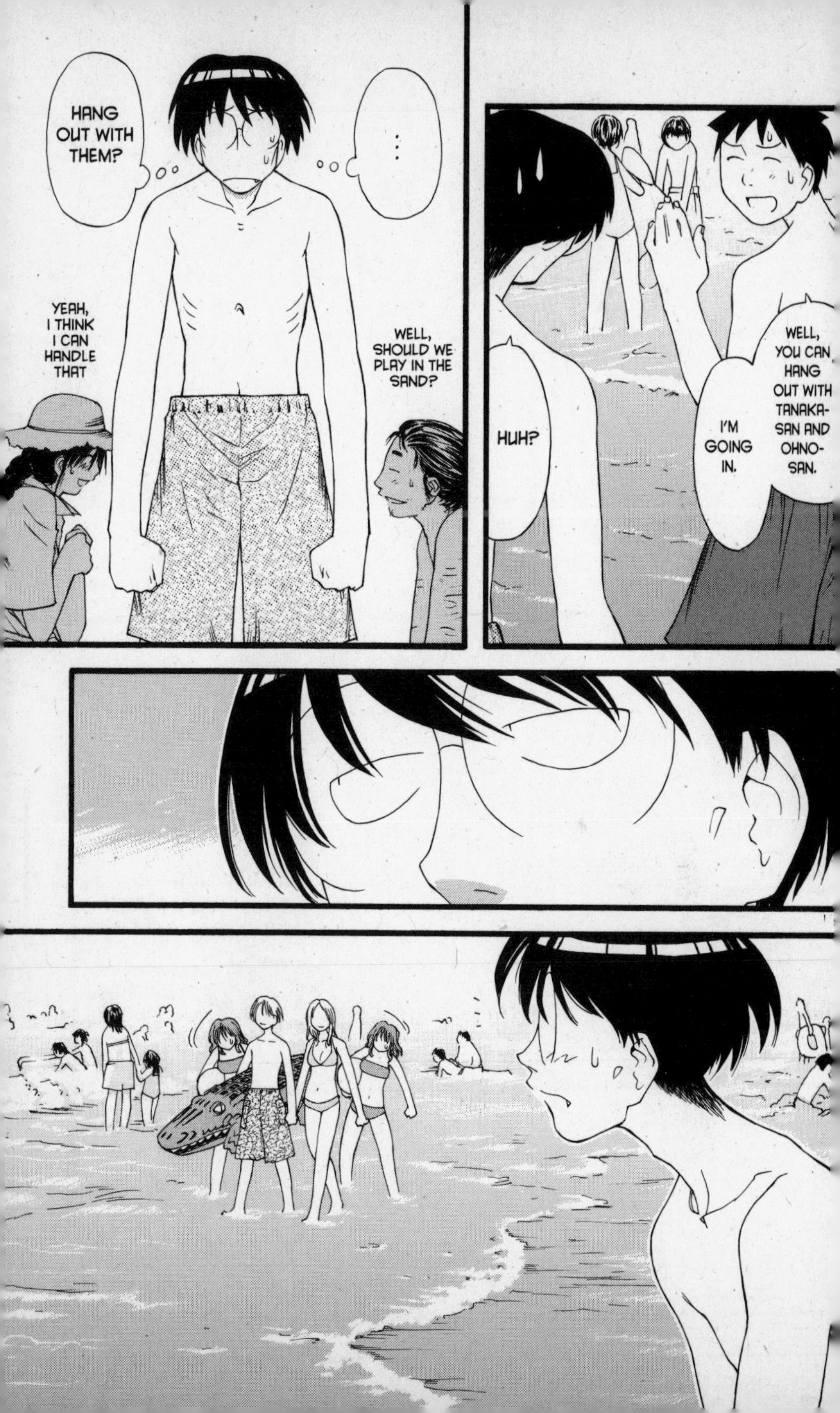
WELL, YOU CAN HANG OUT WITH TANAKA-SAN AND OHNO-SAN.
I'M GOING IN.
HUH?
...
HANG OUT WITH THEM?
WELL, SHOULD WE PLAY IN THE SAND?
YEAH, I THINK I CAN HANDLE THAT

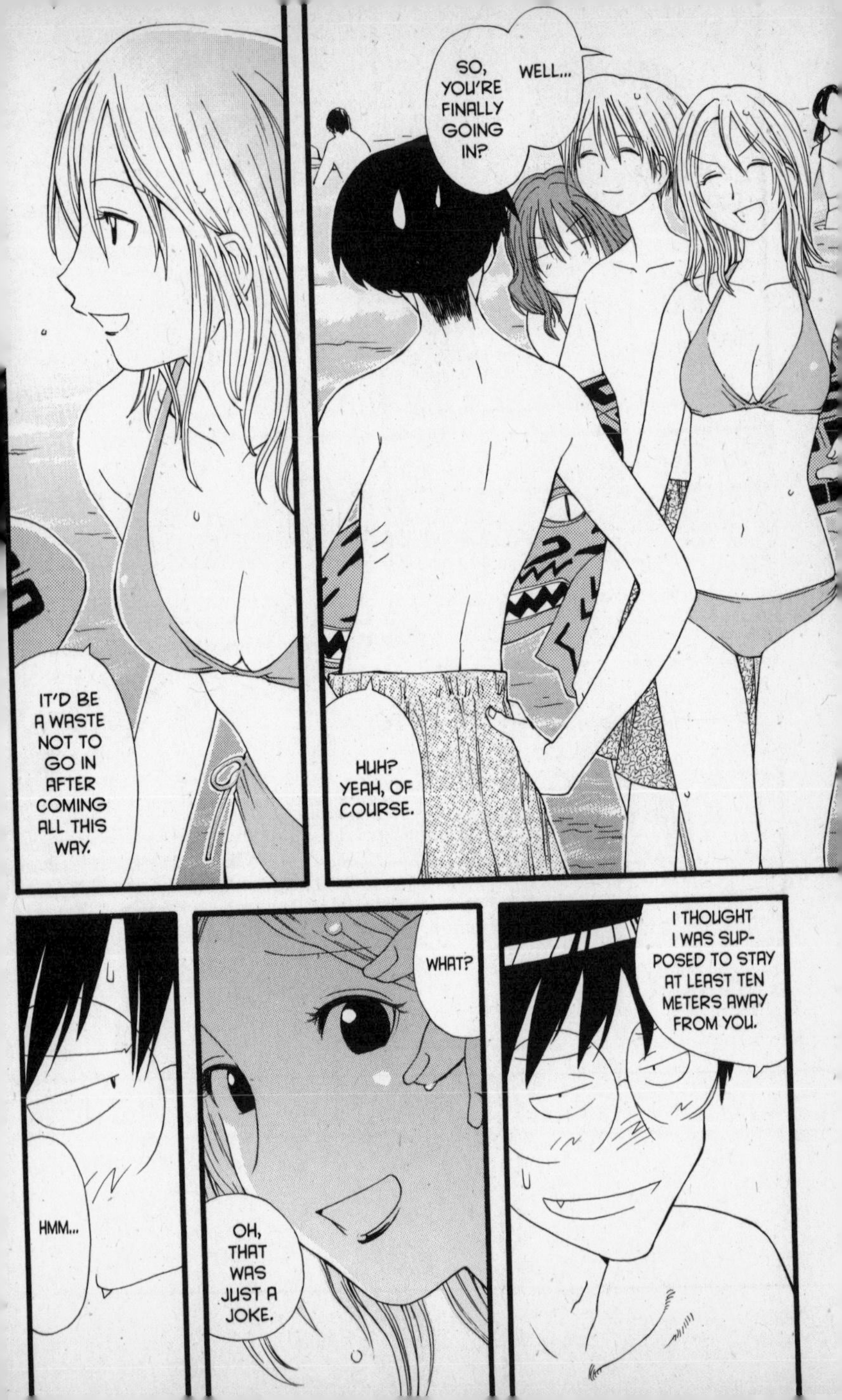
WELL... SO, YOU'RE FINALLY GOING IN?
HUH? YEAH, OF COURSE.
IT'D BE A WASTE NOT TO GO IN AFTER COMING ALL THIS WAY.
I THOUGHT I WAS SUP-POSED TO STAY AT LEAST TEN METERS AWAY FROM YOU.
WHAT?
OH, THAT WAS JUST A JOKE.
HMM...

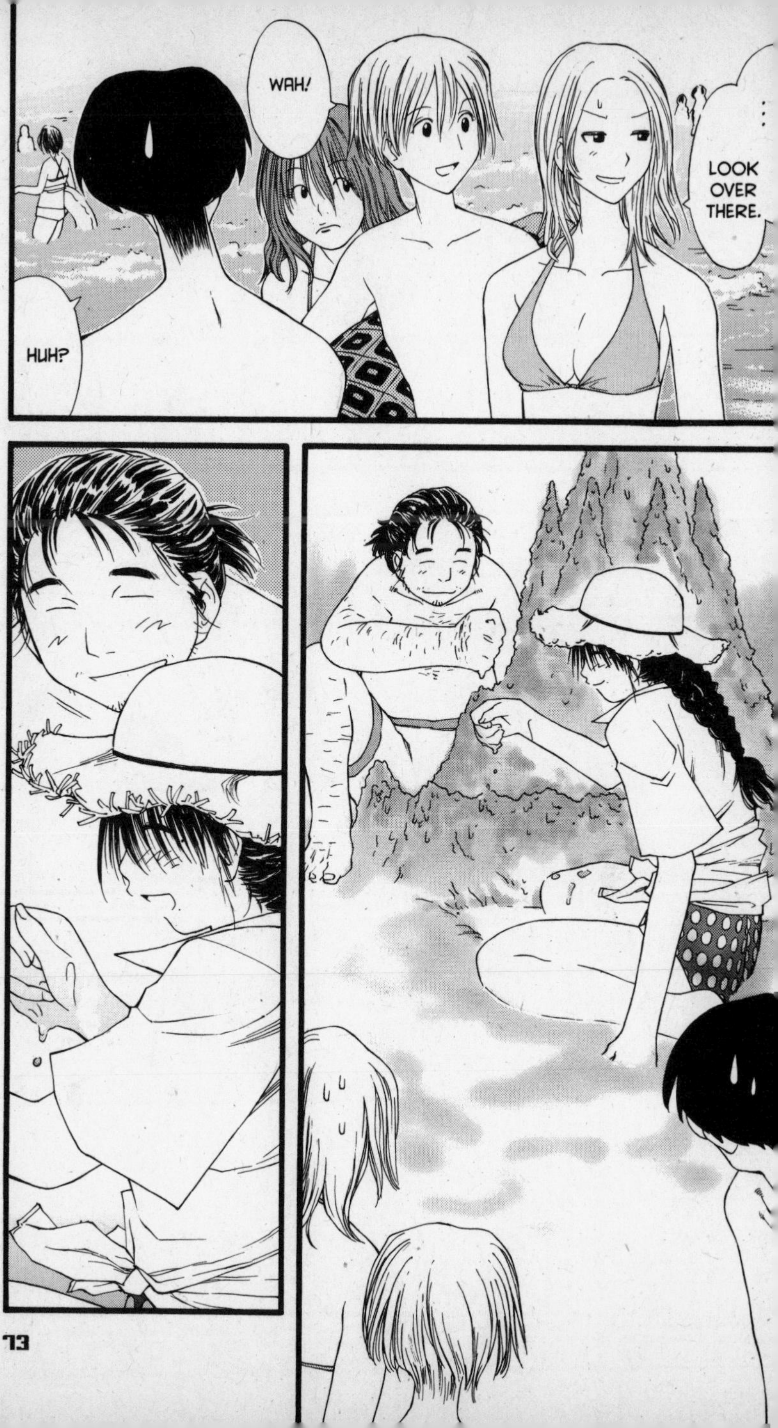
...
LOOK OVER THERE.
WAH!
HUH?

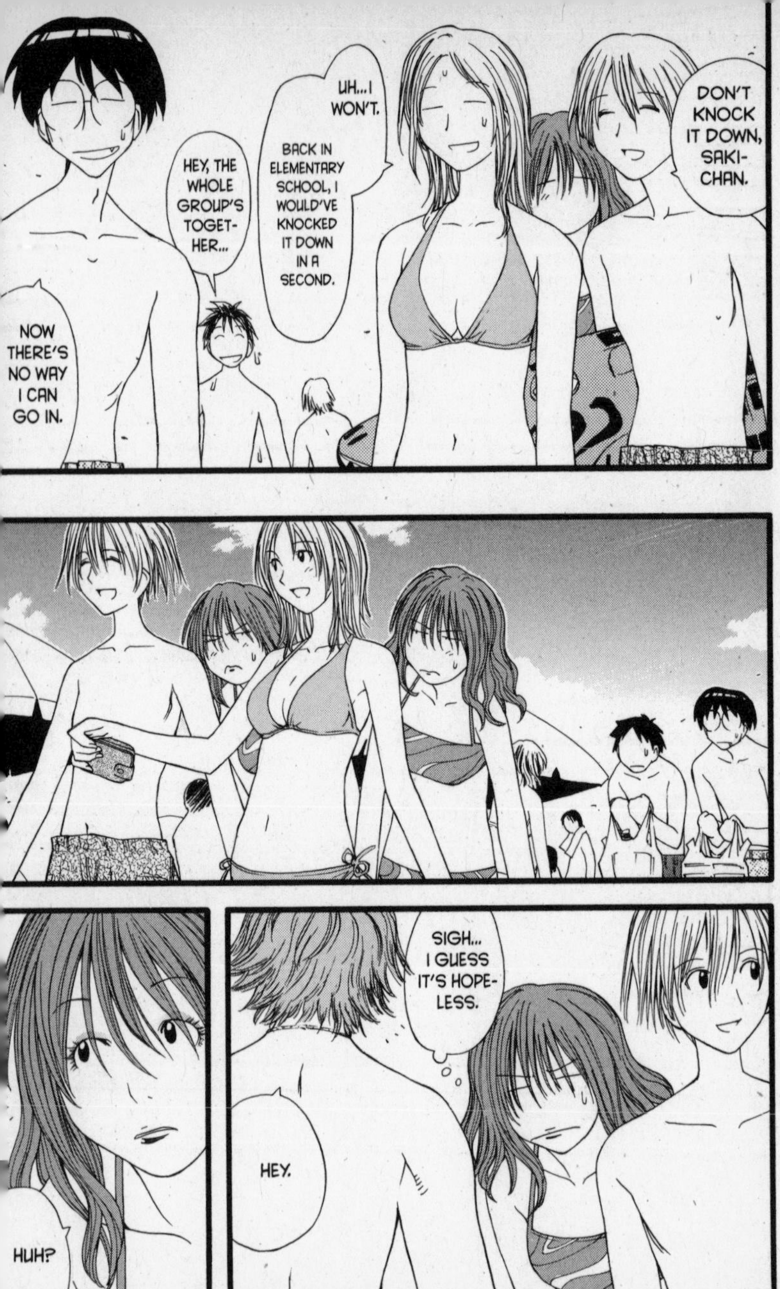
DON'T KNOCK IT DOWN, SAKI-CHAN.
UH...I WON'T.
BACK IN ELEMENTARY SCHOOL, I WOULD'VE KNOCKED IT DOWN IN A SECOND.
HEY, THE WHOLE GROUP'S TOGET-HER...
NOW THERE'S NO WAY I CAN GO IN.
SIGH... I GUESS IT'S HOPE-LESS.
HEY.
HUH?

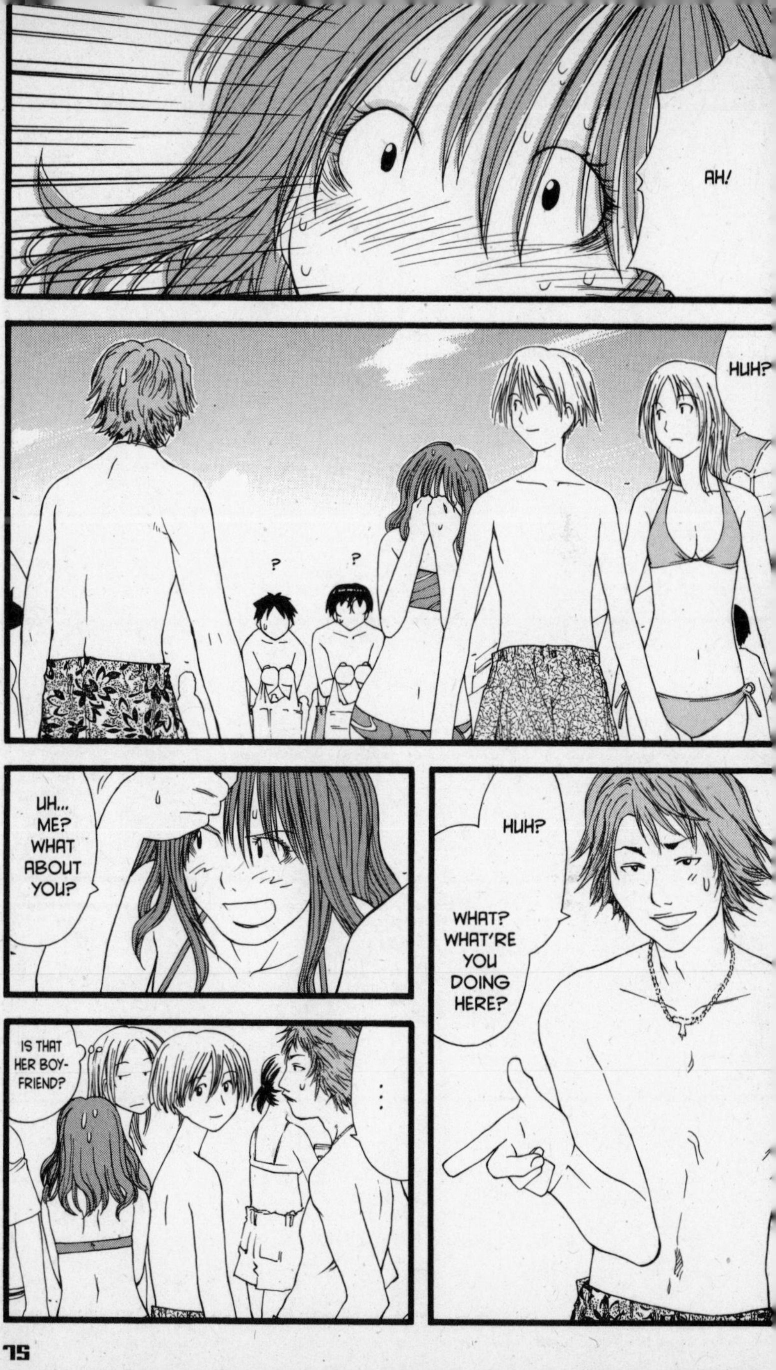
AH!
HUH?
HUH?
WHAT? WHAT'RE YOU DOING HERE?
UH... ME? WHAT ABOUT YOU?
...
IS THAT HER BOY-FRIEND?

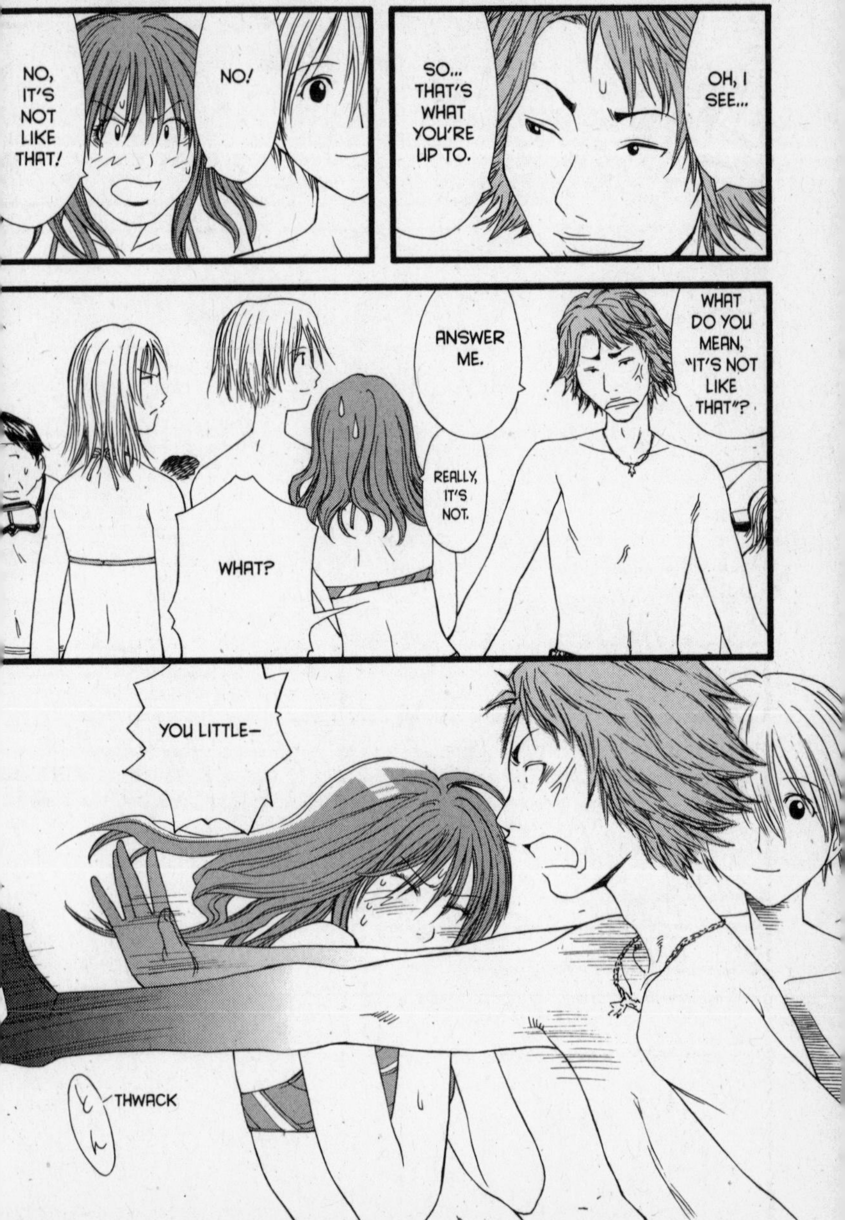
OH, I SEE...
SO... THAT'S WHAT YOU'RE UP TO.
NO!
NO, IT'S NOT LIKE THAT!
WHAT DO YOU MEAN, "IT'S NOT LIKE THAT"?
ANSWER ME.
REALLY, IT'S NOT.
WHAT?
YOU LITTLE—
THWACK

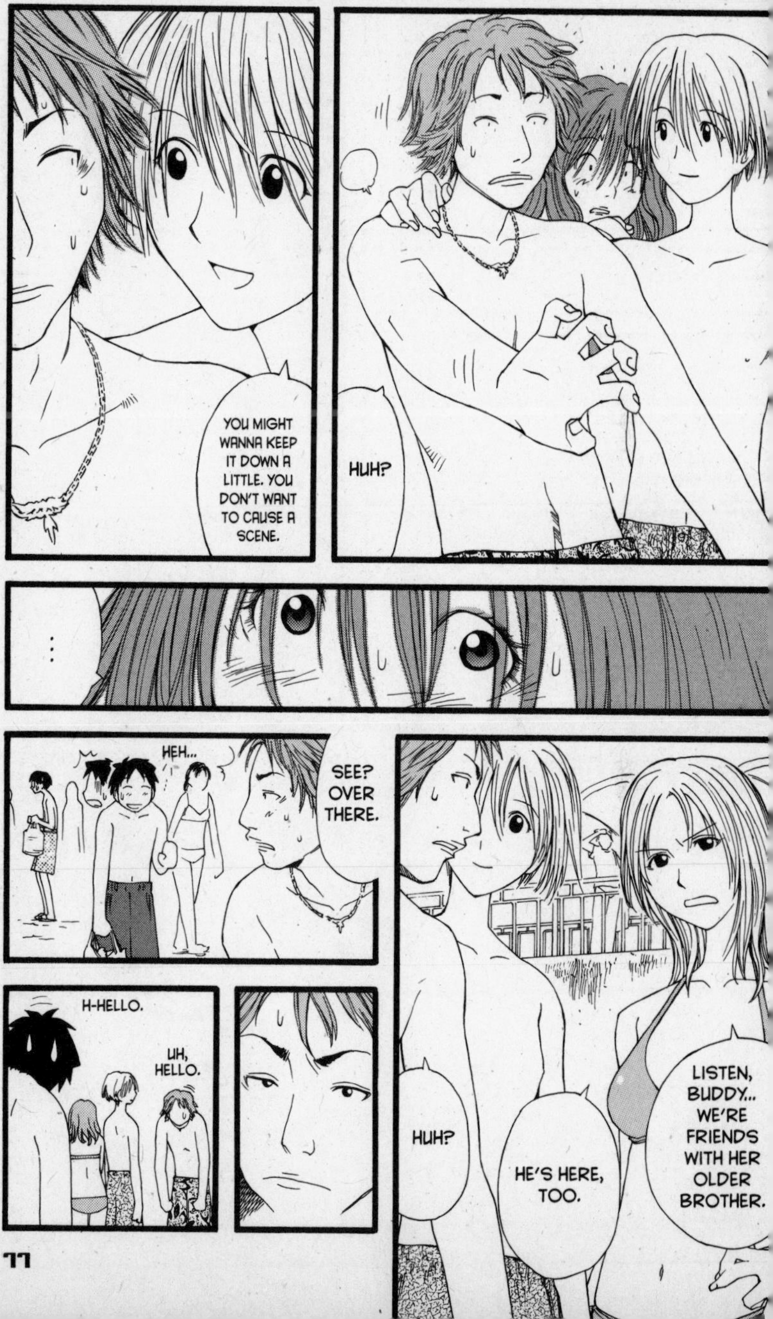
HUH?
YOU MIGHT WANNA KEEP IT DOWN A LITTLE. YOU DON'T WANT TO CAUSE A SCENE.
...
LISTEN, BUDDY... WE'RE FRIENDS WITH HER OLDER BROTHER.
HE'S HERE, TOO.
HUH?
SEE? OVER THERE.
HEH...
H-HELLO.
UH, HELLO.

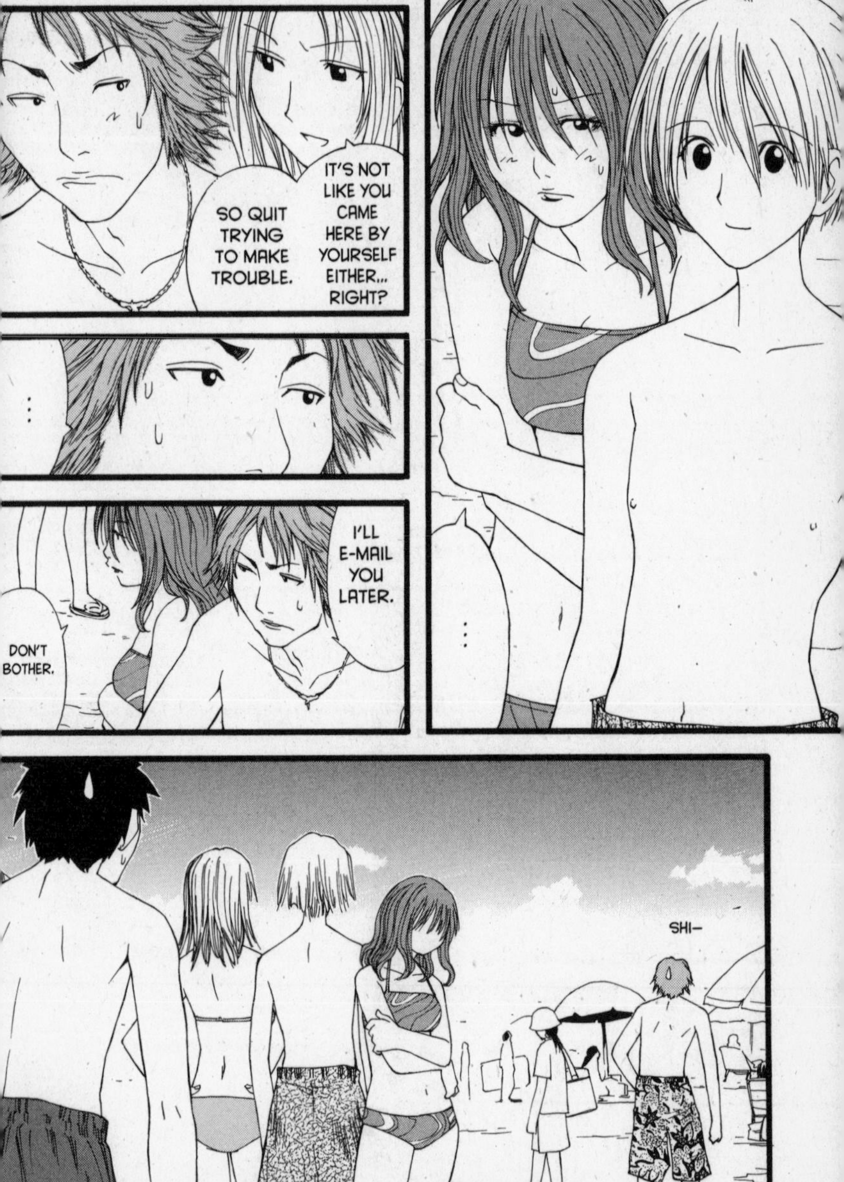
...
IT'S NOT LIKE YOU CAME HERE BY YOURSELF EITHER... RIGHT?
SO QUIT TRYING TO MAKE TROUBLE.
...
I'LL E-MAIL YOU LATER.
DON'T BOTHER.
SHI-

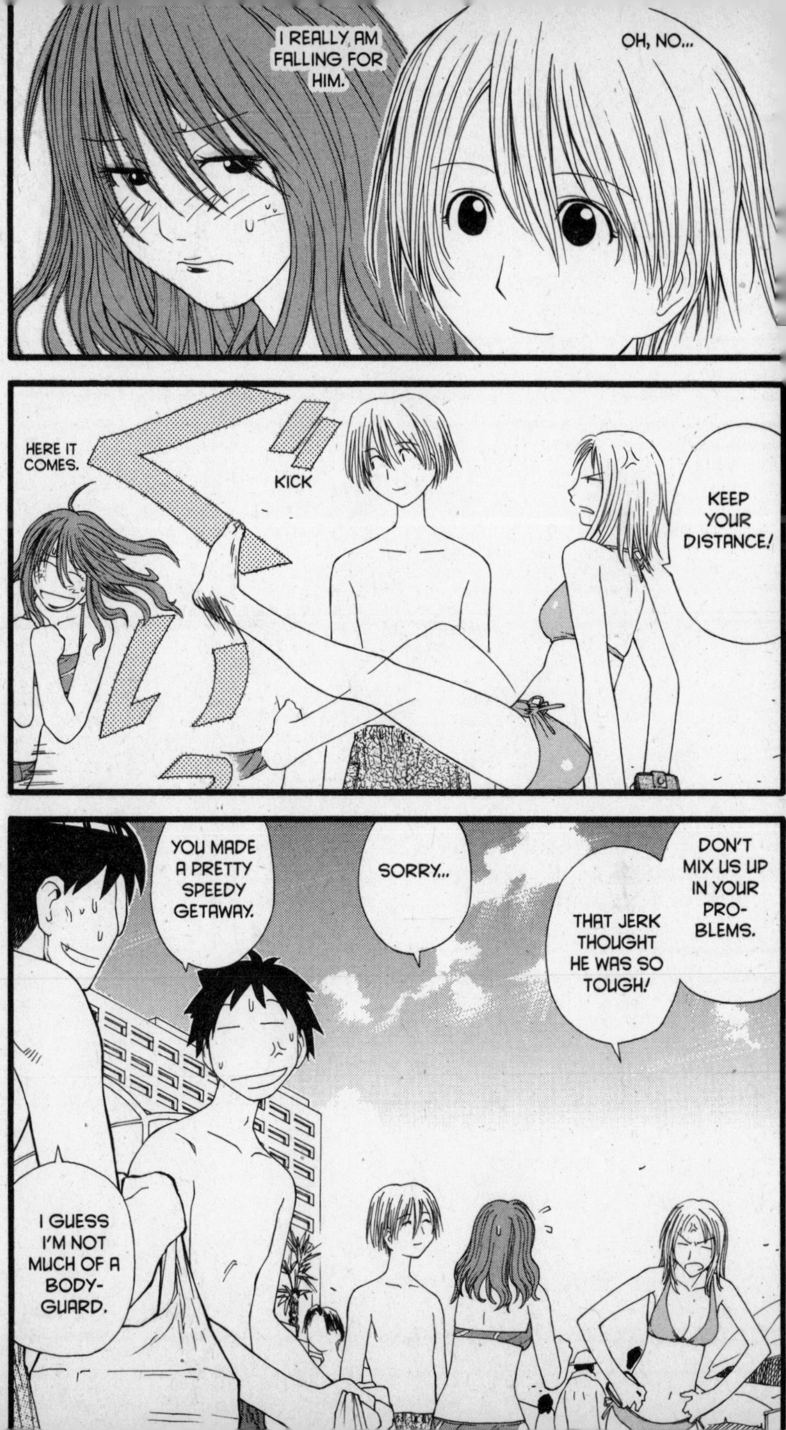
OH, NO...
I REALLY AM FALLING FOR HIM.
KEEP YOUR DISTANCE!
KICK
HERE IT COMES.
DON'T MIX US UP IN YOUR PRO-BLEMS.
THAT JERK THOUGHT HE WAS SO TOUGH!
SORRY...
YOU MADE A PRETTY SPEEDY GETAWAY.
I GUESS I'M NOT MUCH OF A BODY-GUARD.

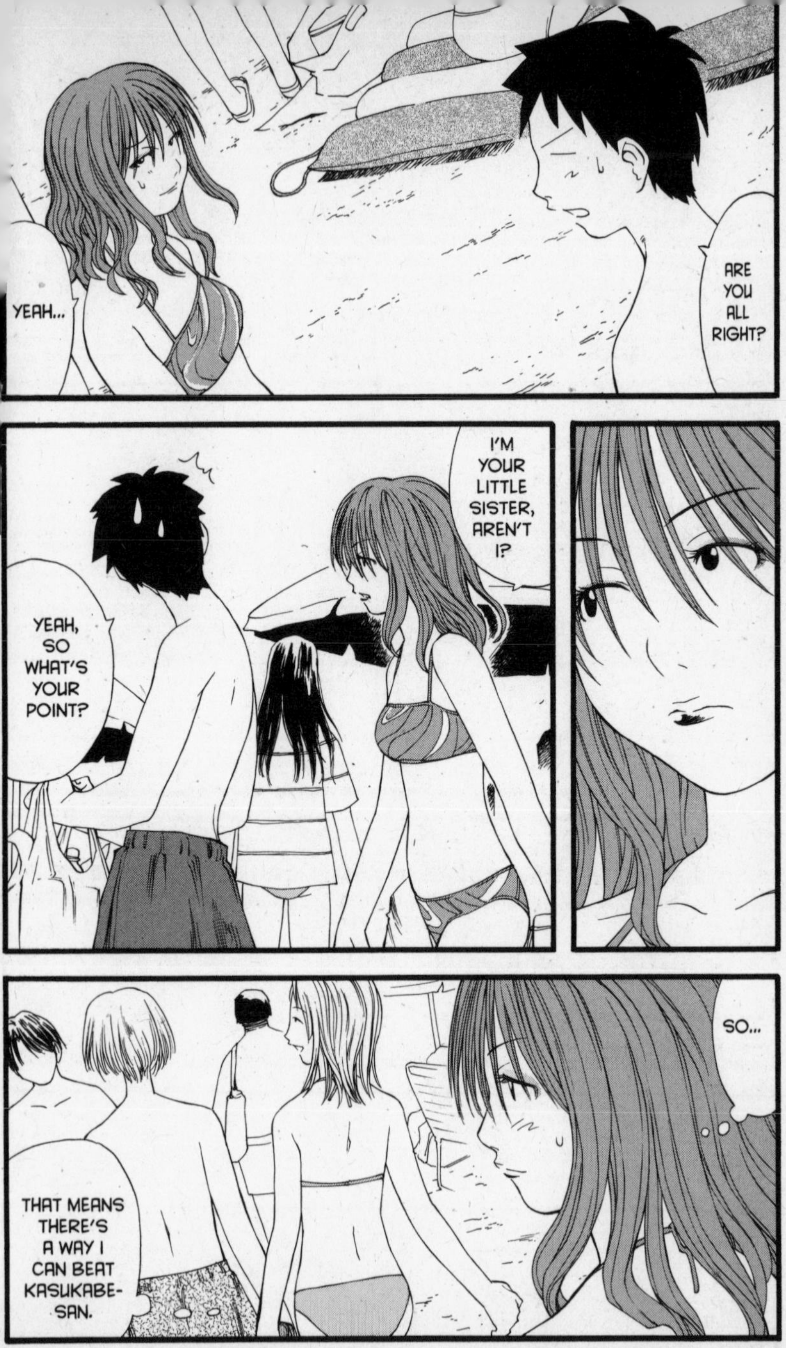
ARE YOU ALL RIGHT?
YEAH...
I'M YOUR LITTLE SISTER, AREN'T I?
YEAH, SO WHAT'S YOUR POINT?
SO...
THAT MEANS THERE'S A WAY I CAN BEAT KASUKABE-SAN.

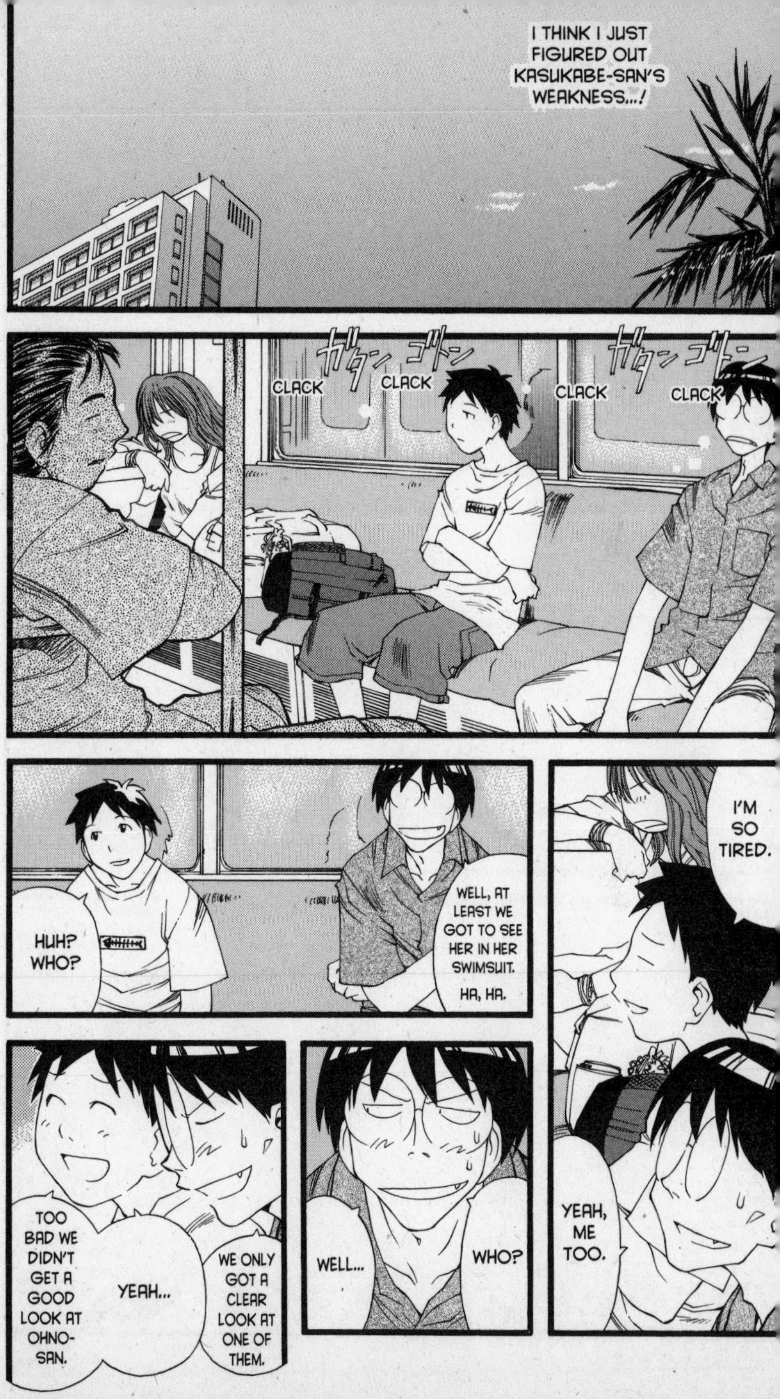
I THINK I JUST FIGURED OUT KASUKABE-SAN'S WEAKNESS...!
ガタンゴトン
CLACK
CLACK
ガタンゴトン
CLACK
CLACK
I'M SO TIRED.
YEAH, ME TOO.
WELL, AT LEAST WE GOT TO SEE HER IN HER SWIMSUIT.
HA, HA.
HUH? WHO?
WHO?
WELL...
WE ONLY GOT A CLEAR LOOK AT ONE OF THEM.
YEAH...
TOO BAD WE DIDN'T GET A GOOD LOOK AT OHNO-SAN.

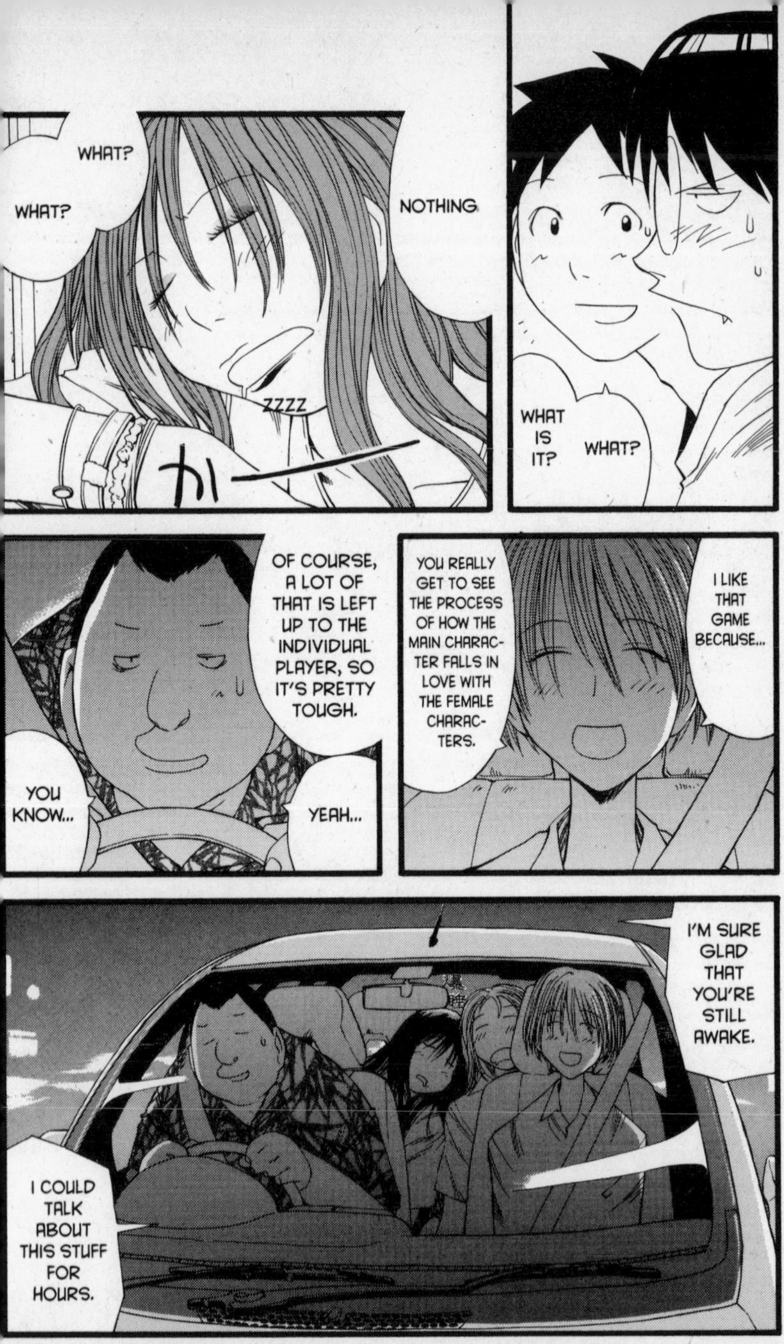
WHAT?
WHAT IS IT?
NOTHING
WHAT?
WHAT?
ZZZZ
かー
I LIKE THAT GAME BECAUSE...
YOU REALLY GET TO SEE THE PROCESS OF HOW THE MAIN CHARACTER FALLS IN LOVE WITH THE FEMALE CHARACTERS.
OF COURSE, A LOT OF THAT IS LEFT UP TO THE INDIVIDUAL PLAYER, SO IT'S PRETTY TOUGH.
YEAH...
YOU KNOW...
I'M SURE GLAD THAT YOU'RE STILL AWAKE.
I COULD TALK ABOUT THIS STUFF FOR HOURS.

END OF CHAPTER 15

3 KASUMI KISARAGI

WRITTEN BY THE OWL

MY CHARACTER IS KASUMI KISARAGI-SAMA A.K.A. THE VICE PRESIDENT. IN THE ACTUAL KUJI-UN SERIES SHE IS OMNIPOTENT AND INVINCIBLE, AS IF SHE'S FROM ANOTHER WORLD. IN THE GAME, SHE TAKES FULL ADVANTAGE OF HER STRENGTH, TO THE EXTENT THAT SHE'S CALLED "RUTHLESS" BY MANY GENSHIKEN MEMBERS. HOWEVER, SHE DOES HAVE WORTHY OPPONENTS, AS WELL AS NUMEROUS WEAKNESSES. IN ANY CASE, HER STRENGTH DOESN'T STOP HER FROM BEING INSTANTLY KILLED BY TOSHIZO'S "OTHER SIDE OF TOKINO" CHARACTER (LAUGH).

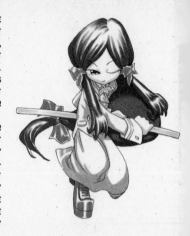

WHAT MAKES HER A POWERFUL CHARACTER IS THAT HER NORMAL FIGHT TECHNIQUES ARE EXTREMELY EFFICIENT. ALMOST ALL OF HER MOVES UTILIZE HER PRICELESS SWORD "ZANSETSU," SO SHE HAS PLENTY OF REACH. HER STANCE LEAVES NO VULNERABILITY, AND SHE HAS EXCELLENT JUDGMENT. I LOVE THE FACT THAT HER ATTACKS ARE SO POWERFUL. YOU CAN WIN PRETTY QUICKLY WITHOUT EVEN USING HER SPECIAL TECHNIQUES. SHE HAS A REPETITIVE KICK TECHNIQUE THAT USES HER TINY LITTLE FEET, AND AS LONG AS YOU GET THE TIMING DOWN, IT'S EASY TO MOVE AHEAD.

AND NOW FOR HER WEAKNESSES... "WHEN SHE GETS THROWN DOWN, SHE BECOMES UNSTABLE." THAT'S THE MAIN ONE. THE VICE PRESIDENT HATES TO BE TOUCHED. WHEN SOMEBODY HOLDS HER SHE PASSES OUT. IT'S AMAZING THAT THEY WERE ABLE TO TRANSLATE THAT WEAKNESS OF HERS INTO THE GAME. WELL DONE! IF SHE GETS THROWN TWICE IN ONE ROUND, THAT'S USUALLY THE END. HER DEFENSIVE ABILITIES ARE VERY WEAK, SO SHE LOSES POWER QUITE RAPIDLY. THAT KIND OF UNBALANCE IS WHAT MAKES THIS GAME GREAT. OBVIOUSLY, HER NORMAL TECHNIQUES DON'T INCLUDE ANY THROWING MOVES (LAUGHS). THE ONLY WAY FOR HER TO DO A THROW IS TO USE THE SPECIAL "IWANAMI" TECHNIQUE.

IT'S IMPORTANT TO CONTROL THE PACE OF THE FIGHT WITHOUT GETTING TOO CLOSE TO THE OPPONENT. HIT THE "A" BUTTON WHILE CROUCHING TO SLIDE FORWARD, AND HIT THE D BUTTON WHILE STANDING TO BLOCK JUMP ATTACKS. IF YOU'RE STILL GETTING HIT BY JUMP ATTACKS THEN YOU CAN ALWAYS RELY ON HITTING THE C BUTTON WHILE STANDING. MAINTAIN THE DISTANCE BETWEEN YOURSELF AND YOUR OPPONENT, AND WHEN THE TIME IS RIGHT, TAKE THEM DOWN WITH THE REPETITIVE KICK ATTACK. I ALWAYS TRY TO SHOOT FOR A FABULOUS VICTORY THAT CAN'T BE CALLED "RUTHLESS." [OWL]

THE VICE PRESIDENT REALLY IS STRONG. ONCE SHE STARTS SETTING THE PACE IT'S REALLY HARD TO BEAT HER. EVEN THOUGH I KNOW HER WEAKNESS IS BEING THROWN DOWN, IT'S SO HARD TO THROW HER, I ALWAYS END UP RELYING SOLELY ON MY CHARACTER'S SPECIAL TECHNIQUES. OF COURSE I'M ALWAYS HAPPY WHEN I GET A DIRECT HIT WITH MY "GIANT SWING." KEEP ON SWINGING! THE REAL PUZZLE IS, WHY IS IT THAT YOU INSIST ON USING THE VICE PRESIDENT CHARACTER. ANSWER THAT ONE. [PIT VIPER]

37

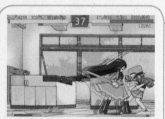

HER "MIST" TECHNIQUE IS UNSTOPPABLE DURING THE FIRST FEW SECONDS OF EACH ROUND. AVOID THE OPPONENT'S JUMP ATTACKS, AND MOVE FORWARD.

49

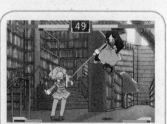

HER TECHNIQUES ARE POWERFUL, BUT HER JUMPS ARE HIGH AND SLOW LEAVING HER VULNERABLE TO ATTACKS. ONLY JUMP WHEN NECESSARY.

THE GIRL NEXT DOOR ♡

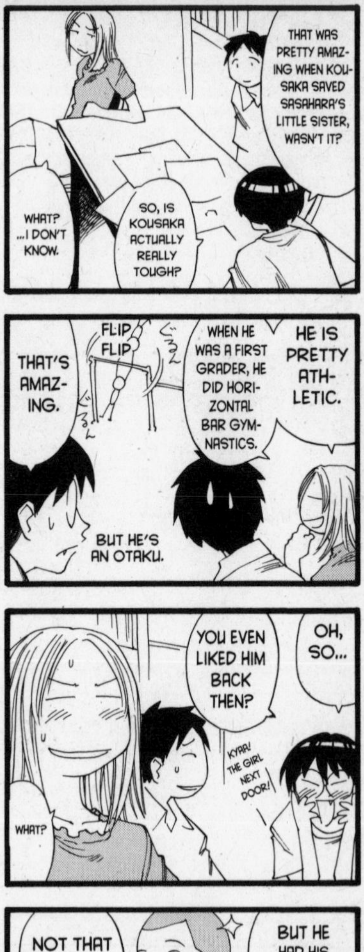
THAT WAS PRETTY AMAZING WHEN KOUSAKA SAVED SASAHARA'S LITTLE SISTER, WASN'T IT?
SO, IS KOUSAKA ACTUALLY REALLY TOUGH?
WHAT? ...I DON'T KNOW.
HE IS PRETTY ATHLETIC.
WHEN HE WAS A FIRST GRADER, HE DID HORIZONTAL BAR GYMNASTICS.
FLIP FLIP
THAT'S AMAZING.
BUT HE'S AN OTAKU.
OH, SO...
YOU EVEN LIKED HIM BACK THEN?
KYAA! THE GIRL NEXT DOOR!
WHAT?
BUT HE HAD HIS HEAD SHAVED BACK THEN.
HUH?
NOT THAT AGAIN.

ADULT CONVERSATION ♡

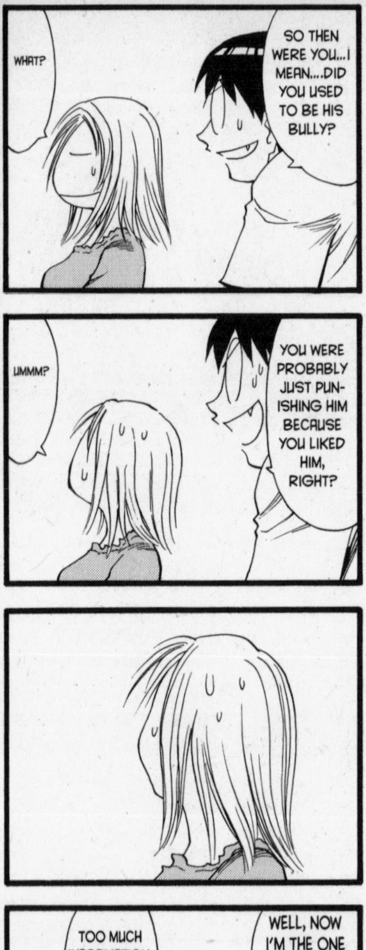
SO THEN WERE YOU...I MEAN....DID YOU USED TO BE HIS BULLY?
WHAT?
YOU WERE PROBABLY JUST PUNISHING HIM BECAUSE YOU LIKED HIM, RIGHT?
UMMM?
WELL, NOW I'M THE ONE WHO GETS PUNISHED EVERY NIGHT. ♡
TOO MUCH INFORMATION. TOO MUCH INFORMATION.

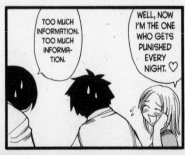

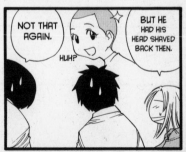

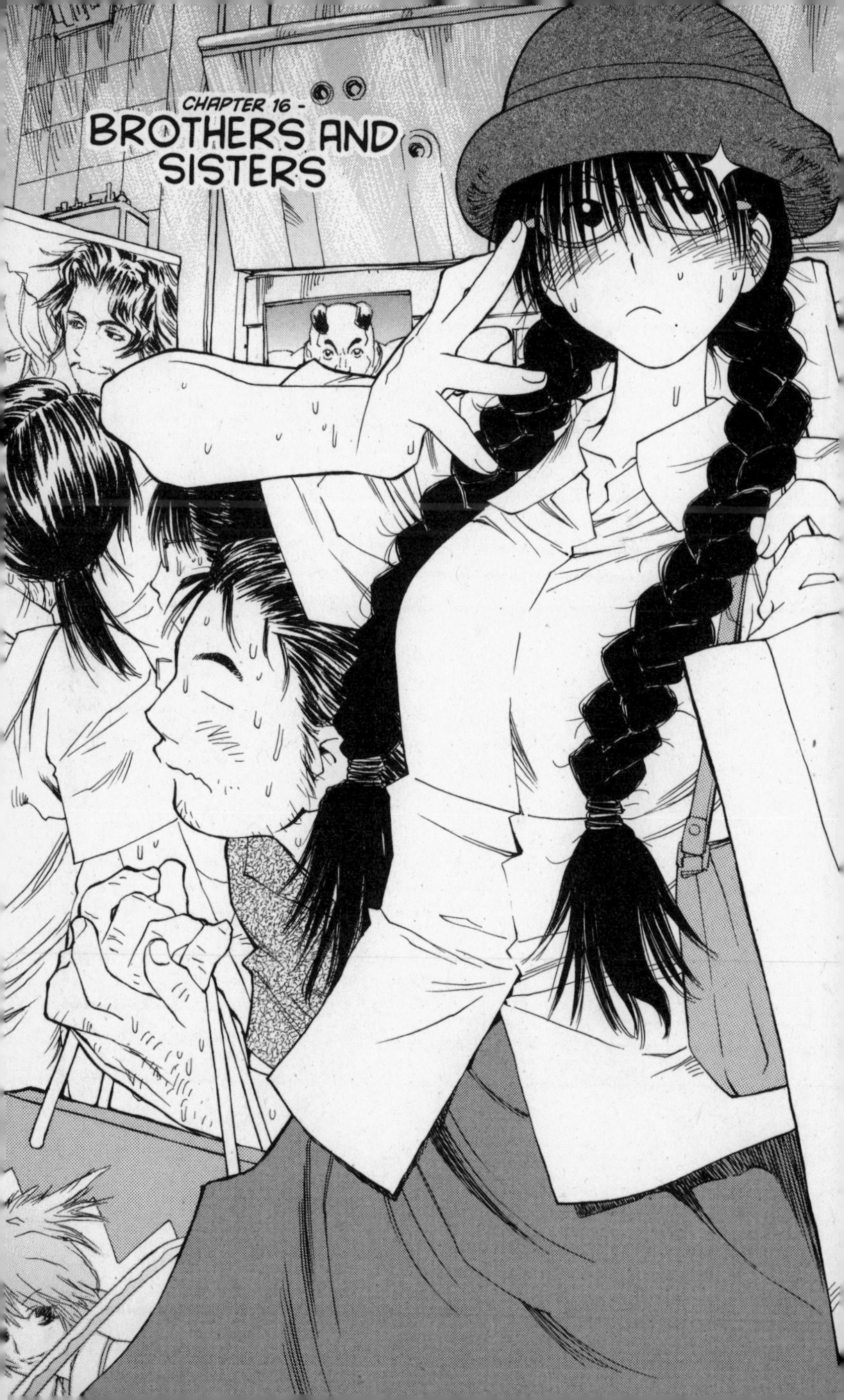
CHAPTER 16 -
BROTHERS AND SISTERS

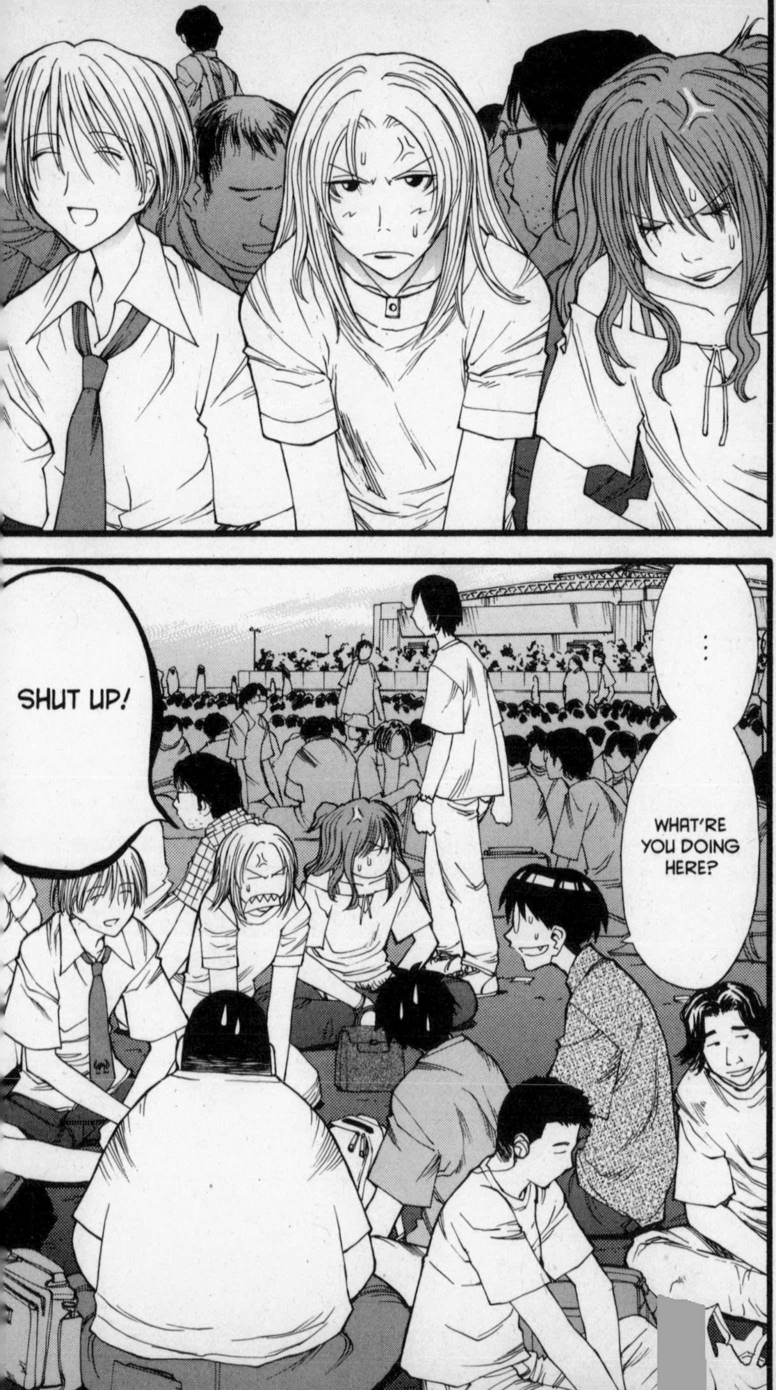
. . .
WHAT'RE YOU DOING HERE?
SHUT UP!

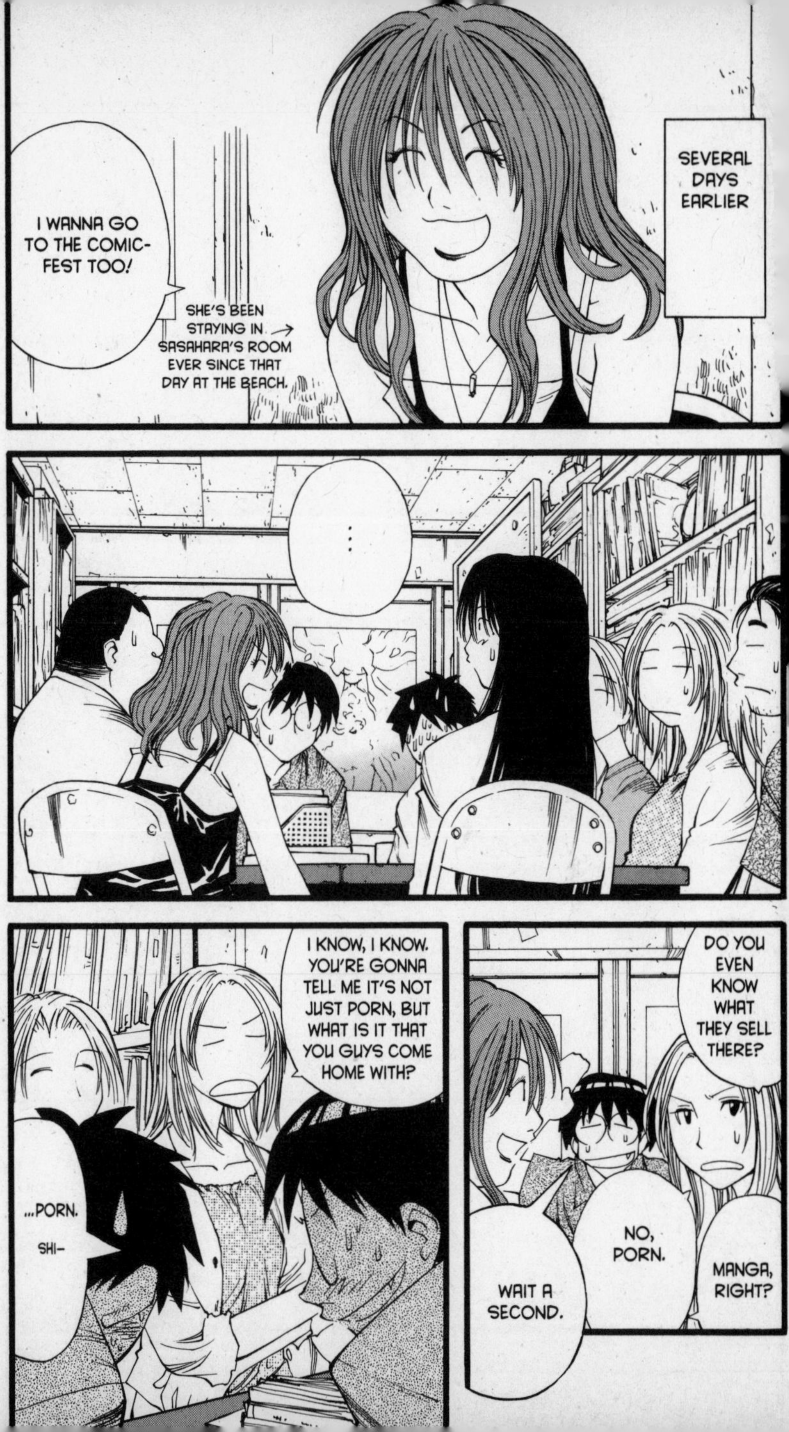
SEVERAL DAYS EARLIER
I WANNA GO TO THE COMIC-FEST TOO!
SHE'S BEEN STAYING IN SASAHARA'S ROOM EVER SINCE THAT DAY AT THE BEACH.
...
DO YOU EVEN KNOW WHAT THEY SELL THERE?
MANGA, RIGHT?
NO, PORN.
WAIT A SECOND.
I KNOW, I KNOW. YOU'RE GONNA TELL ME IT'S NOT JUST PORN, BUT WHAT IS IT THAT YOU GUYS COME HOME WITH?
...PORN.
SHI–

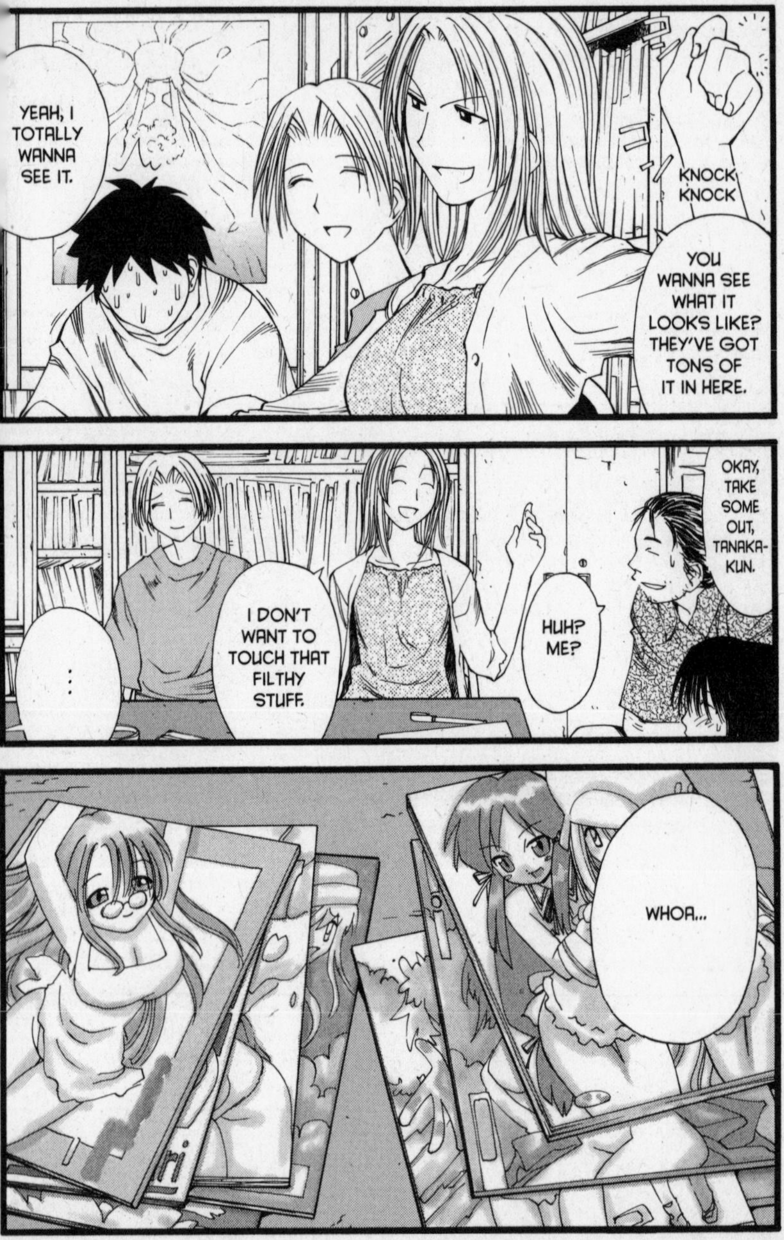
KNOCK KNOCK
YOU WANNA SEE WHAT IT LOOKS LIKE? THEY'VE GOT TONS OF IT IN HERE.
YEAH, I TOTALLY WANNA SEE IT.
OKAY, TAKE SOME OUT, TANAKA-KUN.
HUH? ME?
I DON'T WANT TO TOUCH THAT FILTHY STUFF.
...
WHOA...

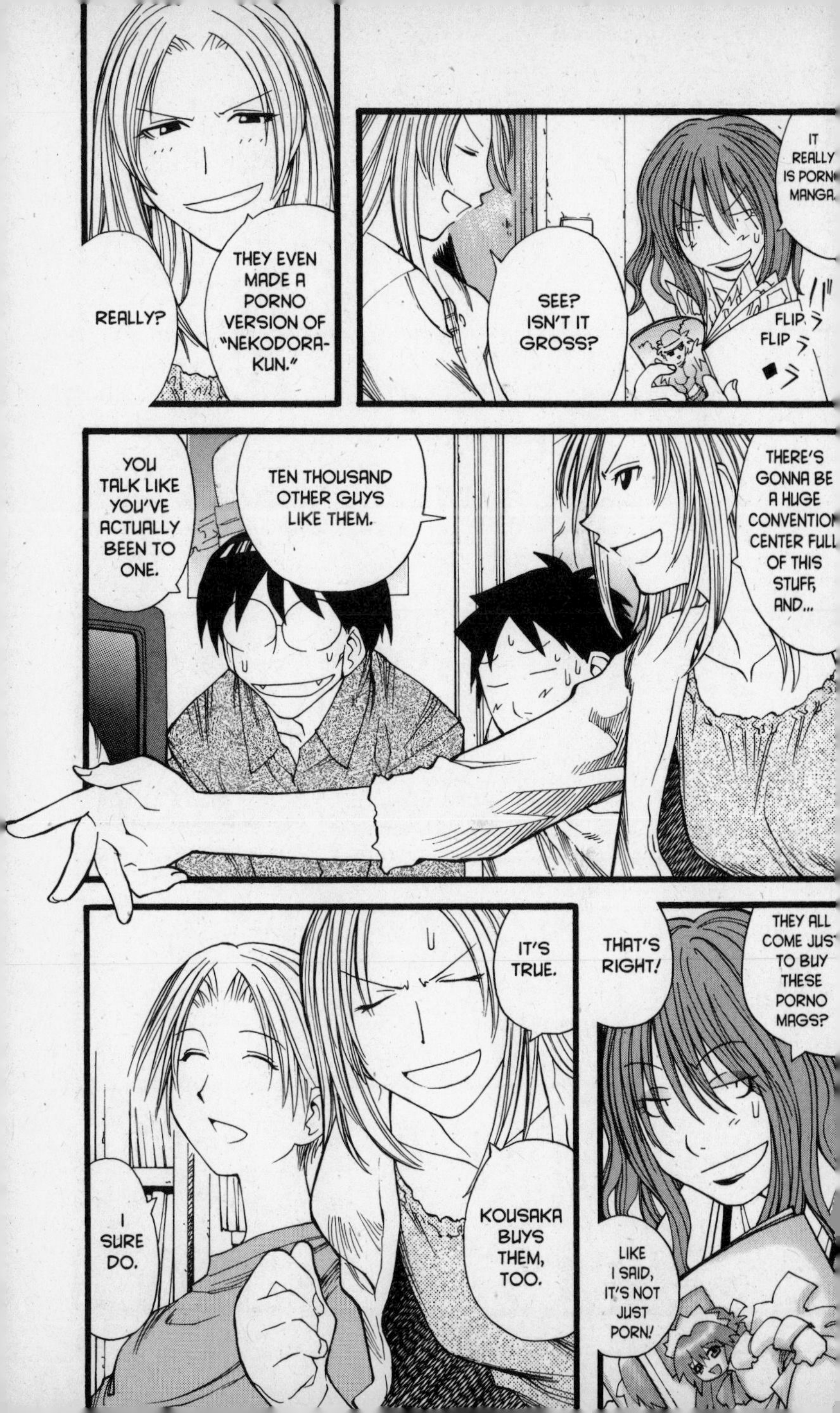
IT REALLY IS PORN MANGA.
FLIP FLIP
SEE? ISN'T IT GROSS?
THEY EVEN MADE A PORNO VERSION OF "NEKODORA-KUN."
REALLY?
THERE'S GONNA BE A HUGE CONVENTION CENTER FULL OF THIS STUFF, AND...
TEN THOUSAND OTHER GUYS LIKE THEM.
YOU TALK LIKE YOU'VE ACTUALLY BEEN TO ONE.
THEY ALL COME JUST TO BUY THESE PORNO MAGS?
LIKE I SAID, IT'S NOT JUST PORN!
THAT'S RIGHT!
IT'S TRUE.
KOUSAKA BUYS THEM, TOO.
I SURE DO.

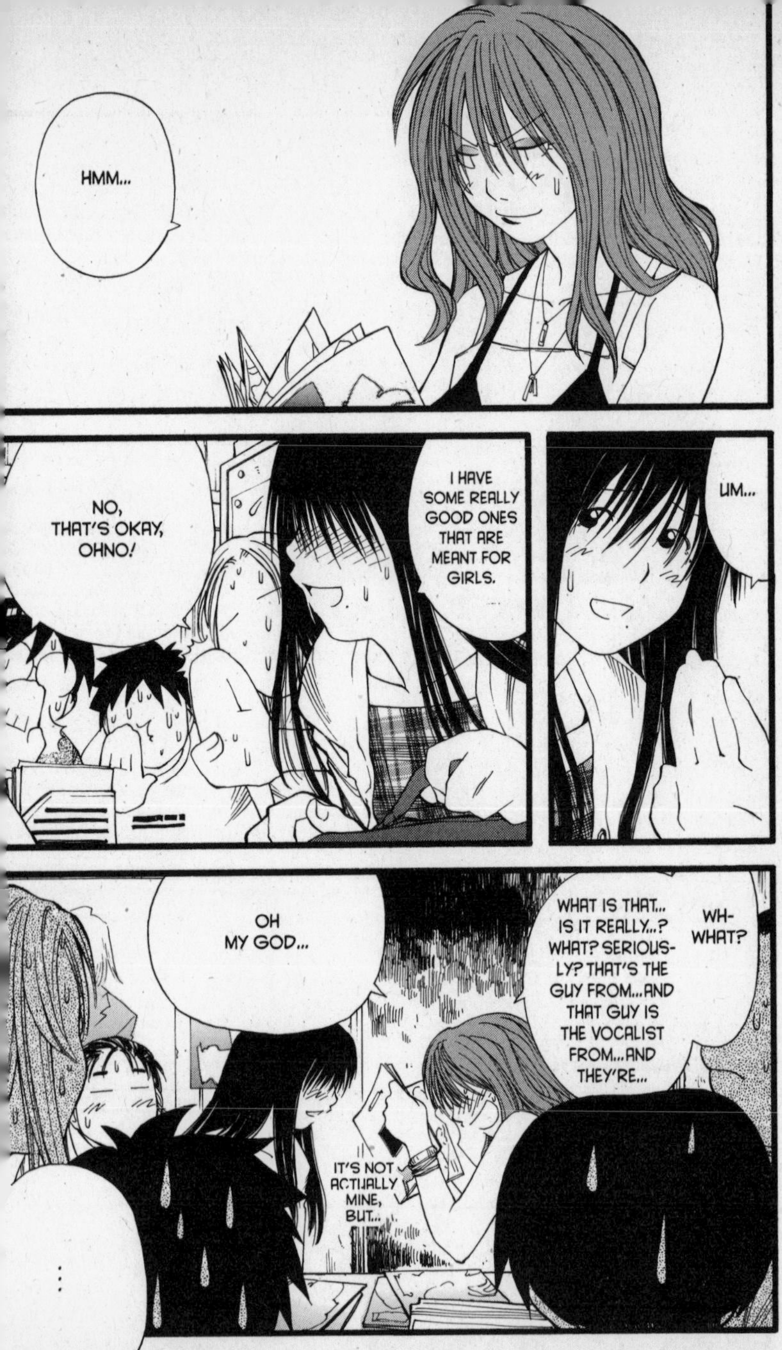
HMM...
UM...
I HAVE SOME REALLY GOOD ONES THAT ARE MEANT FOR GIRLS.
NO, THAT'S OKAY, OHNO!
WH-WHAT?
WHAT IS THAT... IS IT REALLY...? WHAT? SERIOUS-LY? THAT'S THE GUY FROM...AND THAT GUY IS THE VOCALIST FROM...AND THEY'RE...
OH MY GOD...
IT'S NOT ACTUALLY MINE, BUT...
...

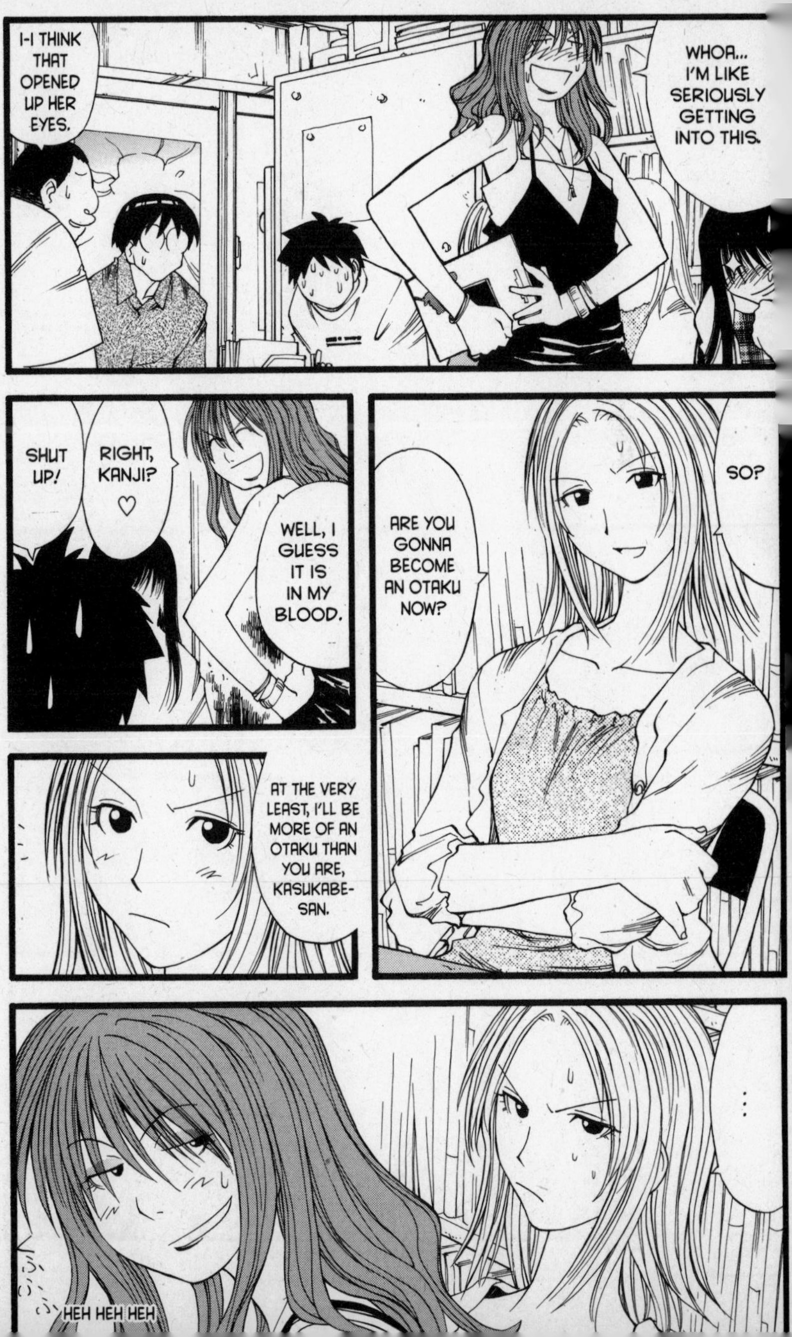
WHOA... I'M LIKE SERIOUSLY GETTING INTO THIS.
I-I THINK THAT OPENED UP HER EYES.
SO?
ARE YOU GONNA BECOME AN OTAKU NOW?
WELL, I GUESS IT IS IN MY BLOOD.
RIGHT, KANJI? ♡
SHUT UP!
AT THE VERY LEAST, I'LL BE MORE OF AN OTAKU THAN YOU ARE, KASUKABE-SAN.
...
HEH HEH HEH

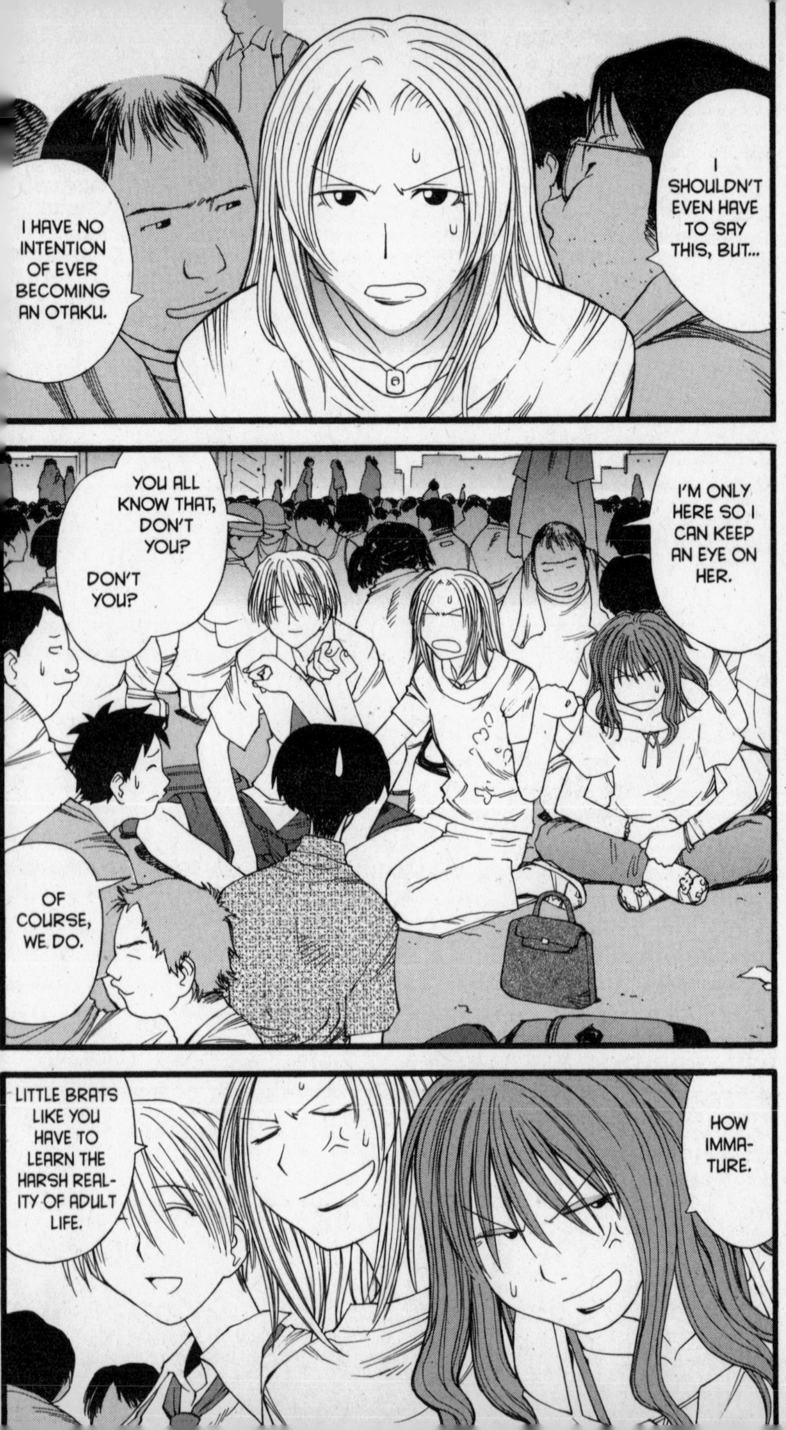
I SHOULDN'T EVEN HAVE TO SAY THIS, BUT...
I HAVE NO INTENTION OF EVER BECOMING AN OTAKU.
I'M ONLY HERE SO I CAN KEEP AN EYE ON HER.
YOU ALL KNOW THAT, DON'T YOU?
DON'T YOU?
OF COURSE, WE DO.
HOW IMMATURE.
LITTLE BRATS LIKE YOU HAVE TO LEARN THE HARSH REALITY OF ADULT LIFE.

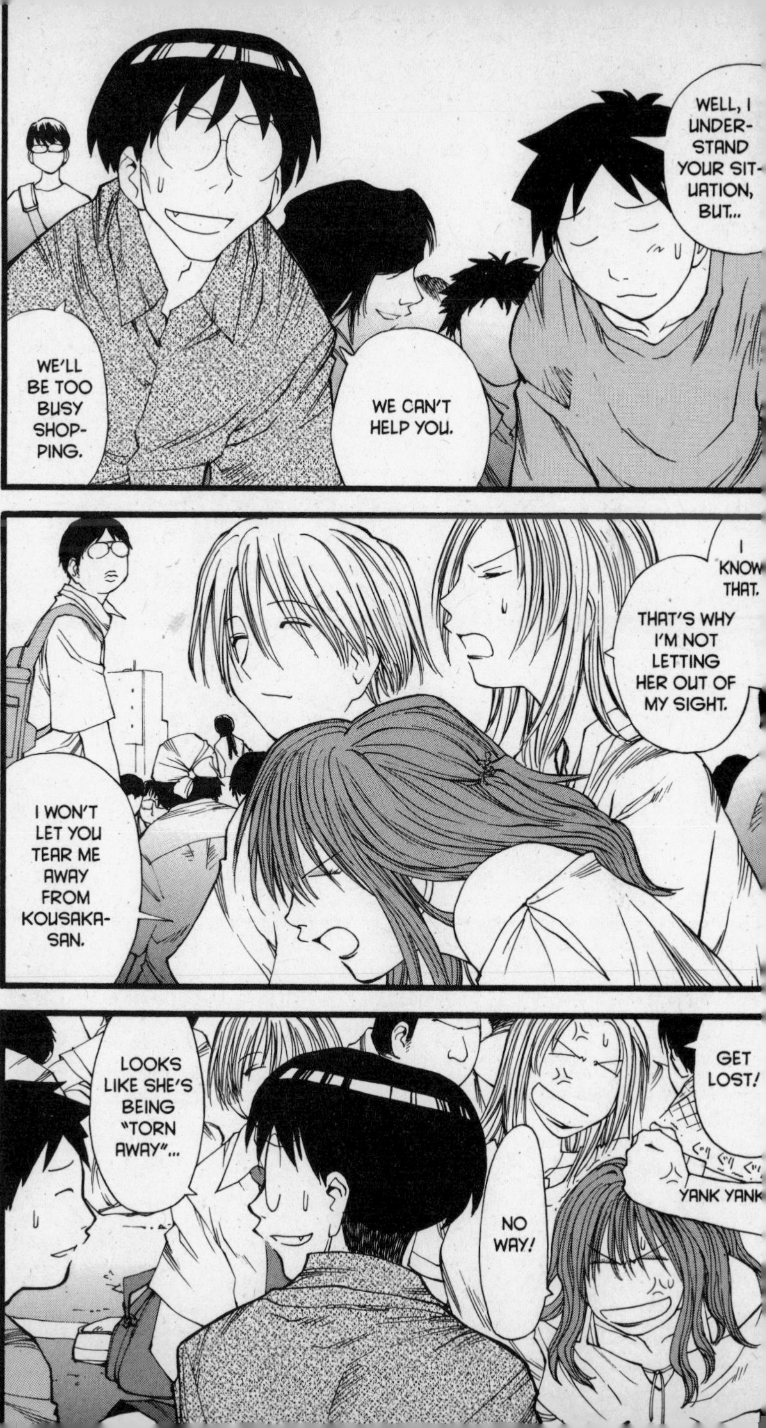
WELL, I UNDERSTAND YOUR SITUATION, BUT...
WE CAN'T HELP YOU.
WE'LL BE TOO BUSY SHOPPING.
I KNOW THAT.
THAT'S WHY I'M NOT LETTING HER OUT OF MY SIGHT.
I WON'T LET YOU TEAR ME AWAY FROM KOUSAKA-SAN.
GET LOST!
YANK YANK
NO WAY!
LOOKS LIKE SHE'S BEING "TORN AWAY"...

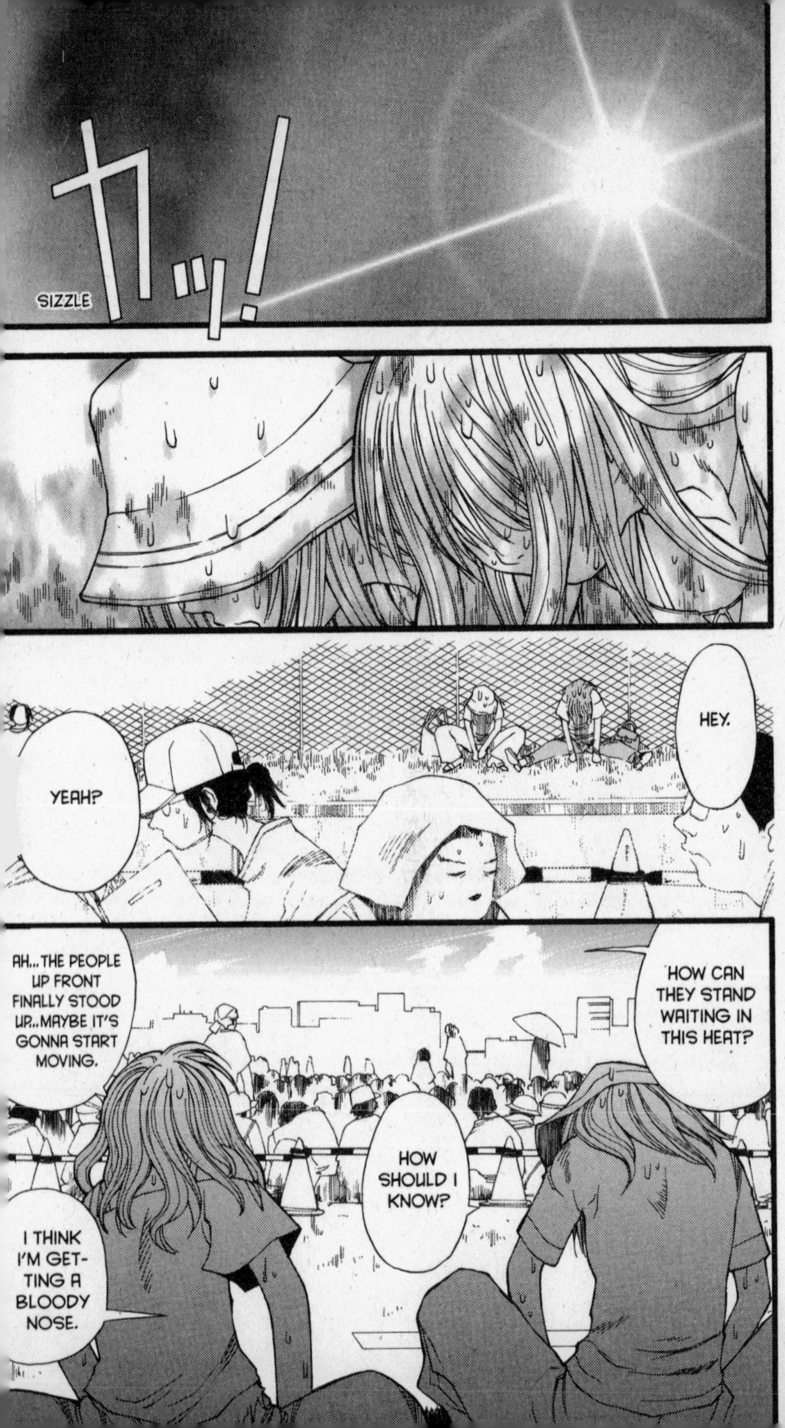
カッ!
SIZZLE
HEY.
YEAH?
HOW CAN THEY STAND WAITING IN THIS HEAT?
HOW SHOULD I KNOW?
AH...THE PEOPLE UP FRONT FINALLY STOOD UP..MAYBE IT'S GONNA START MOVING.
I THINK I'M GETTING A BLOODY NOSE.

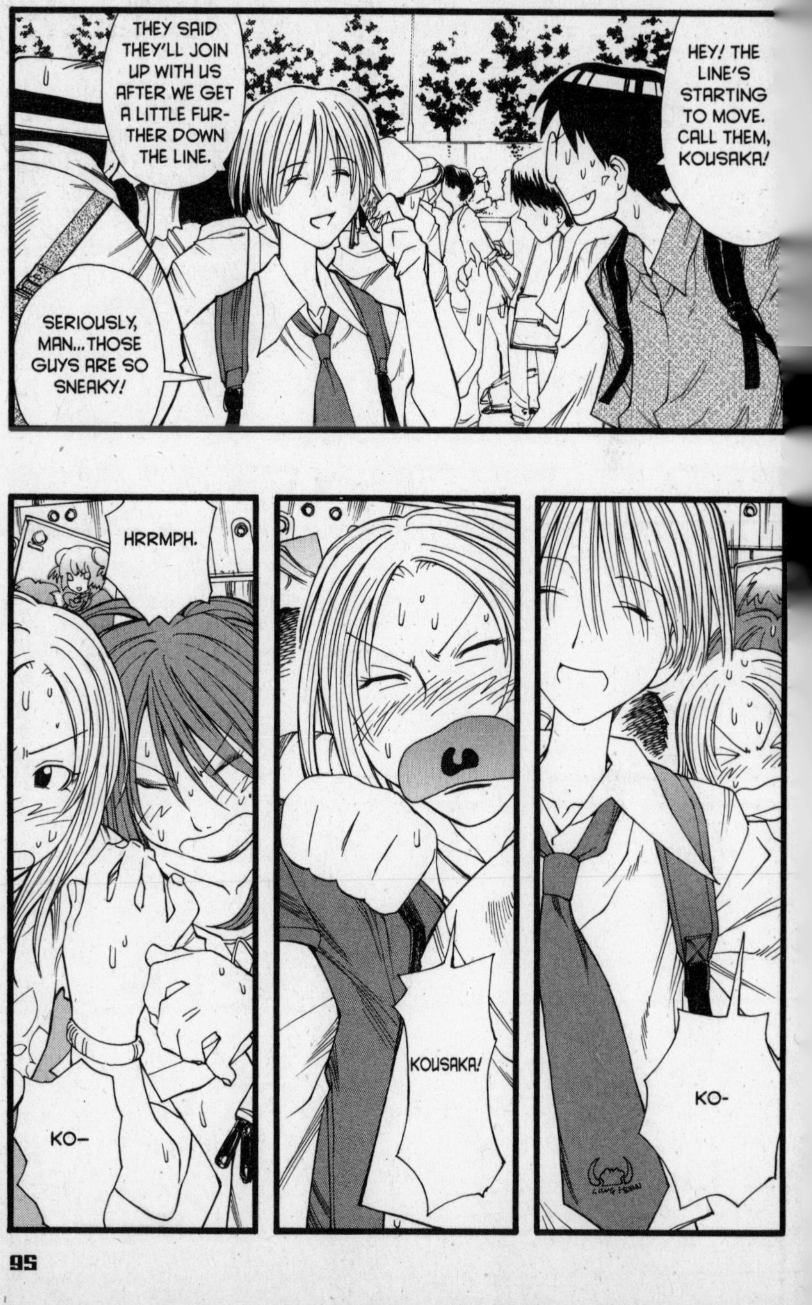
HEY! THE LINE'S STARTING TO MOVE. CALL THEM, KOUSAKA!
THEY SAID THEY'LL JOIN UP WITH US AFTER WE GET A LITTLE FUR-THER DOWN THE LINE.
SERIOUSLY, MAN... THOSE GUYS ARE SO SNEAKY!
KO-
KOUSAKA!
HRRMPH.
KO–

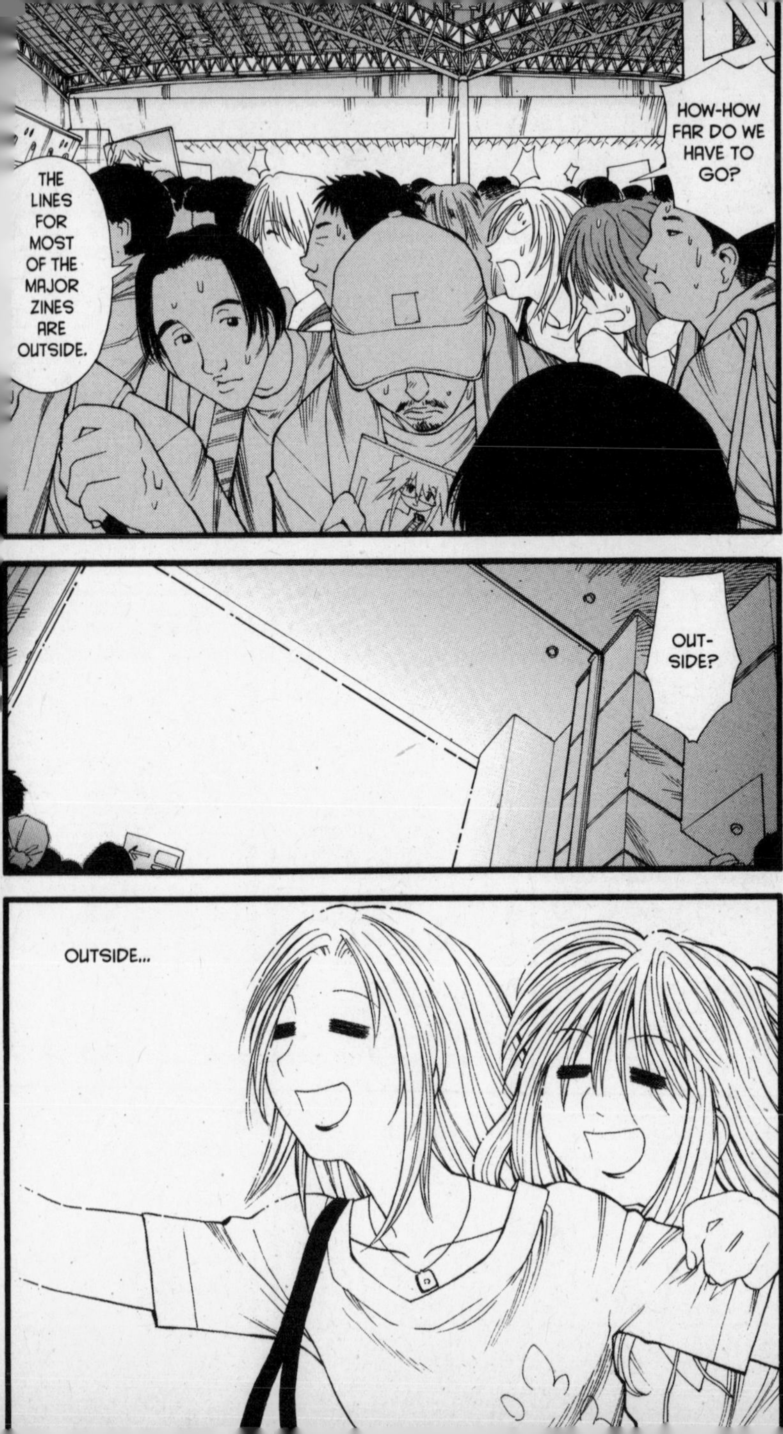
HOW-HOW FAR DO WE HAVE TO GO?
THE LINES FOR MOST OF THE MAJOR ZINES ARE OUTSIDE.
OUT-SIDE?
OUTSIDE...

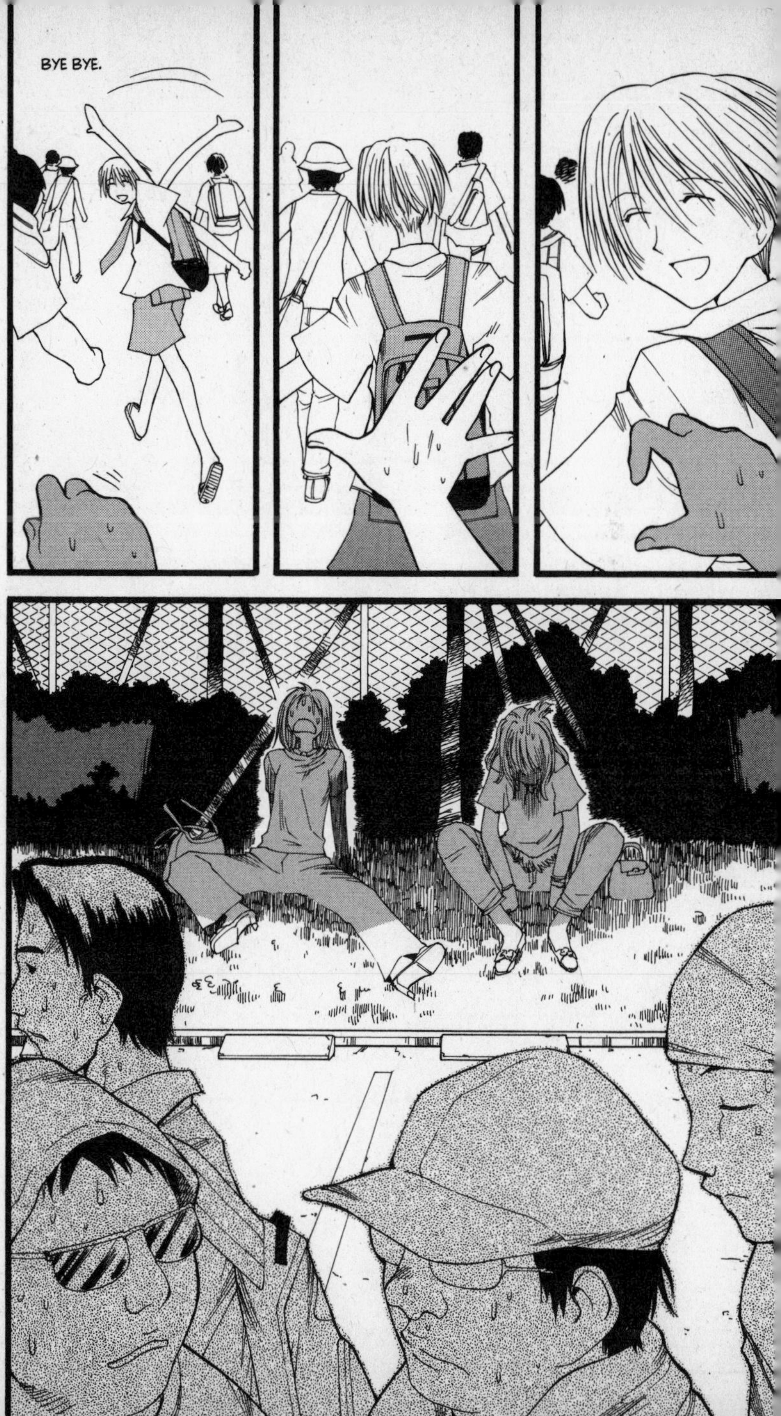
BYE BYE.

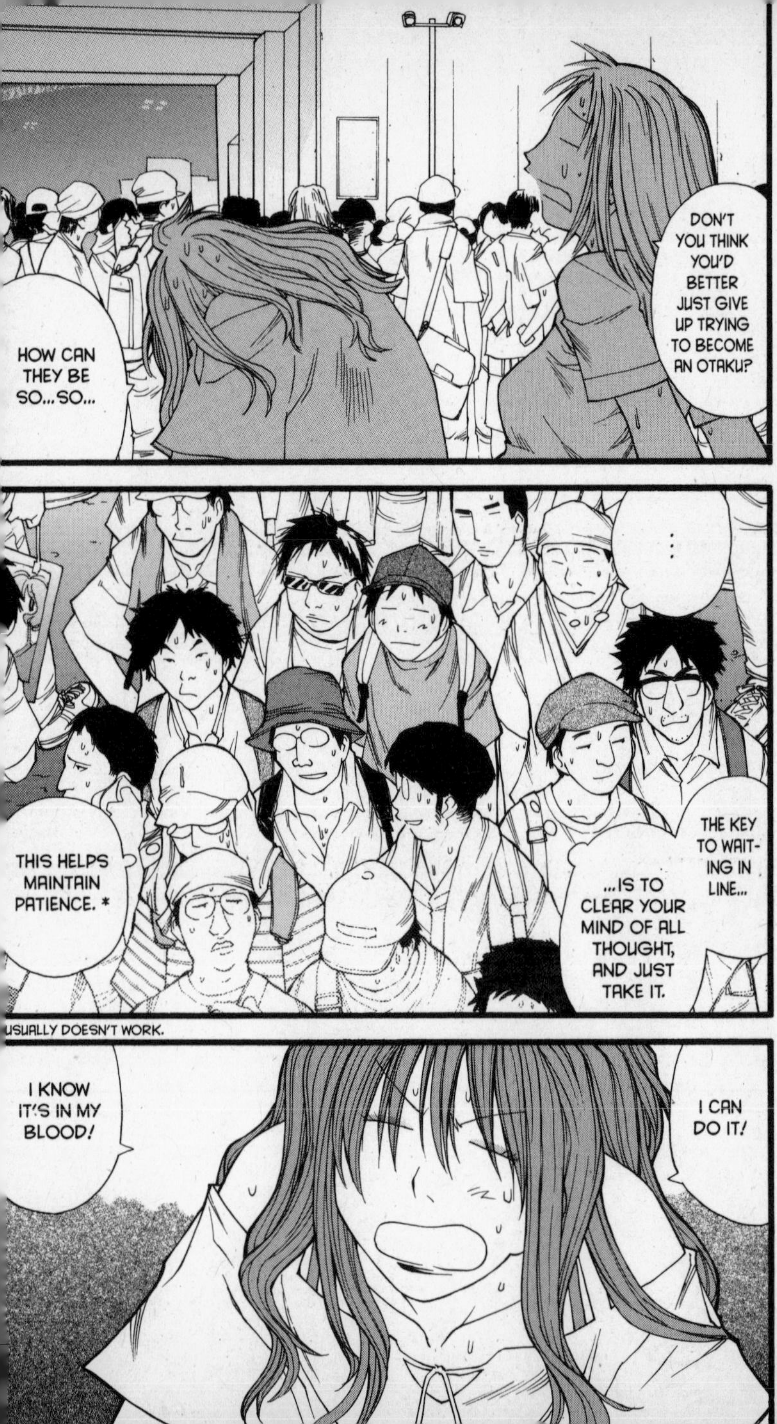
DON'T YOU THINK YOU'D BETTER JUST GIVE UP TRYING TO BECOME AN OTAKU?
HOW CAN THEY BE SO...SO...
...
THE KEY TO WAIT-ING IN LINE...
...IS TO CLEAR YOUR MIND OF ALL THOUGHT, AND JUST TAKE IT.
THIS HELPS MAINTAIN PATIENCE. *
USUALLY DOESN'T WORK.
I CAN DO IT!
I KNOW IT'S IN MY BLOOD!

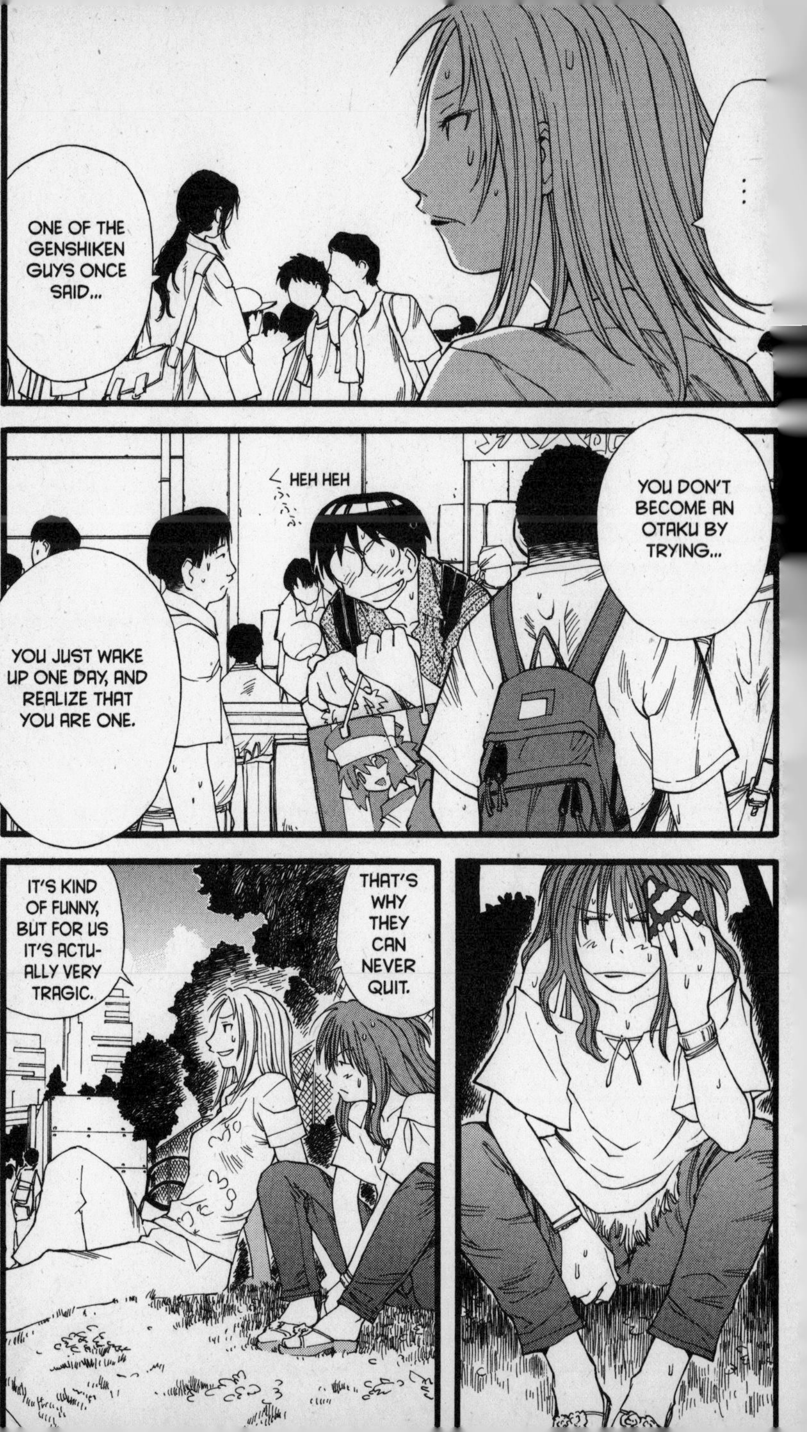
...
ONE OF THE GENSHIKEN GUYS ONCE SAID...
YOU DON'T BECOME AN OTAKU BY TRYING...
HEH HEH
くふふ
YOU JUST WAKE UP ONE DAY, AND REALIZE THAT YOU ARE ONE.
THAT'S WHY THEY CAN NEVER QUIT.
IT'S KIND OF FUNNY, BUT FOR US IT'S ACTU-ALLY VERY TRAGIC.

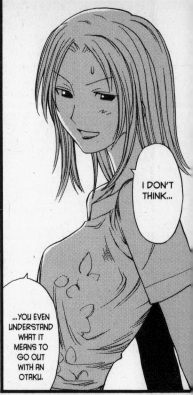

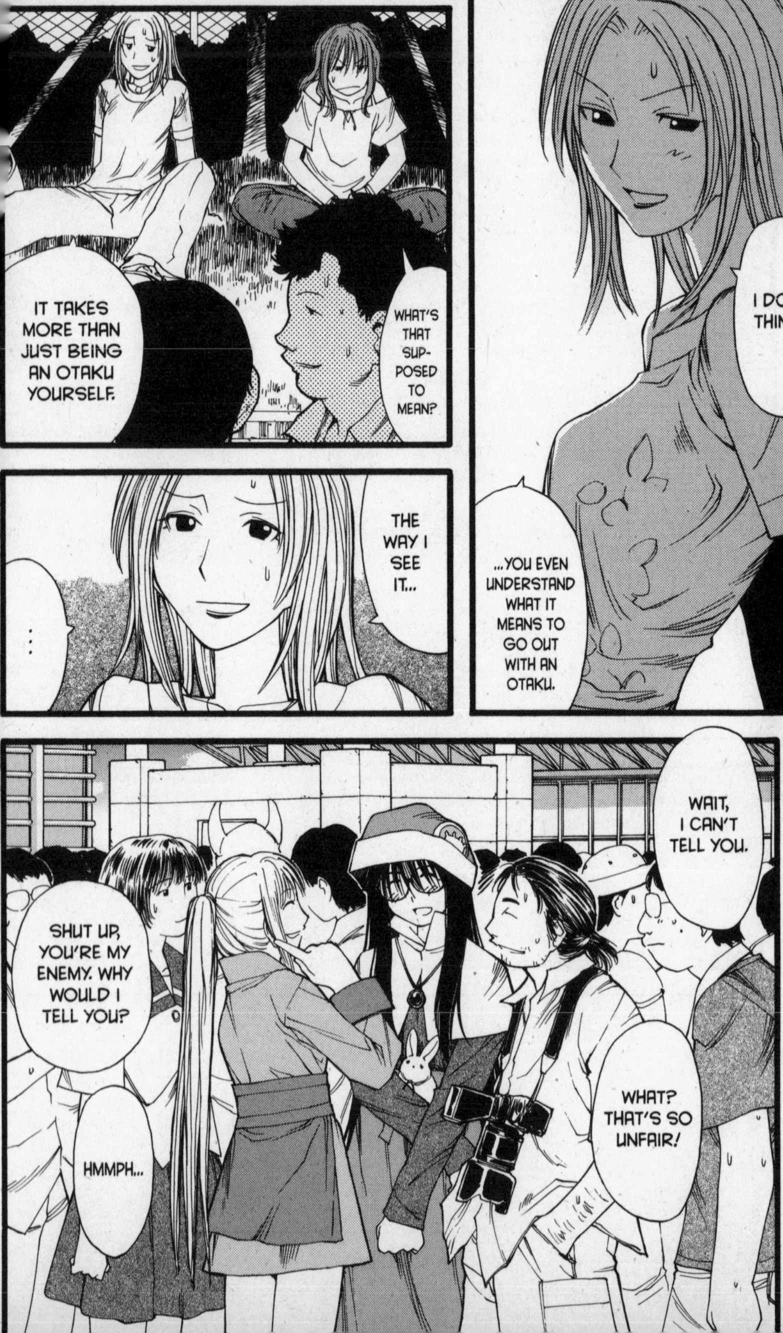
I DON'T THINK...
...YOU EVEN UNDERSTAND WHAT IT MEANS TO GO OUT WITH AN OTAKU.
WHAT'S THAT SUP-POSED TO MEAN?
IT TAKES MORE THAN JUST BEING AN OTAKU YOURSELF.
THE WAY I SEE IT...
...
WAIT, I CAN'T TELL YOU.
WHAT? THAT'S SO UNFAIR!
SHUT UP, YOU'RE MY ENEMY. WHY WOULD I TELL YOU?
HMMPH...

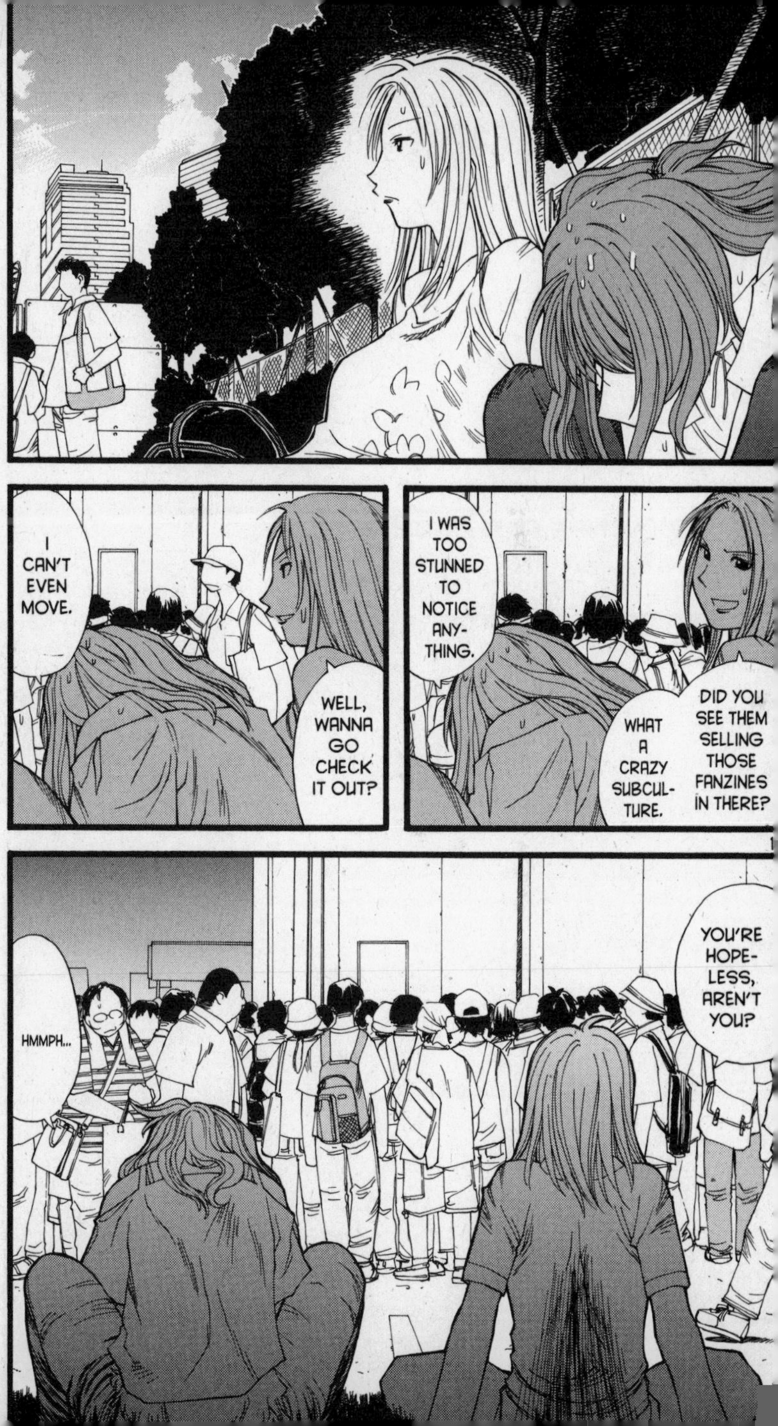
DID YOU SEE THEM SELLING THOSE FANZINES IN THERE?
WHAT A CRAZY SUBCULTURE.
I WAS TOO STUNNED TO NOTICE ANYTHING.
WELL, WANNA GO CHECK IT OUT?
I CAN'T EVEN MOVE.
YOU'RE HOPELESS, AREN'T YOU?
HMMPH...

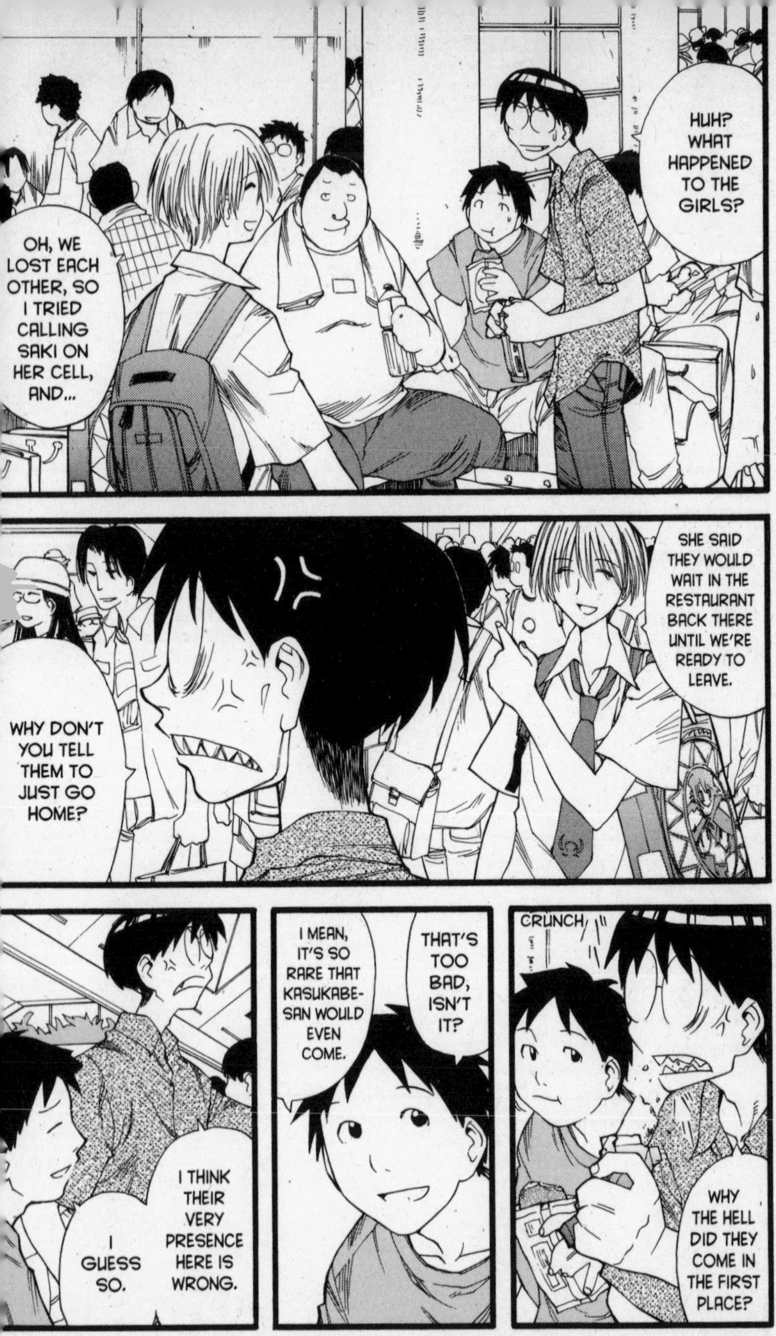
HUH? WHAT HAPPENED TO THE GIRLS?
OH, WE LOST EACH OTHER, SO I TRIED CALLING SAKI ON HER CELL, AND...
SHE SAID THEY WOULD WAIT IN THE RESTAURANT BACK THERE UNTIL WE'RE READY TO LEAVE.
WHY DON'T YOU TELL THEM TO JUST GO HOME?
CRUNCH
WHY THE HELL DID THEY COME IN THE FIRST PLACE?
THAT'S TOO BAD, ISN'T IT?
I MEAN, IT'S SO RARE THAT KASUKABE-SAN WOULD EVEN COME.
I THINK THEIR VERY PRESENCE HERE IS WRONG.
I GUESS SO.

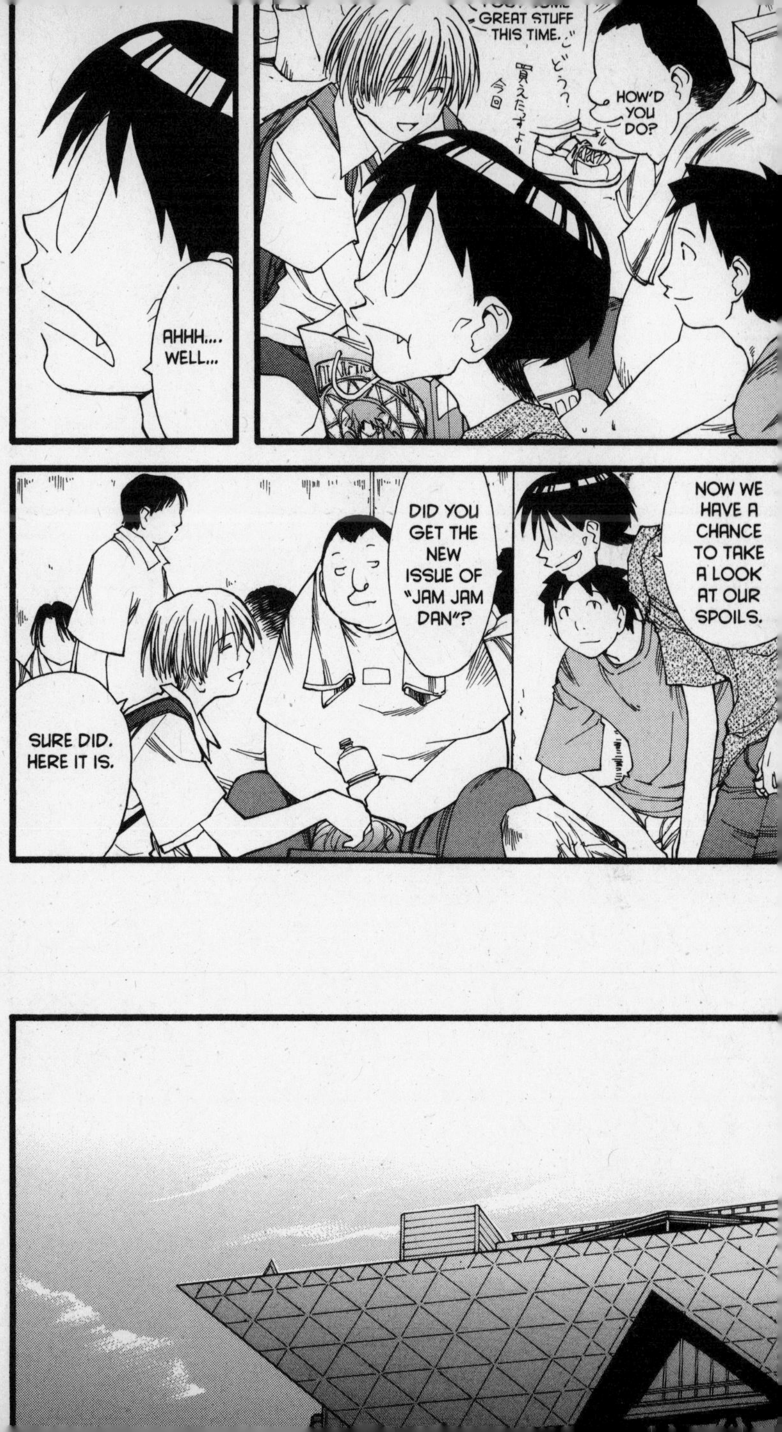
HOW'D YOU DO?
どう？
GREAT STUFF THIS TIME.
今回買えたっすよー
AHHH.... WELL...
NOW WE HAVE A CHANCE TO TAKE A LOOK AT OUR SPOILS.
DID YOU GET THE NEW ISSUE OF "JAM JAM DAN"?
SURE DID. HERE IT IS.

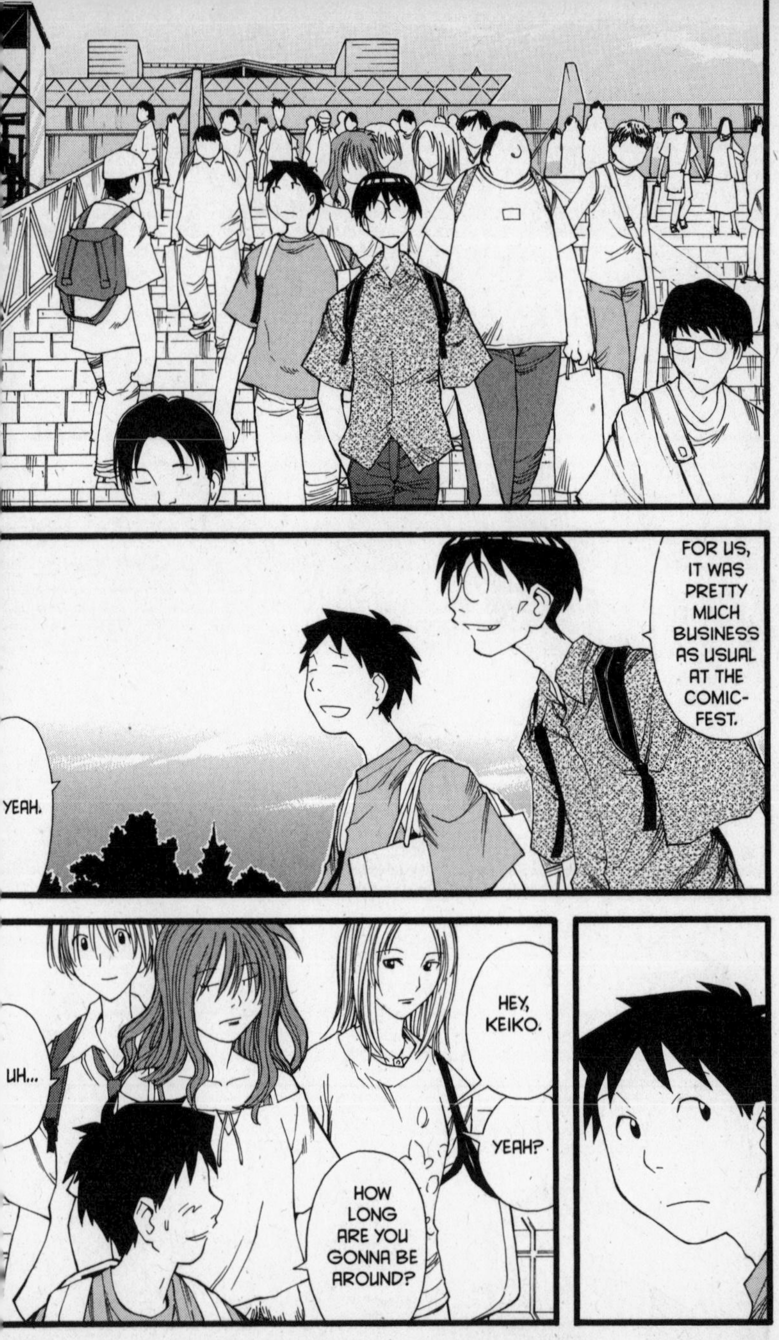
FOR US, IT WAS PRETTY MUCH BUSINESS AS USUAL AT THE COMIC-FEST.
YEAH.
HEY, KEIKO.
YEAH?
HOW LONG ARE YOU GONNA BE AROUND?
UH...

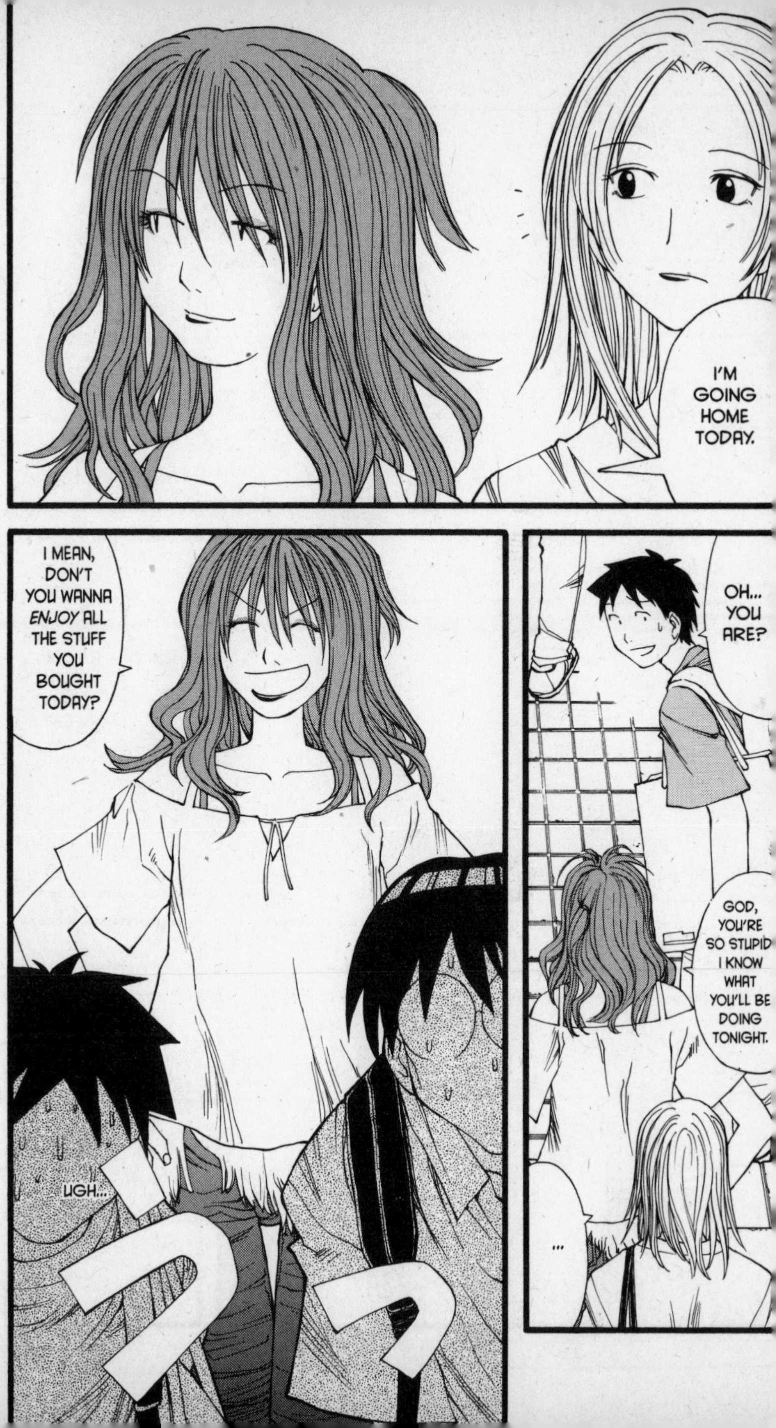
I'M GOING HOME TODAY.
OH... YOU ARE?
GOD, YOU'RE SO STUPID I KNOW WHAT YOU'LL BE DOING TONIGHT.
...
I MEAN, DON'T YOU WANNA *ENJOY* ALL THE STUFF YOU BOUGHT TODAY?
UGH...

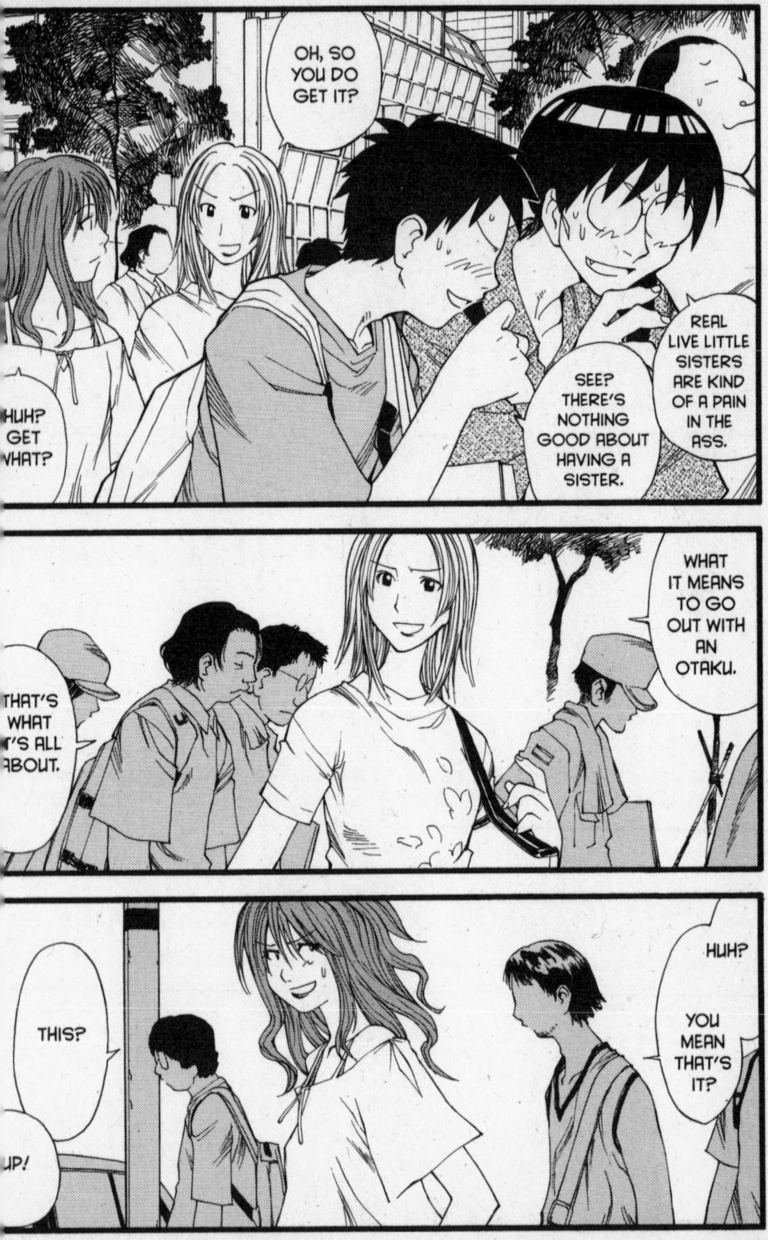
REAL LIVE LITTLE SISTERS ARE KIND OF A PAIN IN THE ASS.
SEE? THERE'S NOTHING GOOD ABOUT HAVING A SISTER.
OH, SO YOU DO GET IT?
HUH? GET WHAT?
WHAT IT MEANS TO GO OUT WITH AN OTAKU.
THAT'S WHAT T'S ALL ABOUT.
HUH?
YOU MEAN THAT'S IT?
THIS?
UP!

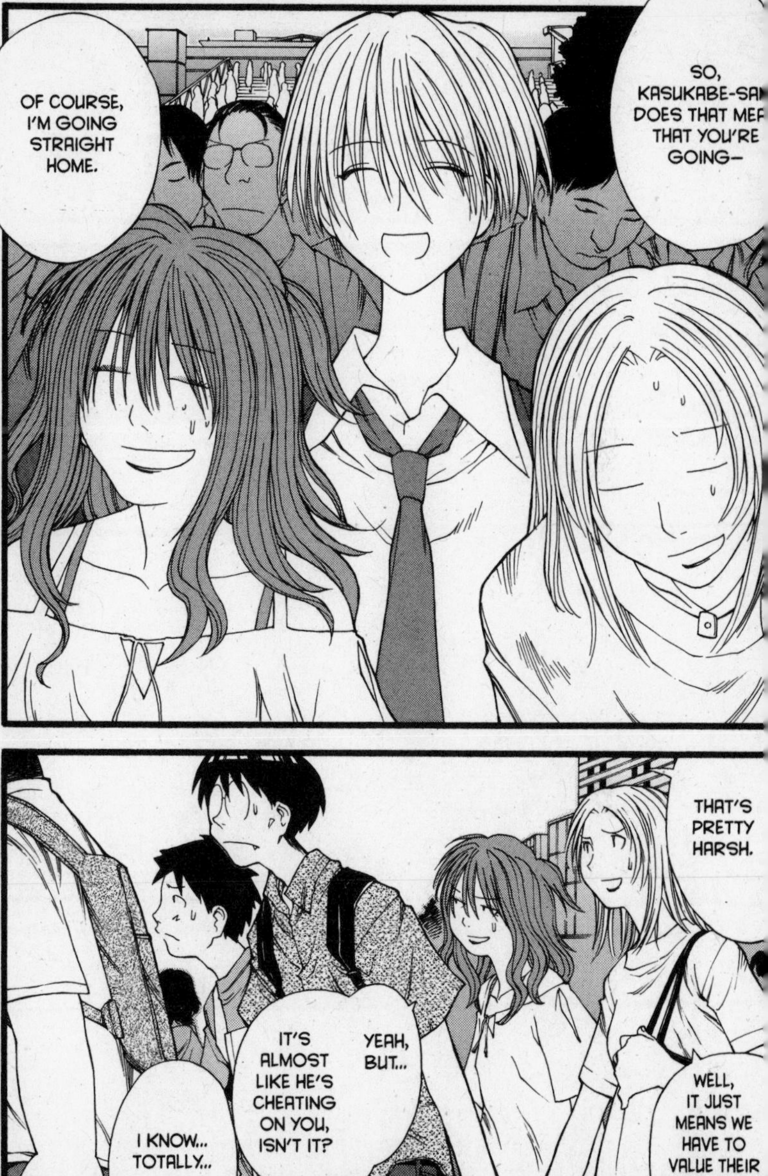
SO, KASUKABE-SA DOES THAT MEA THAT YOU'RE GOING–
OF COURSE, I'M GOING STRAIGHT HOME.
THAT'S PRETTY HARSH.
WELL, IT JUST MEANS WE HAVE TO VALUE THEIR OWN PRIVATE TIME.
YEAH, BUT...
IT'S ALMOST LIKE HE'S CHEATING ON YOU, ISN'T IT?
I KNOW... TOTALLY...

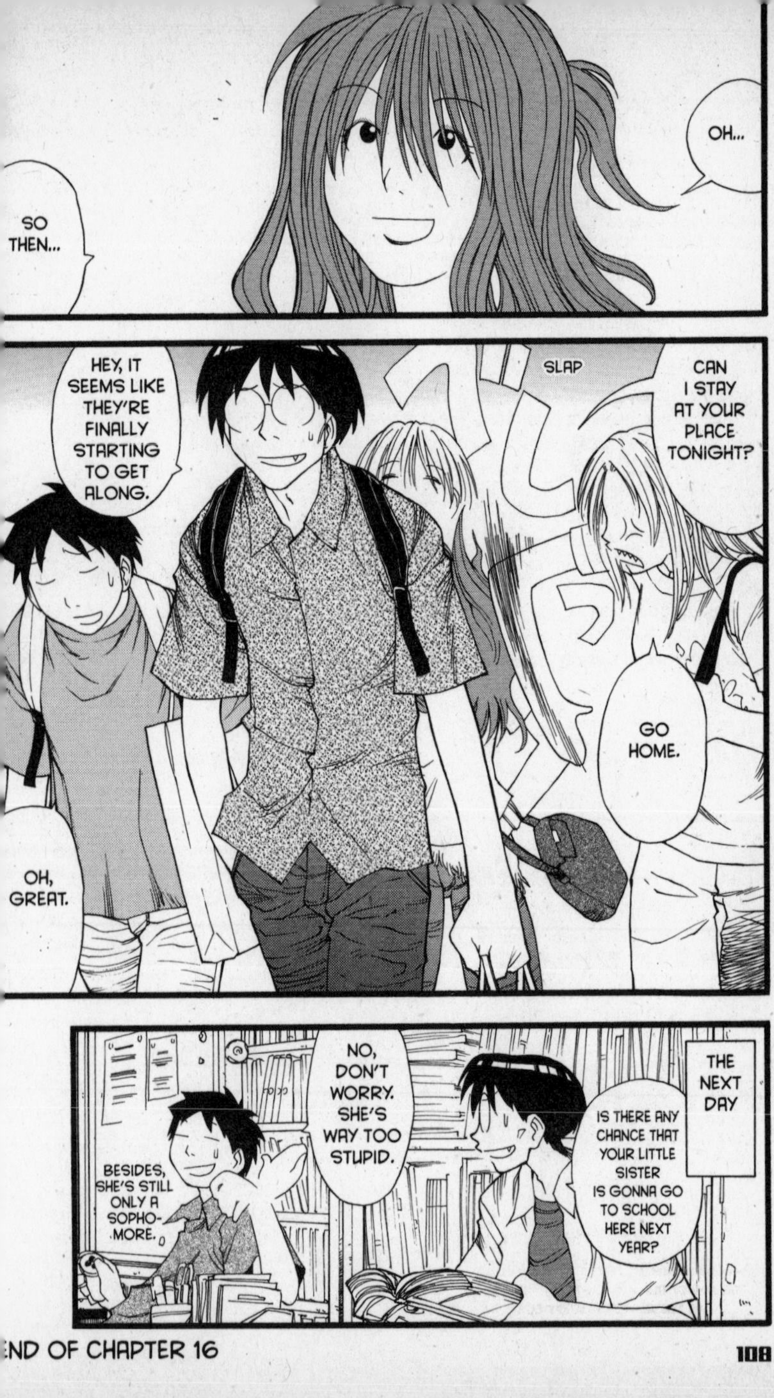
OH...
SO THEN...
CAN I STAY AT YOUR PLACE TONIGHT?
SLAP
GO HOME.
HEY, IT SEEMS LIKE THEY'RE FINALLY STARTING TO GET ALONG.
OH, GREAT.
THE NEXT DAY
IS THERE ANY CHANCE THAT YOUR LITTLE SISTER IS GONNA GO TO SCHOOL HERE NEXT YEAR?
NO, DON'T WORRY. SHE'S WAY TOO STUPID.
BESIDES, SHE'S STILL ONLY A SOPHO-MORE.

ND OF CHAPTER 16

4   LISA HANBII

WRITTEN BY KODAMA

WHY DO I USE LISA HANBII? AT FIRST I DID IT JUST AS A JOKE BECAUSE I THOUGHT THE CRAZY WAY SHE USES HER "SUPER ARMOR" WAS FUNNY. BUT I SOON BEGAN TO REALIZE THAT IT'S ACTUALLY VERY FITTING OF HER RAMBUNCTIOUS PERSONALITY, AND I STARTED THINKING SERIOUSLY ABOUT HOW TO WIN WITH HER. I STARTED OUT USING THE KOMAKI CHARACTER, BUT NOW LISA HAS BECOME MY NUMBER-ONE CHOICE. SORRY, KOMAKI.

WELL, IN ORDER TO WIN WITH LISA, YOU HAVE TO BE ABLE TO DO A REVERSE THROW. I'M NOT VERY GOOD, SO I CAN NEVER GO RIGHT INTO A THROW FROM STANDING POSITION. THE THREE THROWS I CAN DO ARE #1 THROW FROM A DEFENSIVE POS- TURE. #2 THROW WHILE JUMPING. #3 THROW AFTER BLOCKING. WHEN USING SUPER ARMOR AND APPROACHING THE OPPONENT, I USE #1. I USE #3 WHEN I'M TRYING TO BREAK UP AN ATTACK. BUT IF YOU APPROACH YOUR OPPONENT CARELESSLY, YOU'LL BE THROWN DOWN INSTANTLY, SO WATCH YOUR OPPONENT CAREFULLY WHEN YOU'RE MOVING IN. THINGS CAN GET REALLY HOT WHEN YOU START FIGHTING YOUR OPPONENT FROM JUST AN ARM'S LENGTH AWAY. IT'S SO COMPLICATED THAT IT'S HARD TO EXPLAIN IN WRITING, AND IT ALSO DEPENDS GREATLY ON WHICH CHARACTER YOU'RE PLAYING AGAINST. IT'S HARD TO WORK OUT A SYSTEMATIC PLAN OF ATTACK. PLEASE SEE THE WEBSITE FOR MORE DETAILS.

WELL, I'M THE ONLY ONE WHO USES LISA...AT LEAST FOR NOW. [K]

WHEN YOU GO TO PICK UP THE 10 YEN COIN, IT CAN LEAVE YOU VULNERABLE TO ATTACK, SO BE CAREFUL. OF COURSE, YOU CAN ALMOST HEAR THE MAKERS OF THE GAME SCREAMING, "DON'T THROW MONEY WHEN YOU'RE USING LISA."

I CAN'T BELIEVE YOU SAID... "SEE THE WEBSITE"? (LAUGHS) CAN'T YOU WRITE IT IN YOUR OWN WORDS? THIS IS SUPPOSED TO BE YOUR CHANCE TO EXPRESS YOUR LOVE FOR THE GAME...GRR!

ANYWAY, I THINK HER FIGHT STYLE MATCHES UP REALLY WELL WITH RENKO-CHAN'S, AND THAT MAKES FOR FUN BATTLES. I NEVER KNOW WHEN SHE'S GONNA PUT A STOP TO MY REPETITIVE ATTACK. AND THERE'S SOMETHING NERVEWRACKING AND EXCITING ABOUT THAT MOMENT WHEN THE CHARACTERS ARE FACE TO FACE AND LISA IS GETTING READY TO MAKE A THROW. I JUST CAN'T GET OVER IT. BUT THAT KIND OF BATTLE CAN'T LAST LONG. WHEN THINGS HEAT UP, YOU SWITCH TO KOMAKI, AND I THINK THAT'S RUDE TO KOMAKI. WELL, I GUESS THAT'S KIND OF HOW KOMAKI IS ANYWAY. POOR GIRL. OH, BY THE WAY, I THINK LISA MIGHT BE THE VICE PRESIDENT'S NATURAL ENEMY...BECAUSE SHE HAS SUPER ARMOR, AND SHE JUST IGNORES NORMAL ATTACKS AND WAITS FOR A CHANCE TO DO A THROW. WHEN THEY FIGHT, THEY END UP CHASING EACH OTHER, AND IT'S REALLY FUN TO WATCH(LAUGHS). IT'S ALMOST AS IF IT REFLECTS THE GRUDGE THEY HOLD AGAINST EACH OTHER IN THE MANGA. [PIT VIPER]

THE NAME OF THIS SPECIAL ATTACK IS "2000YEN." IS THAT ALL SHE'S WORTH? (TEARS)

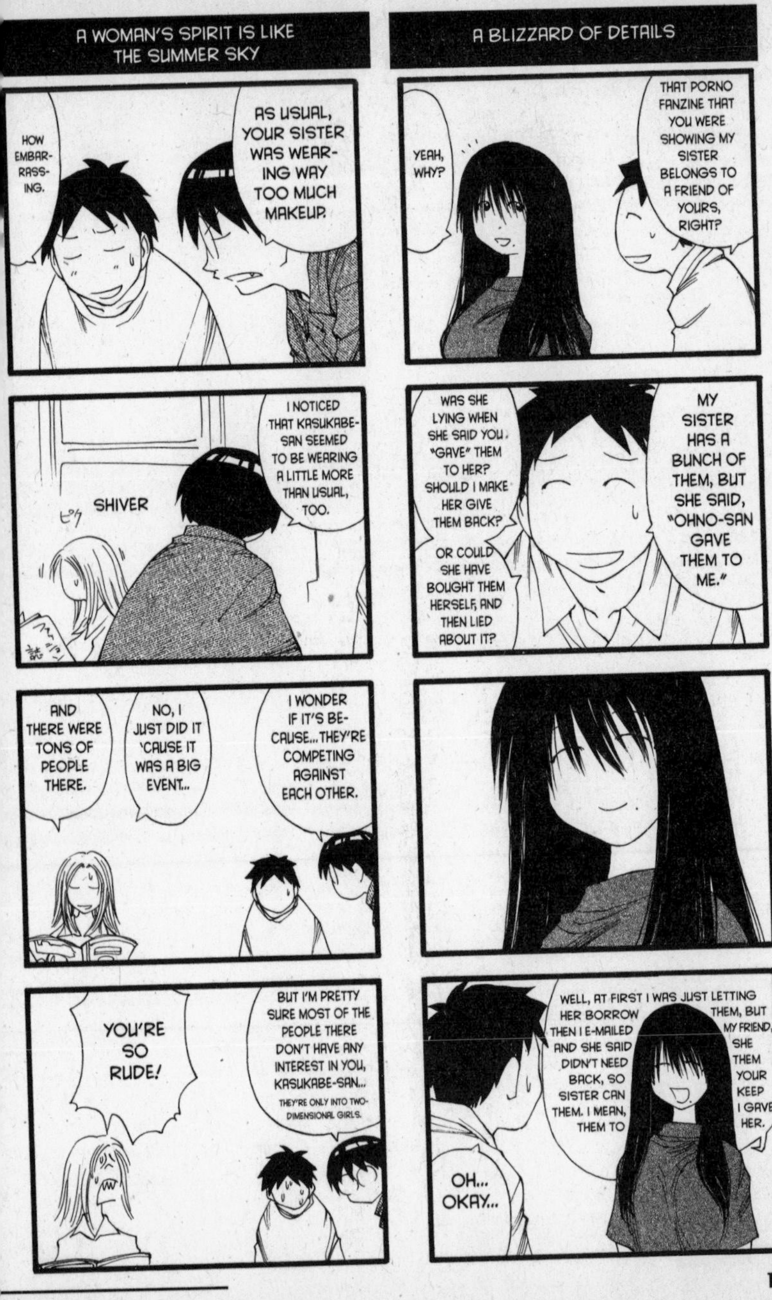
A BLIZZARD OF DETAILS
THAT PORNO FANZINE THAT YOU WERE SHOWING MY SISTER BELONGS TO A FRIEND OF YOURS, RIGHT?
YEAH, WHY?
MY SISTER HAS A BUNCH OF THEM, BUT SHE SAID, "OHNO-SAN GAVE THEM TO ME."
WAS SHE LYING WHEN SHE SAID YOU "GAVE" THEM TO HER? SHOULD I MAKE HER GIVE THEM BACK?
OR COULD SHE HAVE BOUGHT THEM HERSELF, AND THEN LIED ABOUT IT?
WELL, AT FIRST I WAS JUST LETTING HER BORROW THEM, BUT THEN I E-MAILED MY FRIEND, AND SHE SAID SHE DIDN'T NEED THEM BACK, SO YOUR SISTER CAN KEEP THEM. I MEAN, I GAVE THEM TO HER.
OH... OKAY...
A WOMAN'S SPIRIT IS LIKE THE SUMMER SKY
AS USUAL, YOUR SISTER WAS WEARING WAY TOO MUCH MAKEUP.
HOW EMBARRASSING.
I NOTICED THAT KASUKABE-SAN SEEMED TO BE WEARING A LITTLE MORE THAN USUAL, TOO.
SHIVER
I WONDER IF IT'S BECAUSE... THEY'RE COMPETING AGAINST EACH OTHER.
NO, I JUST DID IT 'CAUSE IT WAS A BIG EVENT...
AND THERE WERE TONS OF PEOPLE THERE.
BUT I'M PRETTY SURE MOST OF THE PEOPLE THERE DON'T HAVE ANY INTEREST IN YOU, KASUKABE-SAN...
THEY'RE ONLY INTO TWO-DIMENSIONAL GIRLS.
YOU'RE SO RUDE!

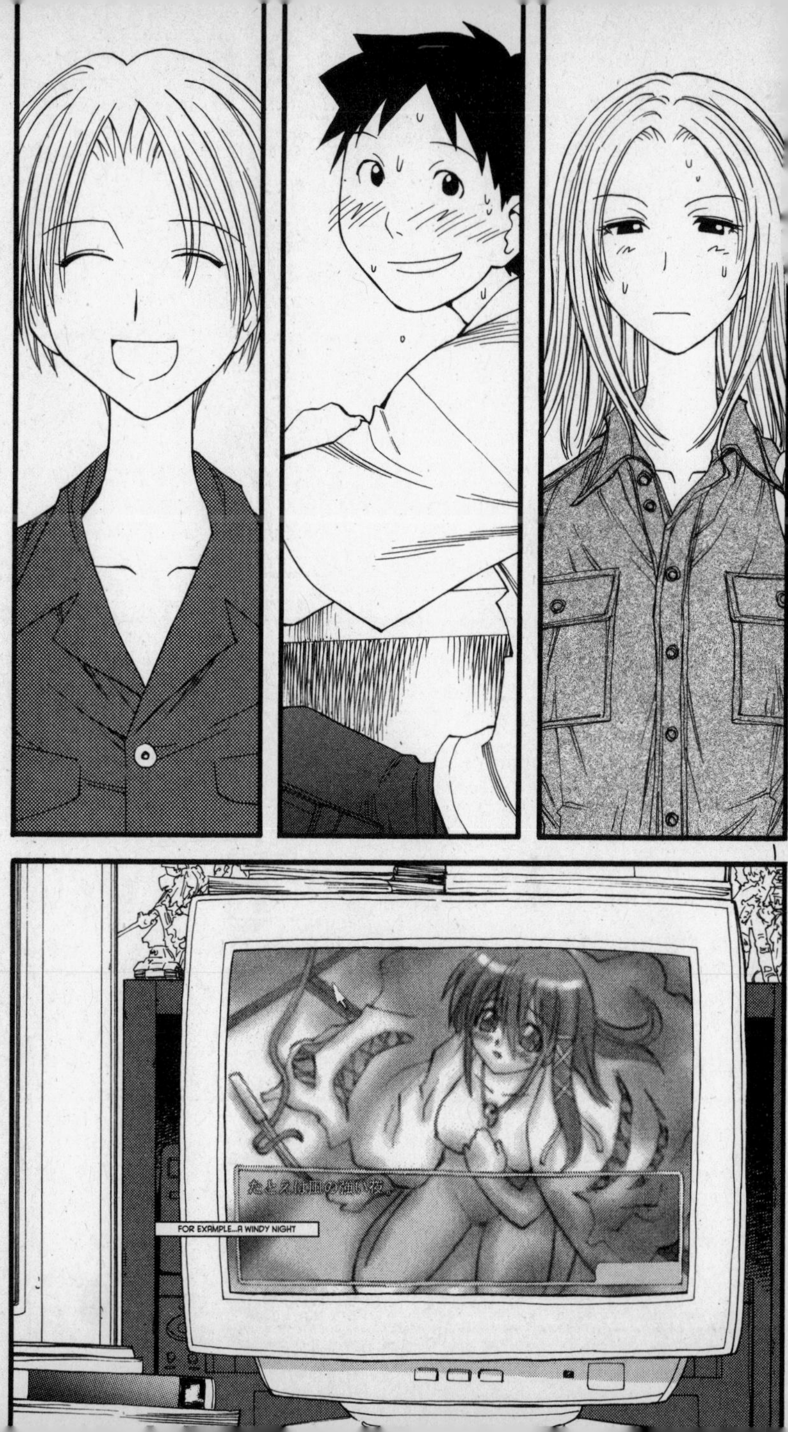
FOR EXAMPLE...A WINDY NIGHT

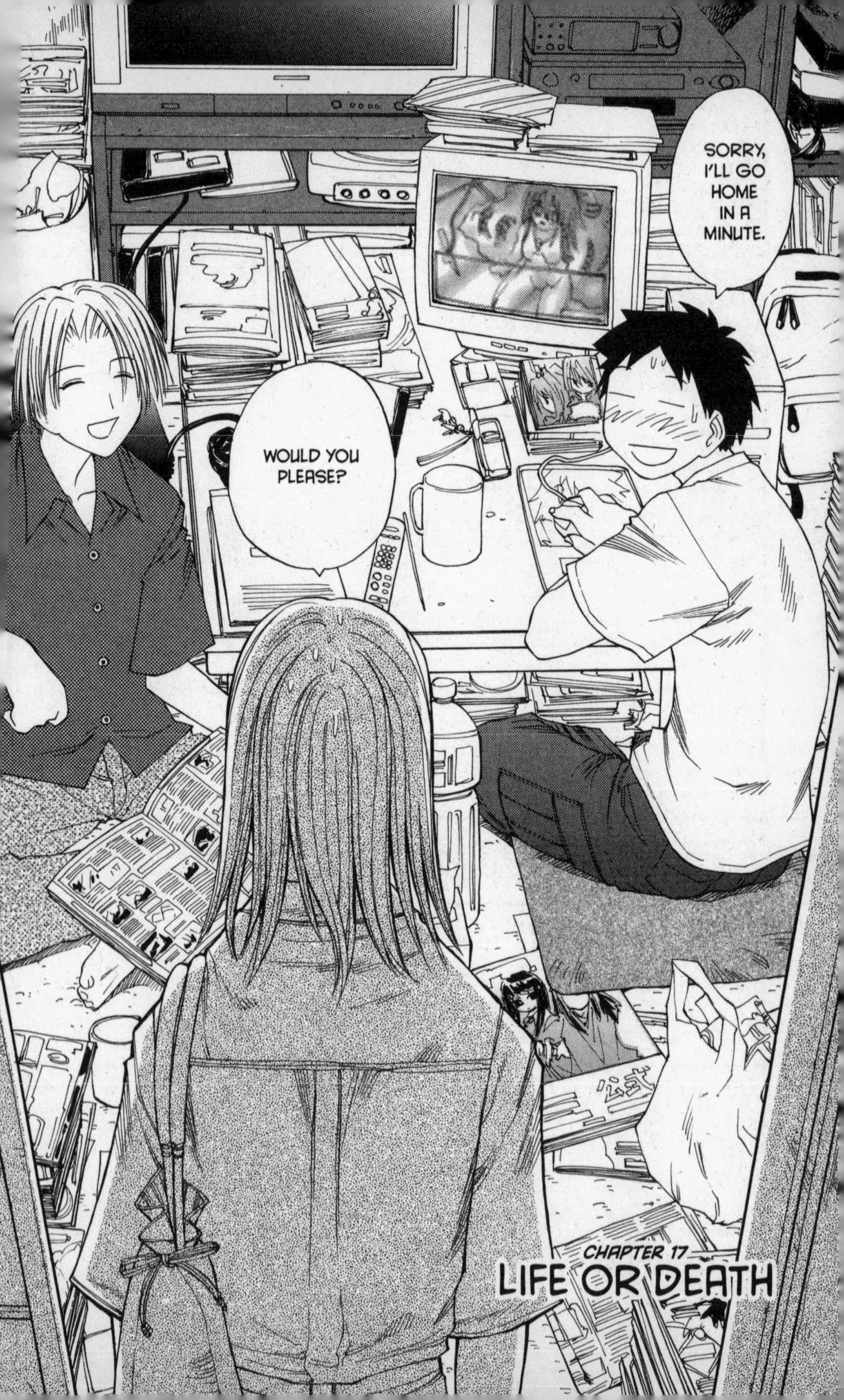
SORRY, I'LL GO HOME IN A MINUTE.
WOULD YOU PLEASE?
CHAPTER 17
LIFE OR DEATH

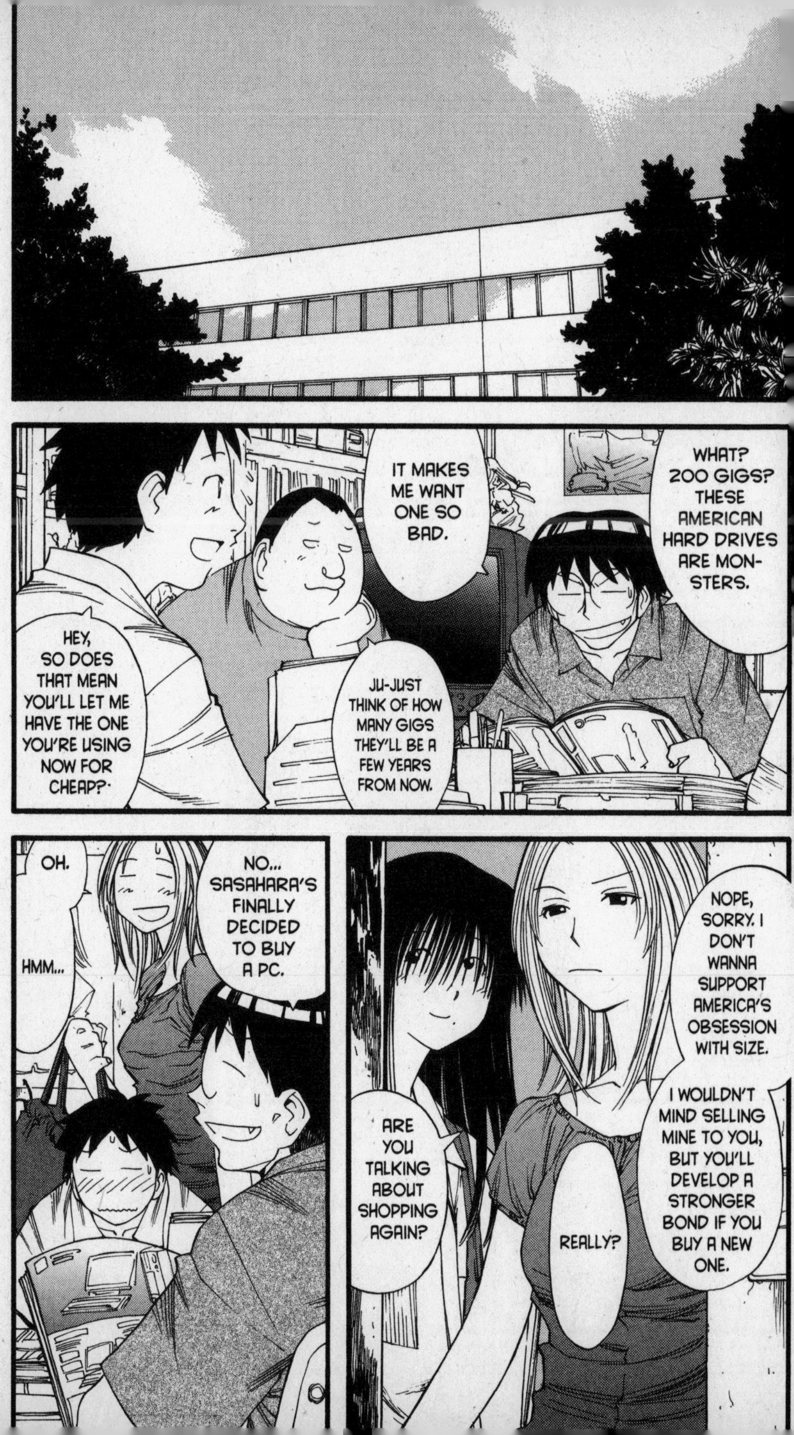
WHAT? 200 GIGS? THESE AMERICAN HARD DRIVES ARE MONSTERS.
IT MAKES ME WANT ONE SO BAD.
JU-JUST THINK OF HOW MANY GIGS THEY'LL BE A FEW YEARS FROM NOW.
HEY, SO DOES THAT MEAN YOU'LL LET ME HAVE THE ONE YOU'RE USING NOW FOR CHEAP?
NOPE, SORRY. I DON'T WANNA SUPPORT AMERICA'S OBSESSION WITH SIZE.
I WOULDN'T MIND SELLING MINE TO YOU, BUT YOU'LL DEVELOP A STRONGER BOND IF YOU BUY A NEW ONE.
ARE YOU TALKING ABOUT SHOPPING AGAIN?
REALLY?
NO... SASAHARA'S FINALLY DECIDED TO BUY A PC.
OH.
HMM...

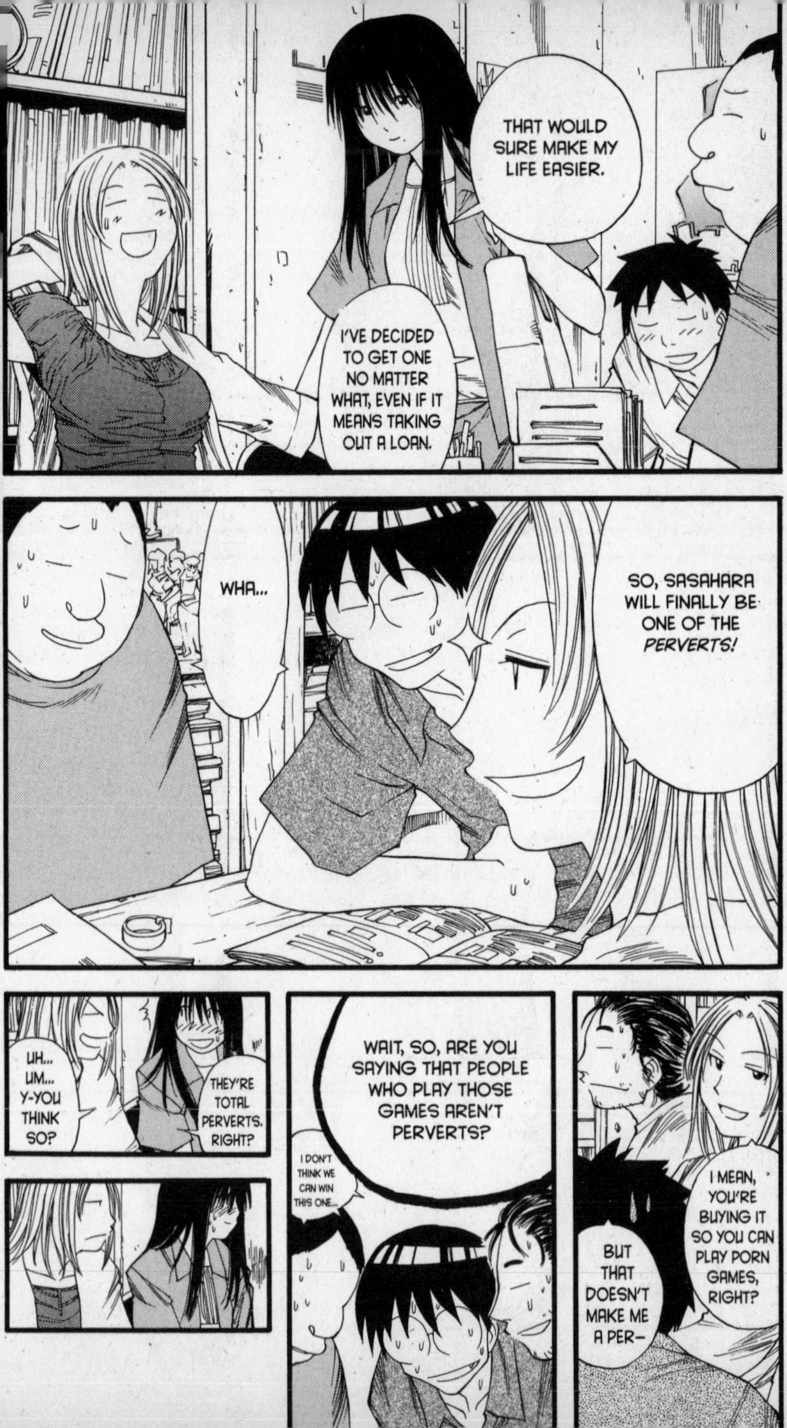
THAT WOULD SURE MAKE MY LIFE EASIER.
I'VE DECIDED TO GET ONE NO MATTER WHAT, EVEN IF IT MEANS TAKING OUT A LOAN.
SO, SASAHARA WILL FINALLY BE ONE OF THE *PERVERTS!*
WHA...
I MEAN, YOU'RE BUYING IT SO YOU CAN PLAY PORN GAMES, RIGHT?
BUT THAT DOESN'T MAKE ME A PER–
WAIT, SO, ARE YOU SAYING THAT PEOPLE WHO PLAY THOSE GAMES AREN'T PERVERTS?
I DON'T THINK WE CAN WIN THIS ONE...
THEY'RE TOTAL PERVERTS. RIGHT?
UH... UM... Y-YOU THINK SO?

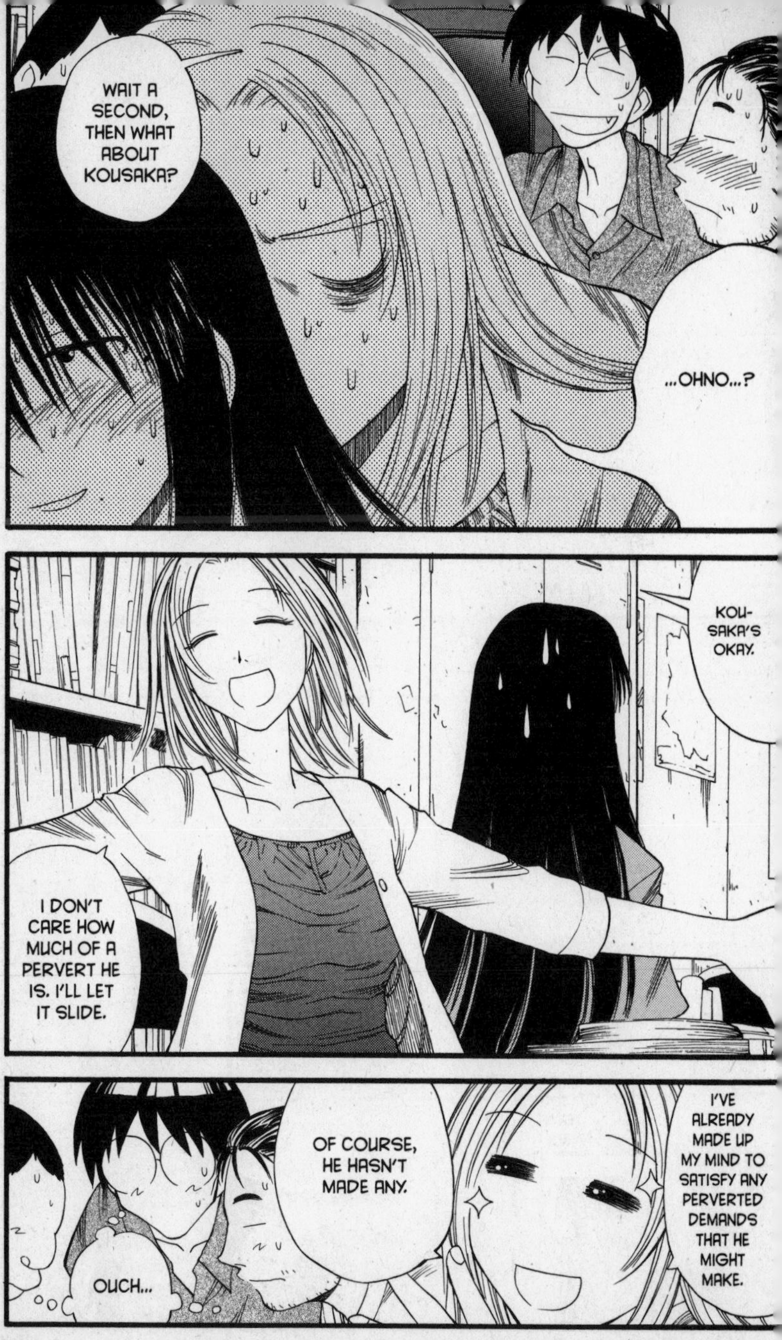
...OHNO...?
WAIT A SECOND, THEN WHAT ABOUT KOUSAKA?
KOUSAKA'S OKAY.
I DON'T CARE HOW MUCH OF A PERVERT HE IS. I'LL LET IT SLIDE.
I'VE ALREADY MADE UP MY MIND TO SATISFY ANY PERVERTED DEMANDS THAT HE MIGHT MAKE.
OF COURSE, HE HASN'T MADE ANY.
OUCH...

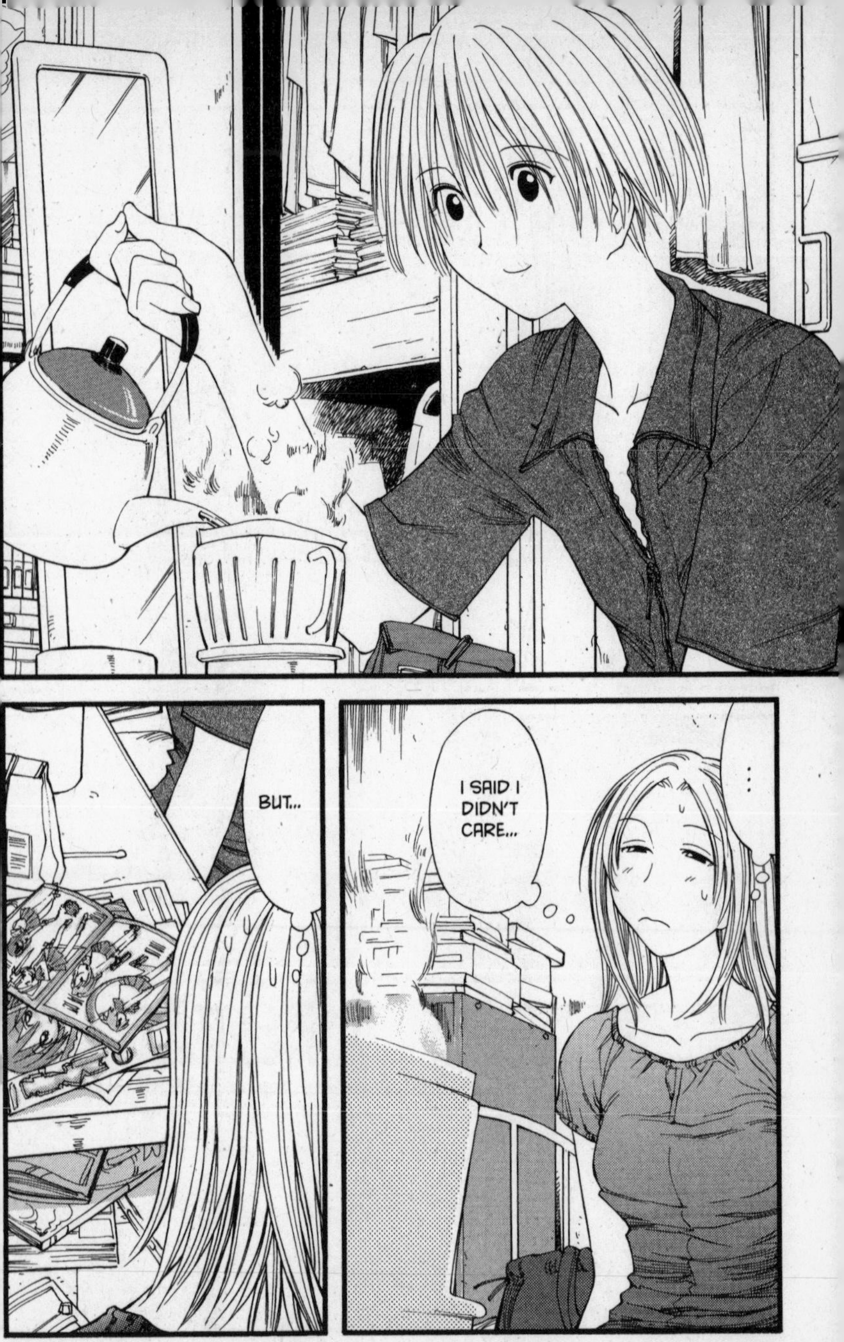
...
I SAID I DIDN'T CARE...
BUT...

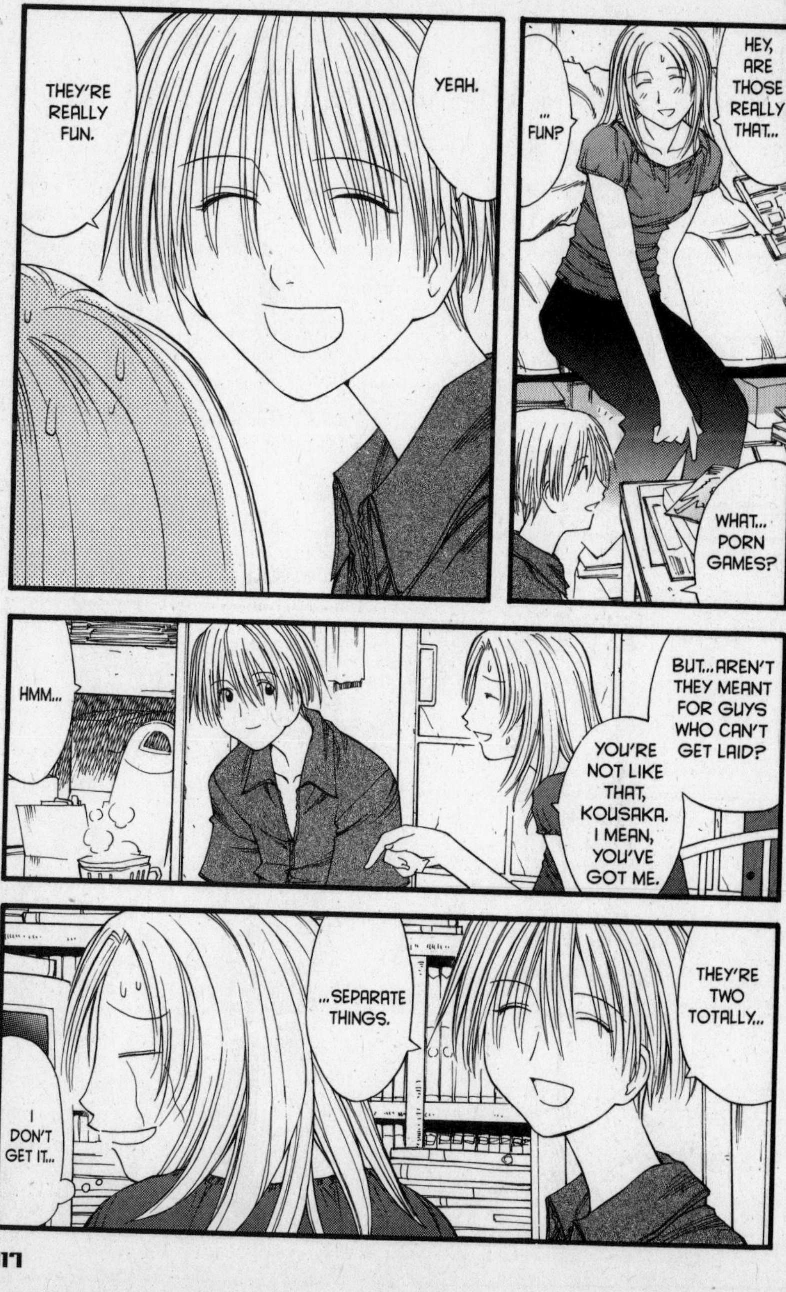
HEY, ARE THOSE REALLY THAT...
... FUN?
WHAT... PORN GAMES?
YEAH.
THEY'RE REALLY FUN.
BUT...AREN'T THEY MEANT FOR GUYS WHO CAN'T GET LAID?
YOU'RE NOT LIKE THAT, KOUSAKA. I MEAN, YOU'VE GOT ME.
HMM...
THEY'RE TWO TOTALLY...
...SEPARATE THINGS.
I DON'T GET IT...

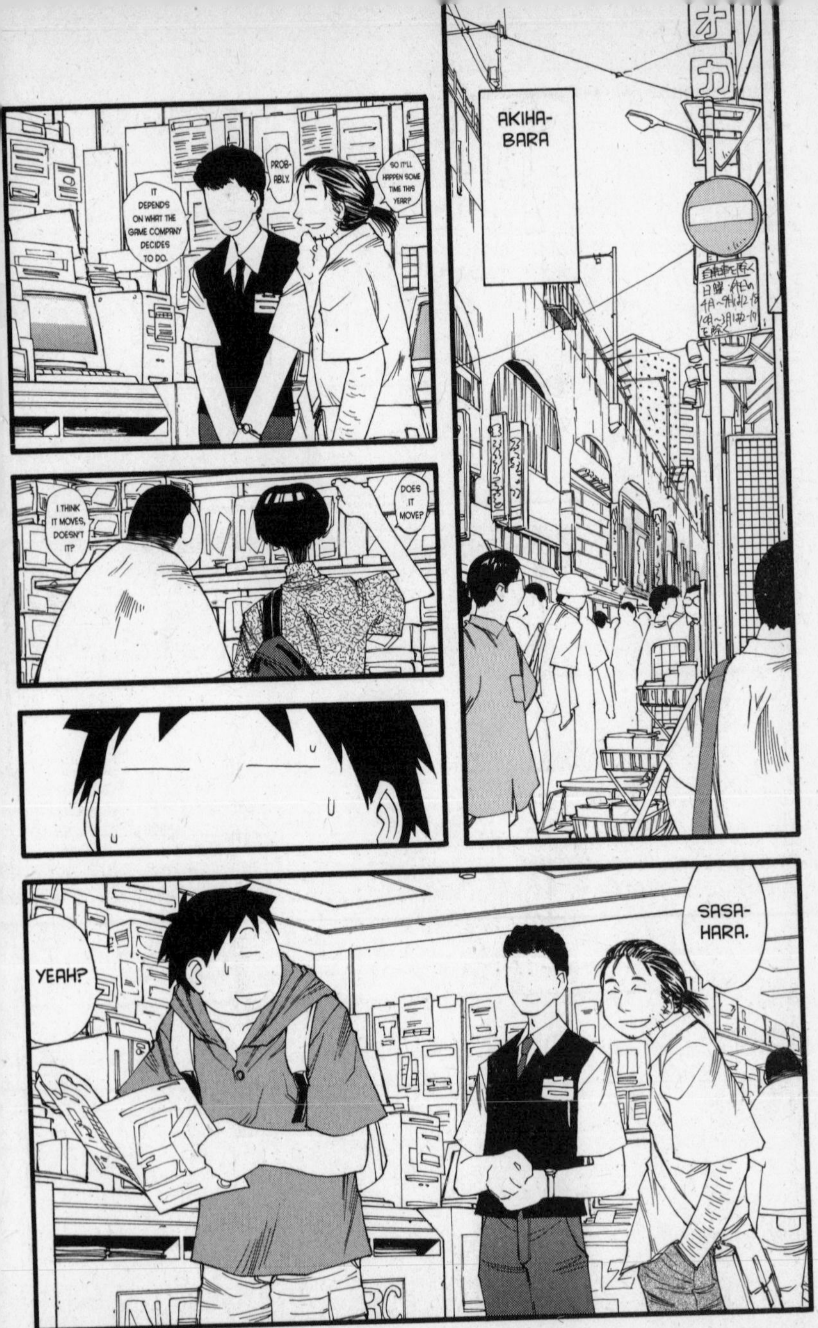
AKIHA-BARA
SO IT'LL HAPPEN SOME TIME THIS YEAR?
PROB-ABLY.
IT DEPENDS ON WHAT THE GAME COMPANY DECIDES TO DO.
DOES IT MOVE?
I THINK IT MOVES, DOESN'T IT?
SASA-HARA.
YEAH?

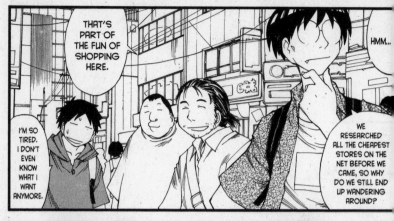

HMM...
WE RESEARCHED ALL THE CHEAPEST STORES ON THE NET BEFORE WE CAME, SO WHY DO WE STILL END UP WANDERING AROUND?
THAT'S PART OF THE FUN OF SHOPPING HERE.
I'M SO TIRED. I DON'T EVEN KNOW WHAT I WANT ANYMORE.
WELL, WHAT'RE YOU GONNA DO? THE PROJECTED DEMAND FOR PORN GAMES HAS BEEN GOING UP LATELY, SO THE MOD-ELS WITH ENOUGH TECHNOLOGY TO LAST FOR AT LEAST TWO YEARS HAVE GOTTEN EXPENSIVE.
DO YOU WANNA GET A MODEL THAT HAS JUST ENOUGH TECH-NOLOGY TO HANDLE THE GAMES THAT ARE OUT NOW?
I DON'T KNOW WHAT TO DO...
YOU'RE TIRED, AREN'T YOU, SASA-HARA?
THAT'S NO GOOD.
THAT'S NO GOOD AT ALL.
WHY DON'T YOU READ THE "TSUKI-JIMA RENEWAL*" MANUAL I JUST BOUGHT? THAT SHOULD PUT YOU IN A GOOD MOOD.
RUSTLE RUSTLE
DON'T TAKE THAT OUT IN THE MIDDLE OF THE STREET.

*A PORN GAME

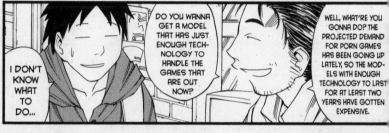

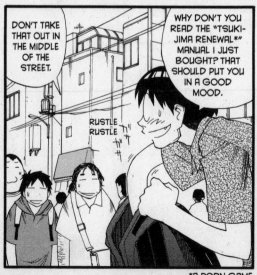

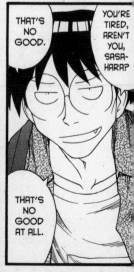

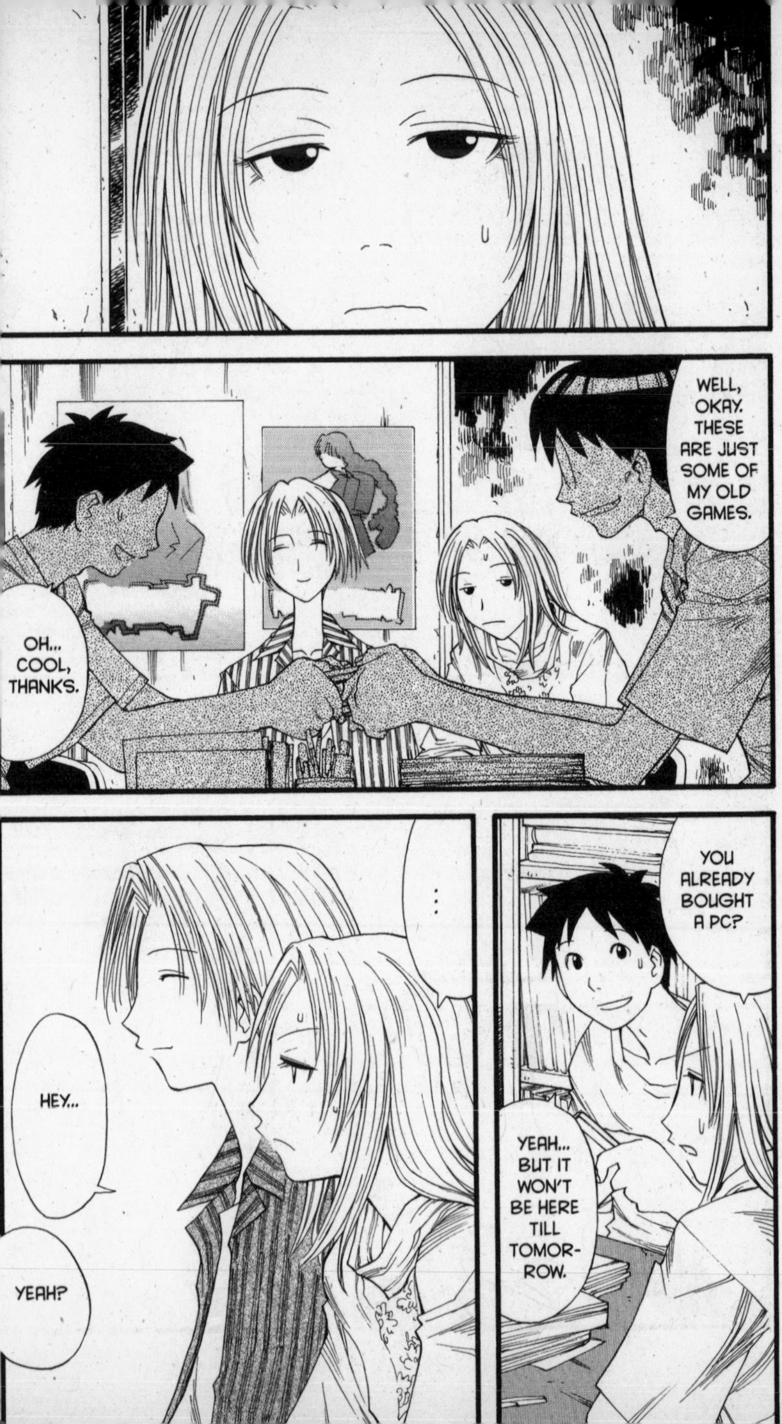
WELL, OKAY. THESE ARE JUST SOME OF MY OLD GAMES.
OH... COOL, THANKS.
YOU ALREADY BOUGHT A PC?
YEAH... BUT IT WON'T BE HERE TILL TOMOR-ROW.
...
HEY...
YEAH?

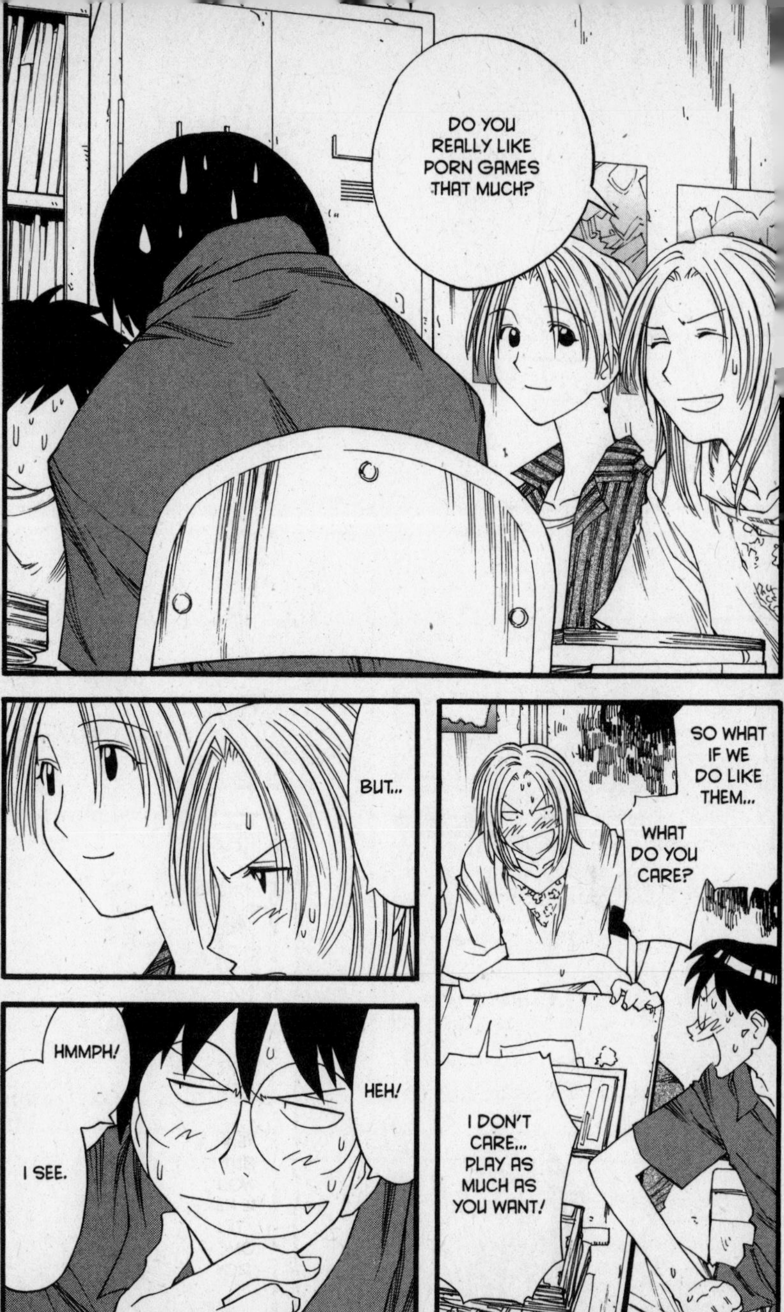
DO YOU REALLY LIKE PORN GAMES THAT MUCH?
SO WHAT IF WE DO LIKE THEM...
WHAT DO YOU CARE?
I DON'T CARE... PLAY AS MUCH AS YOU WANT!
BUT...
HMMPH!
HEH!
I SEE.

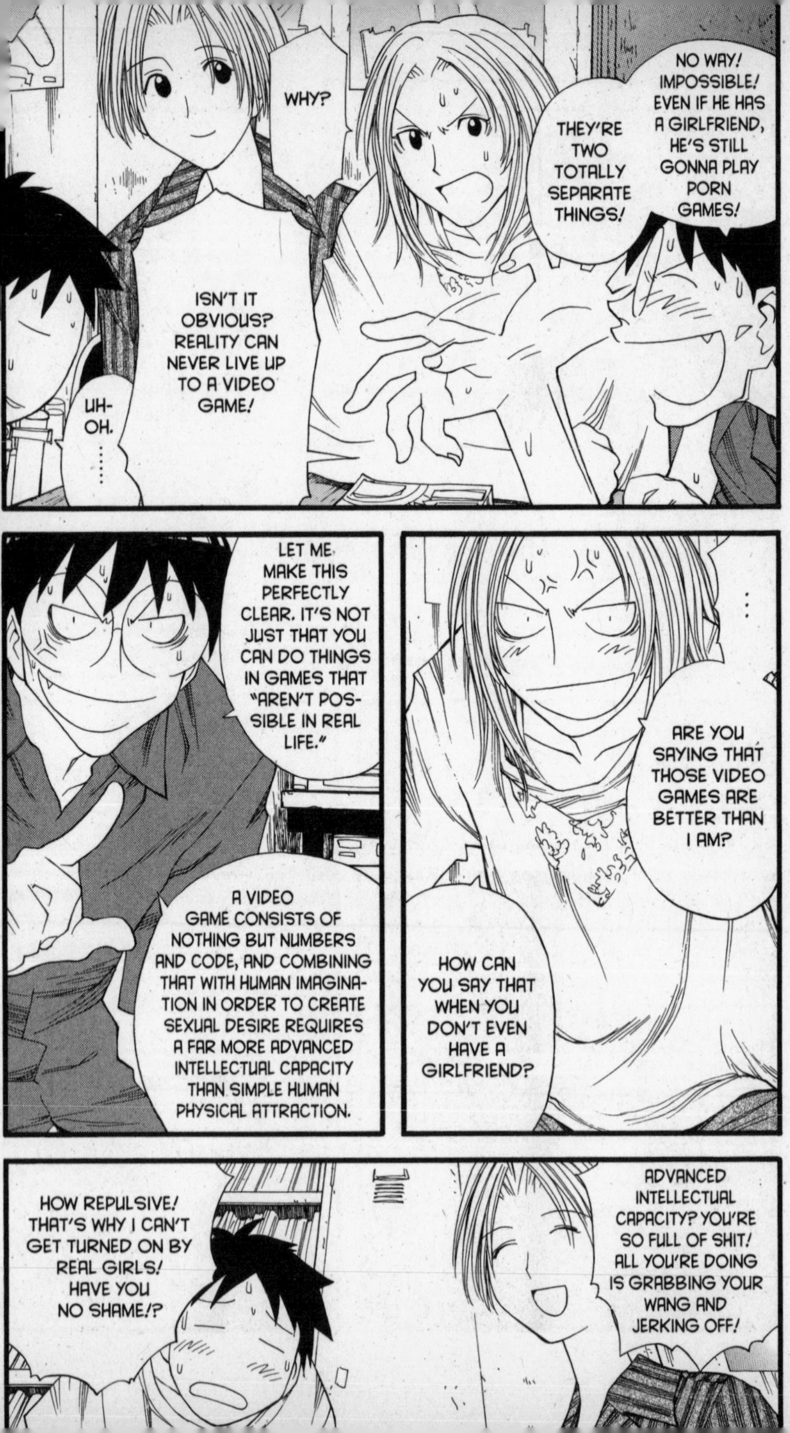
NO WAY! IMPOSSIBLE! EVEN IF HE HAS A GIRLFRIEND, HE'S STILL GONNA PLAY PORN GAMES!
THEY'RE TWO TOTALLY SEPARATE THINGS!
WHY?
ISN'T IT OBVIOUS? REALITY CAN NEVER LIVE UP TO A VIDEO GAME!
UH-OH. ......
...
ARE YOU SAYING THAT THOSE VIDEO GAMES ARE BETTER THAN I AM?
HOW CAN YOU SAY THAT WHEN YOU DON'T EVEN HAVE A GIRLFRIEND?
LET ME MAKE THIS PERFECTLY CLEAR. IT'S NOT JUST THAT YOU CAN DO THINGS IN GAMES THAT "AREN'T POSSIBLE IN REAL LIFE."
A VIDEO GAME CONSISTS OF NOTHING BUT NUMBERS AND CODE, AND COMBINING THAT WITH HUMAN IMAGINATION IN ORDER TO CREATE SEXUAL DESIRE REQUIRES A FAR MORE ADVANCED INTELLECTUAL CAPACITY THAN SIMPLE HUMAN PHYSICAL ATTRACTION.
ADVANCED INTELLECTUAL CAPACITY? YOU'RE SO FULL OF SHIT! ALL YOU'RE DOING IS GRABBING YOUR WANG AND JERKING OFF!
HOW REPULSIVE! THAT'S WHY I CAN'T GET TURNED ON BY REAL GIRLS! HAVE YOU NO SHAME!?

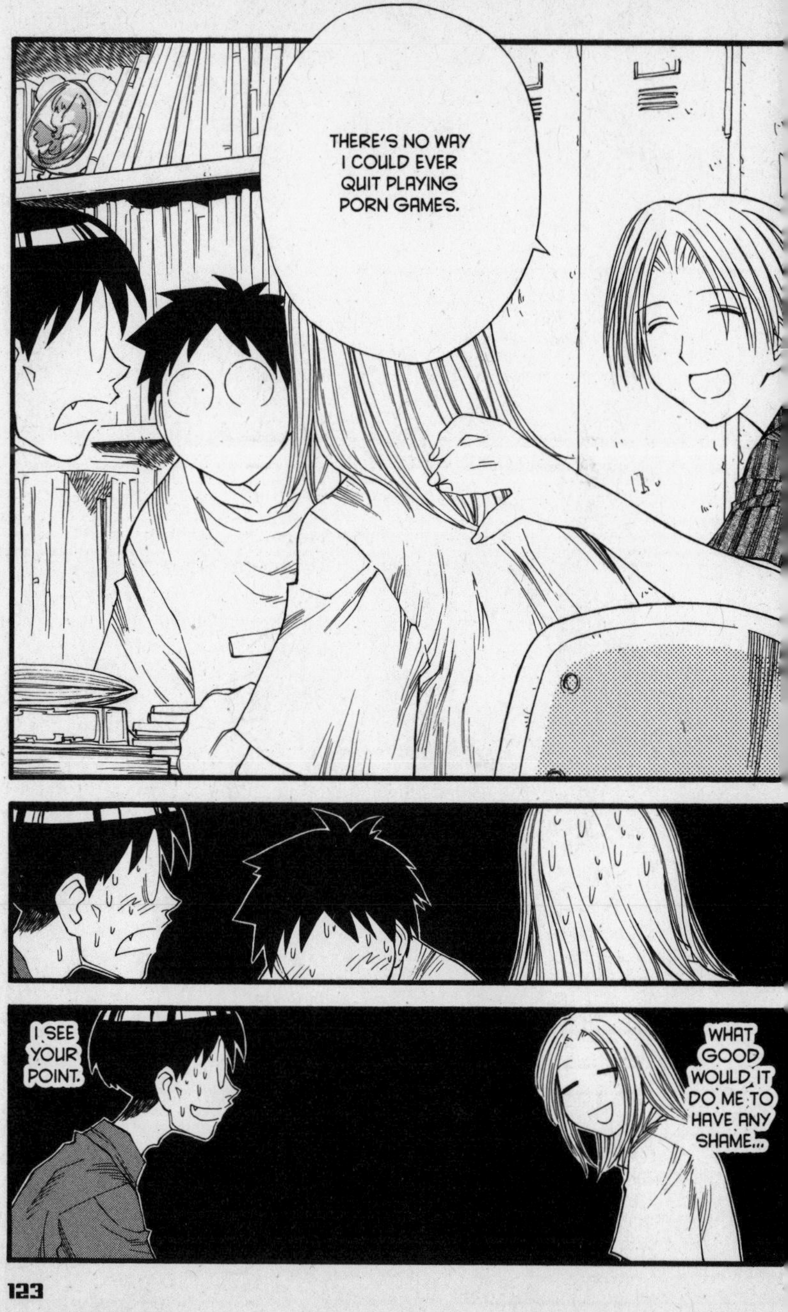
THERE'S NO WAY I COULD EVER QUIT PLAYING PORN GAMES.
WHAT GOOD WOULD IT DO ME TO HAVE ANY SHAME...
I SEE YOUR POINT.

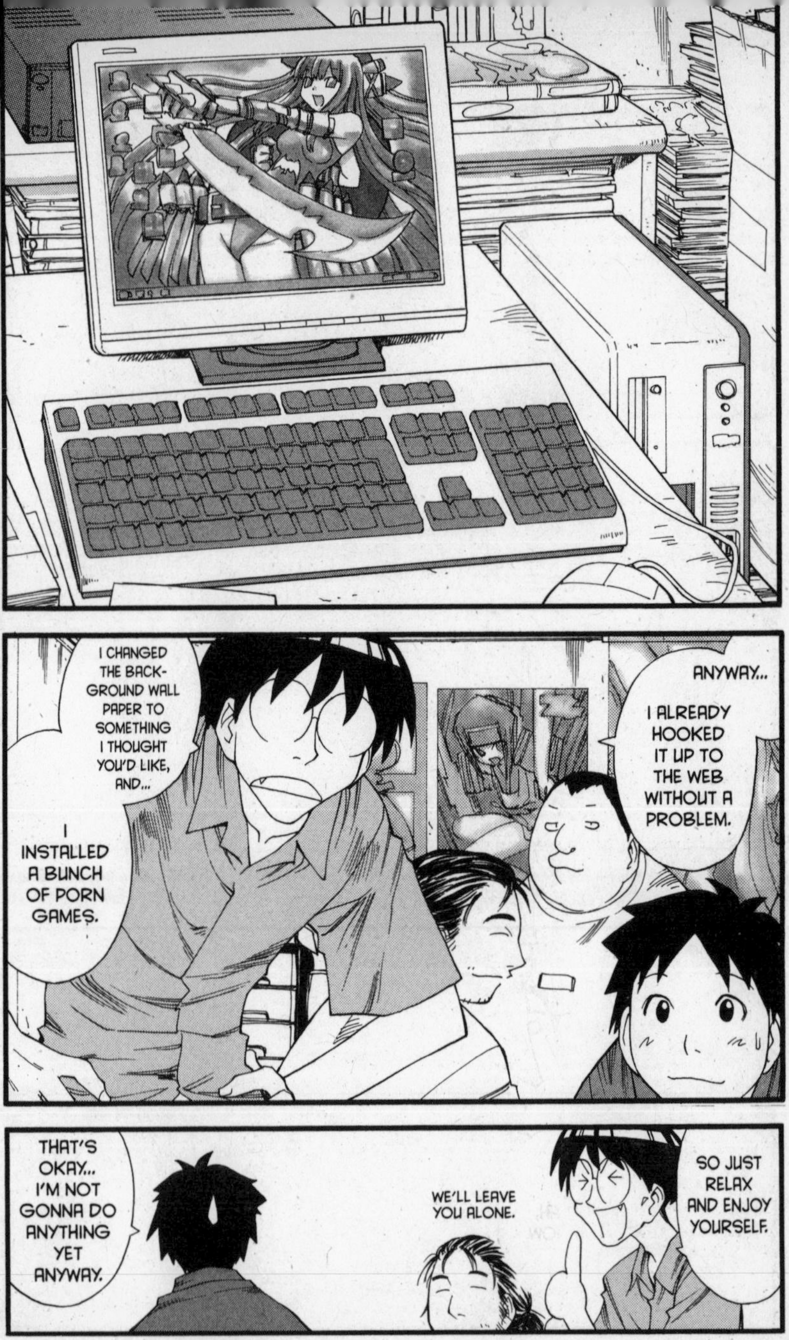
ANYWAY...
I ALREADY HOOKED IT UP TO THE WEB WITHOUT A PROBLEM.
I CHANGED THE BACK-GROUND WALL PAPER TO SOMETHING I THOUGHT YOU'D LIKE, AND...
I INSTALLED A BUNCH OF PORN GAMES.
SO JUST RELAX AND ENJOY YOURSELF.
WE'LL LEAVE YOU ALONE.
THAT'S OKAY... I'M NOT GONNA DO ANYTHING YET ANYWAY.

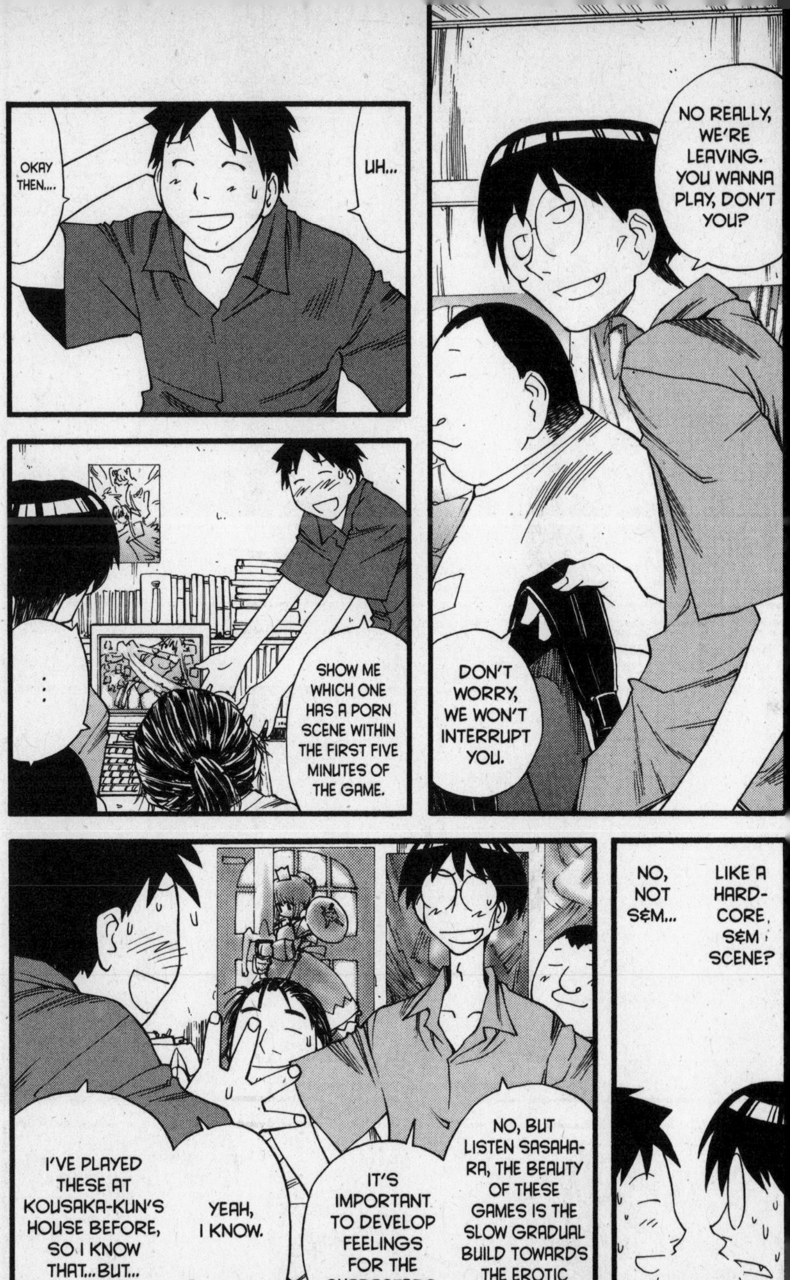
NO REALLY, WE'RE LEAVING. YOU WANNA PLAY, DON'T YOU?
DON'T WORRY, WE WON'T INTERRUPT YOU.
UH...
OKAY THEN....
SHOW ME WHICH ONE HAS A PORN SCENE WITHIN THE FIRST FIVE MINUTES OF THE GAME.
...
LIKE A HARD-CORE S&M SCENE?
NO, NOT S&M...
NO, BUT LISTEN SASAHARA, THE BEAUTY OF THESE GAMES IS THE SLOW GRADUAL BUILD TOWARDS THE EROTIC SCENES.
IT'S IMPORTANT TO DEVELOP FEELINGS FOR THE CHARACTERS.
YEAH, I KNOW.
I'VE PLAYED THESE AT KOUSAKA-KUN'S HOUSE BEFORE, SO I KNOW THAT...BUT...

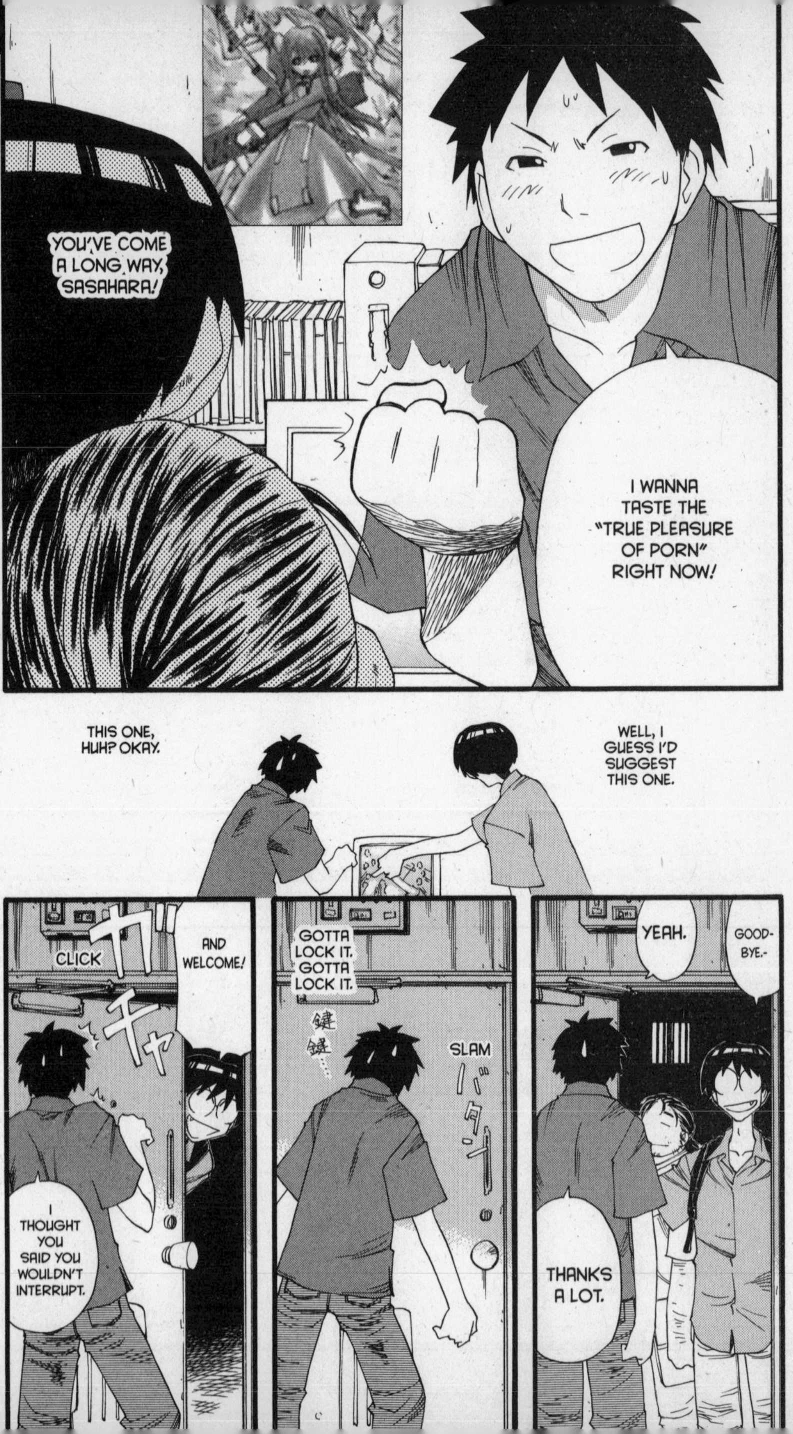
I WANNA TASTE THE "TRUE PLEASURE OF PORN" RIGHT NOW!
YOU'VE COME A LONG WAY, SASAHARA!
WELL, I GUESS I'D SUGGEST THIS ONE.
THIS ONE, HUH? OKAY.
GOOD-BYE.-
YEAH.
THANKS A LOT.
SLAM
バタン
GOTTA LOCK IT. GOTTA LOCK IT.
鍵鍵…
AND WELCOME!
CLICK
ガチャ
I THOUGHT YOU SAID YOU WOULDN'T INTERRUPT.

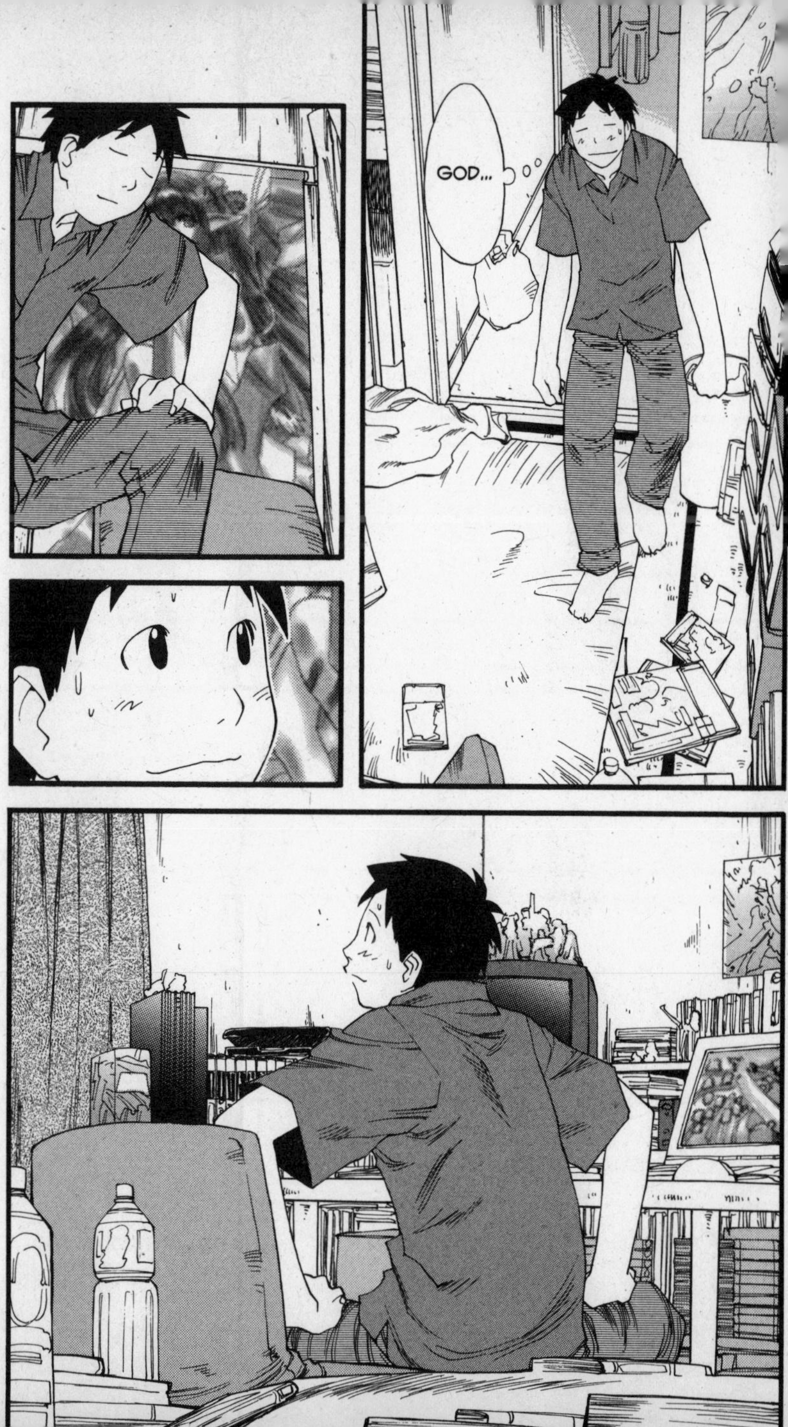
GOD...

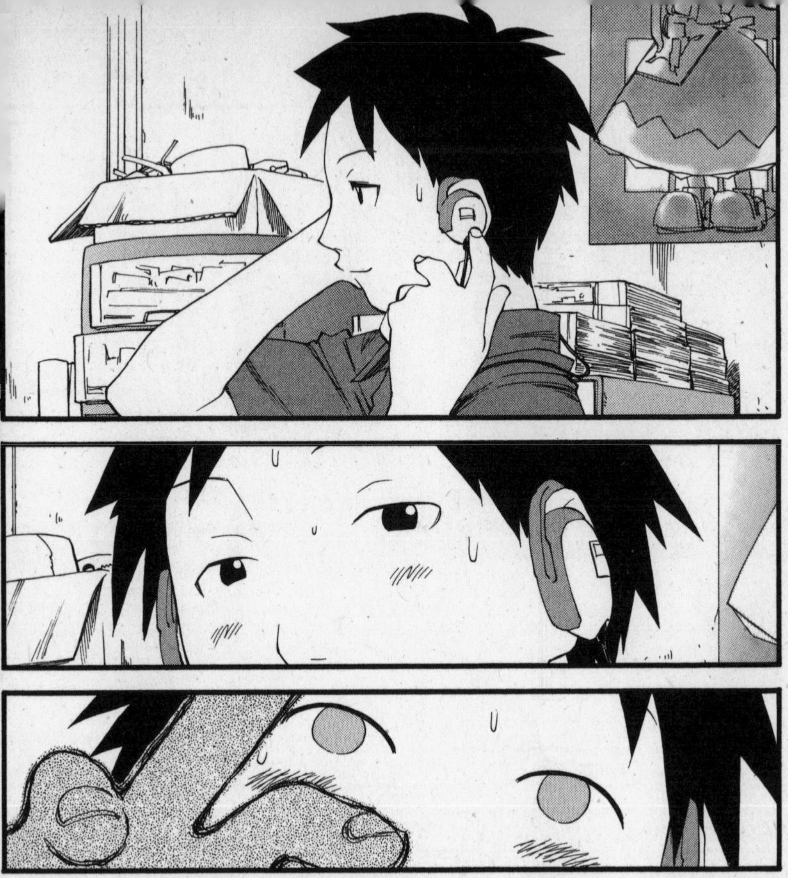

WE ALL KNOW WHAT HE'S ABOUT TO DO, SO...

CUT TO THE NEXT SCENE.

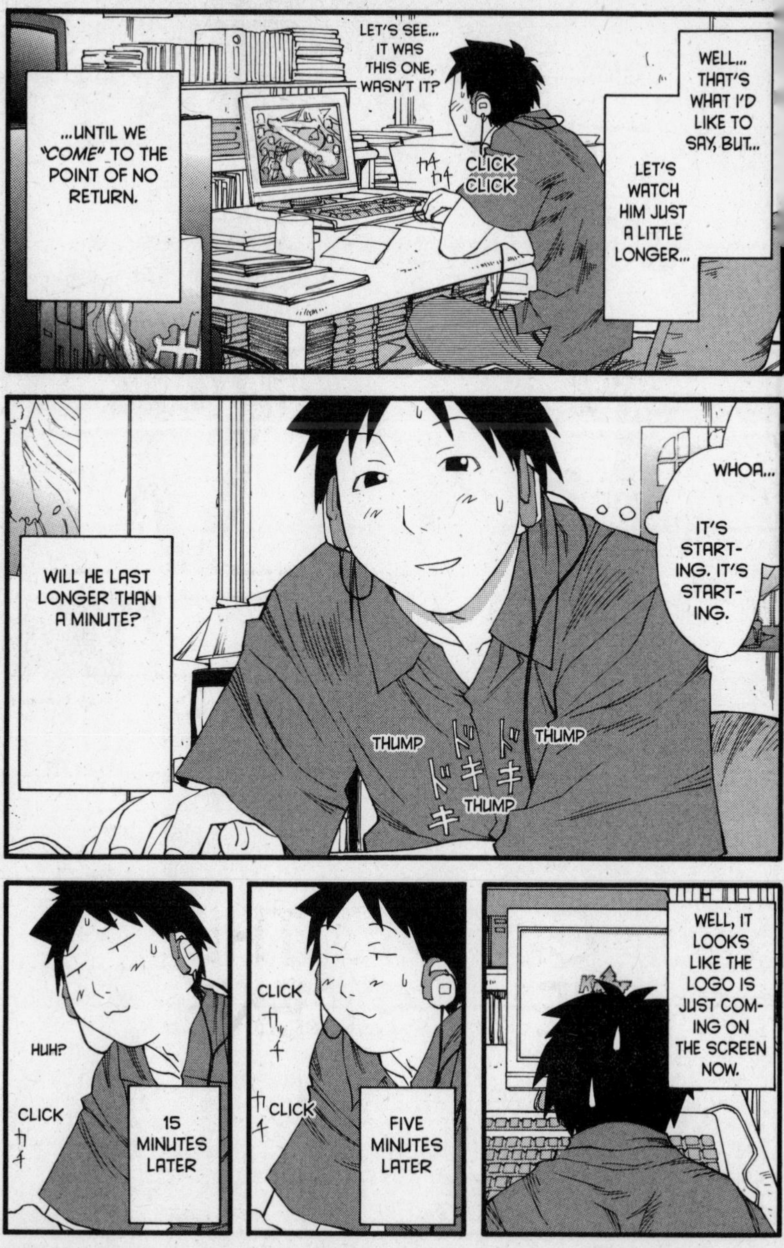
WELL... THAT'S WHAT I'D LIKE TO SAY, BUT...
LET'S WATCH HIM JUST A LITTLE LONGER...
LET'S SEE... IT WAS THIS ONE, WASN'T IT?
CLICK CLICK
...UNTIL WE "COME" TO THE POINT OF NO RETURN.
WHOA...
IT'S START-ING. IT'S START-ING.
THUMP
ドキドキ
THUMP
ドキドキ
THUMP
WILL HE LAST LONGER THAN A MINUTE?
WELL, IT LOOKS LIKE THE LOGO IS JUST COM-ING ON THE SCREEN NOW.
CLICK
CLICK
FIVE MINUTES LATER
HUH?
CLICK
15 MINUTES LATER

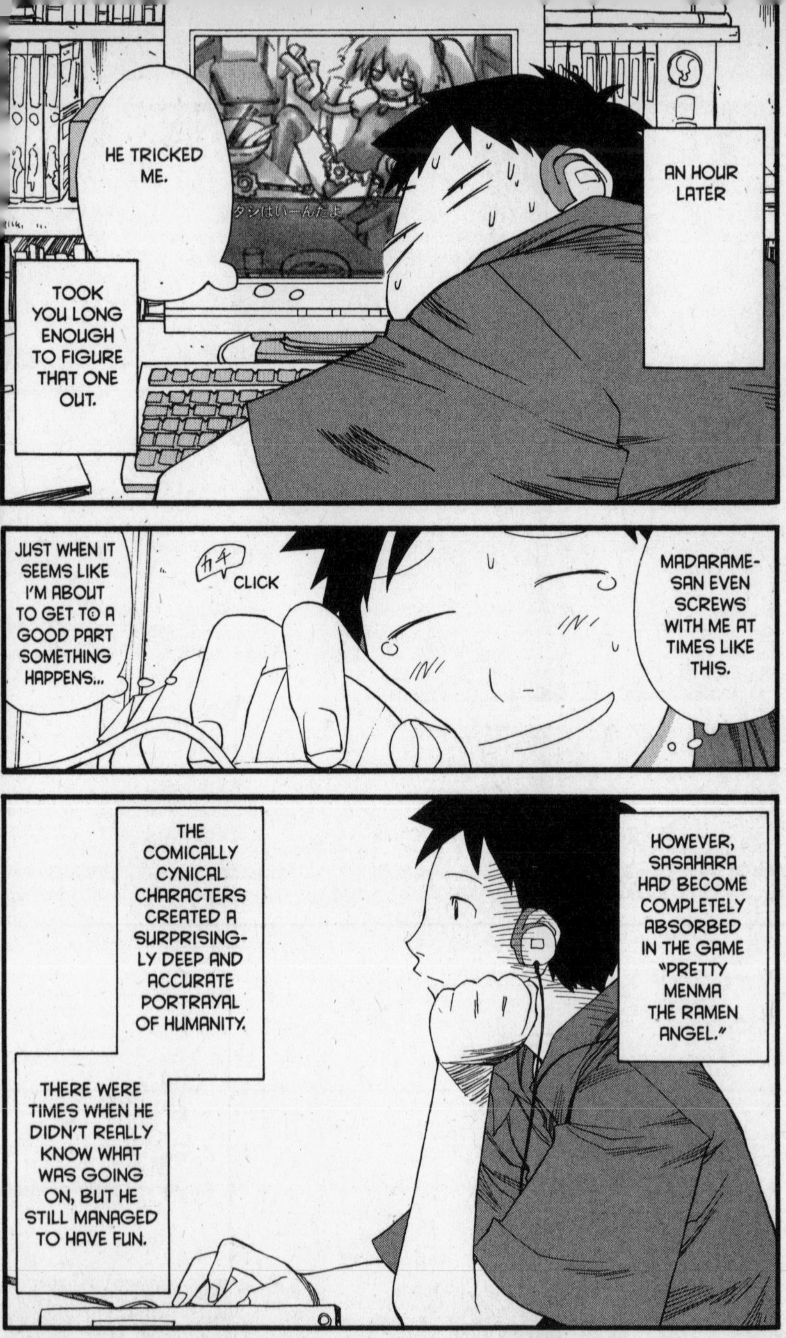
AN HOUR LATER
HE TRICKED ME.
TOOK YOU LONG ENOUGH TO FIGURE THAT ONE OUT.
MADARAME-SAN EVEN SCREWS WITH ME AT TIMES LIKE THIS.
カチ
CLICK
JUST WHEN IT SEEMS LIKE I'M ABOUT TO GET TO A GOOD PART SOMETHING HAPPENS...
HOWEVER, SASAHARA HAD BECOME COMPLETELY ABSORBED IN THE GAME "PRETTY MENMA THE RAMEN ANGEL."
THE COMICALLY CYNICAL CHARACTERS CREATED A SURPRISING-LY DEEP AND ACCURATE PORTRAYAL OF HUMANITY.
THERE WERE TIMES WHEN HE DIDN'T REALLY KNOW WHAT WAS GOING ON, BUT HE STILL MANAGED TO HAVE FUN.

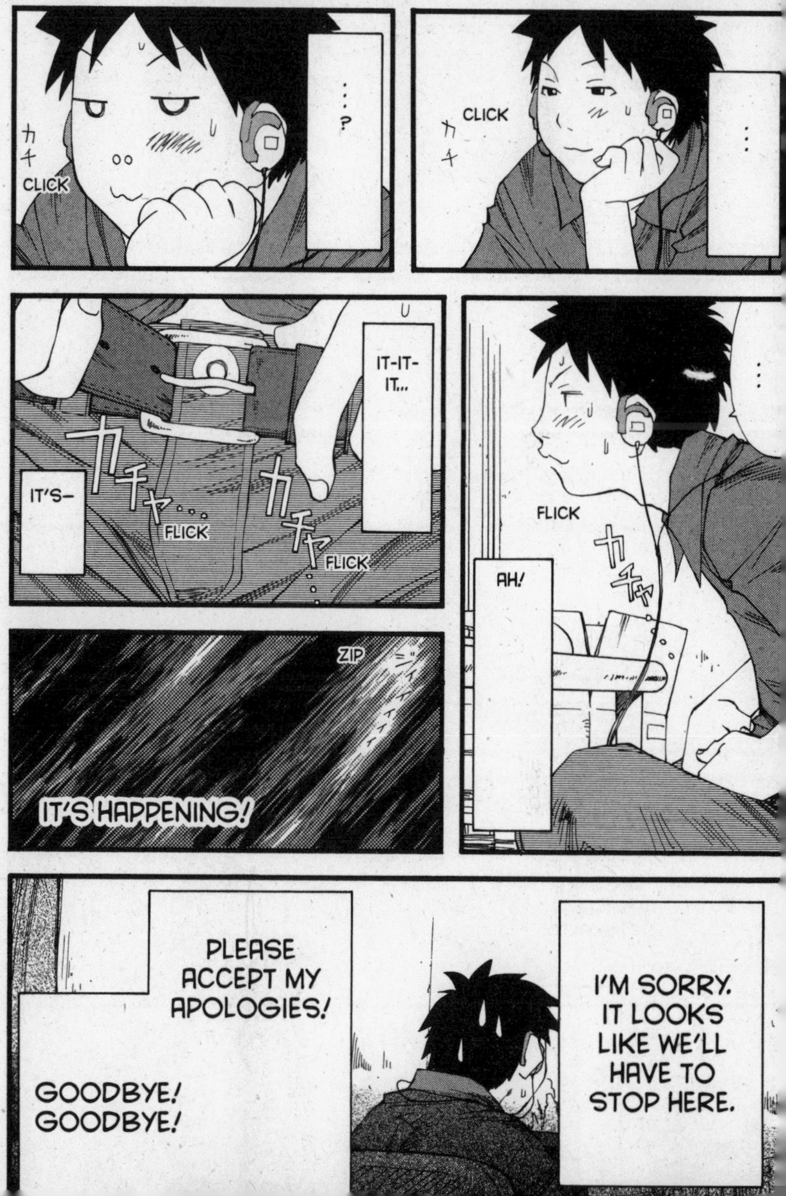
. . .
カチ
CLICK
. . . ?
カチ
CLICK
. . .
FLICK
カチャ
AH!
IT-IT-IT...
IT'S—
カチャ
FLICK
カチャ
FLICK
ZIP
IT'S HAPPENING!
I'M SORRY. IT LOOKS LIKE WE'LL HAVE TO STOP HERE.
PLEASE ACCEPT MY APOLOGIES!
GOODBYE! GOODBYE!

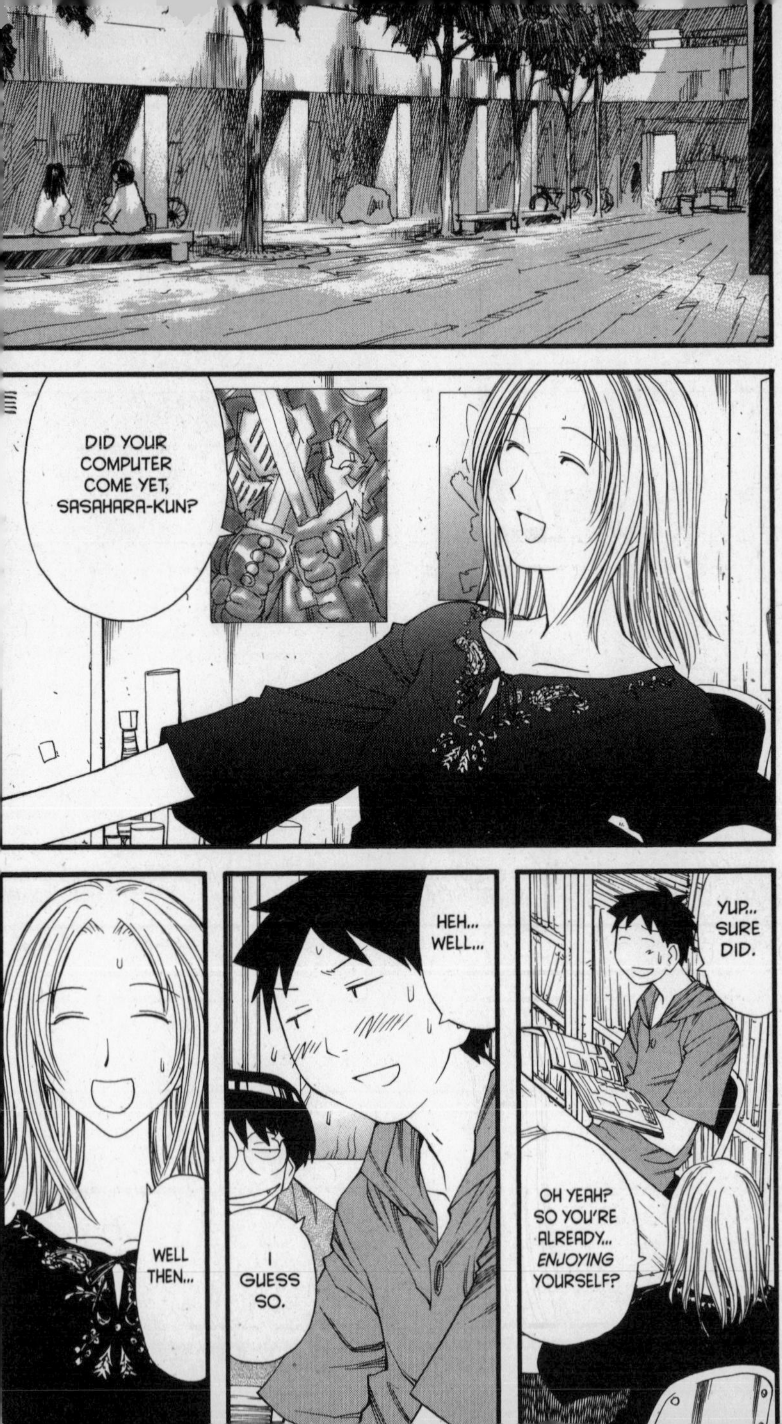
DID YOUR COMPUTER COME YET, SASAHARA-KUN?
YUP... SURE DID.
OH YEAH? SO YOU'RE ALREADY... *ENJOYING* YOURSELF?
HEH... WELL...
I GUESS SO.
WELL THEN...

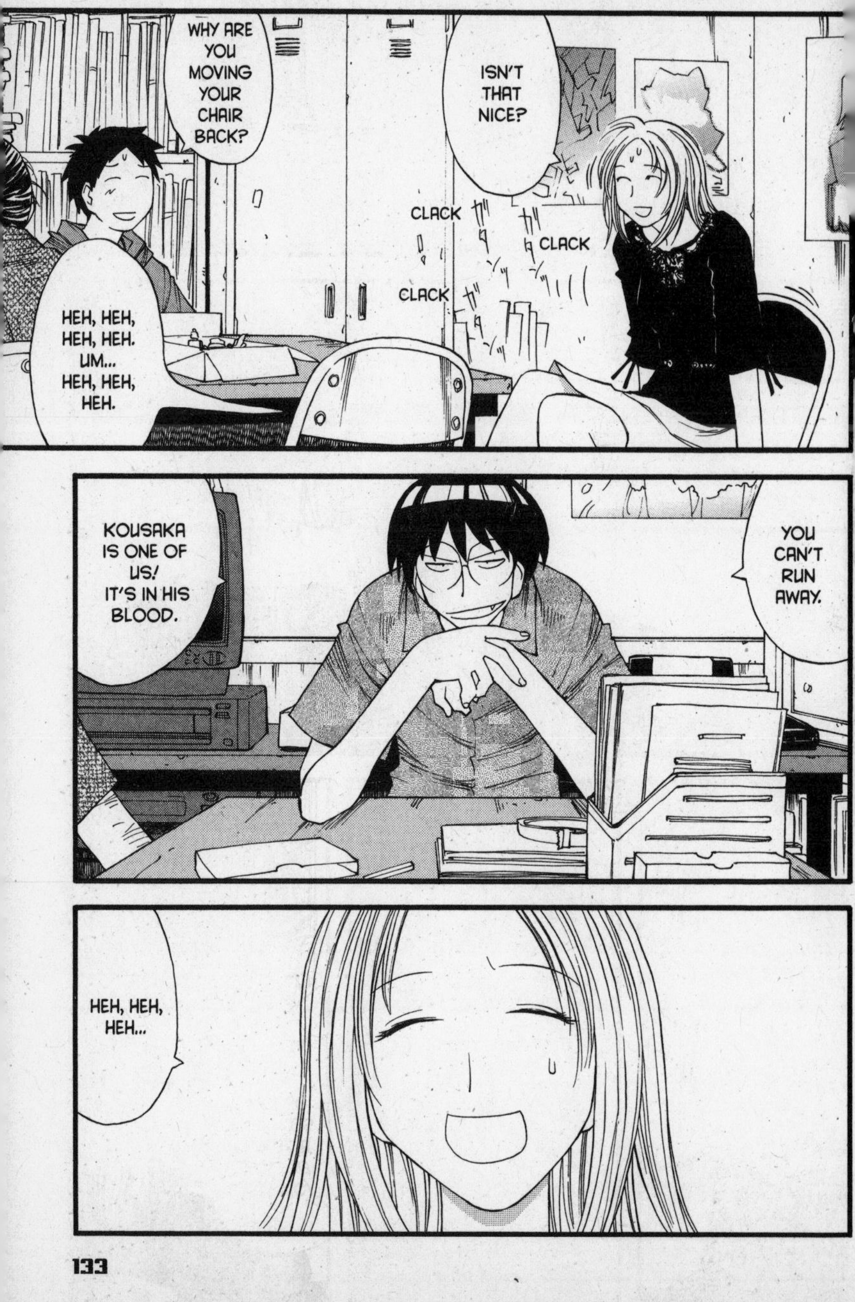
ISN'T THAT NICE?
CLACK
CLACK
CLACK
WHY ARE YOU MOVING YOUR CHAIR BACK?
HEH, HEH, HEH, HEH. UM... HEH, HEH, HEH.
YOU CAN'T RUN AWAY.
KOUSAKA IS ONE OF US! IT'S IN HIS BLOOD.
HEH, HEH, HEH...

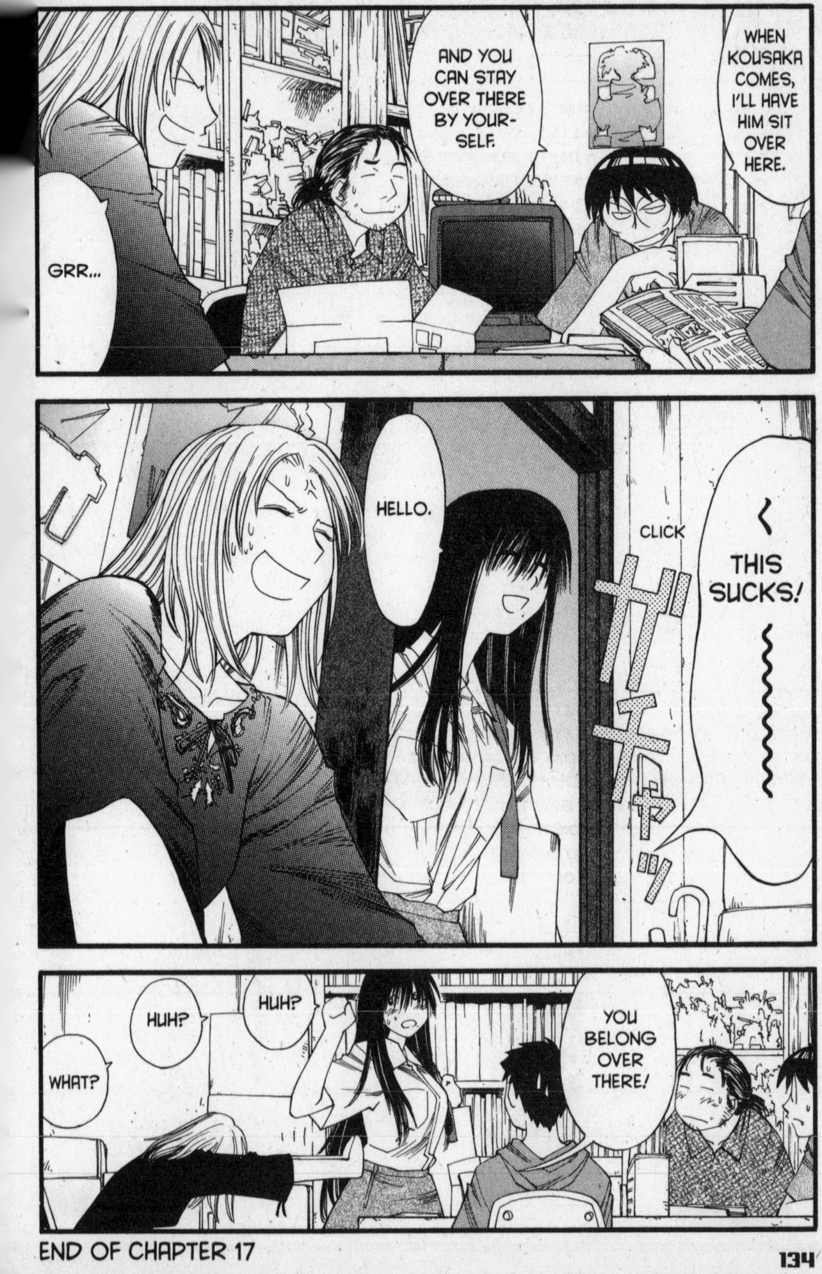

WHEN KOUSAKA COMES, I'LL HAVE HIM SIT OVER HERE.
AND YOU CAN STAY OVER THERE BY YOURSELF.
GRR...
THIS SUCKS!
CLICK
HELLO.
YOU BELONG OVER THERE!
HUH?
HUH?
WHAT?

END OF CHAPTER 17

5 TOKINO — DRUNK ON KOMAKI'S HOMEMADE APPLE CHEESE CAKE (WITH WAY TOO MUCH BRANDY IN IT)

WRITTEN BY TOSHIZO

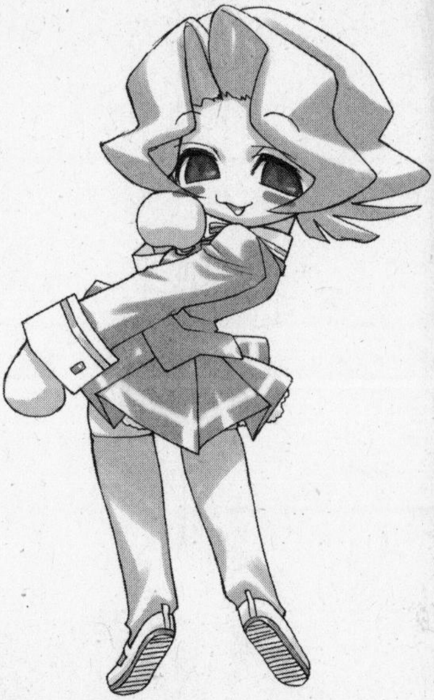

HOLD DOWN JUMP D, AND THEN PRESS THE SECOND D BUTTON WHILE STANDING, AND I'LL ROLL LIKE A STONE. HOLD THE JOY STICK DOWN, PRESS C, AND THEN HIT JUMP D AND I'LL GIVE YOU A KARATE CHOP YOU WON'T BELIEVE. HOLD THE JOY STICK DOWN WHILE PRESSING A AND DOING THE "TOGETHER" MOVE, AND MY OPPONENT DIES INSTANTLY. [TOSHIZO]

...HOW COULD YOU ONLY WRITE ABOUT THOSE TWO MOVES AND THE INSTANT DEATH MANEUVER? EVEN THOUGH TOKINO IS THE HEROINE, SHE IS SO SULTRY. THIS IS A HIDDEN CHARACTER IN THE GAME, ALSO KNOWN AS "THE OTHER SIDE OF TOKINO" OR "TOKINO THE CAT." AS YOU CAN TELL BY HER NAME, SHE'S DRUNK. I THINK IT'S FROM BOOK 2 (WHEN SHE GRABBED HOLD OF THE VICE PRESIDENT AND MADE HER PASS OUT...AHHH, THOSE WERE THE DAYS.)

"THE OTHER SIDE OF TOKINO" IS A COMPLETELY SEPARATE CHARACTER, AND ALL HER MOVES ARE TOTALLY DIFFERENT FROM THE REGULAR TOKINO CHARACTER. SHE MOVES WITH BEWILDERING SPEED AND EFFICIENCY, AND WHEN TOSHIZO USES HER, SHE'S UNSTOPPABLE. HER ATTACKS ARE EXTREMELY POWERFUL BUT SHE'S VERY WEAK WHEN IT COMES TO DEFENSE.

HER ROLLING STONE TECHNIQUE IS A HEAD- FIRST SLIDE. HER KNEELING TECHNIQUE ALLOWS HER TO PULL HER AIRBORNE OPPONENT TO THE GROUND. HER KARATE CHOP TECHNIQUE IS SIMPLY THAT, A KARATE CHOP. SHE CAN ATTACK WHILE MOVING, WHICH IS PRECISELY WHY SHE'S ABLE TO CARRY OUT THE ATTACKS MENTIONED ABOVE. SHE CAN ALSO DO A LOOP MOVE, BUT SINCE TOSHIZO CARES A GREAT DEAL ABOUT HOW HER MOVES LOOK, HE USUALLY FINISHES WITH THE "TOGETHER" MOVE. OH YEAH, "TOGETHER" IS HER SPECIAL THROW. THE "PISTON BLOCK UPPER" IS....WELL...YOU KNOW HOW IN SUXXR MXXIO BRXXHERS YOU GET EXTRA GOLD COINS AFTER YOU HIT THE CEILING? JUST LIKE THAT, IF YOU HIT THE BUTTONS WITH THE RIGHT TIMING, YOU CAN GET MORE PUNCHES IN. WHEN YOUR OPPONENT IS ON THE GROUND, YOU CAN ONLY LAND ONE PUNCH, SO USE THIS TECHNIQUE ONLY WHEN AIRBORNE.

...ANYWAY, TOSHIZO IS THE ONLY ONE IN THE GENSHIKEN WHO REALLY KNOWS

HOW TO USE "THE OTHER SIDE OF TOKINO." IT'S TOTALLY AGAINST THE RULES. [PIT VIPER]

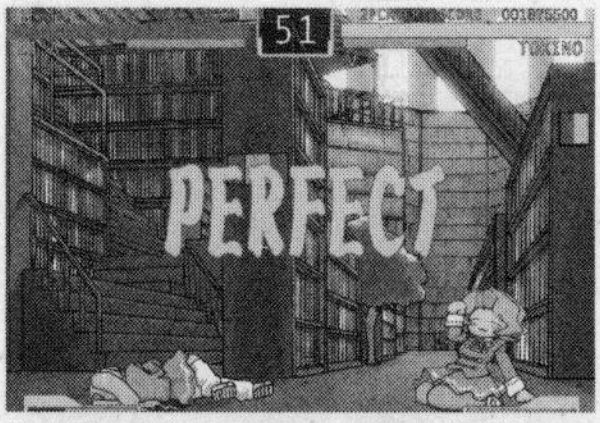
51
TOKINO
PERFECT

SHE'S TOO POWERFUL... [PIT VIPER]

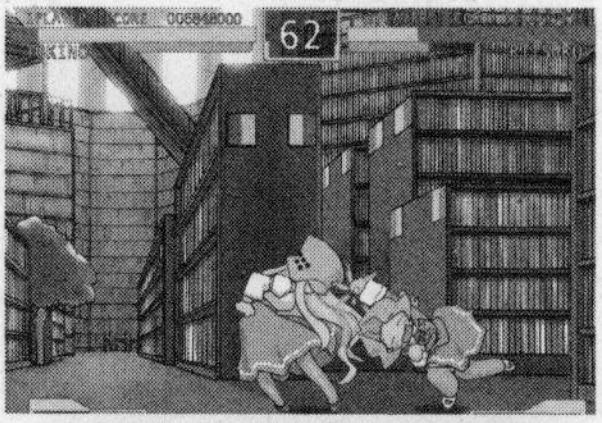
62

IT ALMOST LOOKS LIKE THE "DRUNKEN MONKEY" TECHNIQUE. [PIT VIPER]

NO, AT LEAST THREE PER STORY . . .

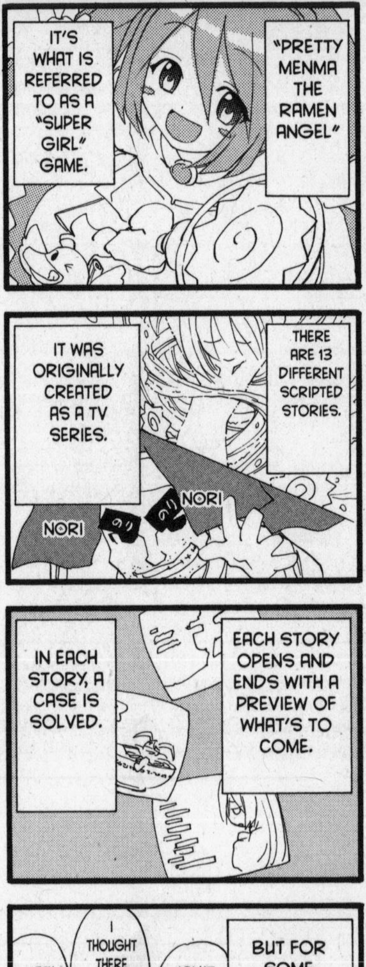
"PRETTY MENMA THE RAMEN ANGEL"
IT'S WHAT IS REFERRED TO AS A "SUPER GIRL" GAME.
THERE ARE 13 DIFFERENT SCRIPTED STORIES.
IT WAS ORIGINALLY CREATED AS A TV SERIES.
NORI
NORI
EACH STORY OPENS AND ENDS WITH A PREVIEW OF WHAT'S TO COME.
IN EACH STORY, A CASE IS SOLVED.
BUT FOR SOME REASON, THERE AREN'T TOO MANY SEX SCENES.
ISN'T THAT WEIRD?
I THOUGHT THERE WOULD BE TONS OF THEM.
YEAH, AT LEAST ONE PER STORY...

STRAIGHT PORN . . . OR GAY PORN

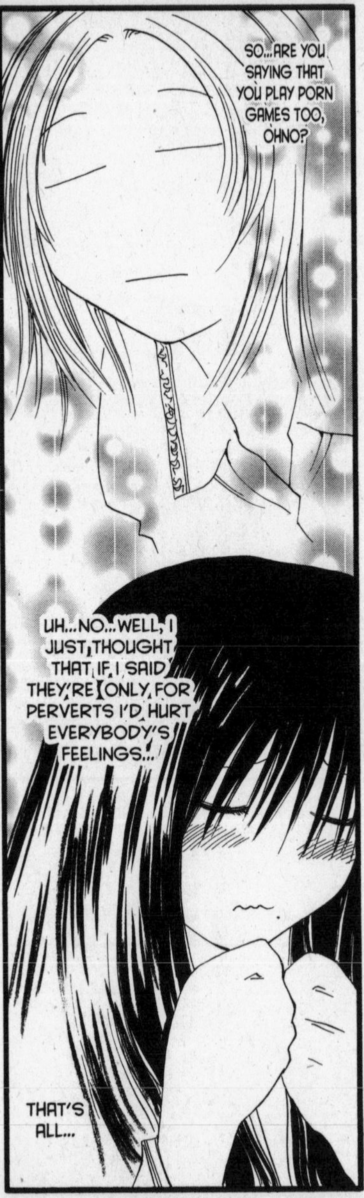
SO...ARE YOU SAYING THAT YOU PLAY PORN GAMES TOO, OHNO?
UH...NO...WELL, I JUST THOUGHT THAT IF I SAID THEY'RE ONLY FOR PERVERTS I'D HURT EVERYBODY'S FEELINGS...
THAT'S ALL...

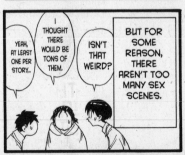

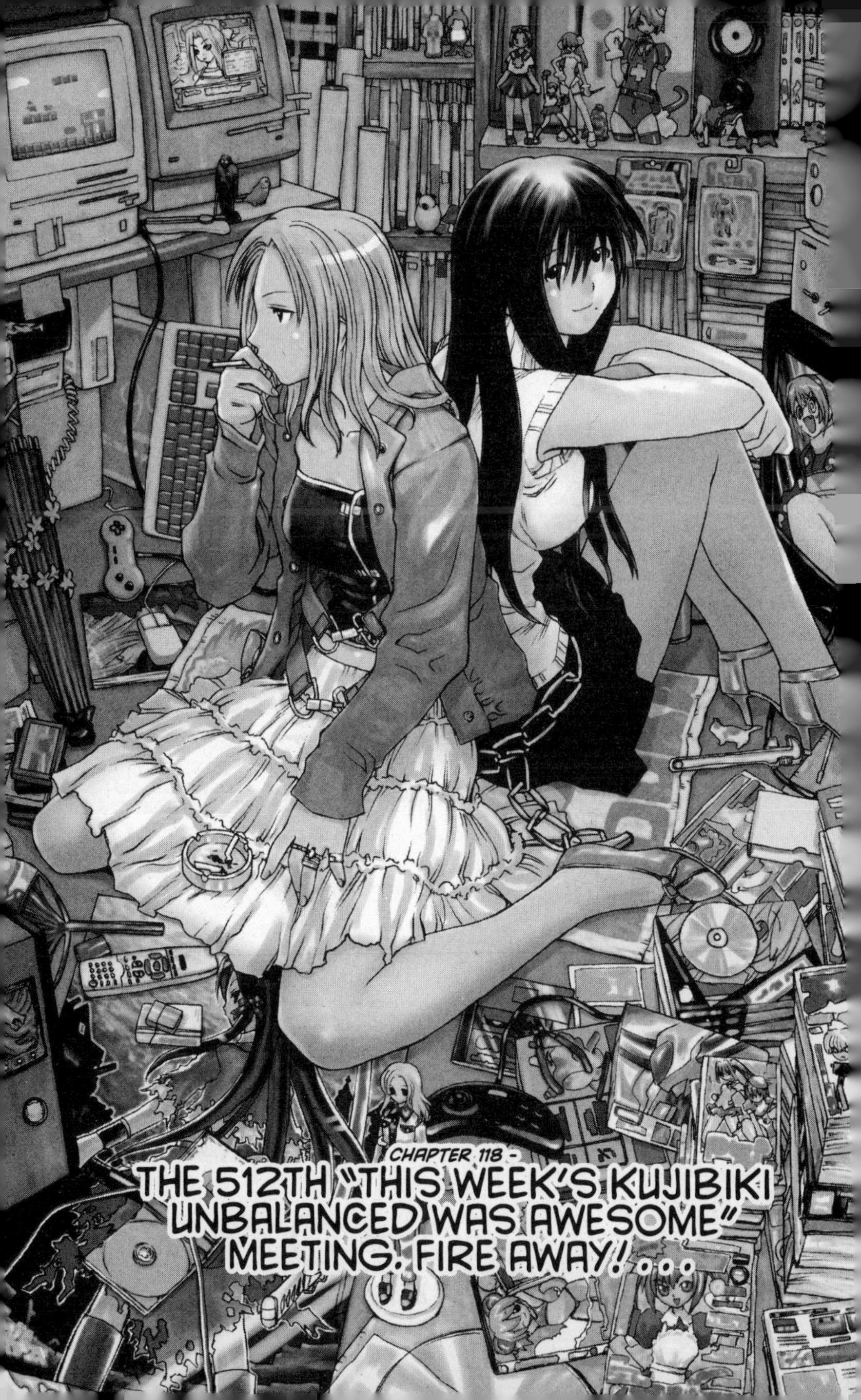
CHAPTER 118 -
THE 512TH "THIS WEEK'S KUJIBIKI UNBALANCED WAS AWESOME" MEETING. FIRE AWAY! . . .

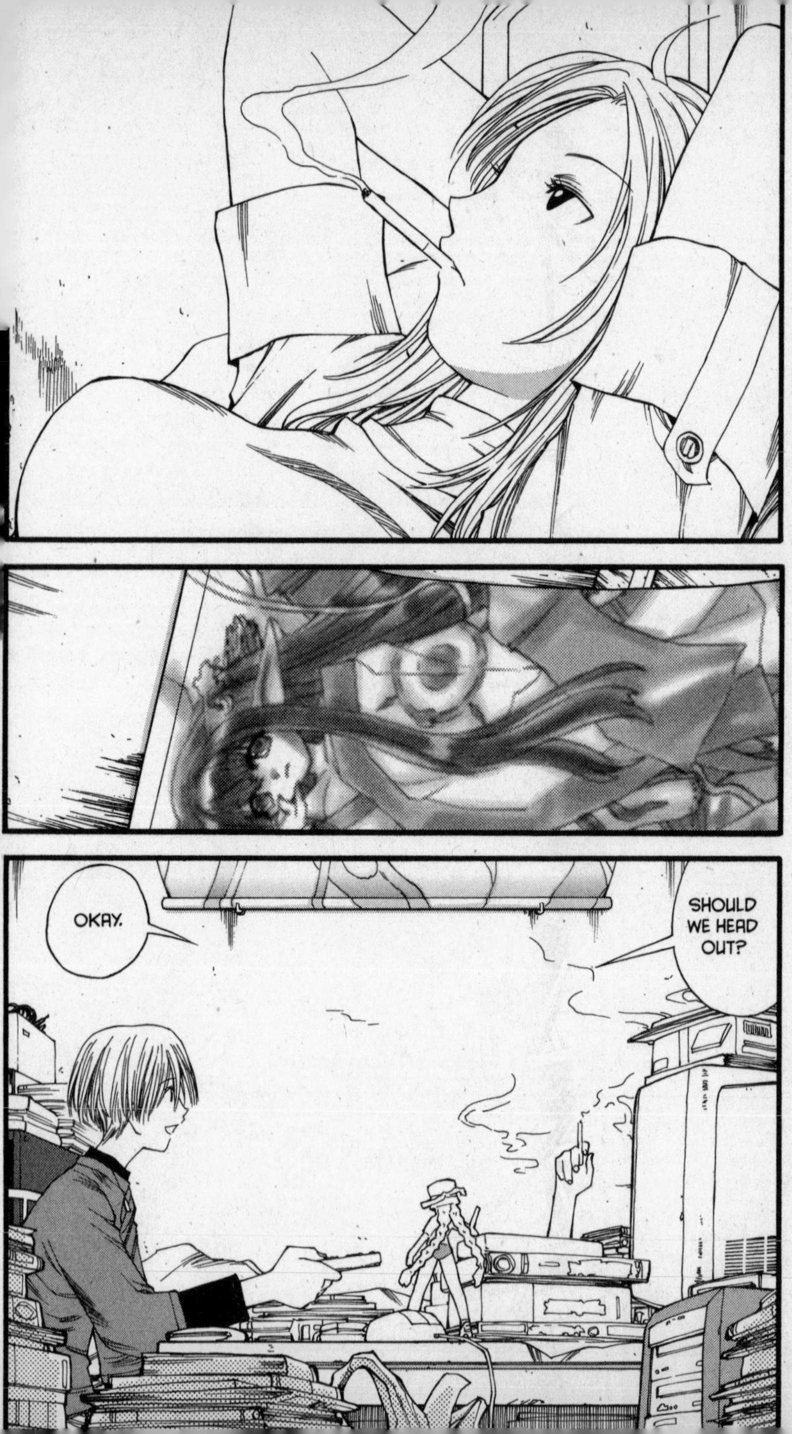
SHOULD WE HEAD OUT?
OKAY.

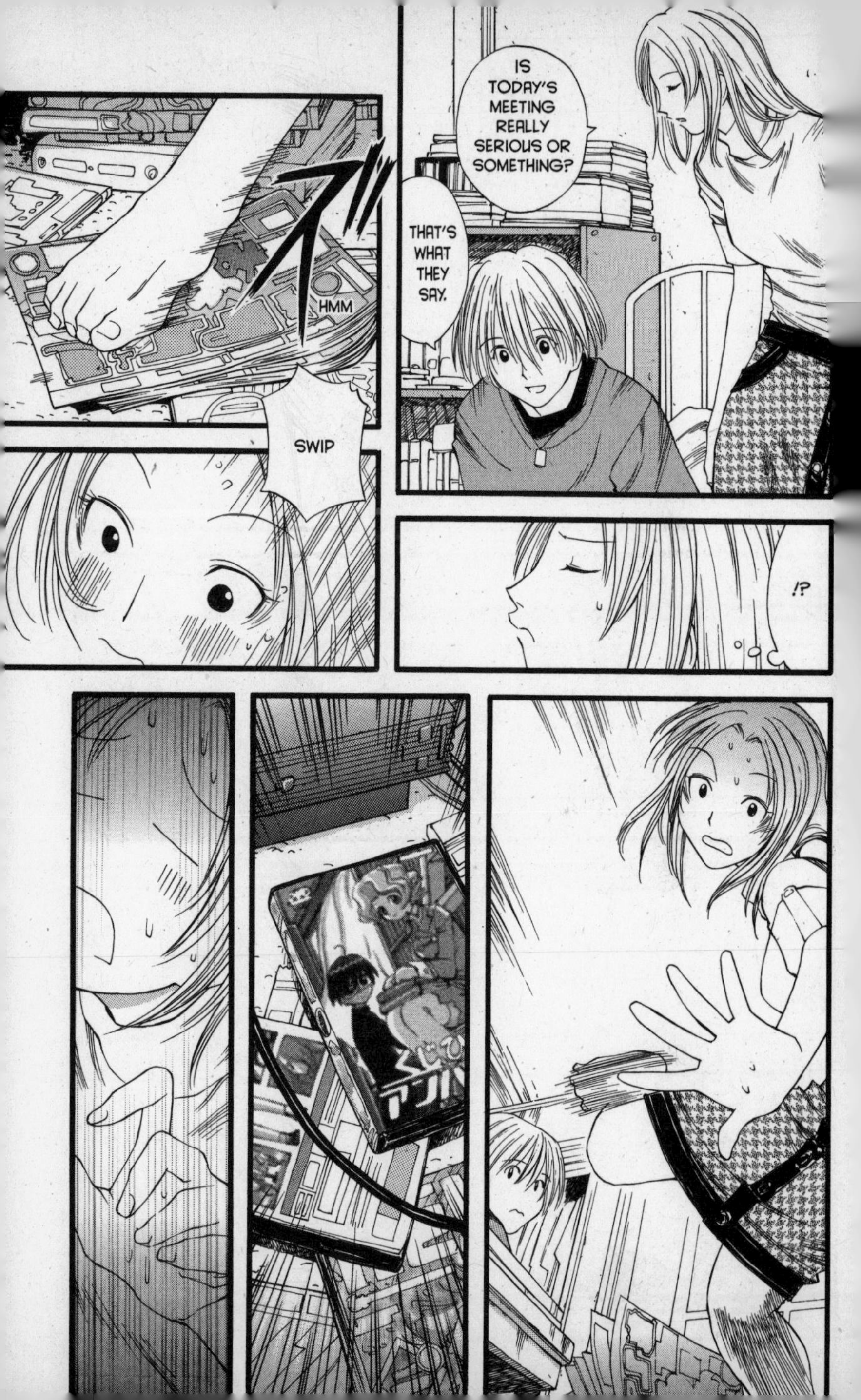
IS TODAY'S MEETING REALLY SERIOUS OR SOMETHING?
THAT'S WHAT THEY SAY.
HMM
SWIP
!?

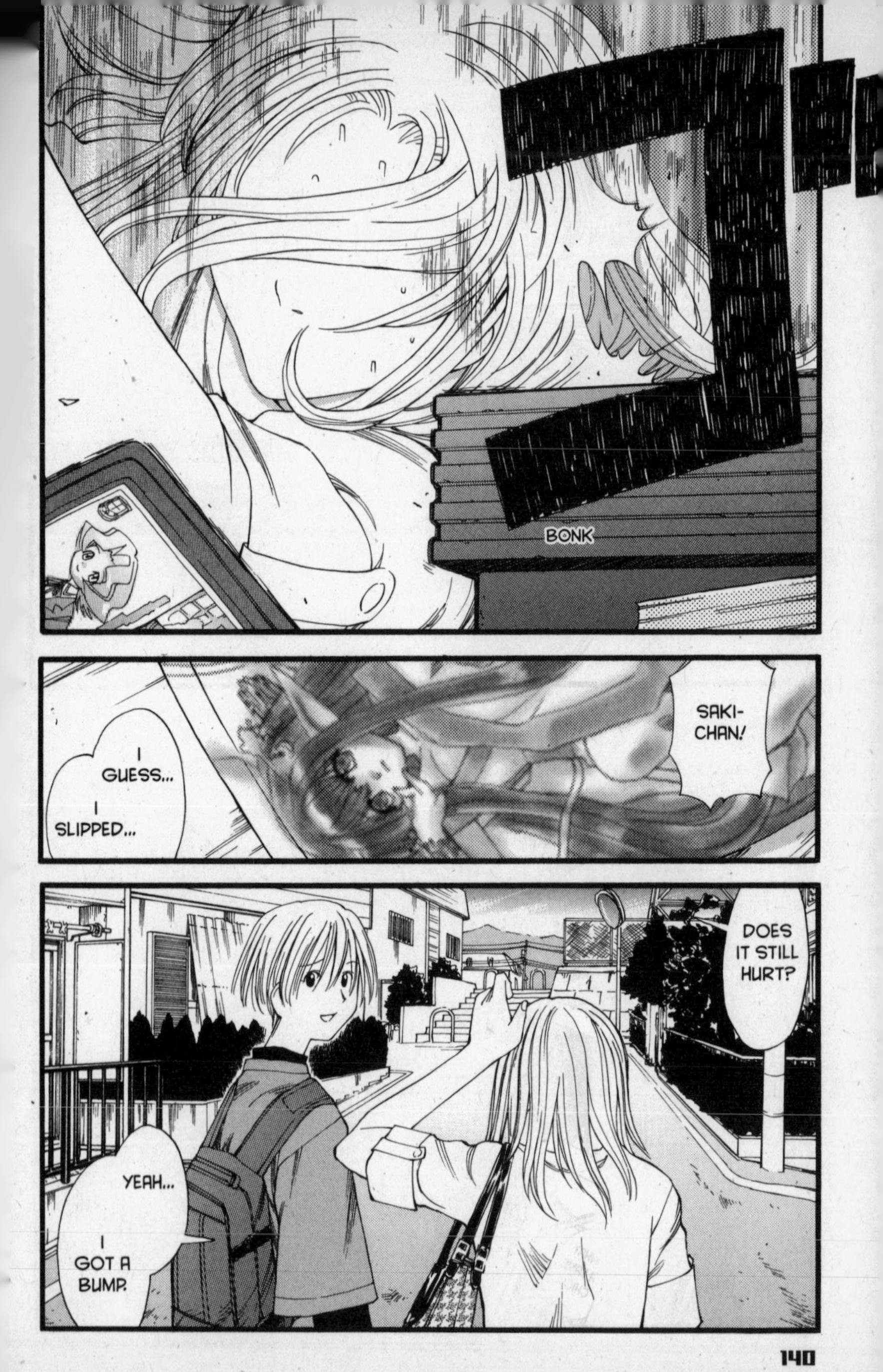
BONK
SAKI-CHAN!
I GUESS... I SLIPPED...
DOES IT STILL HURT?
YEAH... I GOT A BUMP.

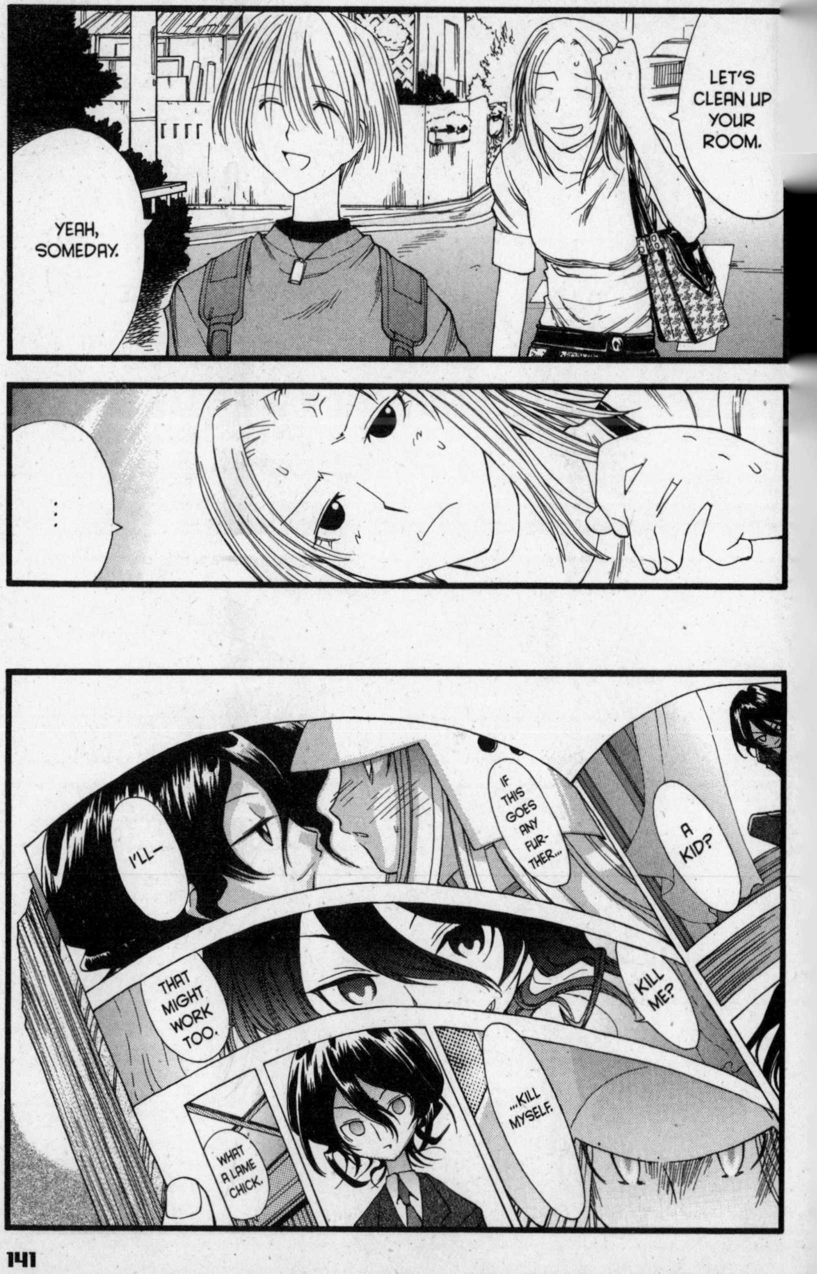
LET'S CLEAN UP YOUR ROOM.
YEAH, SOMEDAY.
...
A KID?
IF THIS GOES ANY FURTHER...
I'LL–
KILL ME?
THAT MIGHT WORK TOO.
...KILL MYSELF.
WHAT A LAME CHICK.

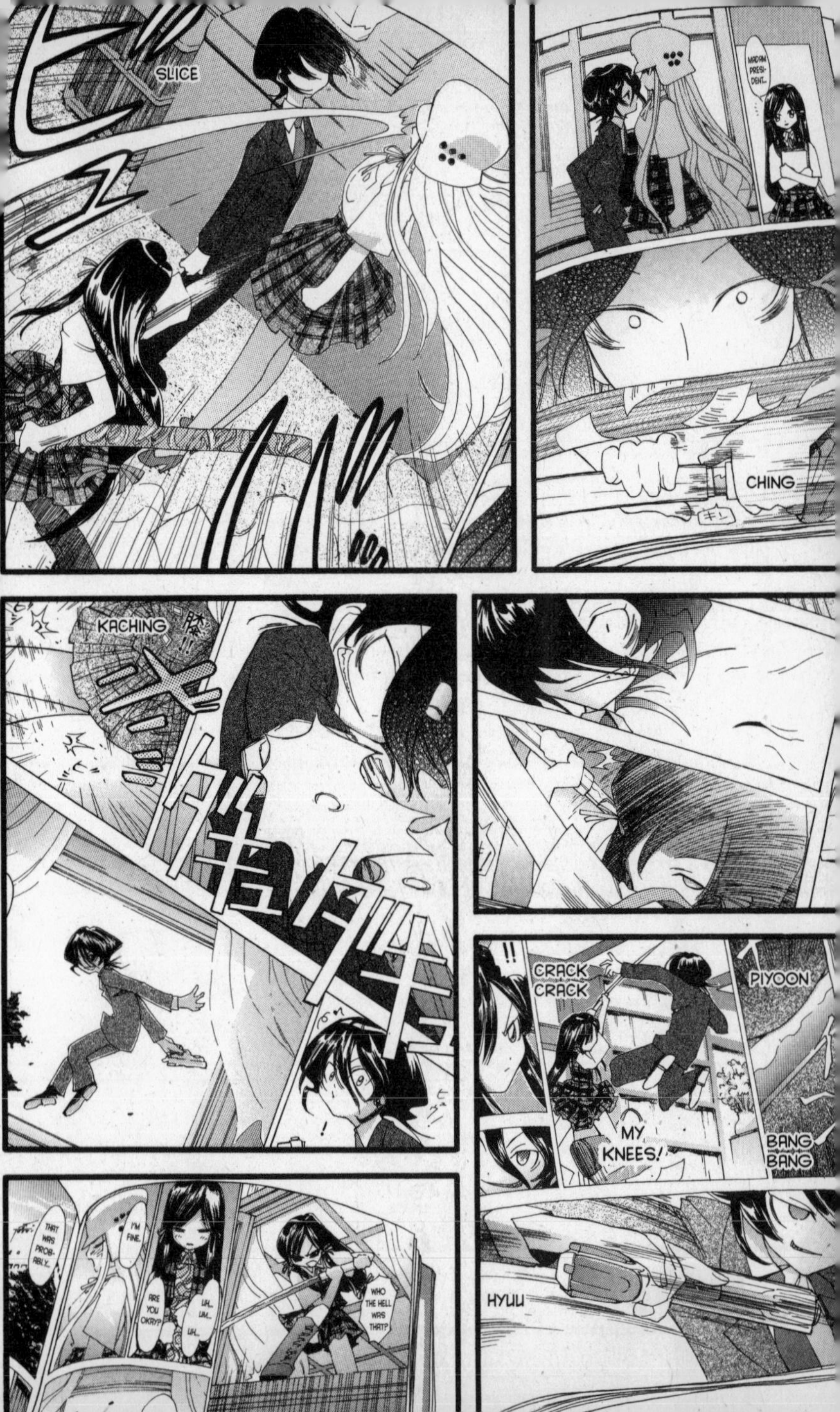
MADAM PRESIDENT...
CHING
SLICE
PIYOON
CRACK CRACK
BANG BANG
MY KNEES!
HYUU
KACHING
WHO THE HELL WAS THAT?
UH... UM... UH...
I'M FINE.
ARE YOU OKAY?
THAT WAS PROBABLY...

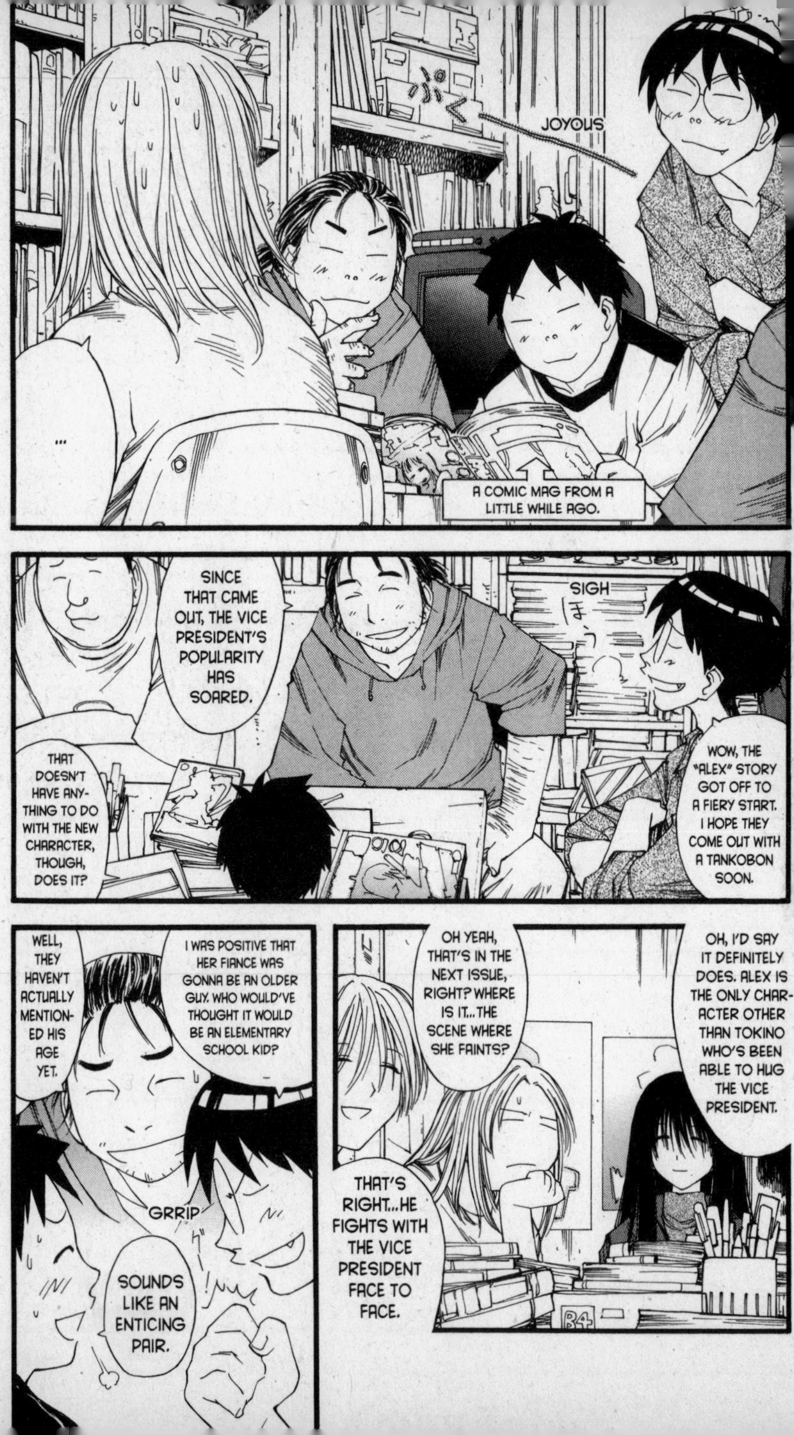
JOYOUS
A COMIC MAG FROM A LITTLE WHILE AGO.
...
SIGH
WOW, THE "ALEX" STORY GOT OFF TO A FIERY START. I HOPE THEY COME OUT WITH A TANKOBON SOON.
SINCE THAT CAME OUT, THE VICE PRESIDENT'S POPULARITY HAS SOARED.
THAT DOESN'T HAVE ANY-THING TO DO WITH THE NEW CHARACTER, THOUGH, DOES IT?
OH, I'D SAY IT DEFINITELY DOES. ALEX IS THE ONLY CHAR-ACTER OTHER THAN TOKINO WHO'S BEEN ABLE TO HUG THE VICE PRESIDENT.
OH YEAH, THAT'S IN THE NEXT ISSUE, RIGHT? WHERE IS IT... THE SCENE WHERE SHE FAINTS?
THAT'S RIGHT...HE FIGHTS WITH THE VICE PRESIDENT FACE TO FACE.
I WAS POSITIVE THAT HER FIANCE WAS GONNA BE AN OLDER GUY. WHO WOULD'VE THOUGHT IT WOULD BE AN ELEMENTARY SCHOOL KID?
WELL, THEY HAVEN'T ACTUALLY MENTION-ED HIS AGE YET.
GRRIP
SOUNDS LIKE AN ENTICING PAIR.

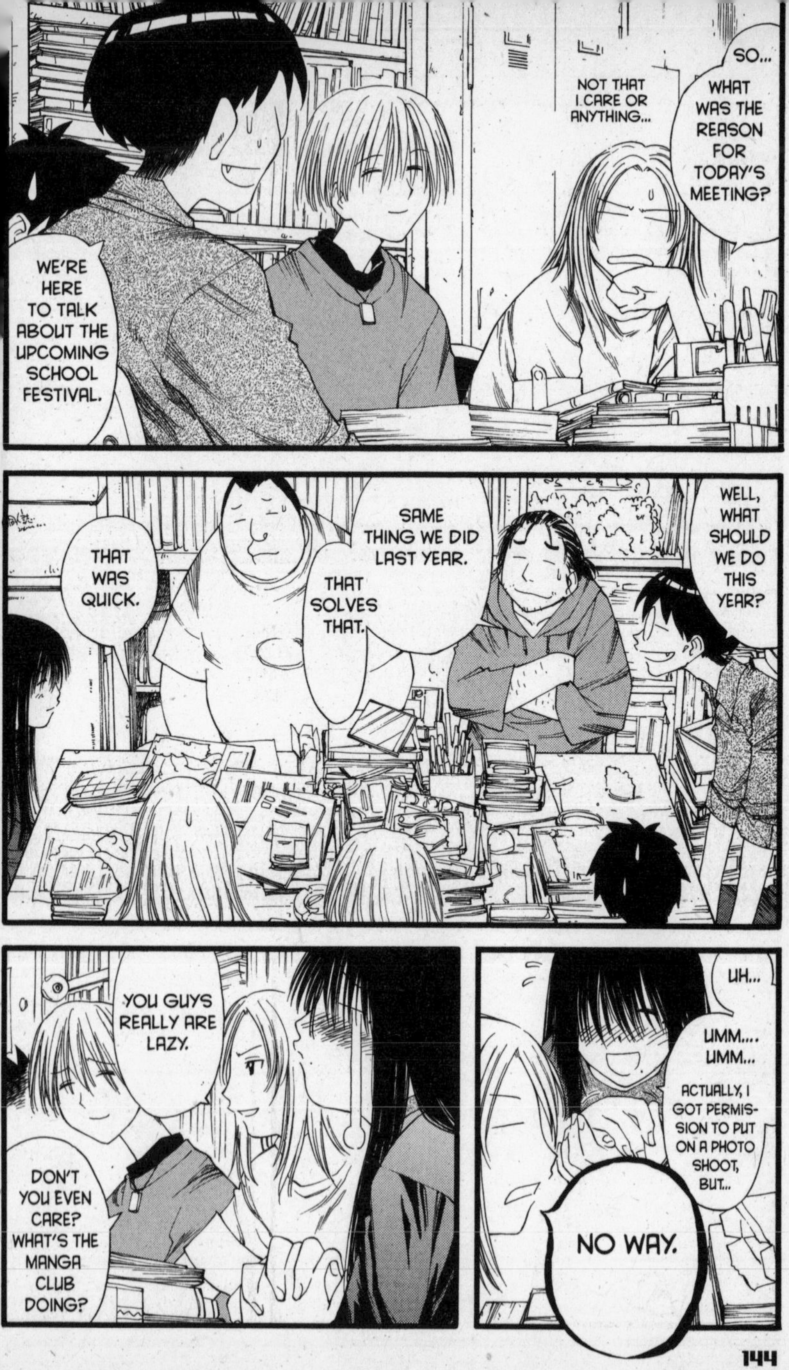
SO... WHAT WAS THE REASON FOR TODAY'S MEETING?
NOT THAT I CARE OR ANYTHING...
WE'RE HERE TO TALK ABOUT THE UPCOMING SCHOOL FESTIVAL.
WELL, WHAT SHOULD WE DO THIS YEAR?
SAME THING WE DID LAST YEAR.
THAT SOLVES THAT.
THAT WAS QUICK.
UH...
UMM.... UMM...
ACTUALLY, I GOT PERMIS-SION TO PUT ON A PHOTO SHOOT, BUT...
NO WAY.
YOU GUYS REALLY ARE LAZY.
DON'T YOU EVEN CARE? WHAT'S THE MANGA CLUB DOING?

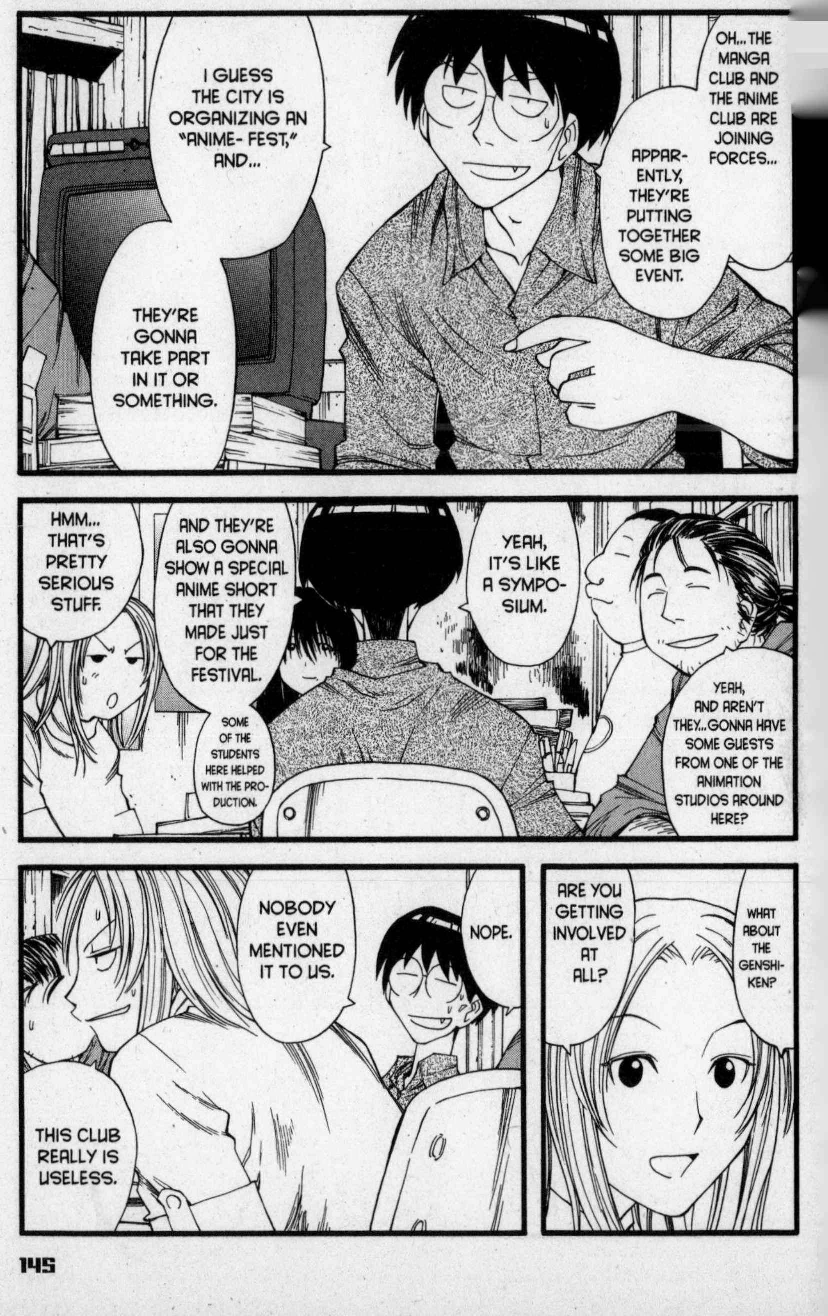
OH...THE MANGA CLUB AND THE ANIME CLUB ARE JOINING FORCES...
APPARENTLY, THEY'RE PUTTING TOGETHER SOME BIG EVENT.
I GUESS THE CITY IS ORGANIZING AN "ANIME- FEST," AND...
THEY'RE GONNA TAKE PART IN IT OR SOMETHING.
YEAH, IT'S LIKE A SYMPOSIUM.
YEAH, AND AREN'T THEY...GONNA HAVE SOME GUESTS FROM ONE OF THE ANIMATION STUDIOS AROUND HERE?
AND THEY'RE ALSO GONNA SHOW A SPECIAL ANIME SHORT THAT THEY MADE JUST FOR THE FESTIVAL.
SOME OF THE STUDENTS HERE HELPED WITH THE PRODUCTION.
HMM... THAT'S PRETTY SERIOUS STUFF.
WHAT ABOUT THE GENSHIKEN?
ARE YOU GETTING INVOLVED AT ALL?
NOPE.
NOBODY EVEN MENTIONED IT TO US.
THIS CLUB REALLY IS USELESS.

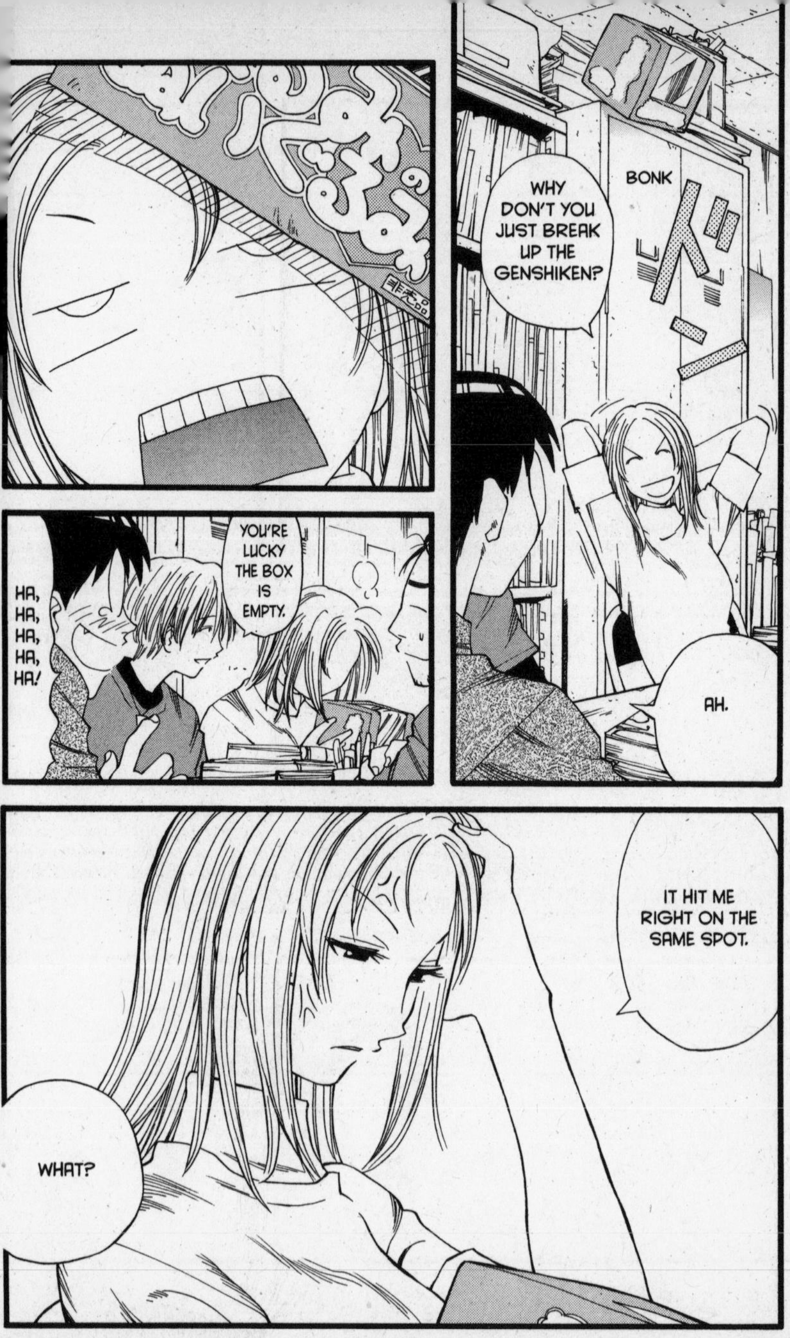
WHY DON'T YOU JUST BREAK UP THE GENSHIKEN?
BONK
AH.
YOU'RE LUCKY THE BOX IS EMPTY.
HA, HA, HA, HA, HA!
IT HIT ME RIGHT ON THE SAME SPOT.
WHAT?

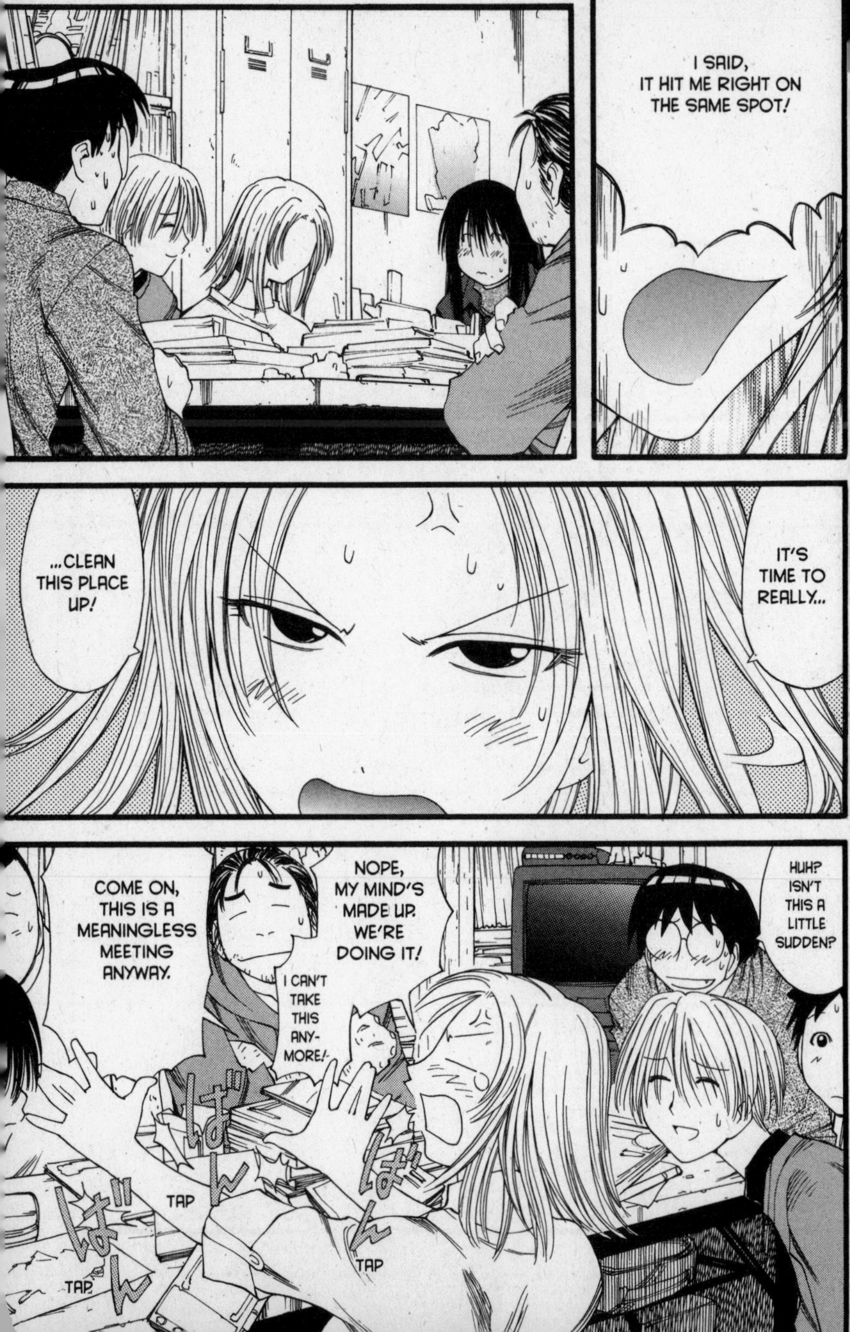
I SAID, IT HIT ME RIGHT ON THE SAME SPOT!
IT'S TIME TO REALLY...
...CLEAN THIS PLACE UP!
HUH? ISN'T THIS A LITTLE SUDDEN?
NOPE, MY MIND'S MADE UP. WE'RE DOING IT!
COME ON, THIS IS A MEANINGLESS MEETING ANYWAY.
I CAN'T TAKE THIS ANY-MORE!
ばん
TAP
ばん
TAP
ばん
TAP

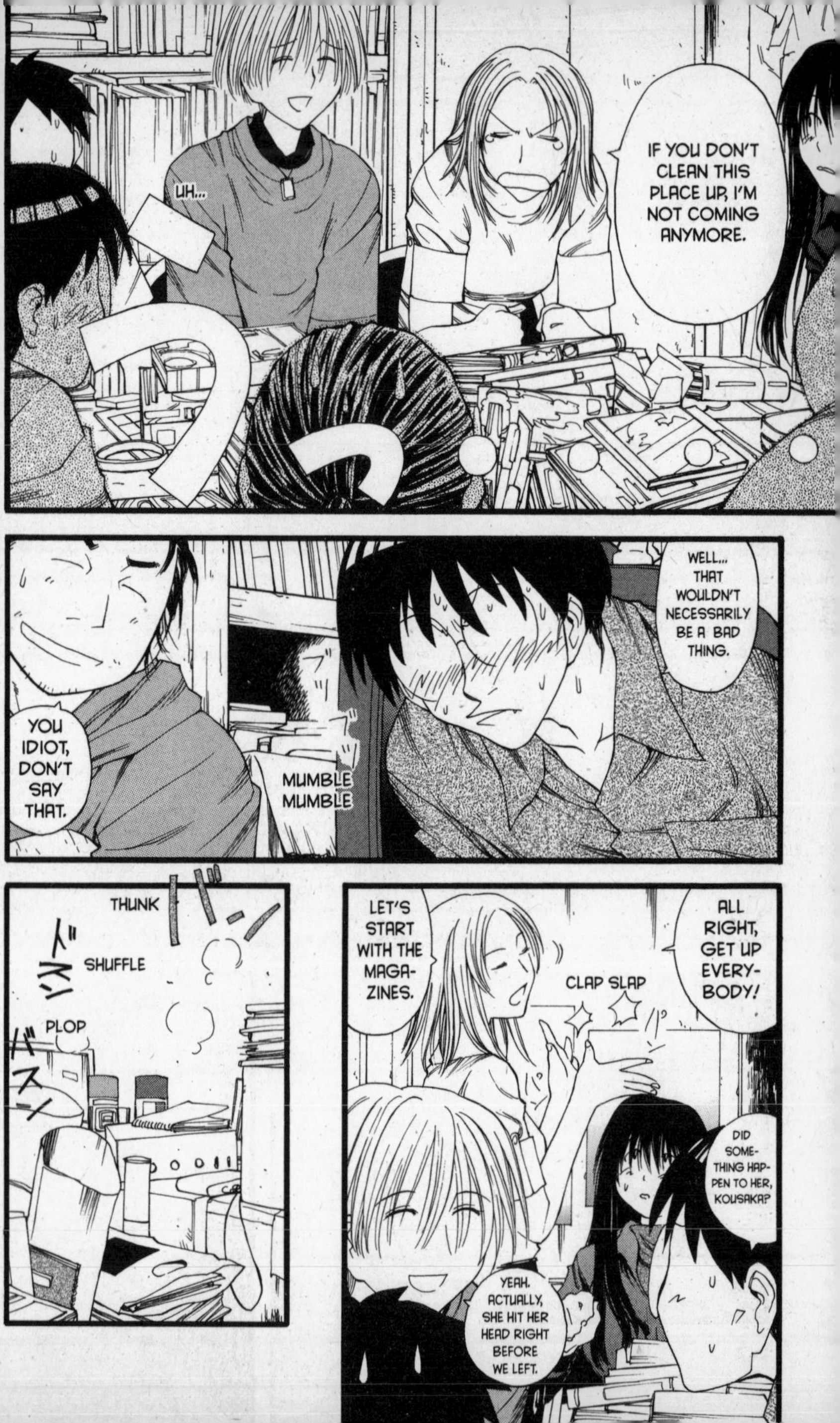
IF YOU DON'T CLEAN THIS PLACE UP, I'M NOT COMING ANYMORE.
UH...
WELL... THAT WOULDN'T NECESSARILY BE A BAD THING.
MUMBLE MUMBLE
YOU IDIOT, DON'T SAY THAT.
ALL RIGHT, GET UP EVERY-BODY!
CLAP SLAP
LET'S START WITH THE MAGA-ZINES.
DID SOME-THING HAP-PEN TO HER, KOUSAKA?
YEAH. ACTUALLY, SHE HIT HER HEAD RIGHT BEFORE WE LEFT.
THUNK
SHUFFLE
PLOP

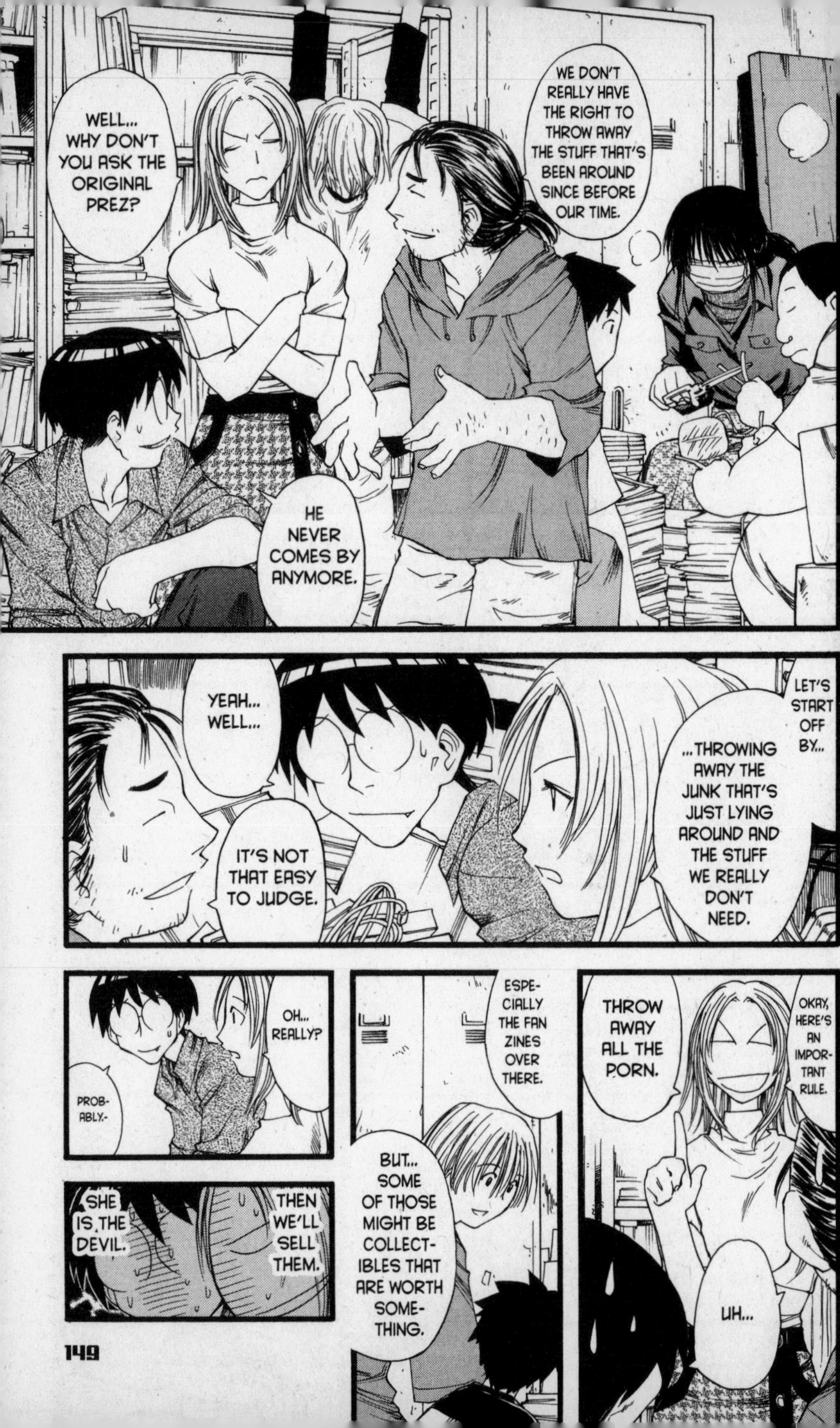
WE DON'T REALLY HAVE THE RIGHT TO THROW AWAY THE STUFF THAT'S BEEN AROUND SINCE BEFORE OUR TIME.
WELL... WHY DON'T YOU ASK THE ORIGINAL PREZ?
HE NEVER COMES BY ANYMORE.
LET'S START OFF BY...
...THROWING AWAY THE JUNK THAT'S JUST LYING AROUND AND THE STUFF WE REALLY DON'T NEED.
YEAH... WELL...
IT'S NOT THAT EASY TO JUDGE.
OKAY, HERE'S AN IMPORTANT RULE.
THROW AWAY ALL THE PORN.
UH...
ESPECIALLY THE FAN ZINES OVER THERE.
BUT... SOME OF THOSE MIGHT BE COLLECTIBLES THAT ARE WORTH SOMETHING.
OH... REALLY?
PROBABLY.-
THEN WE'LL SELL THEM.
SHE IS THE DEVIL.

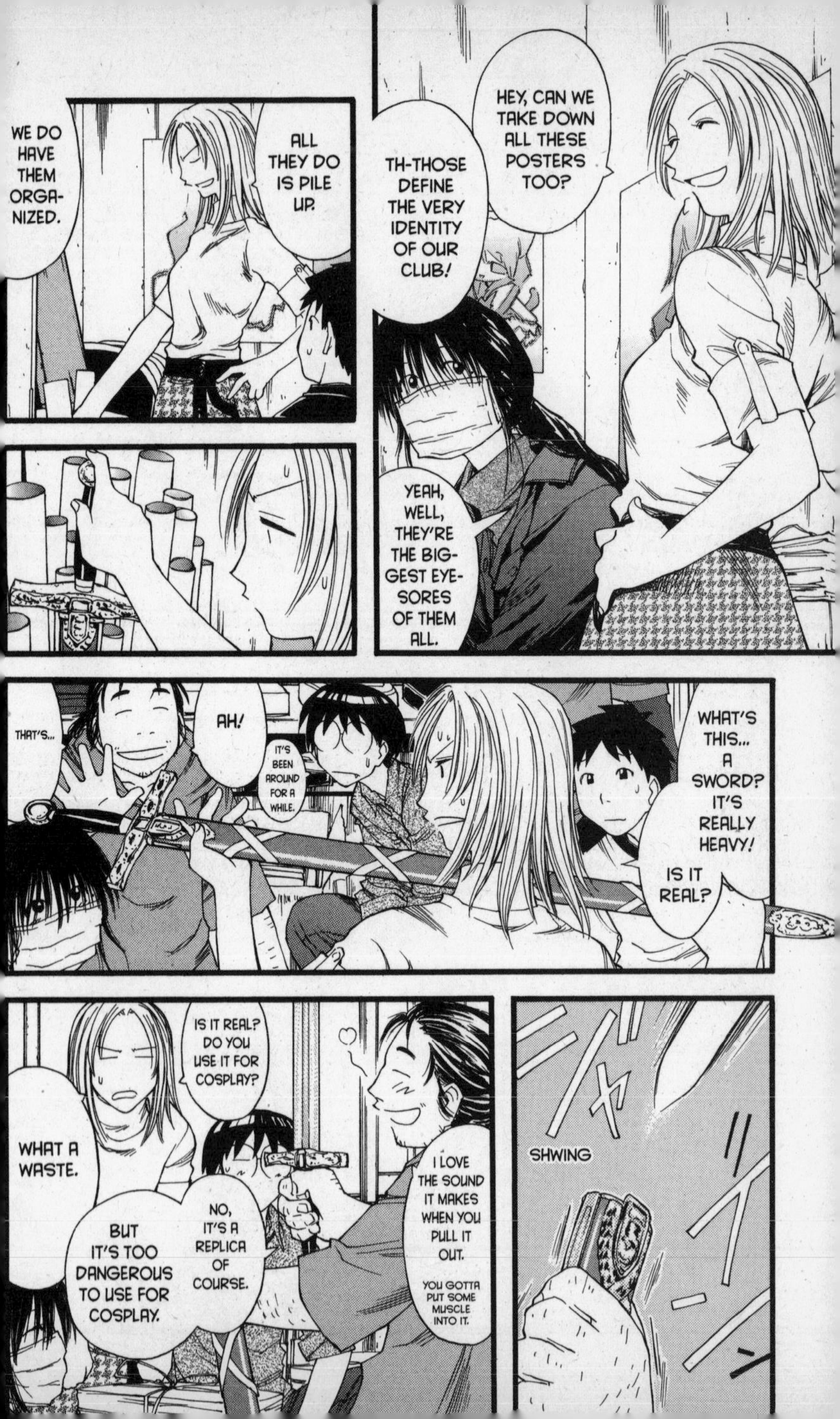
HEY, CAN WE TAKE DOWN ALL THESE POSTERS TOO?
TH-THOSE DEFINE THE VERY IDENTITY OF OUR CLUB!
YEAH, WELL, THEY'RE THE BIG-GEST EYE-SORES OF THEM ALL.
ALL THEY DO IS PILE UP.
WE DO HAVE THEM ORGA-NIZED.
WHAT'S THIS... A SWORD? IT'S REALLY HEAVY!
IS IT REAL?
AH!
IT'S BEEN AROUND FOR A WHILE.
THAT'S...
SHWING
I LOVE THE SOUND IT MAKES WHEN YOU PULL IT OUT.
YOU GOTTA PUT SOME MUSCLE INTO IT.
IS IT REAL? DO YOU USE IT FOR COSPLAY?
NO, IT'S A REPLICA OF COURSE.
BUT IT'S TOO DANGEROUS TO USE FOR COSPLAY.
WHAT A WASTE.

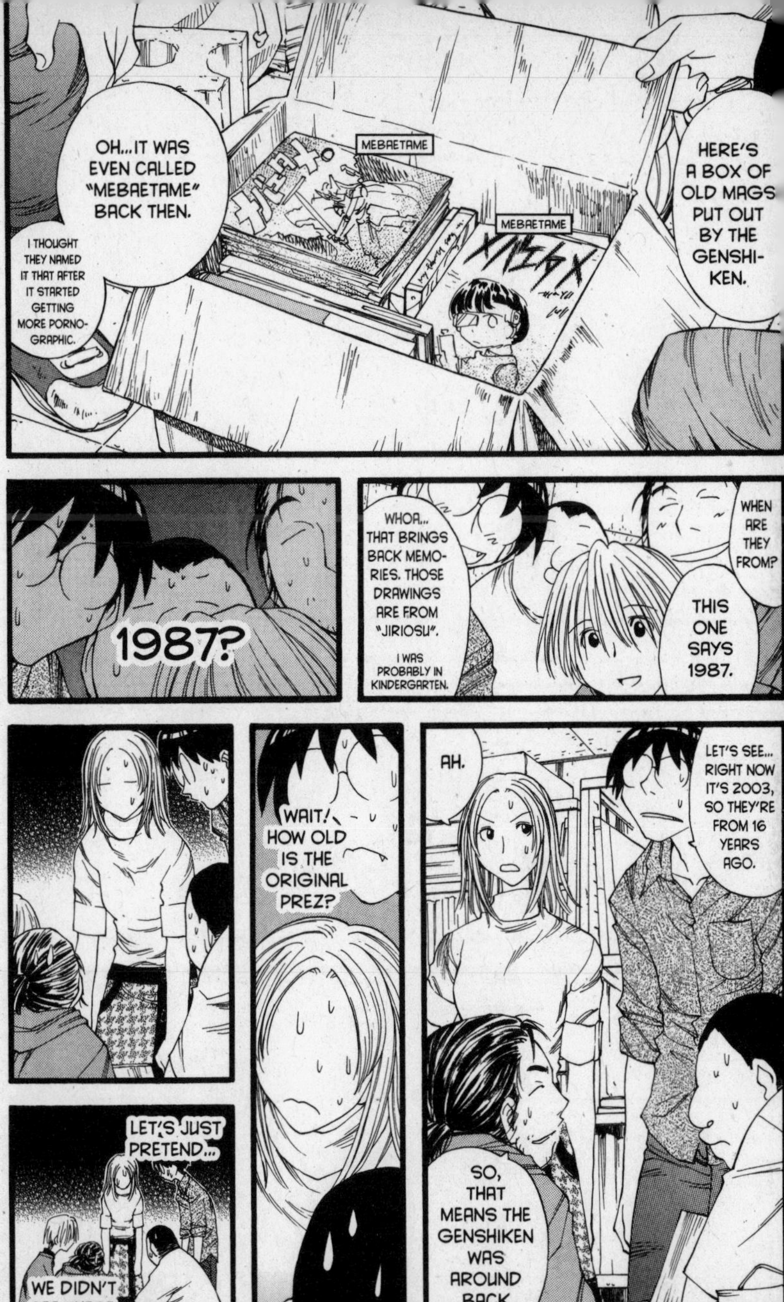
HERE'S A BOX OF OLD MAGS PUT OUT BY THE GENSHIKEN.
MEBAETAME
MEBAETAME
OH...IT WAS EVEN CALLED "MEBAETAME" BACK THEN.
I THOUGHT THEY NAMED IT THAT AFTER IT STARTED GETTING MORE PORNOGRAPHIC.
WHEN ARE THEY FROM?
THIS ONE SAYS 1987.
WHOA... THAT BRINGS BACK MEMORIES. THOSE DRAWINGS ARE FROM "JIRIOSU".
I WAS PROBABLY IN KINDERGARTEN.
1987?
LET'S SEE... RIGHT NOW IT'S 2003, SO THEY'RE FROM 16 YEARS AGO.
AH.
SO, THAT MEANS THE GENSHIKEN WAS AROUND BACK THEN.
WAIT! HOW OLD IS THE ORIGINAL PREZ?
LET'S JUST PRETEND...
WE DIDN'T SEE THESE.

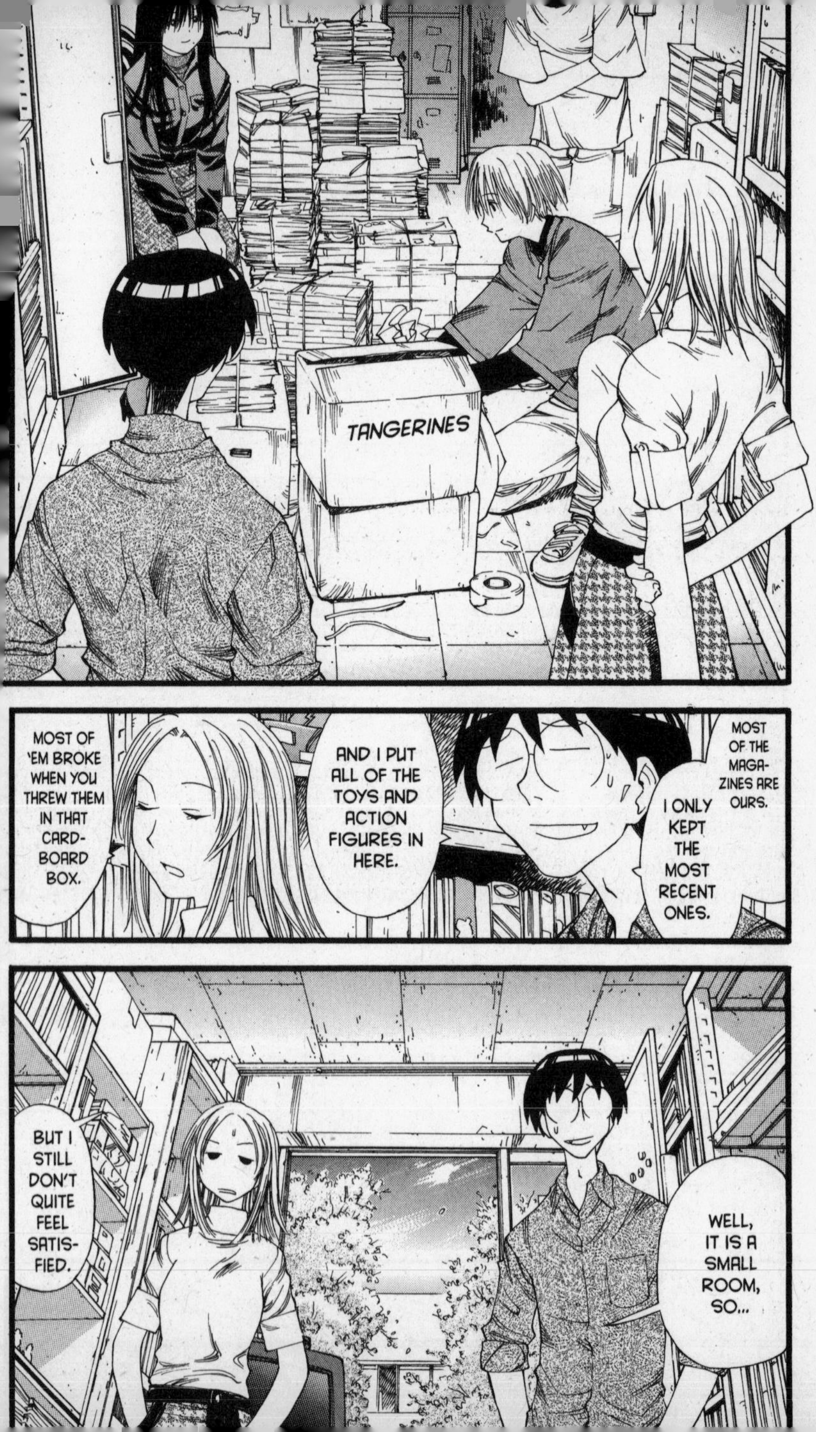
TANGERINES
MOST OF THE MAGAZINES ARE OURS.
I ONLY KEPT THE MOST RECENT ONES.
AND I PUT ALL OF THE TOYS AND ACTION FIGURES IN HERE.
MOST OF 'EM BROKE WHEN YOU THREW THEM IN THAT CARDBOARD BOX.
WELL, IT IS A SMALL ROOM, SO...
BUT I STILL DON'T QUITE FEEL SATISFIED.

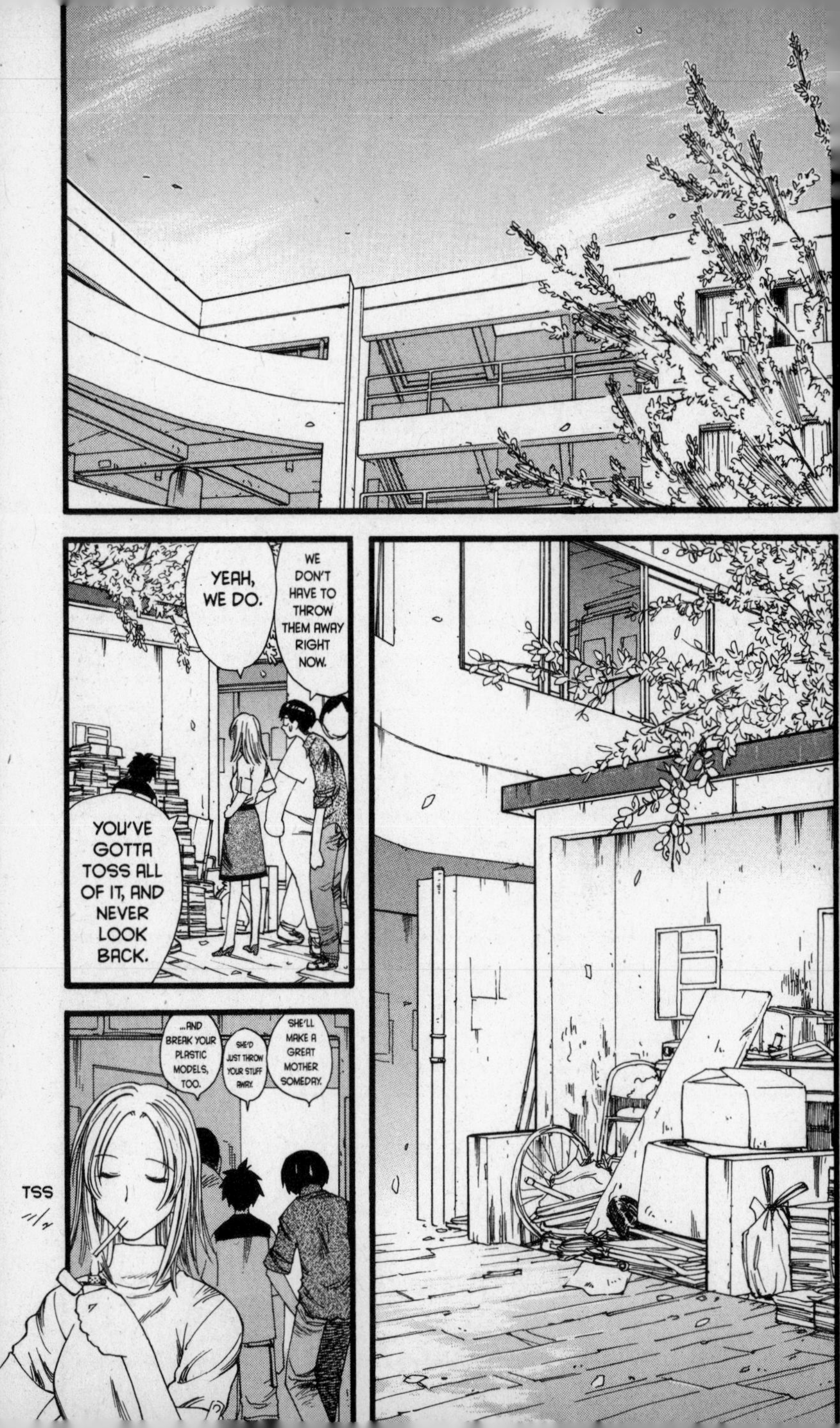
WE DON'T HAVE TO THROW THEM AWAY RIGHT NOW.
YEAH, WE DO.
YOU'VE GOTTA TOSS ALL OF IT, AND NEVER LOOK BACK.
SHE'LL MAKE A GREAT MOTHER SOMEDAY.
SHE'D JUST THROW YOUR STUFF AWAY.
...AND BREAK YOUR PLASTIC MODELS, TOO.
TSS

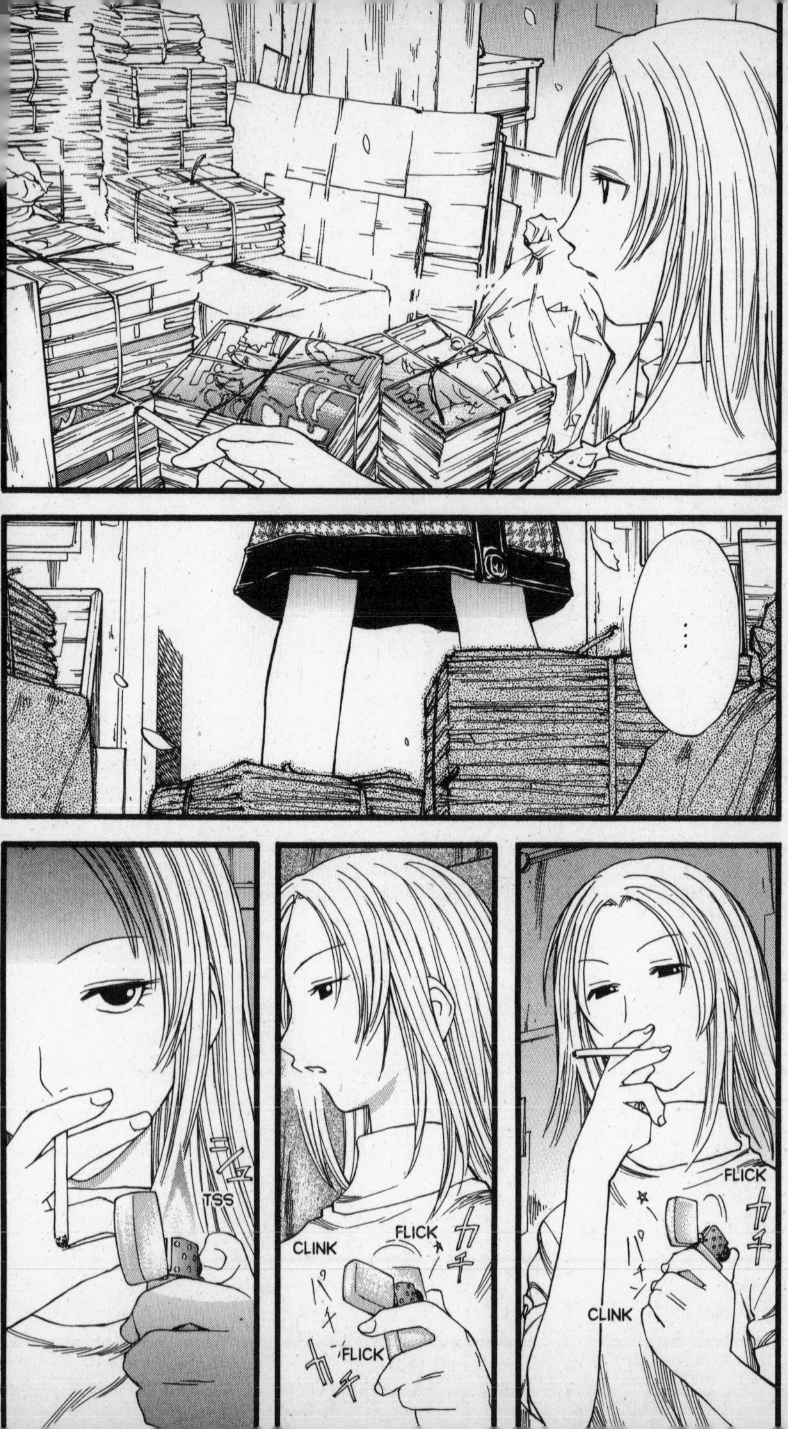
...
FLICK
CLINK
FLICK
CLINK
FLICK
TSS

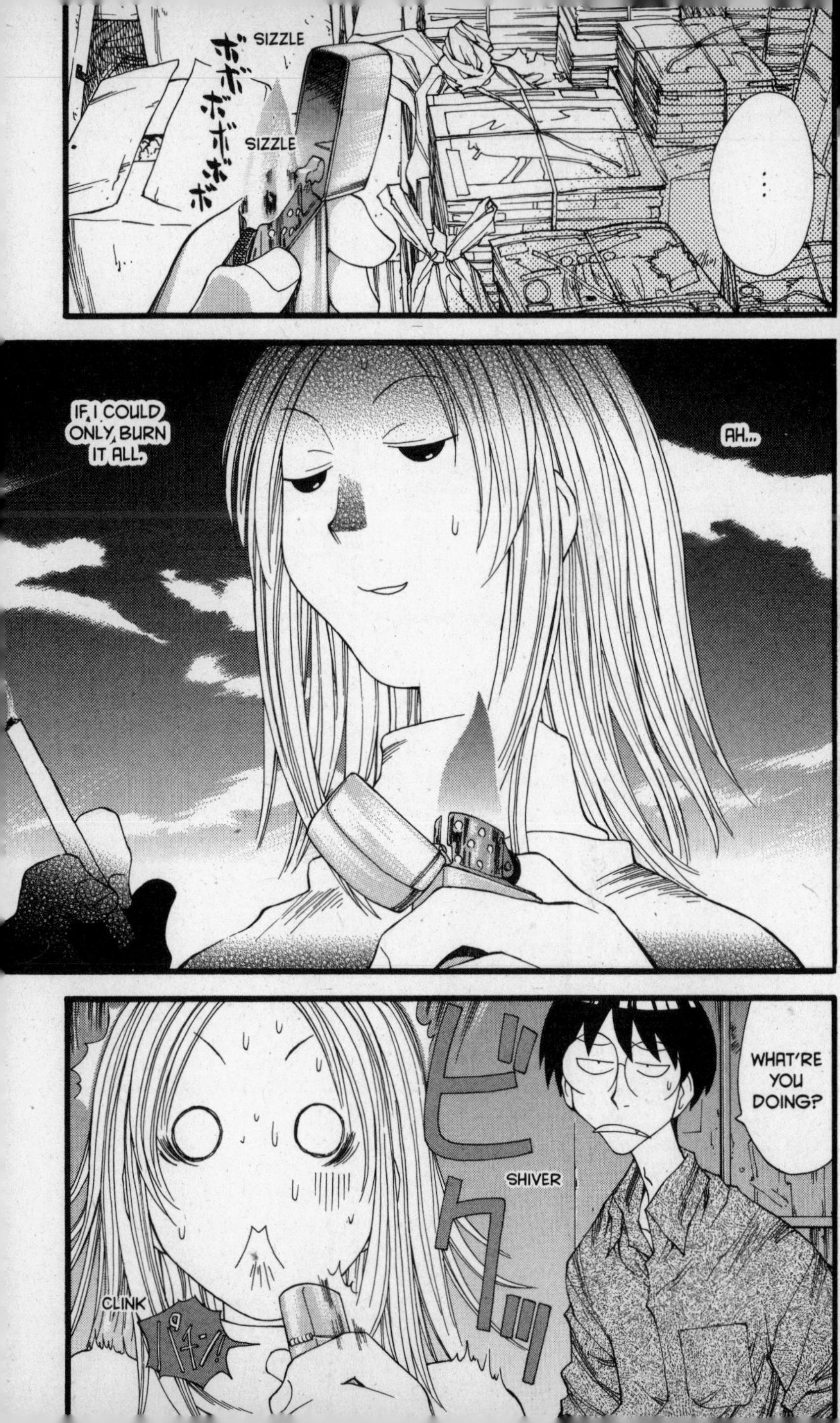
...
SIZZLE
SIZZLE
AH...
IF I COULD ONLY BURN IT ALL.
WHAT'RE YOU DOING?
SHIVER
CLINK

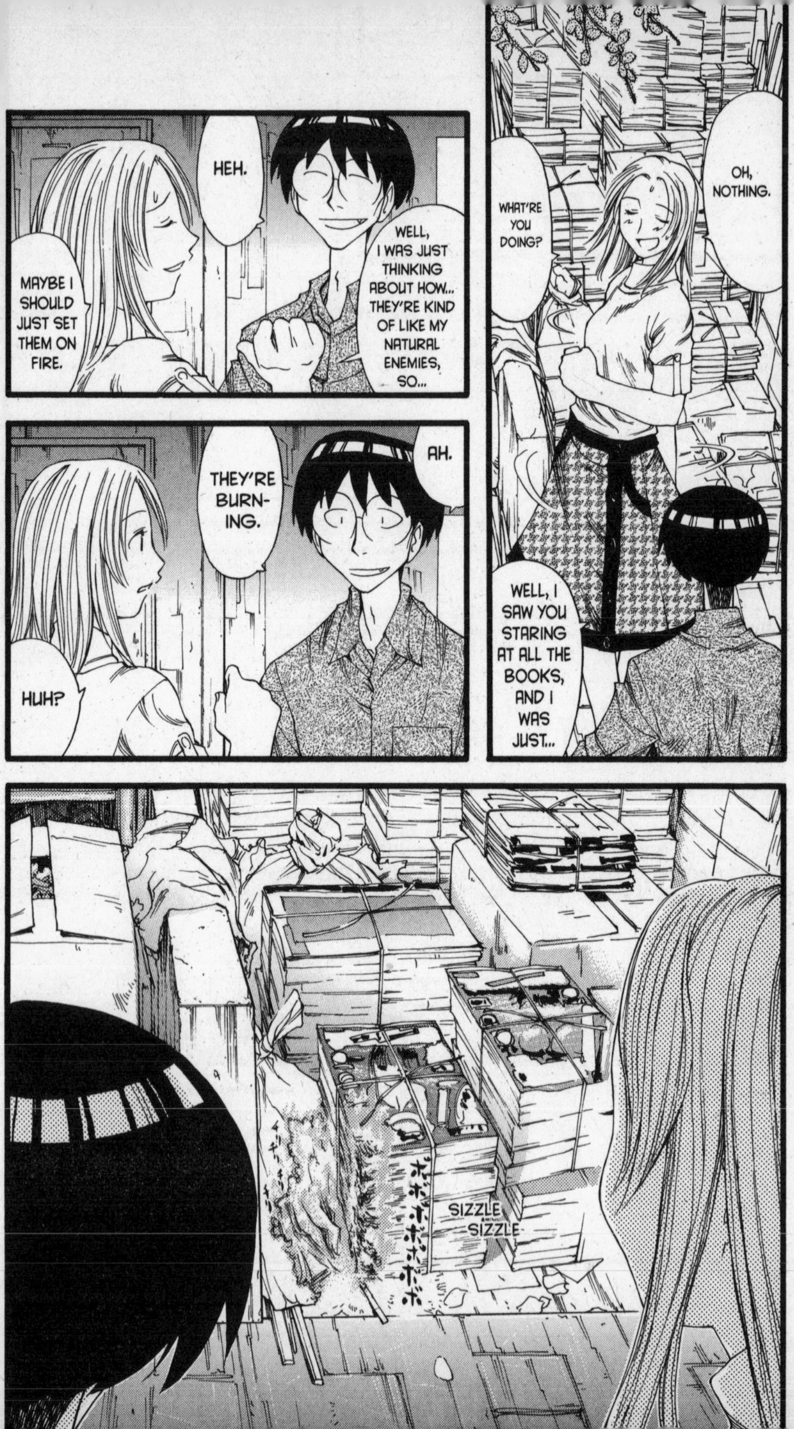
OH, NOTHING.
WHAT'RE YOU DOING?
WELL, I SAW YOU STARING AT ALL THE BOOKS, AND I WAS JUST...
WELL, I WAS JUST THINKING ABOUT HOW... THEY'RE KIND OF LIKE MY NATURAL ENEMIES, SO...
HEH.
MAYBE I SHOULD JUST SET THEM ON FIRE.
AH.
THEY'RE BURNING.
HUH?
SIZZLE SIZZLE

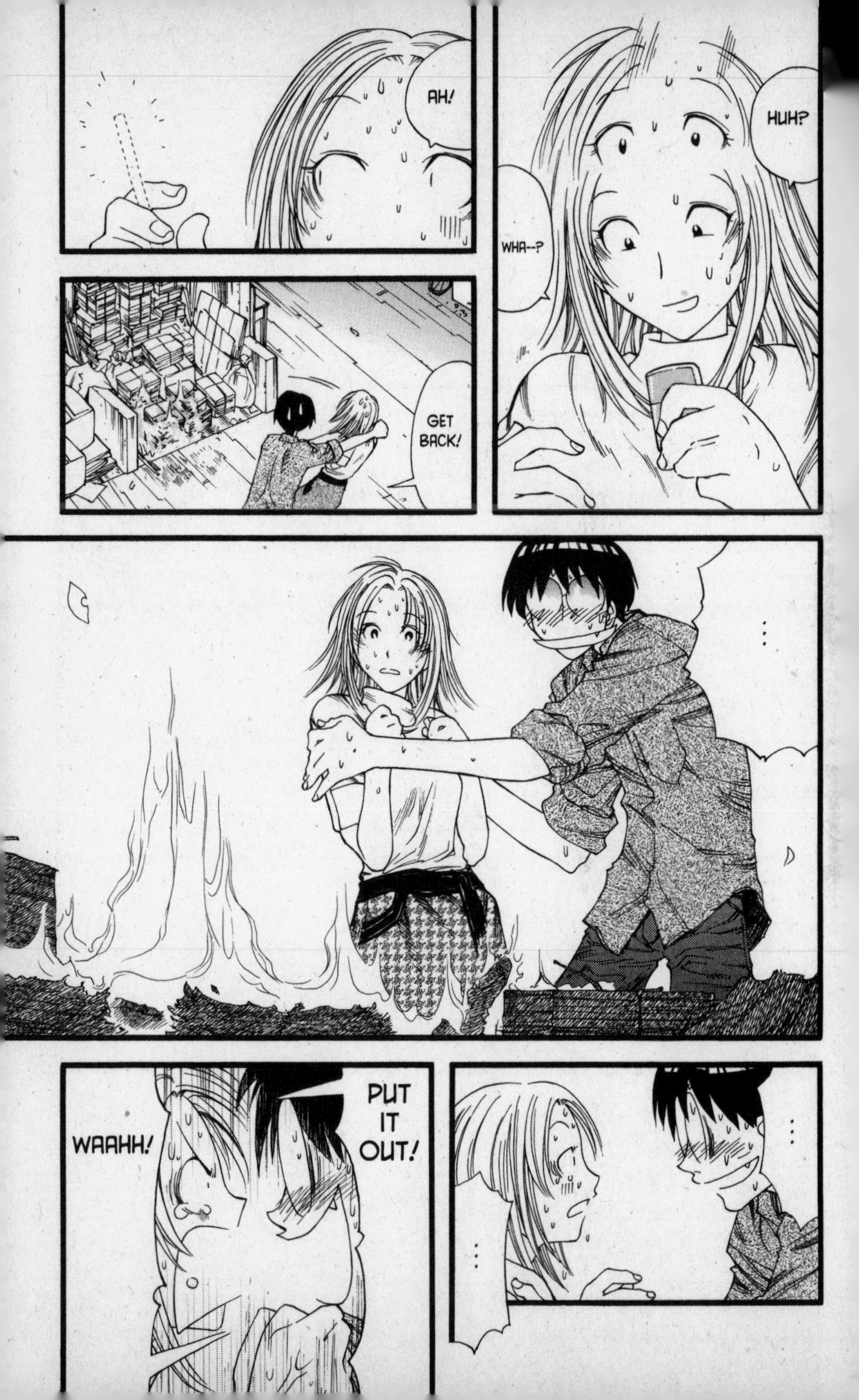
HUH?
WHA--?
AH!
GET BACK!
...
...
...
PUT IT OUT!
WAAHH!

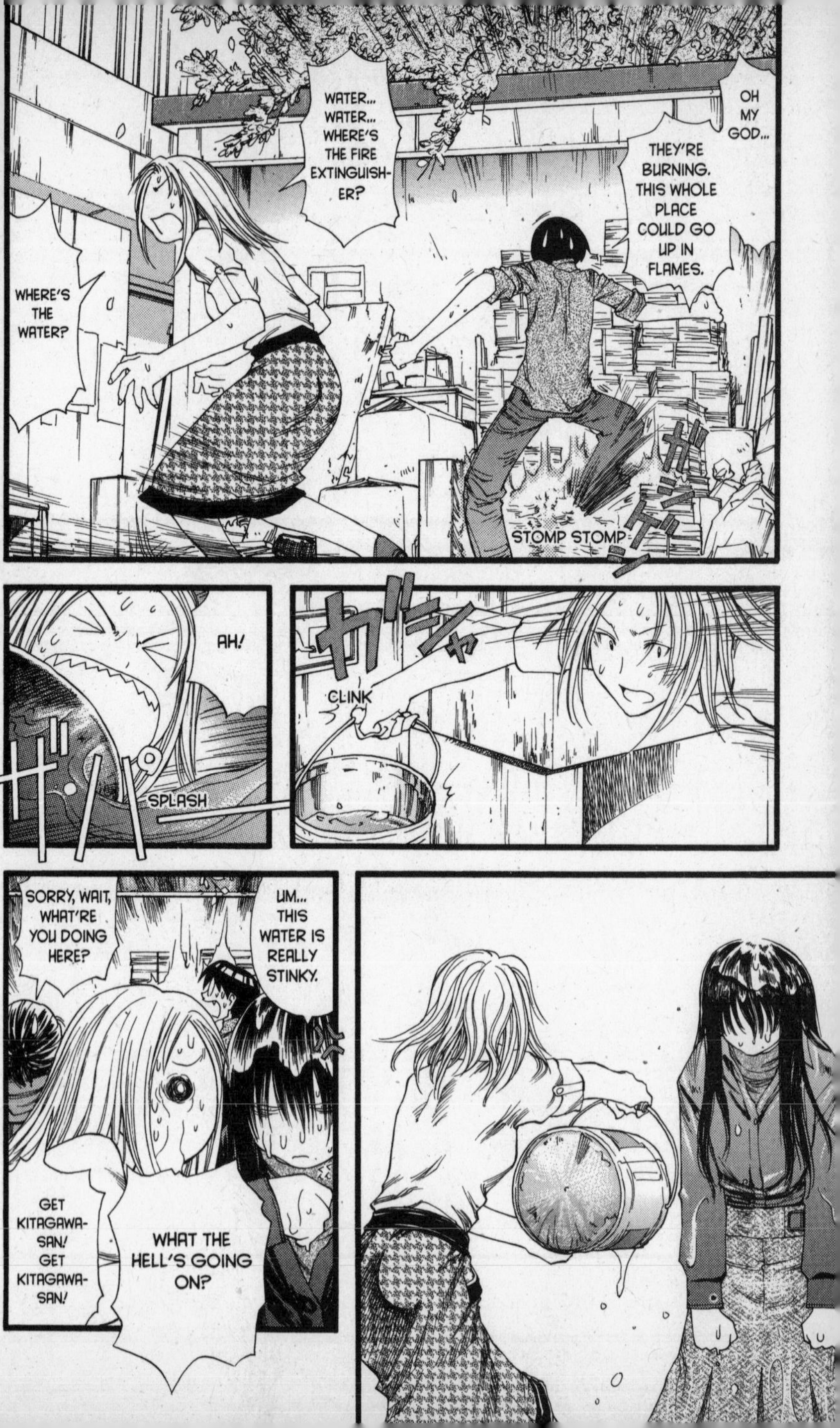
OH MY GOD...
THEY'RE BURNING. THIS WHOLE PLACE COULD GO UP IN FLAMES.
WATER... WATER... WHERE'S THE FIRE EXTINGUISHER?
WHERE'S THE WATER?
STOMP STOMP
CLINK
AH!
SPLASH
UM... THIS WATER IS REALLY STINKY.
SORRY, WAIT, WHAT'RE YOU DOING HERE?
WHAT THE HELL'S GOING ON?
GET KITAGAWA-SAN! GET KITAGAWA-SAN!

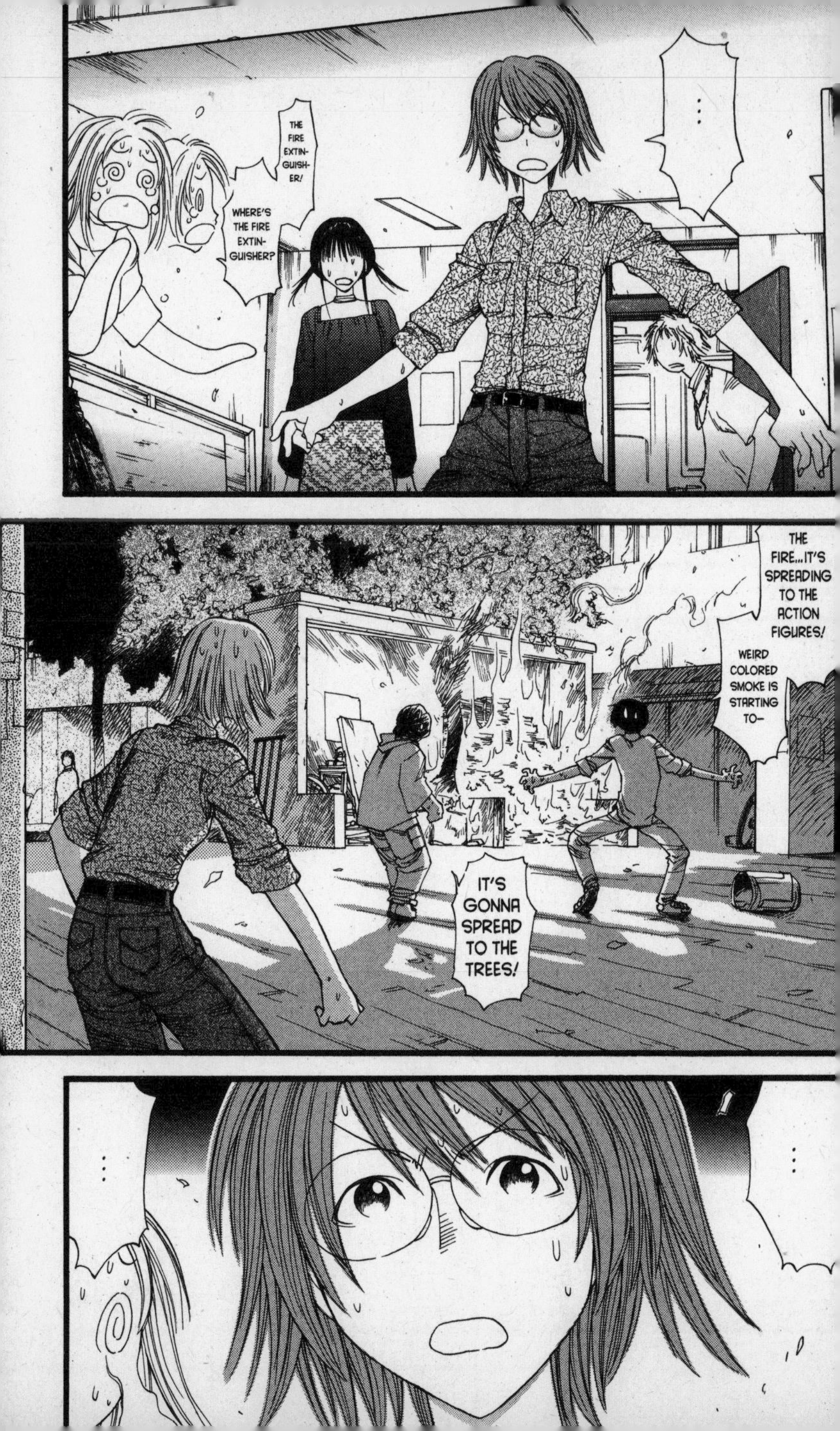
...
THE FIRE EXTINGUISHER!
WHERE'S THE FIRE EXTINGUISHER?
THE FIRE...IT'S SPREADING TO THE ACTION FIGURES!
WEIRD COLORED SMOKE IS STARTING TO—
IT'S GONNA SPREAD TO THE TREES!
...
...

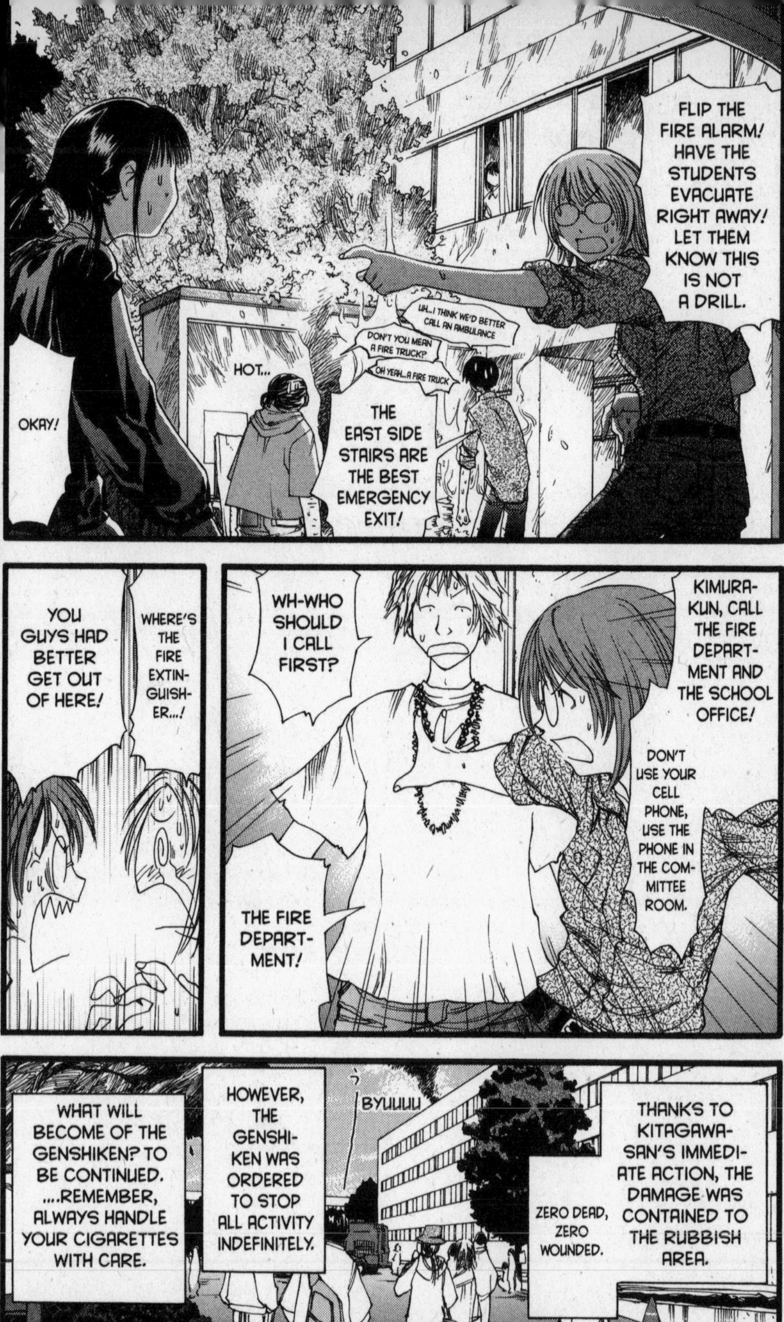
FLIP THE FIRE ALARM! HAVE THE STUDENTS EVACUATE RIGHT AWAY! LET THEM KNOW THIS IS NOT A DRILL.
UH...I THINK WE'D BETTER CALL AN AMBULANCE
DON'T YOU MEAN A FIRE TRUCK?
OH YEAH...A FIRE TRUCK
THE EAST SIDE STAIRS ARE THE BEST EMERGENCY EXIT!
HOT...
OKAY!
KIMURA-KUN, CALL THE FIRE DEPARTMENT AND THE SCHOOL OFFICE!
DON'T USE YOUR CELL PHONE, USE THE PHONE IN THE COMMITTEE ROOM.
WH-WHO SHOULD I CALL FIRST?
THE FIRE DEPARTMENT!
WHERE'S THE FIRE EXTINGUISHER...!
YOU GUYS HAD BETTER GET OUT OF HERE!
THANKS TO KITAGAWA-SAN'S IMMEDIATE ACTION, THE DAMAGE WAS CONTAINED TO THE RUBBISH AREA.
ZERO DEAD, ZERO WOUNDED.
BYUUUU
HOWEVER, THE GENSHIKEN WAS ORDERED TO STOP ALL ACTIVITY INDEFINITELY.
WHAT WILL BECOME OF THE GENSHIKEN? TO BE CONTINUED. ....REMEMBER, ALWAYS HANDLE YOUR CIGARETTES WITH CARE.

END OF CHAPTER 18

6 HERNANDEZ

WRITTEN BY YOKO KANNAZUKI

I WANNA PLAY A HERNANDEZ VS HERNANDEZ MATCH, BUT NOBODY ELSE WILL USE HIM. WHEN THEY PLAY AGAINST EACH OTHER, THEY'RE JOINED AT THE ELBOW IN THE OPENING SCREEN[YOKO]

♡

THEY'RE JOINED TOGETHER. [PIT VIPER]

NOBODY PLAYS WITH HIM. ...WHY IS HERNANDEZ THE ONLY MALE CHARACTER WHEN THEY DON'T EVEN HAVE CHIHIRO OR ROKU-HARA? IF THEY COME OUT WITH A SECOND EDITION, I TOTALLY WANT THEM TO HAVE ALEX AS A CHARACTER.

THAT REMINDS ME...WHEN SHE HIT THE A BUTTON WHILE CROUCHING, AND THEN LAUNCHED HER SPECIAL ATTACK, IT TOTALLY FREAKED ME OUT. [PIT VIPER]

REACHING MODELING

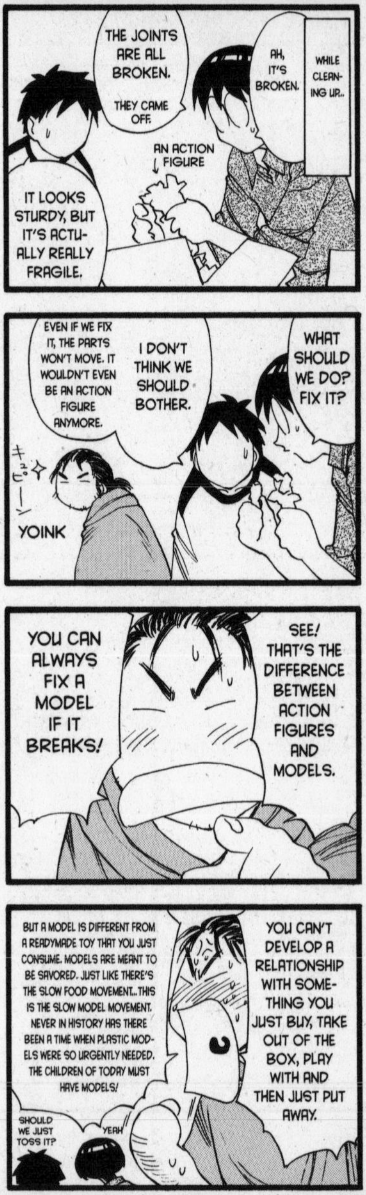
WHILE CLEANING UP...
AH, IT'S BROKEN.
THE JOINTS ARE ALL BROKEN.
THEY CAME OFF.
AN ACTION FIGURE
IT LOOKS STURDY, BUT IT'S ACTUALLY REALLY FRAGILE.
WHAT SHOULD WE DO? FIX IT?
I DON'T THINK WE SHOULD BOTHER.
EVEN IF WE FIX IT, THE PARTS WON'T MOVE. IT WOULDN'T EVEN BE AN ACTION FIGURE ANYMORE.
YOINK
SEE! THAT'S THE DIFFERENCE BETWEEN ACTION FIGURES AND MODELS.
YOU CAN ALWAYS FIX A MODEL IF IT BREAKS!
YOU CAN'T DEVELOP A RELATIONSHIP WITH SOMETHING YOU JUST BUY, TAKE OUT OF THE BOX, PLAY WITH AND THEN JUST PUT AWAY.
BUT A MODEL IS DIFFERENT FROM A READYMADE TOY THAT YOU JUST CONSUME. MODELS ARE MEANT TO BE SAVORED. JUST LIKE THERE'S THE SLOW FOOD MOVEMENT... THIS IS THE SLOW MODEL MOVEMENT. NEVER IN HISTORY HAS THERE BEEN A TIME WHEN PLASTIC MODELS WERE SO URGENTLY NEEDED. THE CHILDREN OF TODAY MUST HAVE MODELS!
YEAH
SHOULD WE JUST TOSS IT?

ICE CLIMBER

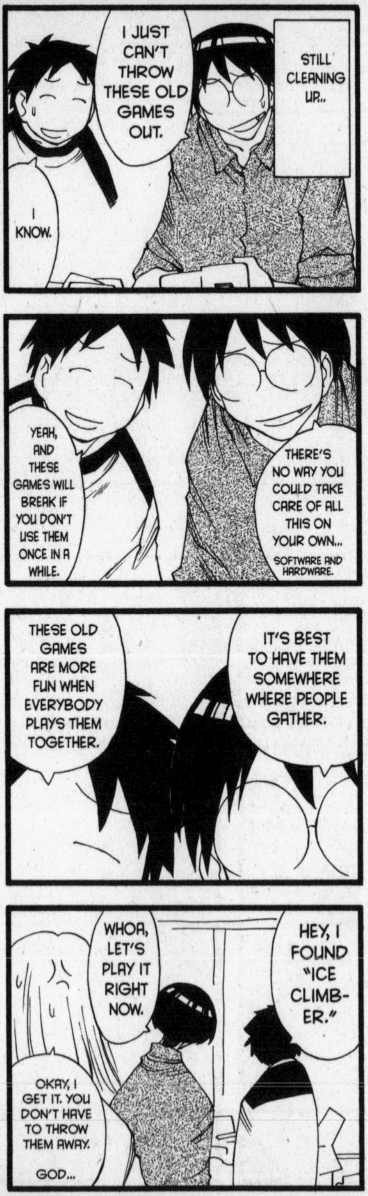
STILL CLEANING UP...
I JUST CAN'T THROW THESE OLD GAMES OUT.
I KNOW.
THERE'S NO WAY YOU COULD TAKE CARE OF ALL THIS ON YOUR OWN...
SOFTWARE AND HARDWARE.
YEAH, AND THESE GAMES WILL BREAK IF YOU DON'T USE THEM ONCE IN A WHILE.
IT'S BEST TO HAVE THEM SOMEWHERE WHERE PEOPLE GATHER.
THESE OLD GAMES ARE MORE FUN WHEN EVERYBODY PLAYS THEM TOGETHER.
HEY, I FOUND "ICE CLIMBER."
WHOA, LET'S PLAY IT RIGHT NOW.
OKAY, I GET IT. YOU DON'T HAVE TO THROW THEM AWAY.
GOD...

THE 8TH "HOW WAS THIS WEEK'S 'KUJI-UN'?" MEETING

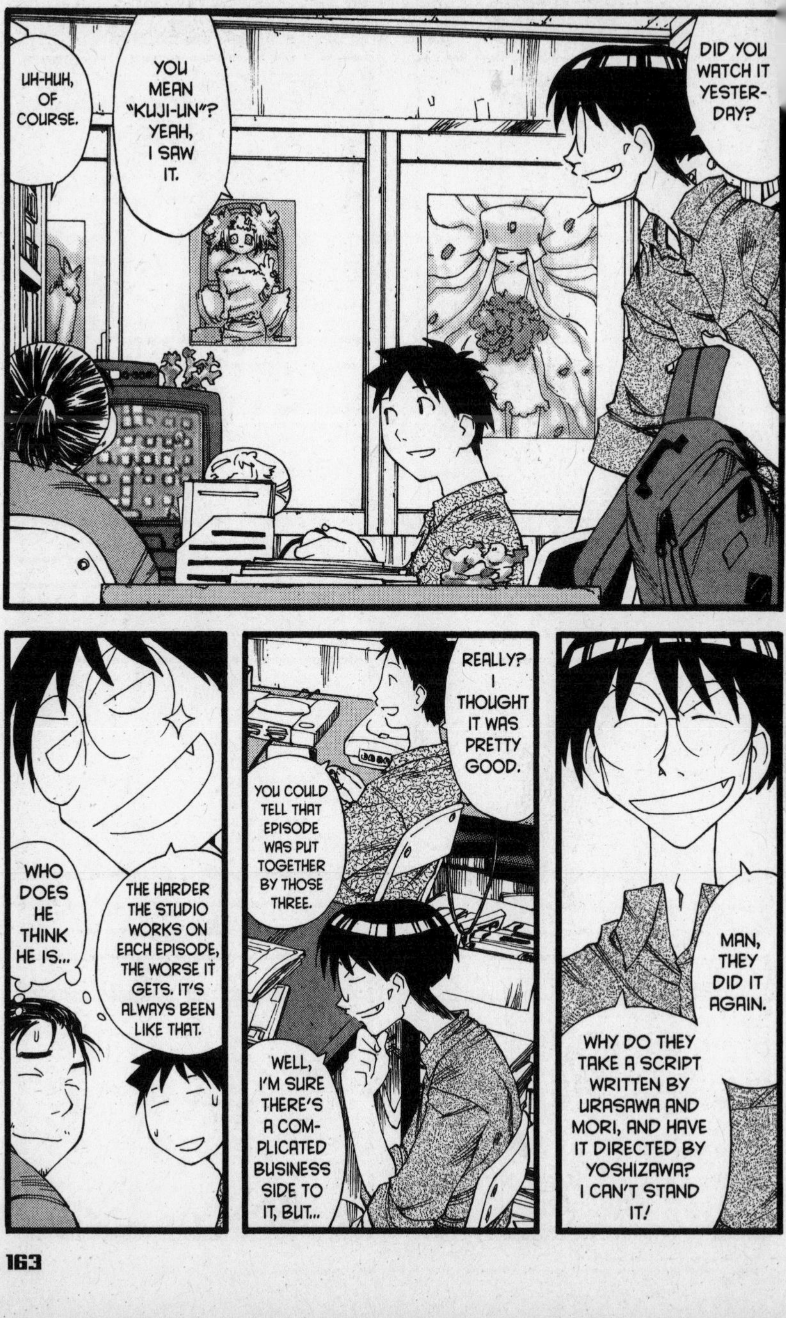
DID YOU WATCH IT YESTERDAY?
YOU MEAN "KUJI-UN"? YEAH, I SAW IT.
UH-HUH, OF COURSE.
MAN, THEY DID IT AGAIN.
WHY DO THEY TAKE A SCRIPT WRITTEN BY URASAWA AND MORI, AND HAVE IT DIRECTED BY YOSHIZAWA? I CAN'T STAND IT!
REALLY? I THOUGHT IT WAS PRETTY GOOD.
YOU COULD TELL THAT EPISODE WAS PUT TOGETHER BY THOSE THREE.
WELL, I'M SURE THERE'S A COMPLICATED BUSINESS SIDE TO IT, BUT...
THE HARDER THE STUDIO WORKS ON EACH EPISODE, THE WORSE IT GETS. IT'S ALWAYS BEEN LIKE THAT.
WHO DOES HE THINK HE IS...

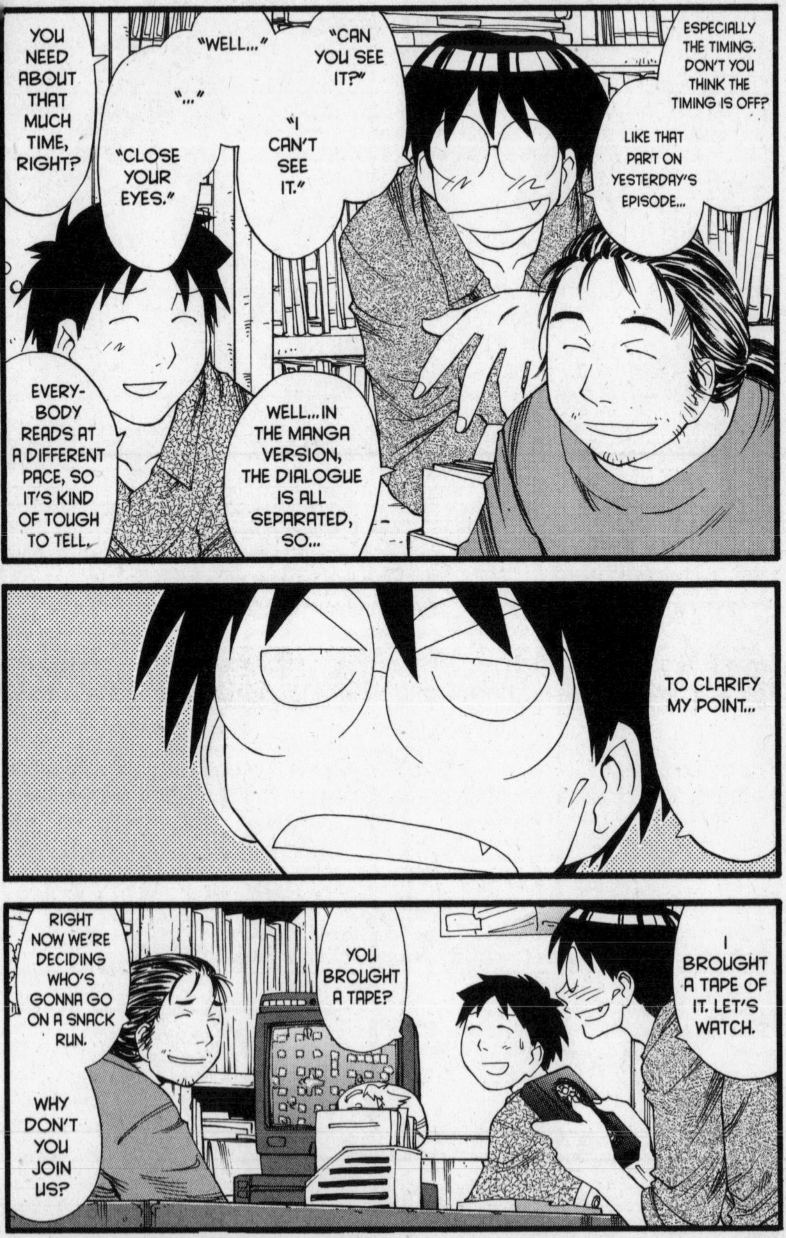
ESPECIALLY THE TIMING. DON'T YOU THINK THE TIMING IS OFF?
LIKE THAT PART ON YESTERDAY'S EPISODE...
"CAN YOU SEE IT?"
"I CAN'T SEE IT."
"WELL..."
"..."
"CLOSE YOUR EYES."
YOU NEED ABOUT THAT MUCH TIME, RIGHT?
WELL...IN THE MANGA VERSION, THE DIALOGUE IS ALL SEPARATED, SO...
EVERY-BODY READS AT A DIFFERENT PACE, SO IT'S KIND OF TOUGH TO TELL.
TO CLARIFY MY POINT...
I BROUGHT A TAPE OF IT. LET'S WATCH.
YOU BROUGHT A TAPE?
RIGHT NOW WE'RE DECIDING WHO'S GONNA GO ON A SNACK RUN.
WHY DON'T YOU JOIN US?

THE MEETING CONTINUES, BUT WE'LL END HERE.

END OF GENSHIKEN BOOK 3

TOKINO AKIYAMA

SPECIAL MOVES	WILD CARD	↓↘→+Ⓐ or Ⓒ
	RED TENGU MUSHROOM	→↘↓+Ⓐ or Ⓒ
	BITTER CHESTNUT MUSHROOM	↓↙←+Ⓑ or Ⓓ
	MOONLIGHT MUSHROOM	→↘↓↘→+Ⓐ or Ⓒ
SUPER SPECIAL MOVES	THE HA HA MUSHROOM	↓↙←↙↓↘→+Ⓐ or Ⓒ
	THE ANGEL OF DEATH	↖↘↓↘↓↙←↓↘→×2 ⒶⒸ 同時押し

RITSUKO K> KETTENKRAD

SPECIAL MOVES	FIERCE TIGER	↓↘→+Ⓐ or Ⓒ
	BACK DOOR	↓↙←+Ⓐ or Ⓒ
	FIERY PASSAGE TO HEAVEN	→↘↓+Ⓐ or Ⓒ
	SIX HEADED ELBOW (ELBOW ATTACK)	↓↙←+Ⓑ or Ⓓ
SUPER SPECIAL MOVES	STEEL MOUNTAIN	↓↙←↓↙←+Ⓑ or Ⓓ
	FIERCE TIGER STRIKE	↓↘→↓↘→+Ⓐ or Ⓒ

KUJIBIKI UNBALANCED

UNBALANCED FIGHTER

IZUMI TACHIBANA

SPECIAL MOVES	MIST GATHERER	↓↘→+Ⓐ or Ⓒ
	SNAKE HANDLER	↓↙←+Ⓐ or Ⓑ or Ⓒ
	SAND STABBER	→↘↓+Ⓑ or Ⓓ
	BOMBER HEAD	→↘↓↘→+Ⓐ or Ⓒ
SUPER SPECIAL MOVES	PURE COLOR	↓↘→↓↘→+Ⓐ or Ⓒ
	HEAVEN'S ASSASSIN	Ⓐ·Ⓐ·→·Ⓑ·Ⓒ

KASUMI KISARAGI

SPECIAL MOVES	CRAZY TIGER BLADE	↓↘→+Ⓐ or Ⓒ
	SIDEWAY'S CLOUD	↓↙←+Ⓐ or Ⓒ (3回連続入力)
	IWANAWI	→↘↓↙←+Ⓑ or Ⓓ
SUPER SPECIAL MOVES	THE BEGGAR	→↘↓↙←↓↘→+Ⓐ or Ⓒ
	MIST	→↘↓↙←→+Ⓑ or Ⓓ· Ⓐ·Ⓒ·Ⓓ·Ⓑ·Ⓒ·Ⓓ·Ⓐ·Ⓑ·↓↘→+Ⓒ

KOMAKI ASAGIRI

SPECIAL MOVES		
KOMAKI FIST	↓↘→+Ⓐ or Ⓒ	(空中可)
KOMAKI BLADE	→↘↓↙+Ⓐ or Ⓒ	
KOMAKI DRAIN	→↓↘←↑+Ⓐ or Ⓒ	
SUPER SPECIAL MOVES		
CARDINAL KOMAKI	↓↘→↓↘→+Ⓑ or Ⓓ	
KOMAKI ILLUSION	Ⓐ·Ⓐ·→·→·Ⓑ·Ⓒ	(空中可)

AIRAWATI CHAKAWARUTII

SPECIAL MOVES		
FIRE	↓↘→+Ⓐ or Ⓒ	
FRAME	→↘↓↙←+Ⓐ or Ⓒ	
TELEPORT	→↘↓↙ or ←↙↓↘→+ⒶⒷⒸ or ⒷⒸⒹ	
SUPER SPECIAL MOVES		
VOLCANO	↓↘→↓↘→+Ⓑ or Ⓓ	
TEMPEST	→↘↓↙←↘→+Ⓐ or Ⓒ	

AFTERNOON COMICS KODANSHA

TOKINO
DRUNK ON KOMAKI'S HOMEMADE APPLE CHEESE CAKE (WITH WAY TOO MUCH BRANDY IN IT)

SPECIAL MOVES		
I'LL ROLL LIKE A STONE (PAUSE)	←タメ→+Ⓐ or Ⓒ	
TONIGHT, I'M GONNA DROP YOU WITH THESE KNEES OF MINE (PAUSE)	↓タメ↑+Ⓑ or Ⓓ	
I'LL GIVE YOU A KARATE CHOP YOU WON'T BELIEVE (WHILE AIRBORNE)	空中で↓↘→+Ⓐ or Ⓒ	
TOGETHER	→↘↓↙←+Ⓐ or Ⓒ	
SUPER SPECIAL MOVES		
PISTON BLOCK UPPER (REPETITIVE HITS)	↓↘→↓↘→+Ⓐ or Ⓒ	(連打でヒット数上昇)

RENKO KAMISHAKUJII
AND HER FOLLOWERS

SPECIAL MOVES		
YAMADA KICK	↓↘→+Ⓑ or Ⓓ	
YAMADA PUNCH	→↓↘+Ⓐ or Ⓒ	
YAMADA MISSILE (1)	→↘↓↙←+Ⓑ or Ⓓ	
YAMADA REVERSE (AFTER)	①後に+ⒶⒷⒸ同時押しで発動	
SUPER SPECIAL MOVES		
YAMADA'S GIANT SWING (2) ROTATE JOY STICK TWICE,	レバー2回転+Ⓒ(レバーで移動可能) (連打で回転数上昇)	
YAMADA FINAL CRUSHER	②中に↓↘→+ⒸⒹ同時押し	
THE BLOOD-COLORED SUNSET I SAW THAT DAY	↓↙←↙↓↘→+Ⓐ or Ⓒ	

Translation Notes

Japanese is a tricky language for most Westerners, and translation is often more art than science. For your edification and reading pleasure, here are notes on some of the places where we could have gone in a different direction in our translation of the work, or where a Japanese cultural reference is used.

Gufu, page 21

"Gufu" is a character from the series *Gundam.*

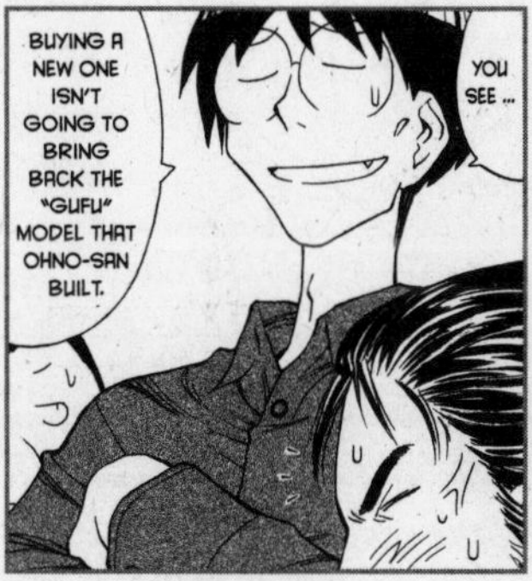
YOU SEE ...
BUYING A NEW ONE ISN'T GOING TO BRING BACK THE "GUFU" MODEL THAT OHNO-SAN BUILT.

Cat Ears, page 25

Saki originally wore the cat ears during the school festival in Chapter 1 of Volume 2. Here, Saki is mad because the cat ears she wore then did not have lace attached. The cat ears with lace are supposed to resemble a French maid's outfit.

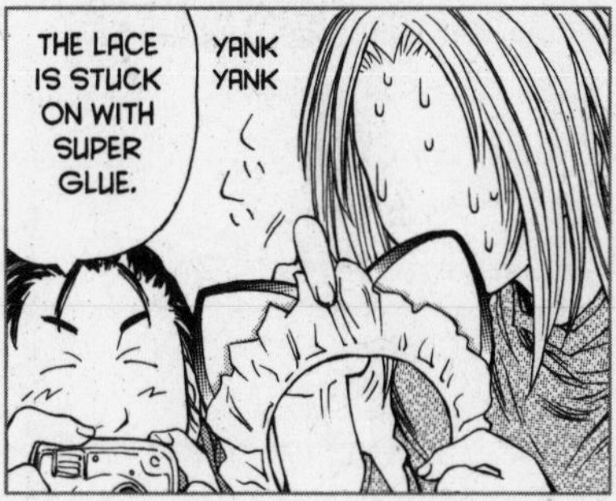
YANK YANK
THE LACE IS STUCK ON WITH SUPER GLUE.

Doujin and Original Combo, page 27

A "doujin" game is a game created by fans, similar to a "doujinshi" fanzine.

Original combo: A technique in games that allows players to mix and match different characters' techniques. Pit Viper (Madarame) actually uses the abbreviation "oricom."

More Gundam, page 28

A "Jimu" is a type of mobile suit from the *Gundam* series. Madarame refers to Raru Ranba, who was the pilot of Gufu (see note for page 21). Hammon Crowley is a female *Gundam* character.

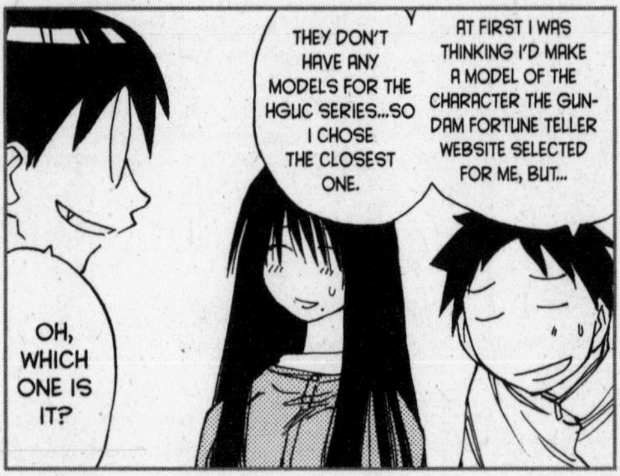

AT FIRST I WAS THINKING I'D MAKE A MODEL OF THE CHARACTER THE GUNDAM FORTUNE TELLER WEBSITE SELECTED FOR ME, BUT...
THEY DON'T HAVE ANY MODELS FOR THE HGUC SERIES...SO I CHOSE THE CLOSEST ONE.
OH, WHICH ONE IS IT?

Apparently there is a website called "*Gundam* uranai" or "*Gundam* fortune teller," which will assign users a *Gundam* character based on the user's birth date, blood type and place of birth. The url for the Japanese-only website is hhtp://www.hinobori.net/gunad/fortune/page0.html

Boru is a *Gundam* character from the HGUC (High Grade Universal Century) series.

Lolita, page 36

"Lolita" refers to Nabokov's novel *Lolita*, a story about a grown man obsessed with a young girl. In Japan, the term "Lolita complex" is commonly used to describe men who take an interest in younger girls. Here, Madarame is probably inferring that he shouldn't be nervous around Kasukabe because she's not a Lolita, and therefore not the type of girl he's interested in.

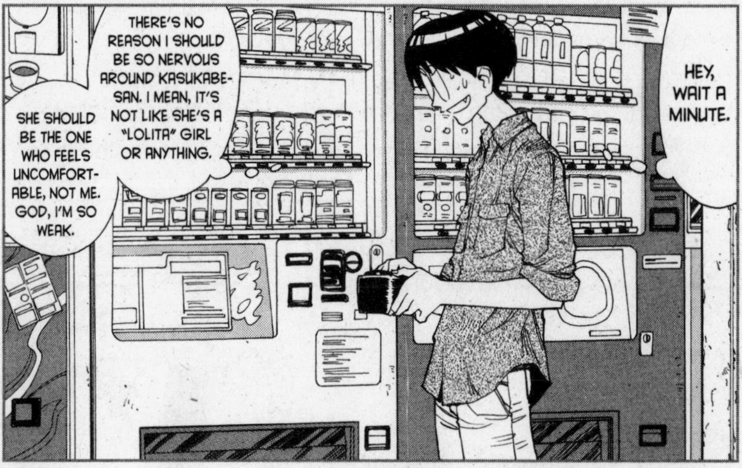
HEY, WAIT A MINUTE.
THERE'S NO REASON I SHOULD BE SO NERVOUS AROUND KASUKABE-SAN. I MEAN, IT'S NOT LIKE SHE'S A "LOLITA" GIRL OR ANYTHING.
SHE SHOULD BE THE ONE WHO FEELS UNCOMFORTABLE, NOT ME. GOD, I'M SO WEAK.

Waterproof make-up, page 58

When Kanji's sister says "waterproof," she uses the katakana word "uouta-puru-fu." This is the Japanese pronunciation of the English word. Apparently, Kanji is not familiar with this word.

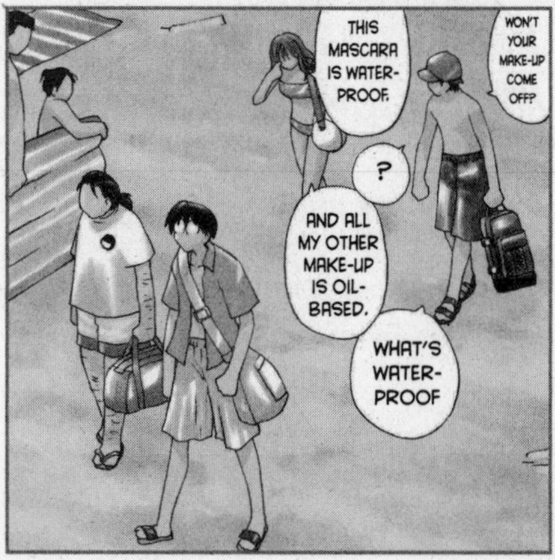
WON'T YOUR MAKE-UP COME OFF?
THIS MASCARA IS WATERPROOF.
?
AND ALL MY OTHER MAKE-UP IS OIL-BASED.
WHAT'S WATERPROOF

Shiritori, page 66

Shiritori is a word game in which players must come up with a word beginning with the last syllable of the previous word used. For example, if one player uses the word "samurai," then the next player needs to respond with a word beginning with "i." A player loses when he or she repeats a word or says a word which ends in "n" (no Japanese words begin with the single character "n," therefore the game cannot be continued.) The Genshiken guys are playing Shiritori using only *Gundam*-related terms.

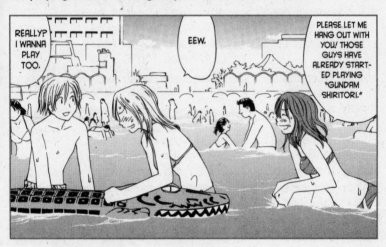

PLEASE LET ME HANG OUT WITH YOU! THOSE GUYS HAVE ALREADY START-ED PLAYING "GUNDAM SHIRITORI."
EEW.
REALLY? I WANNA PLAY TOO.

A Woman's Spirit, page 110

The phrase "a woman's spirit is like the summer sky" is a play on the Japanese proverb "onna gokoro to aki no sora" ("a woman's spirit changes with the fall sky"), which means that a woman's heart/spirit changes as frequently as fall weather.

Honorifics

Throughout the Del Rey Manga books, you will find Japanese honorifics left intact in the translations. For those not familiar with how the Japanese use honorifics and, more importantly, how they differ from American honorifics, we present this brief overview.

Politeness has always been a critical facet of Japanese culture. Ever since the feudal era, when Japan was a highly stratified society, use of honorifics—which can be defined as polite speech that indicates relationship or status—has played an essential role in the Japanese language. When addressing someone in Japanese, an honorific usually takes the form of a suffix attached to one's name (example: "Asuna-san"), or as a title at the end of one's name or in place of the name itself (example: "Negi-sensei," or simply "Sensei!").

Honorifics can be expressions of respect or endearment. In the context of manga and anime, honorifics give insight into the nature of the relationship between characters. Many translations into English leave out these important honorifics, and therefore distort the "feel" of the original Japanese. Because Japanese honorifics contain nuances that English honorifics lack, it is our policy at Del Rey not to translate them. Here, instead, is a guide to some of the honorifics you may encounter in Del Rey Manga.

-san: This is the most common honorific and is equivalent to Mr., Miss, Ms., or Mrs. It is the all-purpose honorific and can be used in any situation where politeness is required.

-sama: This is one level higher than "-san" and is used to confer great respect.

-dono: This comes from the word "tono," which means "lord." It is an even higher level than "-sama" and confers utmost respect.

-kun: This suffix is used at the end of boys' names to express familiarity or endearment. It is also sometimes used by men among friends, or when addressing someone younger or of a lower station.

-chan: This is used to express endearment, mostly toward girls. It is also used for little boys, pets, and even among lovers. It gives a sense of childish cuteness.

Bozu: This is an informal way to refer to a boy, similar to the English term "kid" or "squirt."

Sempai: This title suggests that the addressee is one's senior in a group or organization. It is most often used in a school setting, where underclassmen refer to their upperclassmen as "sempai." It can also be used in the workplace, such as when a newer employee addresses an employee who has seniority in the company.

Kohai: This is the opposite of "sempai" and is used toward underclassmen in school or newcomers in the workplace. It connotes that the addressee is of a lower station.

Sensei: Literally meaning "one who has come before," this title is used for teachers, doctors, or masters of any profession or art.

[blank]: Usually forgotten in these lists, but perhaps the most significant difference between Japanese and English. The lack of honorific means that the speaker has permission to address the person in a very intimate way. Usually, only family, spouses, or very close friends have this kind of permission. Known as *yobisute,* it can be gratifying when someone who has earned the intimacy starts to call one by one's name without an honorific. But when that intimacy hasn't been earned, it can also be very insulting.

Gacha Gacha

BY HIROYUKI TAMAKOSHI

Kouhei is your typical Japanese high school student—he's usually late, he loves beef bowls, he pals around with his buddies, and he's got his first-ever crush on his childhood friend Kurara. Before he can express his feelings, however, Kurara heads off to Hawaii with her mother for summer vacation. When she returns, she seems like a totally different person . . . and that's because she is! While she was away, Kurara somehow developed an alternate personality: Arisa! And where Kurara has no time for boys, Arisa isn't interested in much else. Now Kouhei must help protect his friend's secret, and make sure that Arisa doesn't do anything Kurara would regret!

HIROYUKI TAMAKOSHI

Ages: 16 +

Special extras in each volume! Read them all!

TOMARE!

[STOP!]

You are going the wrong way!

Manga is a completely different type of reading experience.

To start at the *beginning*, go to the *end*!

That's right! Authentic manga is read the traditional Japanese way—from right to left. Exactly the *opposite* of how American books are read. It's easy to follow: Just go to the other end of the book, and read each page—and each panel—from right side to left side, starting at the top right. Now you're experiencing manga as it was meant to be.